3

Grammar in Context

4TH EDITION

SANDRA N. ELBAUM

THOMSON

HEINLE

Australia • Canada • Mexico • Singapore • Spain • United Kingdom • United States

THOMSON
™
HEINLE

Grammar in Context 3, Fourth Edition
ELBAUM

Publisher, Adult & Academic, ESL: *James W. Brown*
Senior Acquisitions Editor, Adult & Academic, ESL: *Sherrise Roehr*
Director of Product Development: *Anita Raducanu*
Associate Development Editor: *Yeny Kim*
Production Manager: *Sally Giangrande*
Director of Marketing: *Amy Mabley*
Marketing Manager: *Laura Needham*
Senior Print Buyer: *Mary Beth Hennebury*

Development Editor: *Charlotte Sturdy*
Compositor: *Nesbitt Graphics, Inc.*
Project Manager: *Julie DeSilva*
Photo Researcher: *Connie Gardner*
Illustrators: *Ralph Canaday, James Edwards, Larry Frederick, and Brock Nichol*
Interior Designer: *Jerilyn Bockorick*
Cover Designer: *Joseph Sherman*
Printer: *Quebecor World*

Cover Image: Edward Hopper: Lighthouse and Buildings, Portland Head. Museum of Fine Arts, Boston, Massachusetts, USA/Bequest of John T. Spaulding/Bridgeman Art Library.

For permission to use material from this text or product, submit a request online at http://www.thomsonrights.com

Any additional questions about permissions can be submitted by email to thomsonrights@thomson.com

Copyright © 2005 by Sandra N. Elbaum

All rights reserved. No part of this work covered by the copyright hereon may be reproduced or used in any form or by any means—graphic, electronic, or mechanical, including photocopying, recording, taping, Web distribution or information storage and retrieval systems—without the written permission of the publisher.

ISBN: 1-4130-0748-1

Library of Congress Control Number: 2004118367

Printed in the United States of America.
5 6 7 8 9 10   09 08 07 06

For more information contact Thomson Heinle, 25 Thomson Place, Boston, Massachusetts 02210 USA, or you can visit our Internet site at elt.thomson.com

Photo credits appear at the end of the book, which constitutes an extension of this copyright page.

Contents

Lesson 4   **137**

Appendices

In memory of
Meyer Shisler—teacher, scholar, inspiration

Acknowledgements

Many thanks to Dennis Hogan, Jim Brown, Sherrise Roehr, Yeny Kim, and Sally Giangrande from Thomson Heinle for their ongoing support of the *Grammar in Context* series. I would especially like to thank my editor, Charlotte Sturdy, for her keen eye to detail and invaluable suggestions.

And many thanks to my students at Truman College, who have increased my understanding of my own language and taught me to see life from another point of view. By sharing their observations, questions, and life stories, they have enriched my life enormously—*Sandra N. Elbaum*

Thomson Heinle would like to thank the following people for their contributions:

Marki Alexander
Oklahoma State
  University
Stillwater, OK

Joan M. Amore
Triton College
River Grove, IL

Edina Pingleton Bagley
Nassau Community
  College
Garden City, NY

Judith A. G. Benka
Normandale Community
  College
Bloomington, MN

Judith Book-Ehrlichman
Bergen Community
  College
Paramus, NJ

Lyn Buchheit
Community College of
  Philadelphia
Philadelphia, PA

Charlotte M. Calobrisi
Northern Virginia
  Community College
Annandale, VA

Sarah A. Carpenter
Normandale Community
  College
Bloomington, MN

Jeanette Clement
Duquesne University
Pittsburgh, PA

Allis Cole
Shoreline Community
  College
Shoreline, WA

Jacqueline M. Cunningham
Triton College
River Grove, IL

Lisa DePaoli
Sierra College
Rocklin, CA

Maha Edlbi
Sierra College
Rocklin, CA

Rhonda J. Farley
Cosumnes River College
Sacramento, CA

Jennifer Farnell
University of Connecticut
American Language
  Program
Stamford, CT

Abigail-Marie Fiattarone
Mesa Community College
Mesa, AZ

Marcia Gethin-Jones
University of Connecticut
American Language
  Program
Storrs, CT

Linda Harlow
Santa Rosa Junior
  College
Santa Rosa, CA

Suha R. Hattab
Triton College
River Grove, IL

Bill Keniston
Normandale Community
  College
Bloomington, MN

Walton King
Arkansas State
  University
Jonesboro, AR

Kathleen Krokar
Truman College
Chicago, IL

John Larkin
NVCC-Community and
  Workforce
  Development
Annandale, VA

Michael Larsen
American River College
Sacramento, CA

Bea C. Lawn
Gavilan College
Gilroy, CA

Rob Lee
Pasadena City College
Pasadena, CA

Oranit Limmaneeprasert
American River College
Sacramento, CA

Gennell Lockwood
Shoreline Community
  College
Shoreline, WA

Linda Louie
Highline Community
  College
Des Moines, WA

Melanie A. Majeski
Naugatuck Valley
  Community College
Waterbury, CT

Maria Marin
De Anza College
Cupertino, CA

Karen Miceli
Cosumnes River College
Sacramento, CA

Jeanie Pavichevich
Triton College
River Grove, IL

Herbert Pierson
St. John's University
New York City, NY

Dina Poggi
De Anza College
Cupertino, CA

Mark Rau
American River College
Sacramento, CA

John W. Roberts
Shoreline Community
  College
Shoreline, WA

Azize R. Ruttler
Bergen Community
  College
Paramus, NJ

Ann Salzmann
University of Illinois,
Urbana, IL

Eva Teagarden
Yuba College
Marysville, CA

Susan Wilson
San Jose City College
San Jose, CA

Martha Yeager-Tobar
Cerritos College
Norwalk, CA

A word from the author

It seems that I was born to be an ESL teacher. My parents immigrated to the U.S. from Poland as adults and were confused not only by the English language but by American culture as well. Born in the U.S., I often had the task as a child to explain the intricacies of the language and allay my parents' fears about the culture. It is no wonder to me that I became an ESL teacher, and later, an ESL writer who focuses on explanations of American culture in order to illustrate grammar. My life growing up in an immigrant neighborhood was very similar to the lives of my students, so I have a feel for what confuses them and what they need to know about American life.

ESL teachers often find themselves explaining confusing customs and providing practical information about life in the U.S. Often, teachers are a student's only source of information about American life. With **Grammar in Context, Fourth Edition,** I enjoy sharing my experiences with you.

Grammar in Context, Fourth Edition connects grammar with American cultural context, providing learners of English with a useful and meaningful skill and knowledge base. Students learn the grammar necessary to communicate verbally and in writing, and learn how American culture plays a role in language, beliefs, and everyday situations.

Enjoy the new edition of **Grammar in Context!**

Sandra N. Elbaum

Grammar in Context

Students learn more, remember more, and use language more effectively when they learn grammar in context.

Learning a language through meaningful themes and practicing it in a contextualized setting promote both linguistic and cognitive development. In **Grammar in Context**, grammar is presented in interesting and culturally informative readings, and the language and context are subsequently practiced throughout the chapter.

New to this edition:

- **New and updated readings** on current American topics such as Instant Messaging and eBay.
- **Updated grammar charts** that now include essential language notes.
- **Updated exercises and activities** that provide contextualized practice using a variety of exercise types, as well as additional practice for more difficult structures.
- **New lower-level** *Grammar in Context Basic* for beginning level students.
- **New wrap-around Teacher's Annotated Edition** with page-by-page, point-of-use teaching suggestions.
- **Expanded Assessment CD-ROM** with ExamView® Pro Test Generator now contains more questions types and assessment options to easily allow teachers to create tests and quizzes.

Distinctive Features of *Grammar in Context:*

Students prepare for academic assignments and everyday language tasks.

Discussions, readings, compositions, and exercises involving higher-level critical thinking skills develop overall language and communication skills.

Students expand their knowledge of American topics and culture.

The readings in **Grammar in Context** help students gain insight into and enrich their knowledge of American culture and history. Students gain ample exposure to the practicalities of American life, such as writing a résumé, dealing with telemarketers and junk mail, and getting student internships. Their new knowledge helps them adapt to everyday life in the U.S.

Students learn to use their new skills to communicate.

The exercises and Expansion Activities in **Grammar in Context** help students learn English while practicing their writing and speaking skills. Students work together in pairs and groups to find more information about topics, to make presentations, to play games, and to role-play. Their confidence in using English increases, as does their ability to communicate effectively.

Welcome to **Grammar in Context, Fourth Edition**

Students learn more, remember more, and use language more effectively when they learn grammar in context.

Grammar in Context, Fourth Edition connects grammar with rich, American cultural context, providing learners of English with a useful and meaningful skill and knowledge base.

An **Audio Program** allows students to hear the readings and dialogs, and provides an opportunity to practice their listening skills.

Readings on American topics such as Instant Messaging, eBay, and The AIDS Ride present and illustrate the grammatical structure in an informative and meaningful context.

Grammar charts offer clear explanations and provide contextualized examples of the structure.

Language Notes refine students' understanding of the target structure.

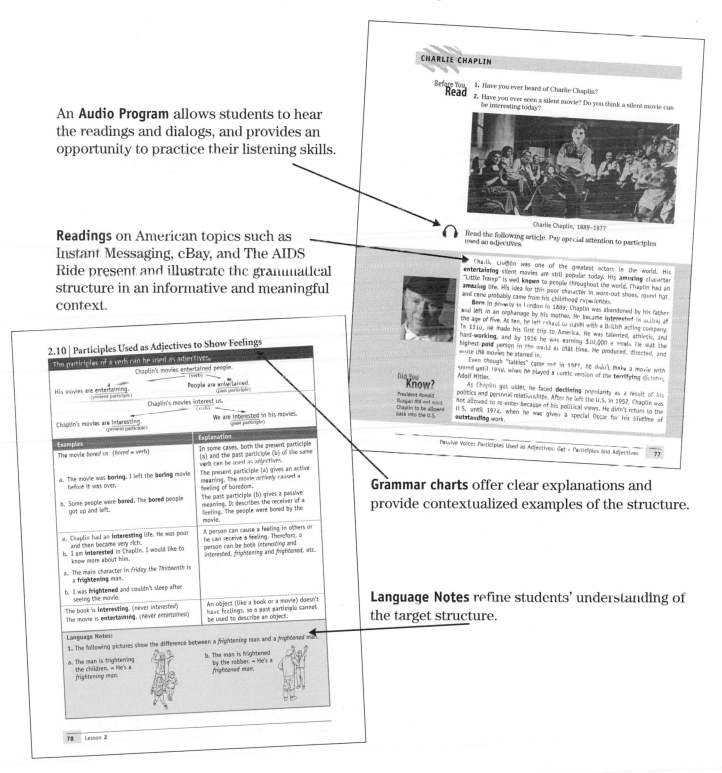

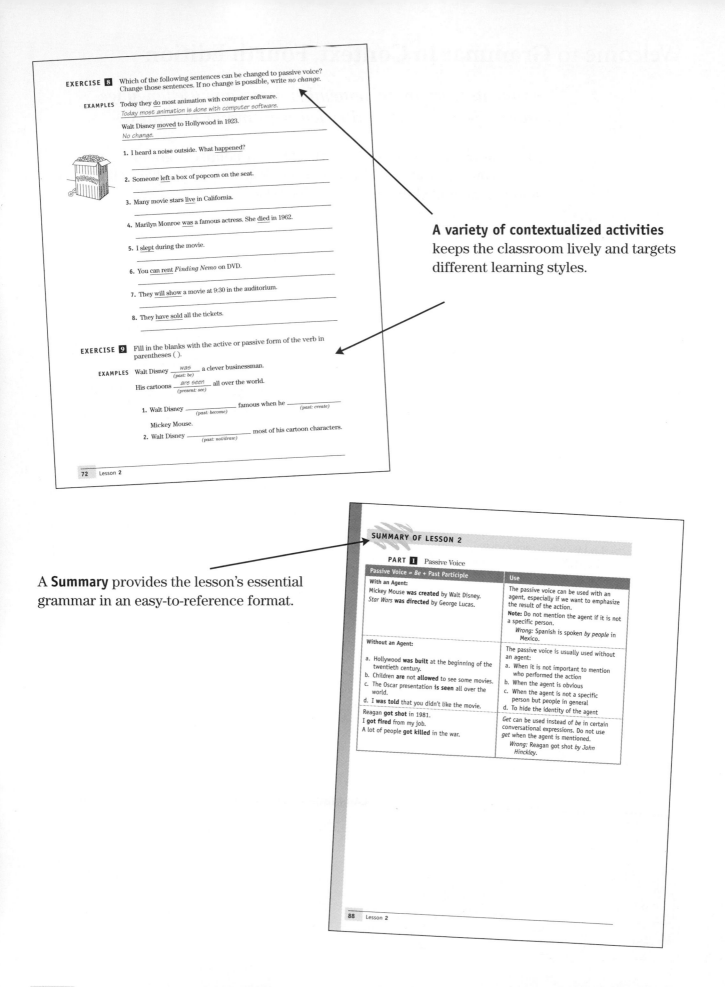

EXERCISE 8 Which of the following sentences can be changed to passive voice? Change those sentences. If no change is possible, write *no change*.

EXAMPLES Today they <u>do</u> most animation with computer software.
Today most animation is done with computer software.

Walt Disney <u>moved</u> to Hollywood in 1923.
No change.

1. I heard a noise outside. What <u>happened</u>?

2. Someone <u>left</u> a box of popcorn on the seat.

3. Many movie stars <u>live</u> in California.

4. Marilyn Monroe <u>was</u> a famous actress. She <u>died</u> in 1962.

5. I <u>slept</u> during the movie.

6. You <u>can rent</u> *Finding Nemo* on DVD.

7. They <u>will show</u> a movie at 9:30 in the auditorium.

8. They <u>have sold</u> all the tickets.

EXERCISE 9 Fill in the blanks with the active or passive form of the verb in parentheses ( ).

EXAMPLES Walt Disney ___*was*___ a clever businessman.
(past: be)

His cartoons ___*are seen*___ all over the world.
(present: see)

1. Walt Disney _____ famous when he _____
(past: become) *(past: create)*
Mickey Mouse.

2. Walt Disney _____ most of his cartoon characters.
(past: not/draw)

A variety of contextualized activities keeps the classroom lively and targets different learning styles.

A **Summary** provides the lesson's essential grammar in an easy-to-reference format.

SUMMARY OF LESSON 2

PART 1 Passive Voice

Passive Voice = *Be* + Past Participle	Use
With an Agent: Mickey Mouse **was created** by Walt Disney. *Star Wars* **was directed** by George Lucas.	The passive voice can be used with an agent, especially if we want to emphasize the result of the action. **Note:** Do not mention the agent if it is not a specific person. *Wrong:* Spanish is spoken *by people* in Mexico.
Without an Agent: a. Hollywood **was built** at the beginning of the twentieth century. b. Children **are** not **allowed** to see some movies. c. The Oscar presentation **is seen** all over the world. d. I **was told** that you didn't like the movie.	The passive voice is usually used without an agent: a. When it is not important to mention who performed the action b. When the agent is obvious c. When the agent is not a specific person but people in general d. To hide the identity of the agent
Reagan **got shot** in 1981. I **got fired** from my job. A lot of people **got killed** in the war.	*Get* can be used instead of *be* in certain conversational expressions. Do not use *get* when the agent is mentioned. *Wrong:* Reagan got shot *by John Hinckley*.

Editing Advice gives students pre-writing practice by alerting them to common errors.

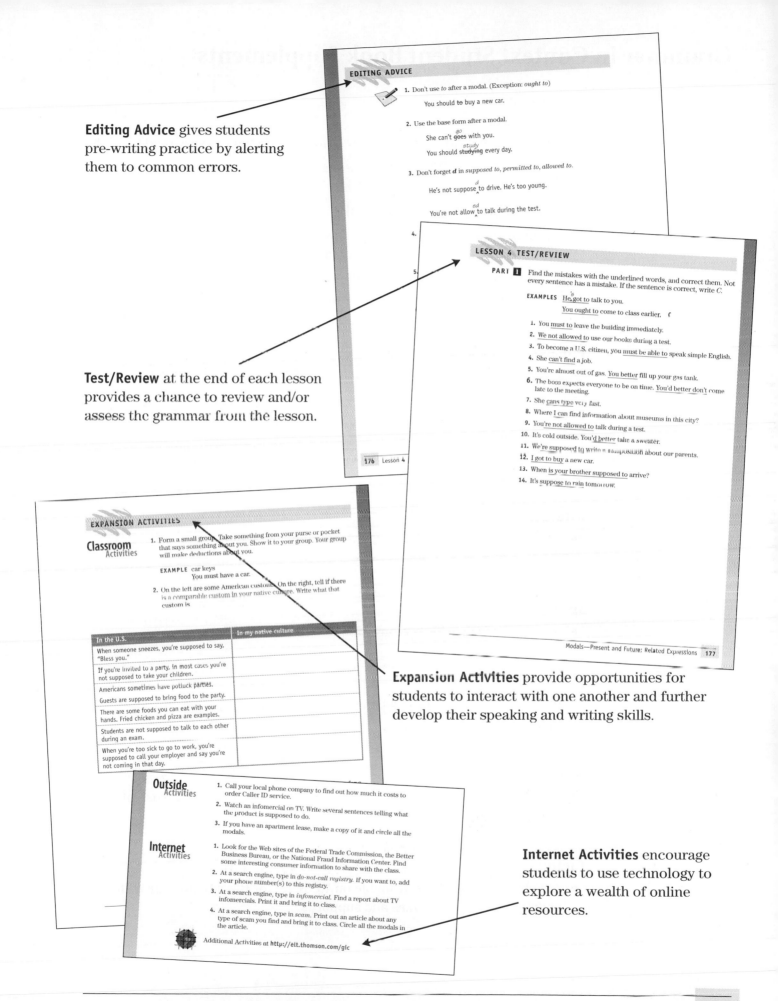

EDITING ADVICE

1. Don't use *to* after a modal. (Exception: *ought to*)

   You should ~~to~~ buy a new car.

2. Use the base form after a modal.

   She can't ~~goes~~ go with you.

   You should ~~studying~~ study every day.

3. Don't forget *d* in *supposed to, permitted to, allowed to.*

   He's not suppose~~d~~ to drive. He's too young.

   You're not allow~~ed~~ to talk during the test.

Test/Review at the end of each lesson provides a chance to review and/or assess the grammar from the lesson.

176 Lesson 4

LESSON 4 TEST/REVIEW

PART 1 Find the mistakes with the underlined words, and correct them. Not every sentence has a mistake. If the sentence is correct, write *C*.

EXAMPLES He got to talk to you.

You ought to come to class earlier. *C*

1. You must to leave the building immediately.
2. We not allowed to use our books during a test.
3. To become a U.S. citizen, you must be able to speak simple English.
4. She can't find a job.
5. You're almost out of gas. You better fill up your gas tank.
6. The boss expects everyone to be on time. You'd better don't come late to the meeting.
7. She cans type very fast.
8. Where I can find information about museums in this city?
9. You're not allowed to talk during a test.
10. It's cold outside. You'd better take a sweater.
11. We're supposed to write a composition about our parents.
12. I got to buy a new car.
13. When is your brother supposed to arrive?
14. It's suppose to rain tomorrow.

Modals—Present and Future; Related Expressions 177

EXPANSION ACTIVITIES

Classroom Activities

1. Form a small group. Take something from your purse or pocket that says something about you. Show it to your group. Your group will make deductions about you.

   EXAMPLE car keys
   You must have a car.

2. On the left are some American customs. On the right, tell if there is a comparable custom in your native culture. Write what that custom is.

In the U.S.	In my native culture
When someone sneezes, you're supposed to say, "Bless you."	
If you're invited to a party, in most cases you're not supposed to take your children.	
Americans sometimes have potluck parties. Guests are supposed to bring food to the party.	
There are some foods you can eat with your hands. Fried chicken and pizza are examples.	
Students are not supposed to talk to each other during an exam.	
When you're too sick to go to work, you're supposed to call your employer and say you're not coming in that day.	

Expansion Activities provide opportunities for students to interact with one another and further develop their speaking and writing skills.

Outside Activities

1. Call your local phone company to find out how much it costs to order Caller ID service.
2. Watch an infomercial on TV. Write several sentences telling what the product is supposed to do.
3. If you have an apartment lease, make a copy of it and circle all the modals.

Internet Activities

1. Look for the Web sites of the Federal Trade Commission, the Better Business Bureau, or the National Fraud Information Center. Find some interesting consumer information to share with the class.
2. At a search engine, type in *do-not-call registry*. If you want to, add your phone number(s) to this registry.
3. At a search engine, type in *infomercial*. Find a report about TV infomercials. Print it and bring it to class.
4. At a search engine, type in *scam*. Print out an article about any type of scam you find and bring it to class. Circle all the modals in the article.

Additional Activities at **http://elt.thomson.com/gic**

Internet Activities encourage students to use technology to explore a wealth of online resources.

Grammar in Context Student Book Supplements

Audio Program
- Audio CDs and Audio Tapes allow students to listen to every reading in the book as well as selected dialogs.

More Grammar Practice Workbooks
- Workbooks can be used with *Grammar in Context* or any skills text to learn and review the essential grammar.
- Great for in-class practice or homework.
- Includes practice on all grammar points in *Grammar in Context*.

Teacher's Annotated Edition
- New component offers page-by-page answers and teaching suggestions.

Assessment CD-ROM with ExamView® Pro Test Generator
- Test Generator allows teachers to create tests and quizzes quickly and easily.

Interactive CD-ROM
- CD-ROM allows for supplemental interactive practice on grammar points from *Grammar in Context*.

Split Editions
- Split editions provide options for short courses.

Instructional Video
- Video offers teaching suggestions and advice on how to use *Grammar in Context*.

Web Site
- Web site gives access to additional activities and promotes the use of the Internet.

Toolbox
- A WebTutor™ Toolbox available on WebCT™ or Blackboard® provides chapter-by-chapter quizzes and support.

LESSON

1

GRAMMAR

The Present Perfect
The Present Perfect Continuous[1]

CONTEXT: Jobs

Job Résumé and Cover Letter
Where Have All the Jobs Gone?
The *Occupational Outlook Handbook*

[1] The Present Perfect Continuous is sometimes called the Present Perfect Progressive.

1.1 | An Overview

Present Perfect Tense

Subject	*Has / Have*	Past Participle	Complement
Daniel	has	had	several jobs.
We	have	been	in the U.S. for three years.
You	have	seen	the manager.

Present Perfect Continuous Tense

Subject	*Has / Have*	*Been*	Present Participle	Complement
Daniel	has	been	living	in the U.S. for many years.
We	have	been	studying	English for three years.
You	have	been	working	hard this year.

JOB RÉSUMÉ AND COVER LETTER

Before You Read

1. Do you have a résumé?

2. Do you have a job now? What do you do? How did you find your job?

3. How can you find and apply for a new job?

Read the résumé and cover letter on the next two pages. In the cover letter, pay special attention to the present perfect and present perfect continuous tenses.

Daniel Mendoza
6965 Troy Avenue
Chicago, Illinois 60659
773-555-1946
E-mail: dmendoza@srv.com

Summary: Hotel professional with proven management skills and successful experience in improving operations, upgrading properties, building teams, and improving customer relations.

Professional Experience

- Developed sales/marketing plans geared towards business travelers
- Handled customer relations, correspondence, and communication
- Coordinated, organized, and supervised front desk operations and food service
- Assisted guests and groups in planning tours and arranging transportation, restaurant accommodations, and reservations
- Designed and maintained hotel Web site
- Managed hotel bookkeeping

Employment History

2004–Present	Town and Country Hotel, Front Office Manager	Chicago, IL
2002–2004	Mid-Town Hotel, Bookkeeper (part-time)	Evanston, IL
1998–2002	Travel Time Hotel, Front Desk Clerk (part-time)	Champaign, IL
1994–1998	Hotel Mendoza, Front Desk Clerk	Mexico City, Mexico

Technical Proficiencies

- Microsoft Office (Word, Excel, Access, PowerPoint); Quicken; Photoshop; Dreamweaver; Flash; Fireworks; Front Page; HTML

Education

- Master of Science: Business Administration, Northwestern University, 2004
- Bachelors of Science: Business Administration, University of Illinois, 2002
- Degree in Hotel Management: National University of Mexico, 1998

Professional Affiliations

- Travel & Tourism Research Association (TTRA)
- Association of Travel Marketing Executives (ATME)
- International Association of Convention & Visitor Bureaus (IACVB)

6965 Troy Avenue
Chicago, Illinois 60659

June 4, 2005

Mr. Ray Johnson, General Manager
Paradise Hotel
226 West Jackson Boulevard
Chicago, Illinois 60606

Dear Mr. Johnson:

I would like to apply for the job of hotel office manager at the Paradise Hotel.

I come from Mexico City, where my family owns a hotel. I worked in the family business part-time when I was in high school. After high school, I studied hotel and restaurant management at the National University of Mexico. I came to the U.S. in 1998 because I wanted to continue my education and learn about managing larger hotels. Since I came to the U.S., I **have worked** in several American hotels. Over the years my English **has improved,** and I now consider myself bilingual. I am fluent in both Spanish and English, and this is a plus in the hotel business. I **have** also **studied** French and can speak it fairly well. I **have been** a U.S. citizen for the past two years.

I received my bachelor's degree from the University of Illinois in 2002 and my master's degree from Northwestern University in 2004. For the past few years, I **have been working** at the Town and Country Hotel. As you can see from my résumé, I **have had** a lot of experience in various aspects of the hotel business. Now that I have my degree in business administration, I am ready to assume[2] more responsibilities.

If you **have** already **filled** the manager's position, I would like you to consider me for any other position at your hotel. I **have** always **loved** the hotel business, and I know I can be an asset[3] to your hotel.

Thank you for considering my application. I look forward to meeting with you soon.

Sincerely,

Daniel Mendoza
Daniel Mendoza

EXERCISE 1 True or False. Based on the cover letter and résumé, decide if the statement is true (*T*) or false (*F*).

EXAMPLES Daniel has worked for his parents. **T**
Daniel has worked in California. **F**

1. Daniel has never worked in a factory.

2. Daniel has had experience with computers.

3. He has been in the U.S. for less than two years.

4. He has included information about his education.

5. He has studied a foreign language.

[2]*Assume* means *take on* or *accept.*
[3]To be an *asset* to a company means to have a talent or ability that will help the company.

6. He has had experience in several hotels.

7. He has already met with Mr. Johnson.

8. He has included his age and marital status in his résumé.

1.2 | The Present Perfect Tense—Forms

Affirmative

Subject	*Have*	Past Participle	Complement	Explanation
I	have	been	in the U.S. for three years.	To form the present perfect, use: *I, you, we, they*, plural noun + *have* + past participle.
You	have	had	a lot of experience.	
We	have	written	a job résumé.	
They	have	seen	the application.	
My parents	have	given	me encouragement.	

Subject	*Has*	Past Participle	Complement	Explanation
My sister	has	been	a doctor for two years.	To form the present perfect, use: *he, she, it*, singular noun + *has* + past participle.
She	has	had	a lot of experience.	
My father	has	visited	me in the U.S.	
It	has	rained	a lot this month.	

Negative

Subject	*Have / Has*	*Not*	Past Participle	Complement	Explanation
He	has	not	found	a job.	To form the negative, put *not* between the auxiliary verb (*has / have*) and the past participle.
The teacher	has	not	given	a test yet.	
We	have	not	done	Lesson Two yet.	
I	have	not	applied	for a job lately.	

With an Adverb

Subject	*Have / Has*	Adverb	Past Participle	Complement	Explanation
You	have	never	worked	in a factory.	You can put an adverb between the auxiliary verb (*have / has*) and the past participle.
We	have	always	wanted	to learn English.	
They	have	already	found	a job.	
My uncle	has	just	arrived	in the U.S.	
The plane	has	probably	arrived	already.	

EXERCISE 2 Read the following paragraph. Underline all present perfect tense verbs.

I am looking for a job. I <u>have been</u> an electrical engineer for the past eight years. I arrived in the U.S. a few months ago, so I have not had much experience with American job interviews. I don't think my English is a problem, because I have studied English since I was a child. But in my country, I found a job right after I graduated from college. I stayed at the same job until I came here. The process of finding a job in the U.S. is a bit different. To learn about this process, I have used the Internet. I have also taken a course at a nearby college on how to prepare for an interview. So far, I have had three interviews, but I have not done well on them. I hope that each interview will help me do better on the next one, and soon I hope to find a good job.

1.3 | The Past Participle

The past participle is the third form of the verb. We use it to form the present perfect tense.

Forms			Explanation
Regular Verbs			
BASE FORM	PAST FORM	PAST PARTICIPLE	The past participle of regular verbs ends in *-ed*. The past form and the past participle of regular verbs are the same.
work	worked	worked	
improve	improved	improved	
Irregular Verbs			
BASE FORM	PAST FORM	PAST PARTICIPLE	The past participle of irregular verbs is sometimes the same as the past form and sometimes different.
have	had	had	
leave	left	left	
		(same as past)	
write	wrote	written	
drive	drove	driven	
		(different from past)	

For some verbs, the past participle is different from the past form.

Base Form	Past Form	Past Participle
become	became	become
come	came	come
run	ran	run
blow	blew	blown
draw	drew	drawn
fly	flew	flown
grow	grew	grown
know	knew	known
throw	threw	thrown
swear	swore	sworn
tear	tore	torn
wear	wore	worn
break	broke	broken
choose	chose	chosen
freeze	froze	frozen
speak	spoke	spoken
steal	stole	stolen
begin	began	begun
drink	drank	drunk
ring	rang	rung
sing	sang	sung
sink	sank	sunk
swim	swam	swum
arise	arose	arisen
bite	bit	bitten
drive	drove	driven
ride	rode	ridden
rise	rose	risen
write	wrote	written
be	was / were	been
do	did	done
eat	ate	eaten
fall	fell	fallen
forget	forgot	forgotten
forgive	forgave	forgiven
get	got	gotten
give	gave	given
go	went	gone
lie	lay	lain
mistake	mistook	mistaken
prove	proved	proven (or proved)
see	saw	seen
shake	shook	shaken
show	showed	shown (or showed)
take	took	taken

Note: For an alphabetical list of irregular past tenses and past participles, see Appendix M.

EXERCISE 3   Fill in the blanks with the past participle of the verb shown.

1. eat _____
2. go _____
3. read _____
4. drive _____
5. work _____
6. see _____
7. believe _____
8. swim _____
9. drink _____
10. steal _____

11. find _____
12. listen _____
13. think _____
14. live _____
15. make _____
16. write _____
17. grow _____
18. begin _____
19. be _____
20. study _____

21. ride _____
22. hid _____
23. look _____
24. leave _____
25. fall _____
26. feel _____
27. choose _____
28. lose _____
29. do _____
30. understand _____

EXERCISE 4   Fill in the blanks with the correct form of the verb in parentheses ( ) to form the present perfect tense.

EXAMPLE   Daniel _____*has sent*_____ three résumés this week.
                                  (send)

1. He _____ several interviews.
       (have)

2. Mr. Johnson _____ a letter from Daniel.
                    (get)

3. There _____ many applicants for the job.
            (be)

4. Daniel's parents _____ in the hotel business.
                      (always/be)

5. Daniel _____ from college.
        (recently/graduate)

6. I _____ Daniel's résumé.
     (read)

7. Daniel _____ as a programmer.
          (never/work)

8. He _____ his résumé to many companies.
      (send)

9. The company _____ 20 applicants so far.
                  (interview)

1.4 | The Present Perfect—Contractions

Examples	Explanation
I've had a lot of experience. **It's** been hard to find a job. **There's** been a change in my plans.	We can make a contraction with subject pronouns and *have* or *has*. I have = I've He has = He's You have = You've She has = She's We have = We've It has = It's They have = They've There has = There's
My father**'s** taught me a lot about the hotel business. The manager**'s** had many job applications.	Most singular nouns can contract with *has*.

I **haven't** had experience in the restaurant business.
 Mr. Johnson **hasn't** called me.
	Negative contractions:
	    have not = haven't
	    has not = hasn't

> **Language Note:**
> The **'s** in *he's, she's, it's,* and *there's* can mean *has* or *is.* The word following the contraction will tell you what the contraction means.
>   He's working. = He **is** working.
>   He's worked. = He **has** worked.

EXERCISE 5   Make a contraction with the subject to fill in the blanks. Use *hasn't* or *haven't* for negative consequences.

EXAMPLE   You*'ve* _____ already sent your application.

1. I _____ applied for many jobs.

2. We _____ seen Daniel's résumé.

3. His father _____ never come to the U.S.

4. It _____ been hard for Daniel to find a job.

5. Daniel _____ had several jobs so far.

6. Mr. Johnson (not) _____ looked at all the résumés.

7. They (not) _____ made a decision yet.

1.5 | The Present Perfect—Question Formation

Compare affirmative statements and questions

Wh- Word	Have / Has	Subject	Have / Has	Past Participle	Complement	Short Answer
		He	has	had	hotel experience.	
	Has	he		had	restaurant experience?	No, he hasn't.
Where	has	he		had	hotel experience?	In Mexico and the U.S.
		You	have	worked	in the U.S.	
	Have	you		worked	in Mexico?	Yes, I have.
How long	have	you		worked	in the U.S.?	For two years.
		Someone	has	read	the résumé.	
		Who	has	read	the résumé?	
		Something	has	happened.		
		What	has	happened?		

Compare negative statements and questions

Wh- Word	Haven't / Hasn't	Subject	Haven't / Hasn't	Past Participle	Complement
		He	hasn't	found	a job yet.
Why	hasn't	he		found	a job?
		You	haven't	seen	my résumé.
Why	haven't	you		seen	my résumé?

EXERCISE 6 Read the job interview with Daniel. Write the missing words in the blanks.

A: I've ___looked at___ your résumé. I see you work in a hotel.
(example)

B: Yes, I do.

A: How long _____ you _____ this job?
(1) (2)

B: I' _____ had this job for only a short time. But I _____
(3) (4)

_____ a lot of experience in the hotel business. In fact, my parents own a hotel in Mexico.

A: How long _____ your parents _____ a hotel?
(5) (6)

B: Most of their lives.

A: _____ you seen your parents recently?
         (7)

B: My mother _____ _____ to the U.S. a few
                      (8)   (9)

times to see me. But my father _____ never
                                       (10)

_____ here because someone has to stay at the
      (11)

hotel all the time. He's _____ me many times, "When
                             (12)

you are an owner of a business, you don't have time for vacations."
But I don't want to be an owner now. I just want a job as a manager.

_____ you filled the position yet?
      (13)

A: No, I haven't. I' _____ already _____
                             (14)   (15)

several people and will interview a few more this week. When we
make our decision, we'll let you know.

1.6 | Uses of the Present Perfect Tense—An Overview

Examples	Explanation
Daniel **has been** in the U.S. since 1998. He **has had** his present job for a short time. He **has** always **loved** the hotel business.	The action started in the past and **continues** to the present.
He **has sent** out 20 résumés so far. He **has had** three interviews this month.	The action **repeats** during a period of time that started in the past and continues to the present.
Mr. Johnson **has received** Daniel's letter. He **hasn't made** his decision yet. **Has** Daniel ever **worked** in a restaurant? Daniel **has studied** French, and he speaks it fairly well.	The action occurred at an **indefinite time** in the past. It still has importance to a present situation.

EXERCISE 7 Fill in the blanks with appropriate words to complete each statement. (Refer to the résumé and cover letter on pages 3–4.)

EXAMPLE Daniel has included ___*his phone number*___ in his résumé.

1. Daniel has been _____ since 1992.

2. He has had his job at the Town and Country Hotel for _____.

3. He has studied in _____ universities.

4. He has never worked in _____.

5. He has had a lot of experience in _____ .

6. In his résumé, he has not included _____ .

7. So far, he has worked in _____ hotels.

8. He hasn't _____ a job yet.

9. Why _____ a job yet?

10. _____ ever organized group transportation?

11. Daniel has _____ hotel bookkeeping.

12. _____ finished his master's degree yet? Yes, he _____ .

13. How long _____ a member of a travel association? He's been a member for several years.

14. How many times _____ worked with business travelers?

15. He has lived in _____ cities in Illinois. He has never _____ in New York.

16. He has _____ French and speaks it fairly well.

1.7 | The Present Perfect with Continuation from Past to Present

We use the present perfect tense to show that an action or state started in the past and continues to the present.

Examples	Explanation
a. Daniel has been a U.S. citizen **for two years.** b. His parents have been in the hotel business **all their lives.** c. He has had his job **for the past few years.**	a. Use *for* + amount of time. b. Omit *for* with an expression beginning with *all.* c. You can say *for the past / last* + time period.
Daniel has been in the U.S. **since 1998.** I have been a citizen **since last March.**	Use *since* + date, month, year, etc. to show when the action began.
I have had my car **since I** *came* **to the U.S.** He has wanted to manage hotels **ever since he** *was* **a teenager.**	Use *since* or *ever since* to begin a clause that shows the start of a continuous action. The verb in the *since*-clause is in the simple past tense.
Daniel went to Chicago in 2002. He has been there **ever since.** My grandfather gave me a watch when I was five years old. I have had it **ever since.**	You can put *ever since* at the end of the sentence. It means "from the past time mentioned to the present."
How long has he been in the U.S.? **How long** have you known your best friend?	Use *how long* to ask an information question about length of time.
Daniel has **always** loved the hotel business. I have **always** wanted to start my own business. I have **never** liked cold weather. Daniel has **never** written to Mr. Johnson before.	We use the present perfect with *always* and *never* to show that an action began in the past and continues to the present. We often use *before* at the end of a *never* statement.

```
                1998                    now
past ←──────────────────────────────────────────────────────→ future
              │ He has been in the │
              │ U.S. since 1998    │
              └────────────────────┘
```

EXERCISE **8** Fill in the blanks with the missing word(s). Not every sentence needs a word.

EXAMPLE I'_ve_____ been in the U.S. for three years.

1. Daniel has _____ in Chicago _____ 2002.

2. How _____ has he been in the U.S.? He'_____ been in the U.S. _____ many years.

3. He found a good job in 2004. He _____ worked at the

   same job ever _____ .

   4. He has worked at a hotel ever _____ he _____
   from high school.

   5. His parents have lived in Mexico _____ all their lives.

   6. Daniel has had his apartment for the _____ ten months.

   7. _____ you always worked in a hotel?

   8. _____ long have you had your job?

   9. Daniel _____ been in the U.S. since he _____ from
   college.

   10. He has wanted to manage a hotel _____ since he was a child.

EXERCISE 9 ABOUT YOU Make statements with *always*.

EXAMPLE Name something you've always thought about.
I've always thought about my future.

   1. Name something you've always disliked.

   2. Name something you've always liked.

   3. Name something you've always wanted to own.

   4. Name something you've always wanted to do.

   5. Name something you've always believed in.

EXERCISE 10 ABOUT YOU Write four **true** sentences telling about things
you've always done or ways you've always been. Share your
answers with the class.

EXAMPLES *I've always worked very hard.* _____

   I've always been very thin. _____

   1. _____

   2. _____

   3. _____

   4. _____

EXERCISE 11 ABOUT YOU Make statements with *never*.

EXAMPLE Name a machine you've never used.
I've never used a sewing machine.

1. Name a food you've never tried.
2. Name something you've never drunk.
3. Name something you've never owned.
4. Name something you've never done.
5. Name something your teacher has never done in class.
6. Name a job you've never had.

EXERCISE 12 ABOUT YOU Write four **true** sentences telling about things you've never done but would like to. Share your answers with the class.

EXAMPLES *I've never gone to Paris, but I'd like to.*

I've never flown in a helicopter, but I'd like to.

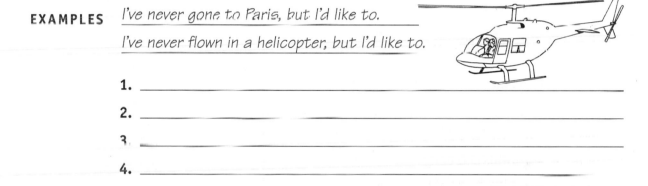

1. _____

2. _____

3. _____

4. _____

1.8 | Negative Statements with *Since, For,* and *In*

We can use *since, for,* and *in* with negative statements.	
Examples	**Explanation**
Daniel hasn't worked in Mexico **since** 1998.	He worked in Mexico until 1998. He stopped in 1998.
Daniel hasn't seen his parents **for** three years. OR Daniel hasn't seen his parents **in** three years.	He saw his parents three years ago. That was the last time. In negative statements, you can use either *for* or *in*.
Language Note: We often say *in ages* to mean "in a long time." Hi Daniel! I haven't seen you **in ages!**	

ABOUT YOU Name something.

EXAMPLE Name something you haven't eaten in a long time.
I haven't eaten fish in a long time.

1. Name someone you haven't seen in a long time.

2. Name a place you haven't visited in a long time.

3. Name a food you haven't eaten in a long time.

4. Name a subject you haven't studied since you were in high school.

5. Name a game you haven't played since you were a child.

6. Name something you haven't had time to do since you started to study English.

1.9 | The Present Perfect vs. the Simple Present

Examples	Explanation
I **am** in the U.S. now. I **have been** in the U.S. *for* two years.	The simple present refers only to the present time. The present perfect with *for, since, always,* or *never* connects the past to the present.
He **has** a car. He **has had** his car *since* March.	
I **love** my job. I **have** *always* **loved** my job.	
I **don't like** to wake up early. I **have** *never* **liked** to wake up early.	

EXERCISE 14 Fill in the blanks to complete the following conversations. Some answers may vary.

EXAMPLES **A:** Do you have a computer?

B: Yes, I do.

A: How long _____have you_____ had your computer?

B: I _'ve had_____ my computer for three years.

1. **A:** Do you have a car?

   B: Yes, I do.

   A: How long _____ your car?

   B: I _____ my car for six months.

2. **A:** Is your sister married?

   B: Yes, she is.

   A: How long _____ married?

   B: She _____ since 1995.

3. **A:** Do you have a bike?

   B: Yes, I _____.

   A: How long _____ your bike?

   B: I _____ my bike _____

   the past _____.

4. **A:** Do you want to learn English?

   B: Of course, I do.

   A: _____ long _____ to learn English?

   B: I _____ to learn English ever since I

   _____ a child.

5. **A:** Does your mother have a driver's license?

   B: Yes, she _____.

   A: How _____ her driver's license?

   B: She _____ her driver's license since _____.

6. **A:** ___ _____ Ms. Foster your teacher?

   B: Yes, she is.

   A: How long _____ _____ _____ your teacher?

   B: For _____.

7. **A:** Does your school have a computer lab?

   B: Yes, it _____ _____.

   A: _____ long _____ a computer lab?

   B: It _____ a computer lab since _____.

8. **A:** Do you know your friend Mark very well?

   B: Yes, I _____.

   A: How long _____ each other?

   B: We _____ each other ever

   _____ we _____ in elementary school.

9. **A:** _____ your son _____ a cell phone?

   B: Yes, he _____.

   A: How long _____?

   B: He bought one when he started going to college and he

   _____ it ever _____

   _____.

10. A: Do you like to dance?

    B: Yes, I _____.

    A: _____ you always _____ to dance?

    B: Yes. I've always liked to dance. But my wife _____

    never _____ to dance.

EXERCISE 15   Read each statement about your teacher. Then ask your teacher a question beginning with the words given. Include *always* in your question. Your teacher will answer.

EXAMPLE   You're a teacher. Have you _____ *always been a teacher?* _____
No. I was a nurse before I became a teacher. I've only been a teacher for five years.

1. You teach adults. Have you _____

2. You work with ESL students. Have you _____

3. You're a teacher at this school. Have you _____

4. You think about grammar. Have you _____

5. English is easy for you. Has English _____

6. Your last name is _____. Has your last name _____

    _____

7. You live in this city. Have you _____

8. You like teaching. Have you _____

EXERCISE 16   ABOUT YOU   Ask a present tense question. Another student will answer. If the answer is *yes*, ask *Have you always . . .?*

EXAMPLE   **A:** Are you interested in learning English?
B: Yes, I am.
A: Have you always been interested in learning English?
B: Yes. I've been interested in learning English since I was a small child.

1. Are you a good student?

2. Do you wear glasses?

3. Do you like to travel?

4. Are you interested in politics?

5. Do you like American movies?

6. Are you an optimist?

7. Do you think about your future?

8. Do you live in an apartment?

9. Are you a friendly person?

10. Do you use credit cards?

11. Do you work hard?

12. Do you want a college degree?

WHERE HAVE ALL THE JOBS GONE?

Before You Read

1. Do you know anyone who has lost a job?

2. Do you think some jobs are more secure than others? Which ones?

Read the following article. Pay special attention to the present perfect and present perfect continuous tenses.

Have you ever **called** an American company for service and **gotten** an answer from someone in another country? Many American companies **have been moving** customer service and technology jobs overseas. Using workers in other countries is called "outsourcing." India is the leading country used in outsourcing. Why India? Because India has a high level of information technology (IT) workers, and many Indians speak English well.

(continued)

Did You Know?

A computer programmer in the U.S. who makes $80,000 a year can be replaced with an Indian worker at $11,000 a year.

Why **has** this shift[4] **occurred?** By using lower wages[5] overseas, U.S. companies can cut labor costs by 25% to 40%. In addition, service is available to customers 24 hours a day by phone or online.

Years ago, American companies started using foreign labor for manufacturing jobs. But college educated workers thought they had nothing to worry about. Then companies started to move call centers abroad[6] to cut costs. But more and more of the jobs going abroad today go to highly skilled, educated people.

Many American workers who **have been working** at the same company for years are losing their jobs. Many educated workers **have had** to take jobs at a lower pay or get more training or education. While U.S. companies **have been benefiting** from outsourcing, American workers **have been losing**. While some American workers in some fields **have become** more insecure about their jobs, educated Indian workers **have become** more confident.

U.S. companies are expected to send 3.4 million jobs overseas by 2015. The U.S. government **has been studying** the impact of outsourcing on the American economy.

1.10 | The Present Perfect Continuous

Forms

Subject	*Have / Has*	*Been*	Present Participle	Complement
I	**have**	**been**	**working**	in a call center.
Workers	**have**	**been**	**losing**	their jobs.
You	**have**	**been**	**getting**	more job experience.
Companies	**have**	**been**	**moving**	jobs overseas.
The U.S.	**has**	**been**	**studying**	the effects of outsourcing.
Daniel	**has**	**been**	**working**	at a hotel.
He	**has**	**been**	**living**	in the U.S.

Language Notes:
1. To form the negative, put *not* between *have* or *has* and *been*.
   You **have *not*** **been** studying.   She **has *not*** **been** working hard.
2. We can make contractions for negative forms.
   have not = haven't   *has not = hasn't*

---

[4] A *shift* is a change.
[5] *Wages* means pay for a job.
[6] *Abroad* means beyond the boundaries of one's country.

Uses

Examples	Explanation
I **have been working** at the same job since 2001. American companies **have been using** workers in foreign countries for many years.	We use the present perfect continuous to talk about an action that started in the past and continues to the present. We use *for* and *since* to show the time spent at an activity.
He **has been working** as a programmer for the past few years. OR He **has worked** as a programmer for the past few years.	With some verbs, we can use either the present perfect or the present perfect continuous with actions that began in the past and continue to the present. There is very little difference in meaning.
He's working now. → He **has been working** for the past eight hours.	If the action is still happening, use the present perfect continuous, not the present perfect.
I have **always** worked as a programmer. I have **never** had another career.	Do not use the continuous form with *always* and *never*.
Americans **have become** insecure about their jobs. (*Not: have been becoming*) I **have known** my friend for 10 years. (*Not: I have been knowing*)	We do not use a continuous tense with nonaction verbs. (See below for a list of nonaction verbs.)

Action: I **have been thinking** *about* starting a new career.
Nonaction: I **have** always **thought** *that* an educated person can find a good job.
	Think can be an action or nonaction verb, depending on its meaning.
	    Think about = action verb
	    Think that = nonaction verb

Nonaction: Daniel **has had** a lot of experience in hotels. Action: Daniel **has been having** problems finding a job.	*Have* is usually a nonaction verb. However, *have* is an action verb in these expressions: *have experience, have a hard time, have a good time, have difficulty, have trouble.*

Nonaction verbs

like	prefer	understand	taste	have (for possession)
love	know	remember	feel	
hate	believe	see	seem	
want	think (that)	smell	cost	
need	care (about)	hear	own	

EXERCISE 17 Fill in the blanks with the present perfect continuous form of the verb in parentheses ( ).

EXAMPLE   Bob ___*has been working*___ as a programmer for the past ten years.
                    (work)

1. His company _____ jobs to India since 2001.
                              (send)

2. He and his coworkers _____ about losing their jobs.
                                    (worry)

3. Bob _____ classes for the past two years to get retrained.
    (take)

4. He _____ a lot of articles about outsourcing.
        (read)

5. He _____ on his résumé for the past two days.
        (work)

6. His friends _____ him to see a job counselor.
            (advise)

EXERCISE 18   Fill in the blanks in the following conversations. Some answers may vary.

EXAMPLE   **A:** Do you ____*play*____ a musical instrument?

B: Yes. I play the guitar.

A: How long ___*have*___ you ___*been playing*___ the guitar?

B: I ___*'ve been playing*___ the guitar since I ___*was*___ ten years old.

1. A: Do you work with computers?

   B: Yes, I do.

   A: How long _____ you _____

   with computers?

   B: I _____ with computers since 1998.

2. A: _____ your father study English?

   B: Yes, he does.

   A: How long _____ he been _____?

   B: He _____ since he _____

   to the U.S.

3. A: Does your teacher have a lot of experience?

   B: Yes, she _____.

   A: How long _____ teaching English?

   B: She _____ English for 20 years.

4. **A:** Do you wear glasses?

   B: Yes, I _____.

   A: How _____ glasses?

   B: I _____ glasses since I _____ in high school.

5. **A:** _____ your parents live in this city?

   B: Yes, they _____.

   A: How _____ in this city?

   B: For _____.

6. **A:** Is your roommate preparing to take the TOEFL[7] test?

   B: Yes, he _____.

   A: How long _____ to take this test?

   B: Since _____.

7. **A:** _____ you studying for your chemistry test?

   B: Yes, I _____.

   A: How _____ for your chemistry test?

   B: I ___ _____ all week.

8. **A:** _____ your roommate using the computer now?

   B: Yes, he _____ .

   A: How long _____ it?

   B: He started to use it when he woke up and _____ it ever _____.

9. **A:** _____ it raining now?

   B: Yes, it _____.

   A: How long _____?

   B: It _____ since _____.

10. **A:** _____ she talking about her children again?

    B: Yes, she _____.

    A: How long _____ about them?

    B: For the past _____.

[7]The *TOEFL* is the Test of English as a Foreign Language. Many U.S. colleges and universities require foreign students to take this test.

EXERCISE 19   ABOUT YOU Fill in the blanks to make a **true** statement about the present. Then make a statement that includes the past by changing to the present perfect continuous form with *for* or *since*.

EXAMPLE   I'm studying _____ *French.*
_____ *I've been studying French for two semesters.*

1. I work in / as _____
   _____

2. I live _____
   _____

3. I attend _____
   _____

4. I'm trying to _____
   _____

5. I'm wearing _____
   _____

6. The teacher is explaining _____
   _____

7. I'm thinking about _____
   _____

8. I'm using _____
   _____

9. I'm studying _____
   _____

10. We're using _____
    _____

1.11 | The Present Perfect vs. the Simple Past

Examples	Explanation
How long **have** you **had** your present car? I've **had** my present car for three months. How long **have** you **been working** at your present job? I've **been working** at my present job for two years.	Use *how long* and *for* with the present perfect or present perfect continuous to include the present.
How long **did** you **have** your last car? I **had** my last car for six years. How long **did** you **work** at your last job? I **worked** at my last job for five years.	Use *how long* and *for* with the simple past tense when you are not including the present.
When did you **come** to the U.S.? I **came** to the U.S. a few years **ago**.	A question that asks *when* usually uses the simple past. A sentence that uses *ago* uses the simple past.
I **came** to this city on January 15. I **have been** in this city since January 15. I **have been living** in this city since January 15.	Use the past tense to refer to a past action that does not continue. Use the present perfect (continuous) to show the continuation of an action from past to present.

EXERCISE 20 Fill in the blanks with the simple past, the present perfect, or the present perfect continuous, using the words in parentheses ( ).

EXAMPLES How long ___*has she had*___ her present computer?
(she/have)

When ___*did she buy*___ her computer?
(she/buy)

1. How long _____ president of the U.S.?
(be/Lincoln)

2. Lincoln _____ president from 1861 to 1865.
(be)

3. How long _____ president of the U.S.?
(be/use the name of the current president)

4. He _____ president since _____.
(be)

5. I _____ English since I was in high school.
(study)

6. When I was a child, I _____ German.
(study)

7. Albert Einstein died in 1955. He _____ in the U.S. for
(live)

22 years.

8. I _____ in this city for _____ years.
(live)

9. When _____ your car?
   (you/buy)

10. I _____ my car two years ago.
    (buy)

11. How long _____ your driver's license?
    (you/have)

12. I _____ my driver's license since May.
    (have)

13. How long _____ our English teacher?
    (you/know)

14. I _____ our teacher for six months.
    (know)

15. When _____ the English teacher?
    (you/meet)

16. I _____ her in September.
    (meet)

17. How long _____ English in your previous school?
    (you/study)

18. How long _____ English in this school?
    (you/study)

EXERCISE 21 Two friends meet on the street. Fill in the blanks in their conversation below. Use the present perfect, the present perfect continuous, or the past. Fill in any other necessary words.

A: Hi, Ivan. I _haven't seen_ you _____ ages. Where _____?
(example: not/see)   *(1)*   *(2 you/be)*

B: I _____ for a job for the last few weeks.
(3 look)

A: What _____ to your old job?
(4 happen)

B: My company is outsourcing, and I _____ laid off last
(5 get)

month. I'm getting depressed. I _____ a paycheck
(6 not/have)

_____ four weeks.
(7)

A: Don't lose hope. You're young and educated and healthy.
B: I know. But jobs here are disappearing, even for educated people.

A: That's true. Look at me. I _____ to be an actor, but
(8 always/want)

I _____ tables in a restaurant for the last three
(9 wait)

years. My friend, Ron, has a degree in accounting, and he

_____ a taxi for the _____ two years.
(10 drive)   *(11)*

B: At least you're earning some money now. For the last month, I

_____ money but I _____ any.
(12 spend)   *(13 not/earn)*

A: If you want, I can ask my boss if there are any openings for a waitperson in the restaurant.

B: I _____ in a restaurant, and I don't really want to.
(14 never/work)

A: It would just be temporary, until you can find a computer job.

B: Temporary? Like your job? You _____ from
(15 graduate)
college three years ago and you _____ tables
(16 wait)
ever _____ .
(17)

A: But I _____ up hope of becoming a famous actor.
(18 never/give)

1.12 | The Present Perfect with Repetition from Past to Present

Examples	Explanation
Daniel is looking for a job. He **has had** three interviews *this month*. We **have studied** two lessons *this semester*.	We use the present perfect to talk about the repetition of an action in a time period that includes the present. The time period is open, and there is a possibility for more repetition to occur. Open time periods include: *today, this week, this month, this year, this semester.*
My company is laying off workers. Three workers **have lost** their jobs *so far.* We are planning to buy a house. *So far*, we **have looked** at five houses. *Up to now*, she **has had** three jobs.	*So far* and *up to now* mean "including this moment." We use these expressions with the present perfect to show that another repetition may occur.
Daniel **has worked** at *several* hotels. You **have had** *a lot of* experience with computers. I **have learned** *many* new words.	We can use *several, many, a lot of,* or a number to show repetition from past to present.
How many interviews **have** you **had** this year? *How much* money **have** you **spent** on career counseling so far? I **haven't spent** *any* money *at all* on career counseling.	We can ask a question about repetition with *how many* and *how much.* A negative statement with *"any . . . at all"* means the number is zero.
We'**ve studied** two lessons so far. *Not: We've been studying* two lessons so far.	Do not use the continuous form for repetition.

now

past ← |——————|———|———| ——————————————→ future

He **has had** three interviews
this month.

EXERCISE 22 Fill in the blanks in the following conversations.

EXAMPLE **A:** How many pages have we ___done___ in this book so far?

B: We _'ve___ done 50 pages so far.

1. **A:** How many tests _____ we had so far this semester?

   B: So far we _____ two tests this semester.

2. **A:** How many compositions have we _____ this semester?

   B: We _____ two compositions this semester.

3. **A:** How many times have you _____ absent this semester?

   B: I _____ absent one time this semester.

4. **A:** How many times _____ the teacher been absent this semester?

   B: The teacher _____ absent at all this semester.

5. **A:** How much money have we _____ this week?

   B: We _____ about $100 so far this week. We

   need to save more.

6. **A:** How _____ phone calls _____

   so far today?

   B: She _____ made ten phone calls so far today.

7. **A:** How _____ water have you _____ today?

   B: I _____ two glasses of water so far today.

8. **A:** How _____ TV shows _____ the children

   _____ today?

   B: They _____ three TV programs today.

9. **A:** How many _____ have you _____

   your teeth today?

   B: I _____ my teeth twice so far today.

10. **A.** How many meals have you _____ in a restaurant this week?

    B: I _____ in a restaurant at all this week.

EXERCISE 23 ABOUT YOU Write a statement to tell how many times you have done something in this city. (If you don't know the exact number, you may use *a few*, *several*, or *many*.)

EXAMPLES live in / apartment(s)

I've lived in one apartment in this city.

get lost / time(s)

I've gotten lost a few times in this city.

1. have / job(s)

_____

2. have / job interview(s)

_____

3. have / traffic ticket(s)

_____

4. buy / car(s)

_____

5. attend / school(s)

_____

6. live in / apartment(s)

_____

7. go downtown / time(s)

_____

EXERCISE 24 ABOUT YOU Ask a question with *How much . . . ?* or *How many . . . ?* and the words given. Talk about today. Another student will answer.

EXAMPLES coffee / have
A: How much coffee have you had today?
B: I've had three cups of coffee today.

glasses of water / drink
A: How many glasses of water have you drunk today?
B: I haven't drunk any water at all today.

1. tea / have

2. glasses of water / have

3. cookies / eat

4. glasses of cola / have

5. times / check your e-mail

6. miles / walk or drive

7. money / spend

8. coffee / have

1.13 | Present Perfect vs. Simple Past with Repetition

Examples	Explanation
How many interviews **have** you **had** this month? I **have had** two interviews **so far** this month. How many times **have** you **been** absent this semester? I **have been** absent twice **so far**.	To show that there is possibility for more repetition, use the present perfect. *This month* and *this semester* are not finished. *So far* indicates that the number given may not be final.
How many interviews **did** you **have** last month? I **had** four interviews last month. How many times **were** you absent last semester? I **was** absent four times last semester.	To show that the number is final, use the simple past tense and a past time expression (*yesterday, last week, last year, last semester,* etc.).
Compare: a. I **have seen** my counselor twice this week. b. I **saw** my counselor twice this week. a. I **have made** five phone calls today. b. I **made** five phone calls today.	With a present time expression (such as *today, this week,* etc.), you may use either the present perfect or the simple past. a. The number may not be final. b. The number seems final.
Compare: a. My grandfather died in 1998. He **had** several jobs in his lifetime. b. My father is a programmer. He **has had** five jobs so far.	a. If you refer to the experiences of a dead person, you must use the simple past tense because nothing more can be added to that person's experience. b. A living person can have more of the same experience.
Compare: a. In my country, I **had** five jobs. b. In the U.S., I **have had** two jobs.	a. To talk about a closed phase of your life, luse the simple past tense. For example, if you do not plan to live in your native country again, use the simple past tense to talk about your experiences there. b. To talk about your experiences in this phase of your life, you can use the present perfect tense.

EXERCISE 25 In the conversation below, fill in the blanks with the correct form of the verb in parentheses ( ).

A: I'm very frustrated about finding a job. I ___*have sent*___ out 100
(example: send)

   résumés so far. And I _____ dozens of phone calls to
   (1 make)

   companies.

B: Have you _____ any answers to your letters and calls?
   (2 have)

A: Yes. Last week I _____ six interviews. But so far, nobody
   (3 have)

   _____ me a job.
   (4 offer)

B: You should call those companies.

A: I know I should. But this week, I _____ (5 be) very busy getting career counseling. I _____ (6 see) my counselor several times in the past few weeks.

B: Has your counselor _____ (7 give) you any advice about looking for a job?

A: Yes. Last week she _____ (8 give) me a lot of advice. But looking for a job is so strange in the U.S. I feel like I have to sell myself.

B: Don't worry. You _____ (9 not/have) much work experience in the U.S. so far. I'm sure you'll get used to the process of finding a job.

A: I don't know. I _____ (10 talk) to a lot of other people looking for work. Even though English is their native language, they _____ (11 not/have) much luck either.

B: _____ (12 it/be) easy for you to find a job when you lived in your native country?

A: In my native country, I _____ (13 never/have) this problem. After I _____ (14 graduate) from college, I _____ (15 find) a job immediately and _____ (16 work) in the same place for many years.

B: In the U.S., people change jobs often. Take me, for example. I _____ (17 have) six jobs, and I'm only 28 years old.

A: I'm 40 years old. But when I lived in my native country, I _____ (18 have) the same job for ten years. And I _____ (19 live) in the same apartment for many years until I came to the U.S. My parents _____ (20 live) in the same apartment from the time they got married until the time they died.

B: Get used to it! Life today is about constant change.

Before You Read

1. Have you ever seen a counselor about finding a job?

2. What careers interest you? What are some jobs you wouldn't want to have?

Read the following conversation between a college student (S) and her counselor (C). Pay special attention to the present perfect tense and the present perfect continuous tense.

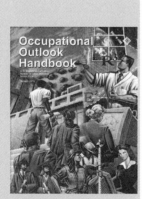

C: I see you're majoring in art. **Have** you **thought** about a career yet for your future?

S: I**'ve thought** about it, but I'm still not sure what I'm going to do when I graduate. I**'ve** always **loved** art, but my parents are worried that I won't be able to make a living as an artist. Lately **I've been thinking** about changing majors.

C: What major **have** you **been considering?**

S: Graphic design or commercial art.

C: **Have** you **taken** any courses in these fields?

S: I**'ve** already **taken** a course in graphic design. But I don't know much about the future of this career. Are there a lot of jobs for graphic artists?

C: **Have** you ever **used** the *Occupational Outlook Handbook*?

S: No, I **haven't.** I**'ve** never even **heard** of it. What is it?

C: It's a government publication that gives you a lot of information about jobs in the U.S. You can find it in the library or on the Internet. If you look up "graphic designer" in this publication, it will tell you the nature of the work, where the jobs are, what salary you can expect, what kind of training you need, what the future will be for graphic designers, and much more.

S: Thanks for the information. Can I come back and see you in a few weeks after I have a chance to check out the *Occupational Outlook Handbook*?

C: Yes, please come back.

> *(A few weeks later)*
>
> **C:** Hi. **Have** you **looked** at the *Occupational Outlook Handbook* yet?
>
> **S:** Yes. Thanks for telling me about it. **I've looked** at many jobs in the art field, but so far I **haven't decided** on anything yet. But I have some ideas.
>
> **C:** **Have** you **talked** to your parents lately? **Have** you **told** them that you're planning on changing majors?
>
> **S:** Oh, yes. They're very happy about it. They don't want me to be a starving[8] artist.

1.14 | The Present Perfect with Indefinite Past Time—An Overview

We use the present perfect to refer to an action that occurred at an indefinite time in the past that still has importance to a present situation.

Questions	Short Answers	Explanation
Has she **ever visited** a counselor? **Have** you **ever used** the *Occupational Outlook Handbook*? **Have** you **ever taken** an art history course?	Yes, she **has.** No, I never **have.** No, I **haven't.**	A question with *ever* asks about any time between the past and the present. Put *ever* between the subject and the main verb in a question.
Have you **decided** on a major **yet**? **Has** she **told** her parents about her decision **yet**?	No, not **yet.** Yes, she **already** has.	*Yet* and *already* refer to an indefinite time in the near past. There is an expectation that an activity took place a short time ago.
Have you **talked** to your parents **lately**? **Have** you **seen** your counselor **recently**?	No, I **haven't.** Yes, I **have.**	Questions with *lately* and *recently* refer to an indefinite time in the near past.

now

past ← ——————————————————————————————— → future

Have you ever **seen** a job counselor?

---

[8]*Starving* means hungry, not having enough to eat.

EXERCISE 26 Read the following conversation. Underline the present perfect and present perfect continuous tenses.

EXAMPLE **A:** There's going to be a job fair at the college next week. <u>Have</u> you ever <u>gone</u> to one?

B: What's a job fair?

A: Representatives from different companies come to one place. You can meet these people, find out about their companies, and give them your résumé. Lately I've been going to a lot of job fairs. And I've been looking for jobs online. I've just rewritten my résumé too. I haven't found a job yet, but I'm hopeful.

B: But you have a good job as an office manager.

A: I'm going to quit in two weeks. I've already given my employer notice. I've worked there for two years, and I haven't had a raise yet. I've realized that I can make more money doing something else. I've talked to a career counselor and I've taken a test to see what I'm good at. I've also taken more courses to upgrade my skills.

B: Have you decided what you want to do?

A: Yes. I've decided to be a legal assistant.

1.15 | Questions with *Ever*

Examples	Explanation

Have you ever **seen** a job counselor?
   Yes, I **have. I've seen** a job counselor a few times.
 Have you ever **used** the Internet to find a job?
   Yes, I**'ve used** the Internet many times.
 Have you ever **worked** in a restaurant?
   No, I never **have.**
	We use *ever* to ask a question about any time in the past.

Have you ever **written** a résumé?
   a. Yes, I **have.**
   b. Yes. I **wrote** my résumé two weeks ago.
 Has he ever **taken** a design course?
   a. Yes. He **has taken** several design courses.
   b. Yes. He **took** one last semester.
	You can answer an *ever* question with the present perfect or the simple past.
	 a. Use the **present perfect** to answer with no reference to time.
	 b. Use the **simple past** to answer with a definite time (*last week, last semester, last Friday, two weeks ago*).

EXERCISE 27 ABOUT YOU Ask a question with *Have you ever . . . ?* and the words given. Use the past participle of the verb. Another student will answer. If the answer is *yes*, ask for more specific information. To answer with a specific time, use the simple past tense. To answer with a frequency response, use the present perfect tense.

EXAMPLE eat a hot dog

A: Have you ever eaten a hot dog?
B: Yes, I have.
A: When did you eat a hot dog?
B: I ate one at a picnic last summer.

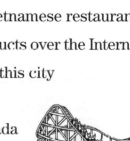

1. find money on the street
2. go to a garage sale
3. meet a famous person
4. study art history
5. get a ticket for speeding
6. be on television
7. win a contest or a prize
8. lend money to a friend
9. lose your keys
10. break an arm or a leg
11. go to a football game
12. go to court
13. hear of [6] Martin Luther King, Jr.
14. eat in a Vietnamese restaurant
15. order products over the Internet
16. get lost in this city
17. tell a lie
18. go to Canada
19. travel by train
20. eat pizza
21. be on a roller coaster
22. see a play in this city
23. eat Chinese food
24. use a digital camer
25. go camping
26. use a scanner

EXERCISE 28 Work with a partner. Use *ever* to write four questions to ask your teacher. Your teacher will answer.

EXAMPLES *Have you ever eaten raw fish?*

Have you ever written a poem?

1. _____

2. _____

3. _____

4. _____

[6]*Hear of* means to recognize a name.

EXERCISE 29 Fill in the blanks with the present perfect or the simple past to complete each dialogue. Sometimes part of the verb (phrase) has already been supplied.

1. **A:** Have you ever _____*studied*_____ algebra?
   (example)

   B: Yes. I studied it in high school.

   A: I like math a lot. Do you?

   B: No, I _____ never_____ math.

2. **A:** Have you ever _____ to Canada?

   B: No, I never have. But I would like to go there some day.

   A: _____ you ever gone to Mexico?

   B: Yes. I _____ there two years ago.

3. **A:** Have you ever broken your arm or leg?

   B: Yes. I _____ my leg when I was ten years old. I
   was climbing a tree.

   A: Which leg _____ you _____?

   B: I broke my left leg.

4. **A:** _____ your parents ever come here to visit you?

   B: No, they never _____. But last year my brother
   _____ to visit me for three weeks.

5. **A:** _____ you ever _____ an Italian
   movie?

   B: No, I haven't. But I _____ seen many French
   movies.

   A: I _____ never _____ a French
   movie.

6. **A:** _____ you ever _____ to the
   public library in this city?

   B: Yes. I _____ gone there many times. Last week I
   _____ there on Monday and checked out a novel
   by Mark Twain. I have never _____ Mark Twain's
   books in English.

   A: _____ you ever_____ his books in
   translation?

   B: Oh, yes. In high school, I_____ two of his novels
   in Spanish.

EXERCISE 30 ABOUT YOU Ask a question with *Have you ever . . . ?* and the words given. Another student will answer.

EXAMPLE ask your boss for a raise
A: Have you ever asked your boss for a raise?
B: No, I never have.

1. fill out a job application

2. have an interview

3. use the *Occupational Outlook Handbook*

4. see a job counselor

5. use a computer on a job

6. use a résumé writing service

7. take courses to train for a job

8. use the Internet to find a job

9. go to a state employment office

10. read a book about finding a job

11. quit a job

12. have your own business

13. be unemployed

14. think about becoming a nurse

15. work in a hotel

16. get job counseling at this school

17. work part-time

18. attend a job fair

1.16 | Yet, Already

Use *yet* and *already* with the present perfect to show an expectation that something took place.

Examples	Explanation
I **have talked** to my job counselor *already*. I **have** *already* **talked** to my job counselor.	For an affirmative statement, use *already*. You can put *already* at the end of the sentence or between the auxiliary verb and the main verb.
I **haven't written** my résumé *yet*. The counselor **hasn't answered** my e-mail *yet*.	For a negative statement, use *yet*. Put *yet* at the end of the statement.

Have you **talked** with your counselor *yet*?
  No, I **haven't**.
Have you **written** your résumé *yet*?
  No, **not yet**.
Have you **filled** out the application *yet*?
  Yes, I **already** have.
	For questions, use *yet*. You can use *yet* in a negative answer. You can use *already* in an affirmative answer.

Has he **eaten** dinner *yet*?
  Yes, he **ate** dinner *two hours ago*.
Have you **seen** the movie *yet*?
  Yes, I **saw** it *two weeks ago*.
	You can answer a *yet* question with a specific time. If you do so, you must use the simple past.

Language Note:
You often hear the simple past tense in questions with *yet* and statements with *already*. There is no difference in meaning between the present perfect and the past.
> **Have** you **eaten** dinner *yet*? = **Did** you **eat** dinner *yet*?
> I **have eaten** dinner *already*. = I **ate** dinner *already*.

EXERCISE 31 Ask a student who has recently moved here questions with the words given and *yet* or *already*. The student who answers should use the simple past tense if the answer has a specific time.

EXAMPLE go downtown
> **A:** Have you gone downtown yet?
> **B:** Yes. I went downtown three weeks ago.

1. buy a computer
2. find an apartment
3. get a library card
4. use public transportation
5. visit any museums
6. meet any of your neighbors

EXERCISE 32   Ask a question with the words given and *yet*. The student who answers should use the simple past tense if the answer has a specific time.

EXAMPLES   the teacher / take attendance

A: Has the teacher taken attendance yet?
B: Yes, he has. He took attendance at the beginning of the class.

the teacher / return the homework

A: Has the teacher returned the homework yet?
B: No, he hasn't. OR No, not yet.

1. we / have an exam

2. we / study modals

3. you / learn the irregular past tenses

4. the teacher / learn the students' names

5. you / learn the other students' names

6. the teacher / teach the past perfect

EXERCISE 33   Daniel is preparing for his job interview. He has made a list of things to do. He has checked those things he has already done. Make sentences about Daniel's list using the present perfect with *yet* or *already*.

EXAMPLES   _____ ✓ _____   prepare his résumé
He has already prepared his résumé.

_____ send his suit to the cleaner's
He hasn't sent his suit to the cleaner's yet.

1. _____ ✓ _____ buy a new tie

2. _____ ✓ _____ wash his white shirt

3. _____ iron his white shirt

4. _____ ✓ _____ get a haircut

5. _____ ✓ _____ rewrite his résumé

6. _____ take his résumé to a copy center

7. _____ ✓ _____ see a job counselor

8. _____ put his papers in his briefcase

9. _____ ✓ _____ send for his transcripts

10. _____ ✓ _____ get letters of recommendation

EXERCISE **34** Fill in the blanks to complete each conversation.

EXAMPLE **A:** Have you bought your textbook yet?

B: No. I ___haven't___ bought it _____yet._____

1. **A:** Have you _____ dinner yet?

   B: No, I haven't. I _____ lunch at 2:30, so I'm not hungry now.

2. **A:** _____ your sister gotten married yet?

   B: Yes. She _____ married two weeks ago. She _____ a beautiful wedding.

   A: Has she _____ back from her honeymoon yet?

   B: Yes. She _____ back last Thursday.

3. **A:** Have your parents _____ an apartment yet?

   B: No. They _____ found one yet. They're still looking.

4. **A:** I'm going to rent the movie *Titanic*. Have you _____ it yet?

   B: Yes, I _____ it a couple of years ago, but I'd like to see it again.

5. **A:** What are you going to do during summer vacation?

   B: I haven't _____ about it yet. It's only April.

   A: I've already _____ plans. I'm going to Niagara Falls. I _____ my ticket last week.

6. **A:** Has the movie _____ yet? I want to buy some popcorn before it begins.

   B: Shhh! It _____ ten minutes ago.

7. **A:** Do you want to go to the museum with me on Saturday?

   B: Sorry. I _____ already _____ other plans for Saturday.

8. **A:** _____ your brother _____ back from Mexico yet?

   B: No, he hasn't. We're expecting him to arrive on Tuesday.

9. **A:** I'd like to talk to the teacher, please.

   B: I'm sorry. She's already _____ for the day.

   A: But she told me to call her before 4 o'clock and it's only 3:30.

   B: She _____ at 2 o'clock because her son was sick.

10. **A:** Is that a good book?

    B: Yes, it is. I haven't _____ it yet, but when I finish it, you can have it.

1.17 | Questions with *Lately* and *Recently*

Questions with *lately* and *recently* ask about an indefinite time in the near past. We can answer a *lately* or *recently* question with the present perfect or the simple past.

Examples	Explanation

Have you **seen** your parents lately?
  No, I **haven't**.
Have you **gotten** a raise recently?
  No. I **haven't gotten** a raise recently.
	When the answer is *no*, we usually use the present perfect.

Have you **seen** any good movies lately?
  Yes. I **saw** a great movie last week.
Have you **gone** to the library recently?
  Yes. I **went** to the library two days ago.
	When the answer is *yes*, we usually give a specific time and use the simple past tense.

EXERCISE **35** ABOUT YOU Ask a *yes / no* question with the words given. Another student will answer. A past-tense statement may be added to a *yes* answer.

EXAMPLE go swimming recently
  A: Have you gone swimming recently?
  B: Yes, I have. I went swimming yesterday.

1. write to your family lately
2. go to the library recently
3. go to the zoo lately
4. see any good movies lately
5. receive any letters lately
6. be absent lately
7. have a job interview lately
8. read any good books recently
9. make any long-distance calls lately
10. take any tests recently

EXERCISE 36   Work with a partner. Write four questions to ask your teacher about what he or she has done lately. Your teacher will answer.

EXAMPLE   *Have you taken a vacation lately (or recently)?*

1. _____

2. _____

3. _____

4. _____

EXERCISE 37   Fill in the blanks with the correct verb forms.

EXAMPLE   A: Have you _____*gotten*_____ a letter from your parents lately?
                        (get)

B: Yes. I _____*got*_____ a letter from them yesterday.

1. A: Have you _____ any pictures lately?
                        (take)

   B: No, I _____. My camera is broken.

2. A: Have you _____ any good movies lately?
                        (see)

   B: Yes. I _____ a great movie last weekend.

3. A: Have you _____ for a walk lately?
                        (go)

   B: Yes. I _____ for a walk yesterday.

4. A: Have you _____ yourself a gift lately?
                        (buy)

   B: Yes. I _____ myself a new CD player last week.

5. A: Have you _____ a good conversation with a friend lately?
                        (have)

   B: No. I _____ time to talk with my friends lately.

6. A: Have you _____ a massage lately?
                        (have)

   B: No. I _____ never _____ a massage.

7. A: Have you _____ the laundry lately?
                        (do)

   B: Yes. I _____ it this morning.

8. A: Have you _____ to any parties lately?
                        (go)

   B: No, I _____. I've been too busy lately.

1.18 | The Present Perfect Continuous with Ongoing Activities

Examples	Explanation
Many American companies **have been sending** jobs abroad. American companies **have been benefiting** from outsourcing. Lately I **have been thinking** about changing majors. My English **has been improving** a lot lately.	We use the present perfect continuous to show that an activity has been ongoing or in progress from a time in the near past to the present. Remember, do not use the continuous form with nonaction verbs: She **has been** absent a lot lately.

EXERCISE 38 ABOUT YOU Fill in the blanks with *have* or *haven't* to tell about your experiences lately. (You may add a sentence telling why.)

EXAMPLE   I ___*haven't*___ been reading a lot lately. *I haven't had much time.*

1. I _____ been getting a lot of sleep recently.

2. I _____ been getting together with my friends lately.

3. I _____ been watching the news a lot lately.

4. I _____ been studying a lot lately.

5. I _____ been learning a lot about English grammar lately.

6. I _____ been worrying a lot lately.

7. I _____ been looking for a job recently.

8. I _____ been watching a lot of TV recently.

9. I _____ been having a lot of problems with my car lately.

10. I _____ been spending a lot of money recently.

11. I _____ been absent a lot lately.

12. I _____ been using a computer a lot lately.

EXERCISE 39 ABOUT YOU Fill in the blanks to make **true** statements about yourself.

EXAMPLES   _____My pronunciation_____ has been getting better.

_____My eyesight_____ has been getting worse.

1. _____ has been improving.

2. _____ has been getting worse.

3. _____ has been increasing.

4. _____ has been helping me with my studies.

5. _____ has been making me tired.

1.19 | The Present Perfect with No Time Mentioned

Examples	Explanation
I **have thought** about my career. **Have** you **told** your parents that you're changing majors? Many educated workers **have lost** their jobs. Many American workers **have become** more insecure about their jobs.	We can use the present perfect to talk about the past without any reference to time. The time is not important or not known or imprecise. Using the present perfect, rather than the past, shows that the past is relevant to a present situation.

EXERCISE 40 ABOUT YOU Fill in the blanks to make a **true** statement about yourself.

EXAMPLE   I've eaten ____pizza____, and I like it a lot.

1. I've visited _____, and I would recommend it to other people.

2. I've tried _____, and I like this food a lot.

3. I've seen the movie _____, and I would recommend it to others.

4. The teacher has said that _____, but some of us forget.

5. I've studied _____, and it has really helped me in my life.

6. I've had a lot of experience with _____ and can help you with it, if you need me to.

EXERCISE 41 ABOUT YOU Place a check mark (✓) next to the work-related experiences you've had. Then at the bottom, write three more things you've done at your present or former job. Write things that would impress an interviewer.

1. _____ I've worked on a team.

2. _____ I've taken programming courses.

3. _____ I've had experience talking with customers on the phone.

4. _____ I've worked overtime when necessary to finish a project.

5. _____ I've worked and gone to school at the same time.

6. _____ I've helped my family financially.

7. _____ I've given oral presentations.

8. _____ I've done research.

9. _____ I've created a Web site.

10. _____ I've done physical labor.

11. _____ I've been in charge of a group of workers.

12. _____ I've traveled as part of my job.

13. _____

14. _____

15. _____

EXERCISE 42 Fill in the blanks with the present perfect (for no time mentioned) or the simple past (if the time is mentioned) of the verb in parentheses ( ).

I _*have had*_ many new experiences since I moved here. I
  (example: have)

_____ some foods for the first time in my life. I _____
    (1 try)   (2 eat)

pizza, but I don't like it much. Yesterday, I _____ Chinese food
                                                  (3 try)

for the first time and thought it was delicious.

I _____ a lot of new people and have some new friends.
   (4 meet)

I _____ some new behaviors. For example, there's a guy in my
   (5 see)

math class who wears torn jeans every day. Yesterday I _____ him
                                                          (6 ask)

if he needs money for new clothes, but he just laughed and said, "Torn

clothes are in style."

I _____ some interesting places. I _____ to the art
(7 visit)   (8 go)

museum and the science museum. I _____ a boat ride on a
                                    (9 take)

nearby river. I _____ to the top of the tallest building.
                (10 even/go)

I _____ about looking for a job. I _____ résumés and
  (11 learn)   (12 write)

_____ job interviews. I _____ to job fairs. I _____
(13 have)   (14 go)   (15 even/use)

the Internet for my job search. Last week I _____ to see a job counselor
                                            (16 go)

at my college, and she _____ me some help with interviewing
                        (17 give)

techniques.

1.20 | The Present Perfect vs. the Present Perfect Continuous with No Time Mentioned

We can use both the present perfect and the present perfect continuous with no time mentioned.

Examples	Explanation
a. My counselor **has helped** me with my résumé. b. My family **has been helping** me a lot.	The (a) examples are present perfect. They refer to a single occurrence at an indefinite time in the past.
a. I **have applied** for a job in New York. b. I **have been applying** for jobs all over the U.S.	The (b) examples are present perfect continuous. They refer to an ongoing activity that is not finished. The activity is still in progress.
a. **Have** you **eaten** in a restaurant lately? b. I**'ve been eating** in restaurants a lot lately.	

EXERCISE 43   Check (✓) the sentence or clause that best completes the idea.

EXAMPLE   I can't sleep. The people in the next apartment . . .

_____ have made a lot of noise.

___✓___ have been making a lot of noise.

1. She's been sick all week.

    _____ She's stayed in bed.

    _____ She's been staying in bed.

2. She is unhappy.

    _____ She has just lost her job.

    _____ She has been losing her job.

3. She lost her job three weeks ago. She hasn't had much free time lately because . . .

    _____ she has looked for a new job.

    _____ she has been looking for a new job.

4. My writing has been improving a lot because . . .

    _____ I have written compositions.

    _____ I have been writing compositions.

5. At first she planned to move, but now she doesn't want to.

    _____ She has changed her mind.

    _____ She has been changing her mind.

6. I meet new people everywhere: in my neighborhood, at my job, at school.

    _____ I have met new people.

    _____ I have been meeting new people.

7. Now I can pay for my car repair because I . . .

    _____ have received a check from my insurance company.

    _____ have been receiving a check from my insurance company.

8. Every week I put 20 percent of my salary in the bank. I plan to buy a house as soon as I can.

    _____ I have saved my money.

    _____ I have been saving my money.

9. I'm going to become an engineer.

    _____ I have made my decision.

    _____ I have been making my decision.

10. **A:** Have you been outside today?

    B: _____ No, I have worked on my composition.

    _____ No, I have been working on my composition.

EXERCISE 44 Fill in the blanks with the simple past, the present perfect, or the present perfect continuous of the verb in parentheses ( ). In some cases, more than one answer is possible.

EXAMPLE I _____worked_____ as a cashier when I was in high school.
          (work)

1. I think I'm qualified for the job of driver because I

    _____ as a driver before.
          (work)

2. I _____ as a pilot many years ago. My job as a pilot
          (work)

    _____ me away from home much of the time.
          (take)

3. I don't like the sight of blood, so I _____ about
                                              (never/think)

    becoming a doctor.

4. I'm a hair stylist. I _____ people's hair for 15 years.
                              (cut)

5. I'm afraid of the interview process because I

    _____ a job interview before.
          (never/have)

6. Many years ago, I _____ as a kindergarten
                            (work)

    teacher. Now I have my own day care center.

7. I'm a car mechanic. I _____ a mechanic for three
                              (be)

    years. I _____ a lot of experience working with
                (have)

    American cars, but I _____ much experience with
                              (not/have)

    foreign cars.

8. I'm 62 years old and I like my job as a lab technician, but I

    _____ about retiring soon.
          (think)

9. When I was in my native country, I _____ an
                                              (be)

    engineer, but now I'm a salesperson.

10. People _____ me why I want to be a funeral
    (often/ask)
    director when I graduate.

11. Lately I _____ the Internet a lot to get
    (use)
    information about jobs.

SUMMARY OF LESSON 1

Compare the Simple Present and the Present Perfect.

Simple Past	Present Perfect
She **has** a job.	She **has had** her job for six months.
She **is** a lab technician.	She **has been** a lab technician since May.

Compare the Present Continuous and the Present Perfect Continuous.

Present Continuous	Present Perfect Continuous
He **is working** now.	He **has been working** for three hours.
She **is sleeping** now.	She **has been sleeping** for 20 minutes.

Compare the Simple Past and the Present Perfect.

Simple Past	Present Perfect
Daniel **worked** in Mexico City from 1994 to 1998.	He **has worked** in the U.S. since 1998.
He **found** a job in 2004.	He **has had** his present job since January, 2004.
He **bought** his car when he came to Chicago.	He **has had** his car since he came to Chicago.
When **did** he **come** to Chicago?	How long **has** he **been** in Chicago?
He **had** three interviews last month.	He **has had** two interviews this month.
He **studied** business in college.	He **has studied** French and speaks it well.
He **went** to New York in July.	He **has gone** to Los Angeles many times.
Did you **go** to the job fair last week?	**Have** you ever **gone** to a job fair?

Compare the Present Perfect and the Present Perfect Continuous.

Present Perfect	Present Perfect Continuous
Ron **has worked** as a programmer for the past five years. *(This sentence has the same meaning as the one on the right.)*	Ron **has been working** as a programmer for the past five years. *(This sentence has the same meaning as the one on the left.)*
I **have lived** in three American cities. *(This sentence refers to a repetition from past to present.)*	I **have been living** in this city for the past two years. *(This sentence shows a continuation from past to present.)*
How many apartments **have** you **had** in this city? *(This question asks about a repetition from past to present.)*	How long **have** you **been living** in your present apartment? *(This question asks about a continuation from past to present.)*
Dan **has studied** French. *(This sentence shows only past activity, with no indication of a continuation.)*	The U.S. government **has been studying** the effect of outsourcing. *(This sentence shows an activity that is still in progress.)*
I **have thought** about changing majors. *(This sentence tells about a time in the indefinite past.)*	I **have been thinking** a lot about my future. *(In this sentence, the phrase "a lot" indicates that this activity is still in progress.)*

EDITING ADVICE

1. Don't confuse the *-ing* form and the past participle.

   taking
   I've been ~~taken~~ English courses for several years.

   been
   Have you ever ~~being~~ in Texas?

2. Don't confuse *for* and *since*.

   for
   He's been in Chicago ~~since~~ three years.

3. Use the simple past, not the present perfect, with a specific past time and in questions and statements with *when*.

wrote
He ~~has written~~ a book five years ago.

She ~~has~~ bought a car when she ~~has~~ found a job.

did he get
When ~~has he gotten~~ his driver's license?

4. Use the present perfect (continuous), not the present tense, if the action started in the past and continues to the present.

have been
I~~'m~~ working in a factory for six months.

have   had
How long ~~do~~ you ~~have~~ your computer?

5. Don't use the continuous form for repetition.

eaten
How many times have you ~~been eating~~ pizza?

6. Use the simple past in a *since*-clause.

came
He's had three jobs since he ~~has come~~ to the U.S.

7. Use correct word order.

never been
He has ~~been never~~ in New York.

ever eaten
Have you ~~eaten ever~~ Chinese food?

8. Use *yet* in negative statements. Use *already* in affirmative statements.

yet
I haven't finished the book ~~already~~.

already
I've finished the book ~~yet~~.

9. Use *how long* for a question about length of time. Don't include the word *time*.

How long ~~time~~ have they been working in a restaurant?

10. If the main verb is *have*, be sure to include the auxiliary verb *have* for the present perfect.

has
He ᴀ had his job since March.

PART 1 Find the mistakes with the underlined words and correct them. Not every sentence has a mistake. If the sentence is correct, write *C*.

EXAMPLES How many times have you ~~seeing~~ *seen* the movie?

Have you ever <u>traveled</u> by train? **C**

1. <u>How long time</u> have you known your best friend?

2. <u>Has</u> your mother <u>been</u> sick lately?

3. She's worked in a restaurant <u>since</u> five months.

4. Have you <u>gone ever</u> to the art museum?

5. How long <u>does</u> our teacher <u>work</u> at this school?

6. I'm <u>studying</u> English <u>for</u> three years.

7. How long <u>you've been living</u> in your present apartment?

8. He's had three jobs since <u>he's come</u> to this city.

9. How many times <u>have you calling</u> your parents this month?

10. When <u>have you come</u> to this city?

11. She <u>bought</u> a car when she <u>found</u> a job.

12. Have you ever <u>giving</u> your sister a present?

13. When her dog <u>died</u>, she felt sad.

14. She <u>has</u> her car since she graduated.

PART 2 Fill in the blanks with the simple present, simple past, present perfect, or present perfect continuous tense of the verb in parentheses ( ).

A: Hi, Ben. I <u>*haven't seen*</u> you in a long time. How <u>*have you been*</u>?
(example: not/see)   (example: you/be)

B: I'm okay. But I _____ a job now, so I feel
(1 not/have)

pretty depressed about it. I _____ for a job for the
(2 look)

past three months, but so far I _____ any success.
(3 not/have)

A: My best friend _____ (4 graduate) from college last year, and he _____ (5 not/find) a job yet. A lot of American jobs _____ (6 disappear) in recent years. Many jobs _____ (7 go) to India and other countries.

B: That's terrible. My family _____ (8 come) to the U.S. last year to find better jobs, but it's not easy anymore.

A: But it's not impossible. _____ you ever _____ (9 use) the *Occupational Outlook Handbook?*

B: No, I never _____ (10 have).

A: You can find it on a Web site. It lists information about professions in the U.S. My counselor _____ (11 tell) me about it when I _____ (12 start) taking courses. I _____ (13 have) a good job now. I _____ (14 work) as a dental assistant.

B: How long _____ (15 you/work) there?

A: Since I _____ (16 get) my certificate two years ago. I don't have to worry about outsourcing. You can't look in people's mouths from another country.

B: You're lucky to have such a good job.

A: It's not luck. I _____ (17 choose) this job carefully before I started taking courses. And I _____ (18 study) hard when I was in the dental program. Now when I _____ (19 go) to work every day, I _____ (20 feel) good because I am helping people and making good money. Also I _____ (21 have) good benefits. In addition, I _____ (22 get) two salary increases so far.

B: That's wonderful! _____ ever _____ about
(23 you/think)

becoming a dentist? They make good money.

A: I _____ about it, but I don't want to spend so much
(24 think)

time studying for a new career. It takes a long time to become a

dentist. And you need to study a lot of science. I _____
(25 never/be)

very good in science.

B: Well, when you have time, will you show me how to use the
Occupational Outlook Handbook?

A: I'd be happy to.

EXPANSION ACTIVITIES

Classroom Activities

1. Walk around the room. Find one person who has done each of these things. Write that person's name in the blank.

   a. _____ has been exercising a lot lately.

   b. _____ has been watching a lot of TV lately.

   c. _____ has never gone to an art museum.

   d. _____ has traveled to more than five countries.

   e. _____ has never owned a car.

   f. _____ hasn't bought the textbook yet.

   g. _____ has been in this city for less than six months.

   h. _____ has just found a job.

   i. _____ has worked in a restaurant.

   j. _____ has never used public transportation in this city.

   k. _____ has eaten raw fish.

   l. _____ has worked out in a gym several times this month.

   m. _____ has never eaten an avocado.

   n. _____ has never used a cell phone.

   o. _____ has been looking for a job.

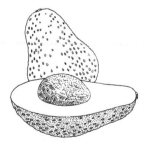

2. **Role Play:** Find a partner. Pretend that one of you is looking for a job and the other one is the interviewer. Ask and answer questions about your experience, education, interests, talents, etc. On the next page are some sample questions that interviewers sometimes ask.

- Why did you leave your last job?

- Why are you applying for this position?

- Where would you like to be five years from now?

- What are your strengths?

- What are your weaknesses?

- Why should we hire you?

3. **Game—True-True-False:** Form a small group. On a piece of paper, write two unusual things you have done in the past. Write one false statement about your past. (Use the present perfect with no mention of time.) Read your statements to the other members of your group. The other members have to guess which is the false statement.

   EXAMPLES I've flown in a helicopter.
   I've worked on a farm.
   I've met the president of my native country.

4. Fill in the blanks and discuss your answers.

   a. I've learned _____ from my experiences in the U.S.

   b. I've thought a lot about _____.

   c. Most people in my native country have never _____.

   d. In the U.S., it's been hard for me to _____.

Talk About it

1. How is looking for a job in the U.S. different from looking for a job in other countries?

2. How is the work environment in your present job different from the work environment in a previous job you had?

3. In other countries, how do people usually select a career? Are there career counselors to help people make a decision?

4. Have you ever used the Internet to search for jobs? Has it been helpful?

5. Look at the list of jobs below. Which ones do you think are interesting and why? What do you think are some good or bad aspects of these jobs?

airplane pilot	funeral director	librarian
architect	gardener	musician
bus driver	immigration officer	newspaper reporter
circus clown	lawyer	police officer
firefighter	letter carrier	veterinarian

Write About it

1. Write about your past work experience.

2. Write about a career that you think is interesting. Explain why you think this career is interesting.

3. Write about a job you would never want to have. Tell why.

4. Write an article giving advice to somebody looking for a job.

Outside Activity

Interview someone about his or her job. Find out the following information and report it to the class.

- how long he or she has been working at this job

- what his / her job responsibilities are

- if he / she likes this job

- how he / she found this job

NOTE: It is not polite to ask about salary.

Internet Activities

1. Type *career* or *jobs* in a search engine. See how many "hits" come up.

2. Find some career counseling Web sites. Find a sample résumé in your field or close to your field. Print it out and bring it to class. What's the difference between a chronological résumé and a functional résumé?

3. From one of the Web sites you found, get information on one or more of the following topics:

- how to write a cover letter

- how to find a career counselor

- how to plan for an interview

- how to network

- what questions to ask the interviewer

4. See if your local newspaper has a Web site. If it does, find the Help Wanted section.

5. Type in *job fair* and the name of your city. Are there any jobs fairs near you?

6. Type in *Occupational Outlook Handbook*. Find information about a job that interests you.

7. Many businesses have pages on the Internet that give information about the company and offer job listings. Find information about a company that interests you.

Additional Activities at **http://elt.thomson.com/gic**

LESSON

2

GRAMMAR

Passive Voice
Participles Used as Adjectives
Get + Participles and Adjectives

CONTEXT: Hollywood

The Oscars
The History of Animation
Charlie Chaplin
Being Famous

2.1 | Passive Voice—An Overview

Examples	Explanation
American films **are made** in Hollywood. The winner's name **will be announced.** Popcorn **is sold** in movie theaters.	Passive = a form of *be* + past participle
subject verb object **Active:** The children **saw** the movie. subject verb by agent **Passive:** The movie **was seen** by the children.	Compare active and passive. The object of the active sentence (*movie*) is the subject of the passive sentence. If the agent of the action (the person who performs the action) is mentioned, it follows *by*.

THE OSCARS

Before You Read

1. Who is your favorite actor? Who is your favorite actress?

2. What movies have you seen recently?

Read the following article. Pay special attention to verbs in the passive voice.

The Academy Awards **are given** out every year to recognize outstanding work of movie actors, directors, and others who are part of the movie-making industry. These awards, called Oscars, **are presented** in a formal ceremony in Hollywood. Several people **are nominated** in specific categories, such as Best Movie, Best Actor, Best Music, Best Costumes. One person **is chosen** to receive an award in each category.

When the awards ceremony started in 1929, 15 awards **were presented** and the ceremony **was attended** by only 250 people. Tickets cost $10, and anyone who could afford a ticket could attend. Today about two dozen Oscars **are presented.** Tickets **are** no longer **sold** to the general public; invitations **are sent** only to people involved in making the movies and to their guests. Today the awards **are presented** in the 3400-seat Kodak Auditorium in Hollywood.

Until 1941, the winners' names **were** already **known** before the ceremony and **published** in newspapers the night before the ceremony. Now the winners' names **are placed** in sealed envelopes and the envelopes **are** not **opened** until the night of the ceremony.

Since 1953, Oscar night **has been televised** and **broadcast** all over the world. This show **is seen** by hundreds of millions of people. Viewers watch as their favorite movie stars arrive looking beautiful and hopeful.

Did You Know?

Walt Disney has won the most Oscars ever: 26.

2.2 | Passive Voice—Form

Both the active voice and the passive voice can be used with different tenses and with modals. The tense of the passive sentence is shown in the verb *be*. Use the past participle with every tense. Compare active voice and passive voice in different tenses.

Tense	Active	Passive = *Be* + Past Participle
Simple Present	A committee **chooses** the best actor.	The best actor **is chosen** by a committee.
Present Continuous	They **are presenting** an award now.	An award **is being presented** now.
Future	They **will pick** the best movie. They **are going to pick** the best movie.	The best movie **will be picked**. The best movie **is going to be picked**.
Simple Past	They **announced** the winner's name.	The winner's name **was announced**.
Past Continuous	They **were taking** photographs.	Photographs **were being taken**.
Present Perfect	They **have chosen** the best movie.	The best movie **has been chosen**.
Modal	They **should announce** the winner's name.	The winner's name **should be announced**.

Examples	Explanation
Before 1941, the winners' names **were** *already* **known** before the ceremony. Today the winners **are** *never* **announced** ahead of time.	An adverb can be placed between the auxiliary verb and the main verb.
Affirmative: The movie **was filmed** in the U.S. **Negative:** It **wasn't filmed** in Canada. **Question: Was it filmed** in Hollywood? **Short Answer:** No, it **wasn't**. *Wh-* **Question:** Where **was** it **filmed**?	Observe affirmative statements, negative statements, and questions with the passive voice. Never use do, does, or did with the passive voice. (*Wrong:* The movie **didn't** filmed in Canada.)
The Oscar ceremony **is televised and seen** by millions of people.	If two verbs in the passive voice are connected with *and*, do not repeat *be*.
Active: **She** saw **him**. **Passive:** **He** was seen by **her**. **Active:** **They** helped **us**. **Passive:** **We** were helped by **them**.	Notice the difference in pronouns in an active sentence and a passive sentence. After *by*, the object pronoun is used.

EXERCISE 1 Read the following sentences. Decide if the underlined verb is active (A) or passive (P).

EXAMPLES The actress <u>received</u> an Oscar. A

The actress <u>was given</u> an Oscar. P

1. The actress <u>wore</u> a beautiful gown.

2. The gown <u>was designed</u> by Anne Klein.

3. Julia Roberts <u>presented</u> an Oscar.

4. Julia Roberts <u>was presented</u> an Oscar.

5. Julia Roberts <u>has been seen</u> in many movies.

6. The director <u>has been nominated</u> many times.

7. The movie <u>was filmed</u> in black and white.

8. Many actors <u>live</u> in California.

9. Movies <u>are made</u> in Hollywood.

10. The names of the winners <u>will be printed</u> in tomorrow's newspaper.

11. The actress <u>thanked</u> all the people who helped her win.

12. The actress <u>was driven</u> to the ceremony in a white limousine.

13. Hollywood <u>was built</u> at the beginning of the twentieth century.

14. Hollywood <u>has become</u> the movie capital of the U.S.

15. Movie reviewers <u>make</u> predictions about the winners.

EXERCISE 2 Fill in the blanks with the passive voice of the verb, using the tense given.

EXAMPLE (simple present: *give*)

The best actor ___*is given*___ an Oscar.

1. (simple present: *see*)

   The awards ceremony _____ _____ by millions of people.

2. (future: *choose*)

   Which actor _____ _____ _____ next year?

3. (modal: *can / see*)

The movie _____ _____ _____ at many theaters.

4. (present perfect: *make*)

Many movies _____ _____ _____ about World War II.

5. (simple past: *give*)

James Cameron _____ _____ an award in 1997 for Best Director, for *Titanic*.

6. (present continuous: *show*)

A good movie _____ _____ _____ at a theater near my house.

7. (simple past: *make*)

Star Wars _____ _____ in 1977.

8. (present perfect: *show*)

The movie _____ _____ _____ on TV many times.

9. (present perfect: *give*)

Over 2,000 Academy Awards _____ _____

_____ out since 1929.

10. (simple past: *give*)

In 1929, only one award _____ _____ to a woman.

11. (simple past: *add*)

When _____ sound _____ to movies?

It _____ _____ in 1927.

12. (simple present: *often / make*)

Movies _____ _____ _____ in Hollywood.

13. (present perfect: *film*)

How many movies _____ _____ _____ in black and white?

2.3 | Passive and Active Voice—Uses

Examples	Explanation
Compare: **Active:** The man **ate** the fish. **Passive:** The man **was eaten** by the fish.	When the verb is in the active voice, the subject performs the action. When the verb is in the passive voice, the subject receives the action.
A. **Active:** I **see** the Academy Awards ceremony every year. **Passive:** The Academy Awards ceremony **is seen** by millions. **B.** **Active:** **Do** you **know** the winners' names? **Passive:** The winners' names **are not known** until the night of the ceremony. **C.** **Active:** The Academy **presents** awards to the best actors and directors. **Passive:** The awards **are presented** every year.	The active voice focuses on the person who does the action. The passive voice focuses on the receiver or the result of the action. Sometimes the passive voice mentions the agent, the person who does the action (A). Sometimes it is not necessary to mention the agent (B and C).

EXERCISE **3** Write an active sentence and a passive sentence for each subject. Choose an appropriate tense.

EXAMPLE *Active:* The test _____ *has 12 questions.* _____

Passive: The test _____ *will be given in a large auditorium.* _____

1. *Active:* My textbook _____
   Passive: My textbook _____
2. *Active:* My best friend _____
   Passive: My best friend _____
3. *Active:* Some students _____
   Passive: Some students _____
4. *Active:* I _____
   Passive: I _____
5. *Active:* Actors _____
   Passive: Actors _____
6. *Active:* Movies _____
   Passive: Movies _____

2.4 | The Passive Voice Without an Agent

The passive voice is used more frequently without an agent than with an agent.

Examples	Explanation
The invitations **have been sent** out. The winners' names **are placed** in envelopes.	The passive voice is used when it is not important to mention who performed the action.
A. Active: *Someone* **stole** my wallet. Passive: My wallet **was stolen** last week. **B.** Active: *Someone* **told** me that you like movies. Passive: I **was told** that you like movies.	The passive voice is used when we do not know the agent (A) or when we prefer not to mention the agent (B).
a. One person **is chosen** to receive the award. b. Oscar night **has been televised** since 1953.	The passive voice is used when the agent is obvious and doesn't need to be mentioned. a. It is obvious that the Academy chooses the winner. h. It is obvious that TV studios have televised Oscar night.
Compare Active (A) and Passive (P): A: *You* **can rent** DVDs at many stores. P: DVDs **can be rented** at many stores. A: *They* **sell** popcorn in movie theaters. P: Popcorn **is sold** in movie theaters.	In conversation, the active voice is often used with the impersonal subjects *people, you, we,* or *they*. In more formal speech and writing, the passive is used with no agent.

EXERCISE 4 Fill in the blanks with the passive voice of the verb in parentheses ( ). Choose an appropriate tense.

EXAMPLE Hollywood _____*was built*_____ in the early 1900s.
(build)

1. Most American movies _____ in Hollywood.
(make)

2. Let's get some popcorn. It's fresh. It _____ right now.
(make)

3. Movie listings _____ in the newspaper.
(can/find)

4. Children _____ to see some movies.
(not/allow)

5. Hurry! The winners _____ in ten minutes.
(announce)

6. In 1929, only fifteen Oscars _____.
 (present)

7. Before 1941, the winners' names _____ in
 (publish)
newspapers the night before the ceremony.

8. A new theater _____ near my house at this time.
 (build)

9. We can't get into the movie theater because all the tickets
_____ already.
 (sell)

10. Did you see the movie *Jaws*? Where _____ it
_____?
 (film)

11. I went to the lobby to buy popcorn, and my seat
_____.
 (take)

12. No one knows why the award _____ "Oscar."
 (call)

13. *Lord of the Rings* _____ the best film of 2004.
 (choose)

14. In a movie theater, coming attractions[1] _____
 (show)
before the feature film begins.

15. Sound _____ to movies in 1927.
 (add)

16. The Kodak Theater, where the awards _____
 (present)
each year, _____ in 2001.
 (build)

[1]*Coming attractions* are short previews of new movies. Theaters show coming attractions to get your
interest in returning to the theater to see a new movie.

2.5 | The Passive Voice with an Agent

Sometimes the passive voice is used with an agent.

Active	Passive
Active: Billy Crystal **has hosted** the Oscar ceremony many times. **Passive:** The Oscar ceremony **has been hosted** by Billy Crystal many times. **Active:** Ralph Lauren **designs** many of the actresses' gowns. **Passive:** Many of the actresses' gowns **are designed** by Ralph Lauren.	When the sentence has a strong agent (a specific person: Billy Crystal, Ralph Lauren), we can use either the active or the passive voice. The active voice puts more emphasis on the person who performs the action. The passive voice puts more emphasis on the action or the result. In general, the active voice is more common than the passive voice when an agent is mentioned. Billy Crystal
Active: *The first Oscar ceremony* **took** place in 1929. **Passive:** *It* **was** *attended* by 250 people. **Active:** *The Oscar ceremony* **is** popular all over the world. **Passive:** *It* **is seen** by millions of viewers each year.	Sometimes the passive voice is used to continue with the same subject of the preceding sentence.
Active: Steven Spielberg **directed** *Star Wars,* didn't he? **Passive:** No. *Star Wars* **was directed** by George Lucas.	We can use the passive voice to shift the emphasis to the object of the preceding sentence.
Passive: The dress **was designed** by Vera Wang. **Passive:** The music **was composed** by Bob Dylan. **Passive:** The movie camera **was invented** by Thomas Edison.	We often use the passive voice when the agent *made, discovered, invented, designed, built, wrote, painted,* or *composed* something.
The 2004 Oscar ceremony **was hosted** *by Billy Crystal.* The 2003 ceremony **was not hosted** *by him.* It was hosted by Steve Martin.	When the agent is included, use *by* + noun or object pronoun.

EXERCISE 5 *Test Your Knowledge.* Fill in the blanks with the past-tense passive voice and the name of the agent. Choose an agent from the box below.

Pablo Picasso	Christopher Columbus	Leonardo Da Vinci
Alexander Graham Bell	Thomas Edison	William Shakespeare
Celine Dion	Barbra Streisand	Steven Spielberg
George Lucas	Walt Disney	Mark Twain

1. Mickey Mouse _____ by _____.
        (create)

2. The *Mona Lisa* _____ by _____.
        (paint)

3. America _____ by _____.
        (discover)

4. The electric light _____ by _____.
        (invent)

5. *Romeo and Juliet* _____ by _____.
        (write)

6. The telephone _____ by _____.
        (invent)

7. *My Heart Will Go On* _____ by _____.
        (sing)

8. *Star Wars* _____ by _____.
        (direct)

EXERCISE 6 Fill in the blanks with the active or passive of the verb in parentheses ( ). Use the tense indicated.

EXAMPLES   I _____*saw*_____ an old movie on TV last night.
                      (past: see)

The movie _____*was filmed*_____ in black and white.
                      (past: film)

It _____*will be shown*_____ again on TV tonight.
      (future: show)

1. Many movies _____ in Hollywood.
                            (present: make)

2. Steven Spielberg _____ many movies.
                              (present perfect: make)

3. We _____ a DVD this weekend.
              (future: rent)

4. Vera Wang _____ beautiful dresses.
                        (present: design)

5. The actress _____ a dress that

   that _____ by Ralph Lauren.
   (past: design)

   (past continuous: wear)

6. Who _____ the music for the movie? The music
   (past: write)

   _____ by Randy Newman.
   (past: write)

7. The first Academy Awards presentation _____
   (past: have)

   250 guests.

8. I _____ *Star Wars.*
   (present perfect: never/see)

9. Computer animation _____ in many movies.
   (present: use)

10. Movie reviewers _____ the winners weeks
    (present: predict)

    before the Oscar presentation.

11. Oscar winners _____ _____ the people who helped them.
    (present: always/thank)

2.6 | Verbs with Two Objects

Some verbs have two objects: a direct object (D.O.) and an indirect object (I.O.).

Examples	Explanation
I.O. **D.O.** **Active:** They gave Spielberg an award. **Passive 1:** *Spielberg* was given an award. **Passive 2:** *An award* was given to Spielberg.	When an active sentence has two objects, the passive sentence can begin with either object. Notice that if the direct object (*an award*) becomes the subject of the passive sentence, *to* is used before the indirect object.

Some verbs that use two objects are:

bring	lend	pay	serve	teach
give	offer	sell	show	tell
hand	owe	send	take	write

EXERCISE 7   Change the following sentences to passive voice in two ways. Omit the agent.

EXAMPLE   They gave the actress an award.

The actress was given an award.

The award was given to the actress.

1. They handed the actress an Oscar.

_____

_____

2. Someone served the guests dinner.

_____

_____

3. Someone told the students the answers.

_____

_____

4. Someone will send you an invitation.

_____

_____

5. They have shown us the movie.

_____

_____

6. They will give the winners flowers.

_____

_____

7. Someone has given you the key.

_____

_____

THE HISTORY OF ANIMATION

Before You Read

1. Do you like cartoons? Which cartoons do you like?
2. Do you know how cartoons are created?
3. Are cartoons just for children? Do adults enjoy cartoons too?

Gertie the Dinosaur
Winsor McCay

Animated movies **have changed** a lot over the last 100 years. Winsor McCay **is considered** the father of animation. In the early 1900s, McCay **animated** his films by himself. He **drew** every picture separately and had them photographed, one at a time. Hundreds of photographs **were needed** to make a one-minute film. Sometimes it would take him more than a year to make a five-minute cartoon.

Walt Disney

In 1913, the development of celluloid (a transparent material) made animation easier. Instead of drawing each picture separately, the animator could make a drawing of the background, which **remained** motionless, while only the characters **moved.**

Walt Disney **took** animation to a new level. He **created** Mickey Mouse, **added** sound and music to his movies, and **produced** the first full-length animated film, *Snow White and the Seven Dwarfs*. Many people think he was a great cartoonist, but he wasn't. Instead, he was a great story editor and clever businessman who had other artists do most of the drawings.

Today most animated films **are** not **drawn** by hand. The animation **is done** by computer software. Also special effects for movies, such as *Star Wars,* **are done** by computer animation. To create the illusion of move-

ment, an image **is put** on the computer and then quickly **replaced** by a similar image with a small change. While this technique is similar to hand-drawn animation, the work **can be done** much faster by computer. In fact, anyone with a home computer and special software can create a simple animation.

1901	Walt Disney was born.
1914	Winsor McCay created the first animation on film, *Gertie the Dinosaur.*
1918	Walt Disney opened a cartoon studio in Kansas City, Missouri.
1923	Disney moved his studio to Hollywood.
1928	The first Mickey Mouse cartoon was introduced. It was the first talking cartoon.
1937	Disney produced *Snow White and the Seven Dwarfs,* the first full-length animated cartoon.
1966	Walt Disney died.
1995	*Toy Story* became the first full-length film animated entirely on computers.
2004	*Finding Nemo* won the Academy Award for best animated film.

2.7 | Transitive and Intransitive Verbs

Examples	Explanation
Compare: 　　　　verb　　　　　　object **Active:** McCay **created** the first animated film. **Passive:** The first animated film **was created** in 1913. 　　　　　verb　　　object **Active:** Walt Disney **didn't draw** his cartoons. **Passive:** His cartoons **were drawn** by studio artists.	Most active verbs are followed by an object. They can be used in the active and passive voice. These verbs are called *transitive* verbs.
Active Only: Disney **lived** in Hollywood most of his life. He **became** famous when he created Mickey Mouse. He **worked** with many artists. What **happened** to the first Mickey Mouse cartoon? I'd like to see it.	Some verbs have no object. We cannot use the passive voice with these verbs. agree　　　die　　　　look　　　seem arrive　　fall　　　occur　　sleep be　　　　go　　　　rain　　　stay become　happen　recover　walk come　　live　　　remain　work These are called *intransitive* verbs.
Compare: a. Disney **left** Kansas City in 1923. b. The books **were left** on the floor.	*Leave* can be intransitive or transitive, depending on its meaning. In sentence (a), *leave* means "go away from." It is an intransitive verb. It has no passive form. In sentence (b), leave means "not taken." It is a transitive verb. It has a passive form.
Compare: a. Cartoons **have changed** a lot over the years. b. The light bulb **was changed** by the janitor. a. In a cartoon, it looks like the characters **are moving**, but they are not. b. The chairs **were moved** to another room.	*Change* and *move* can be intransitive or transitive. When a change happens through a natural process (a), it is intransitive. When someone specific causes the change (b), it is transitive.
Compare: Walt Disney **was born** in 1901. He **died** in 1966.	Notice that we use *was / were* with *born,* but we don't use the passive voice with *die.*

Note: *Born is not a verb. It is a past participle used as an adjective.

EXERCISE 8 Which of the following sentences can be changed to passive voice? Change those sentences. If no change is possible, write *no change*.

EXAMPLES Today they <u>do</u> most animation with computer software.

Today most animation is done with computer software.

Walt Disney <u>moved</u> to Hollywood in 1923.
No change.

1. I heard a noise outside. What <u>happened</u>?

_____

2. Someone <u>left</u> a box of popcorn on the seat.

_____

3. Many movie stars <u>live</u> in California.

_____

4. Marilyn Monroe <u>was</u> a famous actress. She <u>died</u> in 1962.

_____

5. I <u>slept</u> during the movie.

_____

6. You <u>can rent</u> *Finding Nemo* on DVD.

_____

7. They <u>will show</u> a movie at 9:30 in the auditorium.

_____

8. They <u>have sold</u> all the tickets.

_____

EXERCISE 9 Fill in the blanks with the active or passive form of the verb in parentheses ( ).

EXAMPLES Walt Disney ____*was*____ a clever businessman.
                           (past: be)

His cartoons ___*are seen*___ all over the world.
                      (present: see)

   1. Walt Disney _____ famous when he _____
                              (past: become)   *(past: create)*

   Mickey Mouse.

   2. Walt Disney _____ most of his cartoon characters.
                              (past: not/draw)

3. Most of his cartoons _____ by studio artists.
(past: draw)

4. Walt Disney _____ 26 Oscars.
(past: give)

5. Walt Disney _____ his studio to Hollywood.
(past: move)

6. Walt Disney _____ in Hollywood most of his life.
(past: live)

7. Disney _____ in 1966.
(past: die)

8. Today's animations _____ by computer.
(present: create)

9. Cartoon characters look like they _____.
(present continuous: move)

10. Even today, Disney's old cartoons _____ beautiful.
(present: look)

EXERCISE 10

Fill in the blanks with the active or passive form of the verb in parentheses ( ). Use the past tense.

Ronald Reagan ___*was elected*___ president of the United States in
(example: elect)

1980. Before he ___*became*___ president, he was governor of
(example: become)

California. Even before that, he _____ as a Hollywood
(1 work)

actor. He _____ in 53 Hollywood movies between 1937
(2 appear)

and 1964. He _____ a great actor, and he never
(3 not/consider)

_____ an Oscar.
(4 win)

On March 20, 1981, the day the Oscar ceremony _____
(5 schedule)

to take place, something terrible _____. Reagan
(6 happen)

_____ in an assassination attempt. Fortunately, he
(7 shoot)

_____ from his wounds. However, one of his
(8 past: not die)

aides, who was with him at the time, _____ . Out
(9 wound)

of respect for the president, the Academy Awards show

_____ for one day. Reagan _____ and continued
(postpone)   *(recover)*

to serve as president until he _____ his second term
(finish)

in 1989. He _____ in 2004 at the age of 93.
(die)

EXERCISE 11   Find the mistakes with the verbs in the sentences below and correct them. Not every sentence has a mistake. If the sentence is correct, write *C*.

EXAMPLES
were
Before the 1950s, most movies filmed in black and white.

I like old movies.   **C**

1. We went to see a movie.

2. I don't like scary movies. I can't be slept afterwards.

3. Did the movie directed by Steven Spielberg?

4. People in the audience are eaten popcorn.

5. The popcorn is fresh. It is been popped right now.

6. Popcorn sells in the lobby of the theater.

7. Before the movie, coming attractions are show.

8. At the end of the movie, we were left the theater and went home.

9. A lot of popcorn containers and candy wrappers was left on the floor of the theater.

10. Some movies can be enjoy by the whole family.

11. Tickets can bought online ahead of time.

12. What was happened? I can't find my ticket.

13. The theater is big. Fourteen movies are shown at the same time.

14. The movie is for adults. Children don't permitted to enter.

15. I enjoyed the movie. Did you?

16. Parking is free at the theater, but the parking pass must be validated in the theater.

17. Some movies should not seen by children.

18. Senior citizens can get a discount on tickets.

19. At the Oscar ceremony, the actors are arrived in limousines.

20. The actresses wear beautiful dresses.

PARKING PASS
Boston Parking Authority
Auto Park Garage
6th and Maple Streets

12/15/05 8:30pm
Apply date/time stamp here

2.8 | Passive with *Get*

Examples	Explanation
Actors **get paid** a lot of money. I don't like violent movies. A lot of people **get shot** and **killed.**	In conversation, we sometimes use *get* instead of *be* with the passive. 　*get paid = are paid* 　*get shot = are shot* 　*get killed = are killed* We usually omit the agent after *get*. **Compare:** 　He **was shot** by a cowboy. 　He **got shot** three times.
How much **do** actors **get paid** for a movie? She **didn't get paid** last Friday.	When *get* is used with the passive voice, questions and negatives are formed with *do, does, did,* and other auxiliaries. *Be* is not used with *get*. 　*Wrong:* She *wasn't* get paid last Friday.
She **got hired** for the job. He **got laid off** last month.	*Get* is frequently used with: *killed, injured, wounded, paid, hired, fired, laid off.*

EXERCISE 12　Fill in the blanks with *get* + the past participle of the verb in parentheses ( ).

EXAMPLE　Who _____*got chosen*_____ for the part in the movie?
　　　　　　　　　　　(choose)

1. Reagan _____ on the day of the Oscars.
　　　　　　　(shoot)

2. No one _____.
　　　　　　(kill)

3. Did you _____ for the job?
　　　　　　(hire)

4. How often do you _____?
　　　　　　　　　　(pay)

5. His car _____ from in front of his house.
　　　　　　(steal)

6. The little boy told a lie, and he _____.
　　　　　　　　　　　　(punish)

7. We have so much to do, but I'm not worried. Everything will

_____ little by little.
   (do)

8. The results of the exam _____ to the wrong
   (send)

person by mistake.

9. One student _____ cheating on the exam.
   (catch)

10. If you leave your car in a no-parking zone, it might

_____.
   (tow)

2.9 | Participles Used as Adjectives

A present participle is verb + -ing. A past participle is the third form of the verb (usually -ed or -en). Both present participles and past participles can be used as adjectives.

Examples	Explanation
We saw an **entertaining** movie. *Star Wars* is an **exciting** movie. *The Matrix* has **amazing** visual effects.	In these examples, a *present participle* is used as an adjective.
The winners' names are placed in **sealed** envelopes. I wasn't **bored** during the movie. Are you **interested** in action movies? Do you like **animated** films?	In these examples, a *past participle* is used as an adjective.

Before You
Read

1. Have you ever heard of Charlie Chaplin?

2. Have you ever seen a silent movie? Do you think a silent movie can be interesting today?

Charlie Chaplin, 1889–1977

Read the following article. Pay special attention to participles used as adjectives.

Did You
Know?

President Ronald Reagan did not want Chaplin to be allowed back into the U.S.

Charlie Chaplin was one of the greatest actors in the world. His **entertaining** silent movies are still popular today. His **amusing** character "Little Tramp" is well **known** to people throughout the world. Chaplin had an **amazing** life. His idea for this poor character in worn-out shoes, round hat, and cane probably came from his childhood experiences.

Born in poverty in London in 1889, Chaplin was abandoned by his father and left in an orphanage by his mother. He became **interested** in acting at the age of five. At ten, he left school to travel with a British acting company. In 1910, he made his first trip to America. He was talented, athletic, and hard-**working,** and by 1916 he was earning $10,000 a week. He was the highest-**paid** person in the world at that time. He produced, directed, and wrote the movies he starred in.

Even though "talkies" came out in 1927, he didn't make a movie with sound until 1940, when he played a comic version of the **terrifying** dictator, Adolf Hitler.

As Chaplin got older, he faced **declining** popularity as a result of his politics and personal relationships. After he left the U.S. in 1952, Chaplin was not allowed to re-enter because of his political views. He didn't return to the U.S. until 1972, when he was given a special Oscar for his lifetime of **outstanding** work.

2.10 | Participles Used as Adjectives to Show Feelings

The participles of a verb can be used as adjectives.

Chaplin's movies <u>entertained</u> people.
(verb)

His movies are <u>entertaining</u>.
(present participle)

People are <u>entertained</u>.
(past participle)

Chaplin's movies <u>interest</u> us.
(verb)

Chaplin's movies are <u>interesting</u>.
(present participle)

We are <u>interested</u> in his movies.
(past participle)

Examples	Explanation
The movie *bored* us. (*bored* = verb)	In some cases, both the present participle (a) and the past participle (b) of the same verb can be used as adjectives.
a. The movie was **boring.** I left the **boring** movie before it was over.	The present participle (a) gives an active meaning. The movie *actively* caused a feeling of boredom.
b. Some people were **bored.** The **bored** people got up and left.	The past participle (b) gives a passive meaning. It describes the receiver of a feeling. The people were bored by the movie.
a. Chaplin had an **interesting** life. He was poor and then became very rich. b. I am **interested** in Chaplin. I would like to know more about him. a. The main character in *Friday the Thirteenth* is a **frightening** man. b. I was **frightened** and couldn't sleep after seeing the movie.	A person can cause a feeling in others or he can receive a feeling. Therefore, a person can be both *interesting* and *interested, frightening* and *frightened,* etc.
The book is **interesting.** (never *interested*) The movie is **entertaining.** (never *entertained*)	An object (like a book or a movie) doesn't have feelings, so a past participle cannot be used to describe an object.

Language Notes:

1. The following pictures show the difference between a *frightening* man and a *frightened* man.

a. The man is frightening the children. = He's a *frightening man.*

b. The man is frightened by the robber. = He's a *frightened man.*

2. Common paired participles are:

amazing	amazed	exhausting	exhausted
amusing	amused	frightening	frightened
annoying	annoyed	frustrating	frustrated
boring	bored	interesting	interested
confusing	confused	puzzling	puzzled
convincing	convinced	satisfying	satisfied
disappointing	disappointed	surprising	surprised
embarrassing	embarrassed	terrifying	terrified
exciting	excited	tiring	tired

EXERCISE 13 Use the verb in each sentence to make two new sentences. In one sentence, use the present participle. In the other, use the past participle.

EXAMPLE The game entertains the children.

The game is entertaining.

The children are entertained.

1. The movie frightened the children.

2. The book interests the children.

3. The children are amusing the adults.

4. The trip tired the children.

5. The game excited the children.

6. The vacation exhausted the adults.

7. The movie bored the adults.

_____

_____

8. Chaplin interests me.

_____

_____

EXERCISE 14 Fill in the blanks with the correct participle, present or past, of the verb in parentheses ( ).

Last night my friend and I went to see a new movie. We thought it

was _____ _boring_ _____. It had a lot of stupid car chases, which
(example: bore)

were not _____ at all. And I didn't like the characters.
(1 excite)

They weren't very _____.
(2 convince)

We were pretty _____ because the reviewers said it was a
(3 disappoint)

good movie. They said it had _____ visual effects. But for
(4 amaze)

me, it wasn't _____ at all. I was _____ that I
(5 interest)   (6 annoy)

wasted $10 and a whole evening for such a _____ movie.
(7 disappoint)

The only thing that was _____ was the popcorn.
(8 satisfy)

EXERCISE 15 Fill in the blanks and discuss your answers.

EXAMPLE I'm interested in _____ *sports* _____.

1. I'm interested in _____ movies.

2. Now I'm worried about _____.

3. In the past, I was worried about _____.

4. In my opinion, _____ is an amazing (*choose one*) actor / athlete / politician.

5. Married people _____ than single people.

6. Children shouldn't be allowed to _____.

7. I'm not interested in _____.

8. I'm annoyed when people _____.

9. _____ is a boring subject for me.

10. I feel frustrated when _____.

11. I am amazed that _____ in the U.S.

12. It's not surprising that _____ in the U.S.

13. Sometimes I feel embarrassed when I _____.

14. I was very excited when _____.

15. When I came to this school, I was surprised _____.

2.11 | Other Past Participles Used as Adjectives

Some sentences look passive (*be* + past participle), but there is no action in the sentence. The past participles are used as adjectives.

Examples	Explanation
a. No one knows the winners' names because the envelope is **sealed.** b. Is this seat **taken?** c. Chaplin was **born** in England. d. The dress is **made** of silk. e. The door is **locked** now. f. He bought a **used** car.	In some cases, we are looking at the result of a previous action. We no longer know or care about the agent of the action or even the action.[2] a. **Previous Action:** Someone *sealed* the envelope. b. **Previous Action:** Someone *took (occupied)* the seat. c. **Previous Action:** His mother *bore* a child. d. **Previous Action:** The dress *was made* by someone. **Previous Action:** The door *was locked* by the janitor. f. **Previous Action:** The car *was used* by another owner.
Many people are **involved** in making a movie. Hollywood is **located** in California. Is Geraldine Chaplin **related** to Charlie Chaplin? We are **done** with the video. When you are **finished** with the video, return it to the store. Is the theater **air-conditioned?** The theater was very **crowded.**	In some cases, we use a past participle as an adjective even though there is no previous action. The sentences to the left have no equivalent active form.
a. The glass is **broken.** b. Don't touch the **broken** glass. a. The child is **lost** in the park. b. Let's take the **lost** child to the park office. a. The child seems **tired.** b. Let's put the **tired** child to bed.	Past participles can be used: a. after *be* and other linking verbs (*seem, look, feel, sound,* etc.). OR b. before a noun.

---

[2]These forms are sometimes called "stative passives."

Examples	Explanation
Chaplin was a **well known** actor. He was a **highly paid** actor. He was **well liked** by millions.	To emphasize and further describe the adjectives used as past participles, an adverb can be added. Common phrases include: • a well known actor • a well educated person • a well behaved child • a well dressed woman • a well fed dog • a highly paid actor • a closely watched experiment • a slightly used book • closely related languages

The following are some common combinations of *be* + past participle:

be air-conditioned	be filled (with)	be married
be accustomed (to)	be finished	be permitted (to)
be allowed (to)	be gone	be pleased
be born	be injured	be prepared
be broken	be insured	be related (to)
be closed	be interested (in)	be taken (*occupied*)
be concerned (about)	be involved (in)	be used
be crowded	be known	be used to
be divorced	be located	be worried (about)
be done	be locked	be wounded
be dressed	be lost	
be educated	be made (of, in)	

EXERCISE 16 Underline the past participle in the following sentences.

EXAMPLE Movie theaters are <u>crowded</u> on Saturday night

1. The movie theater is closed in the morning.

2. Where is the movie theater located?

3. Charlie Chaplin was married several times.

4. Chaplin was not an educated man.

5. Children are not allowed to see some movies.

6. Many movies are made in Hollywood.

7. How many people were involved in making *Toy Story*?

8. Chaplin was a well paid actor.

9. Chaplin was born in England.

10. He was well known all over the world.

11. Ronald Reagan was involved in movies before he became a politician.

Find the mistakes and correct them. Not every sentence has a mistake. If the sentence is correct, write *C*.

EXAMPLES The theater _∧ *is* located near my house.

Are you interested in action movies?   **C**

1. Is Julia Roberts marry?

2. I'm concerned about the violence in movies.

3. Movie theaters crowded on Friday nights.

4. Children aren't allow to enter some movies.

5. How many people are involved in making a movie?

6. Walt Disney born in 1901.

7. When you're finish with the DVD, please return it to the video store.

8. Is the Oscar make of gold?

BEING FAMOUS

Before You **Read**

1. In the U.S., movie stars get divorced a lot. Is this true in other countries?

2. Is the divorce rate for Hollywood stars higher than for average people?

3. Do you think being famous would be fun?

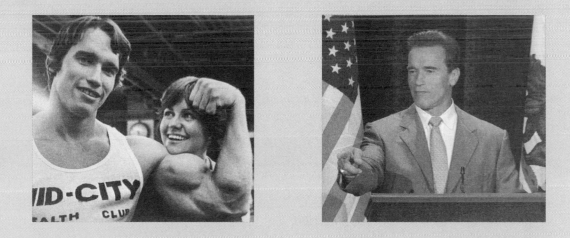

Read the following article. Pay special attention to *be* and *get* before past participles and adjectives.

Becoming a Hollywood star is a dream for many. Glamour, money, beauty, and even power make the occupation very attractive. However, actually living the Hollywood star life can **be difficult** and **challenging,** both personally and professionally.

Hollywood stars are known for their short and frequent marriages—and divorces. Elizabeth Taylor **got married** eight times. In fact, she married the same man (Richard Burton) twice—and divorced him twice. Britney Spears **got married** one day and **got divorced** the next day. One Hollywood couple is an exception—Paul Newman and Joanne Woodward. They **have been married** since 1958. What few people know is that Newman **was married** once before, from 1949 to 1958.

Why is being famous so difficult? Some actors **get rich** overnight and don't handle their sudden wealth and fame easily. Life can **be difficult** in the public eye, when reporters record an actor's every moment. Also, Hollywood stars need to look great to stay on top. They do not like to **get old.** Many Hollywood stars use cosmetic surgery to look young. Many work out with a personal trainer because they don't want to **get fat** or out of shape.

Some Hollywood actors go into politics when they **get tired** of acting. They use their popularity as actors to win elections. Ronald Reagan and Arnold Schwarzenegger both went from being actors to becoming governor of California. Ronald Reagan went on to become president of the U.S.[3] A famous wrestler, Jessie Ventura, even got to be governor of Minnesota.

Life in the public eye seems wonderful, but it can be difficult at times.

[3]Schwarzenegger can't become president because he was not born in the U.S.

2.12 | Past Participles and Other Adjectives with *Get*[4]

Examples	Explanation
a. **Is** Julia Roberts **married?** b. When did she **get married?**	a. *Be* + past participle describes the status of a noun over a period of time.
a. The actress is **divorced.** b. She **got divorced** soon after she **got married.**	b. *Get* + past participle shows the specific point at which this status began. There is no reference to the continuation of this status.
a. You're yawning. I see you **are tired.** b. When Arnold Schwarzenegger **got tired** of acting, he went into politics.	
a. Movie stars **are rich.** b. A lot of people buy a lottery ticket because they want to **get rich** quickly.	a. *Be* + adjective describes the status of a noun over a period of time.
a. Paul Newman **is old.** b. Most stars don't want to **get old.** They want to look young forever.	b. *Get* + adjective shows the specific point at which this status began. *Get* means *become*.

Usage Note:
Notice the difference between *to be married, to marry, to get married.*

Paul Newman **is married.** He **has been married** to the same woman for many years. (status)

He **married** Joanne Woodward in 1958. (The verb *marry* is followed by an object.)

Paul and Joanne **got married** in 1958. (*Get married* is not followed by an object.)

Past Participles with *get*		Adjectives with *get*	
get accustomed to	get hurt	get angry	get old
get acquainted	get lost	get dark	get rich
get bored	get married	get fat	get sleepy
get confused	get scared	get hungry	get upset
get divorced	get tired	get nervous	get well
get dressed	get used to		
get engaged	get worried		

[4]For a list of expressions with *get*, see Appendix C.

EXERCISE 18 Circle the correct words to complete this conversation between two young men.

A: Jennifer Lopez is my favorite actress. When she (was / (got)) married a
(example)

few years ago, I felt so sad. But then she (was / got) divorced just a
(1)

year later. I was so happy.

B: Happy? Sad? Do you think Jennifer (is / gets) interested in you? She
(2)

doesn't even know you!

A: I keep sending her letters. I would like to (be / get) acquainted with
(3)

her.

B: She's not going to answer your letters. She (is / gets) too rich and
(4)

famous to pay attention to you.

A: Well, I'm an actor too, you know.

B: Mostly you're just a waiter.

A: I'm not always going to be a waiter. When acting studios discover

me, I'm going to (get / be) famous, and Jennifer will notice me.
(5)

B: You will be an old man by the time you (get / are) famous.
(6)

A: That doesn't matter. Someday it will happen, and I'll meet Jennifer.

B: By that time, she (will be / will get) old and you won't be interested
(7)

in her anymore.

A: I will always (get / be) interested in her. She's my one true love.
(8)

B: Oh really? What does your girlfriend have to say about that?

A: I never talk to her about Jennifer. One time I told her how much

I like Jennifer, and she (was / got) angry.
(9)

B: I don't think your girlfriend has anything to worry about.

PART 1   Passive Voice

Passive Voice = *Be* + Past Participle	Use
With an Agent: Mickey Mouse **was created** by Walt Disney. *Star Wars* **was directed** by George Lucas.	The passive voice can be used with an agent, especially if we want to emphasize the result of the action. **Note:** Do not mention the agent if it is not a specific person. *Wrong:* Spanish is spoken *by people* in Mexico.
Without an Agent: a. Hollywood **was built** at the beginning of the twentieth century. b. Children **are** not **allowed** to see some movies. c. The Oscar presentation **is seen** all over the world. d. I **was told** that you didn't like the movie.	The passive voice is usually used without an agent: a. When it is not important to mention who performed the action b. When the agent is obvious c. When the agent is not a specific person but people in general d. To hide the identity of the agent
Reagan **got shot** in 1981. I **got fired** from my job. A lot of people **got killed** in the war.	*Get* can be used instead of *be* in certain conversational expressions. Do not use *get* when the agent is mentioned. *Wrong:* Reagan got shot *by John* *Hinckley.*

PART 2 Participles Used as Adjectives

Examples	Explanation
Silent movies are very **interesting.** We are **interested** in the life of Charlie Chaplin.	Use the present participle to show that the noun produced a feeling. Use the past participle to show that the noun received a feeling.
I'm tired of your **broken** promises. Is this seat **taken?**	Use the past participle to show the result of a previous action. **Previous Actions:** Someone *broke* the promise. Someone *took* the seat.
The child is **lost.** The bus is **crowded.** Where is Hollywood **located?**	Some past participles are not related to a previous action.
She **got confused** when the teacher explained participles. I **got lost** on my way to your house. She **got upset** when she couldn't find her keys.	Use *get* with past participles and other adjectives to mean *become*.

EDITING ADVICE

PART 1 Passive Voice

1. Use *be*, not *do / does / did* to make negatives and questions with the passive voice.

   My watch ~~didn't~~ *wasn't* made in Japan.

   When ~~did~~ *was* the movie filmed?

2. Don't use the passive voice with intransitive verbs.

   The accident ~~was~~ happened at 10:30 p.m.

   Her grandfather ~~was~~ died three years ago.

3. Don't confuse the *-ing* form with the past participle.

   The candy was ~~eating~~ *eaten* by the child.

4. Don't forget the *-ed* ending for a regular past participle.

   The floor was wash *ed* by the janitor.

5. Don't forget to use a form of *be* in a passive sentence.

> *was*
> The movie͜seen by everyone in my family.

6. Use *by* to show the agent of the action.

> *by*
> *Tom Sawyer* was written ~~for~~ Mark Twain.

7. Use an object pronoun after *by*.

> *her*
> My mother prepared the soup. The salad was prepared by ~~she~~ too.

8. Use *do*, *does*, or *did* when you use *get* in questions and negatives with the passive voice.

> *Did*
> ~~Were~~ you get fired from your job?

PART 2 Participles and Other Adjectives

1. Don't forget the *-ed* ending for past participles used as adjectives.

> *d*
> I'm very tire͜now. I have to go to sleep.

> *ied*
> When did you get marry͜?

2. Don't forget to include a verb (usually *be*) before a participle used as an adjective.

> *is*
> My college͜located on the corner of Broadway and Wilson Avenues.

> *was*
> The movie͜boring, so we left.

3. Participles used as adjectives are used with *be*, not *do*.

> *isn't*
> My sister ~~doesn't~~ married.

> *Are*
> ~~Do~~ you bored in your math class?

PART 1 Find the mistakes with the underlined words, and correct them.

Not every sentence has a mistake. If the sentence is correct, write *C*.

EXAMPLES   The movie ~~filmed~~ *was* in Mexico last year.

A good movie <u>is being shown</u> this week in a theater near my house.   **C**

1. The composition <u>didn't written</u> by Jim. It was written by his brother.

2. The criminal <u>was taking</u> to the police station.

3. A dictionary <u>found</u> on the floor of the classroom.

4. The janitor <u>found</u> a dictionary on the floor of the classroom.

5. Where <u>was</u> the accident <u>happened</u>?

6. Where <u>was</u> the movie <u>filmed</u>?

7. I <u>wasn't given</u> any information about the final exam.

8. The answers <u>can find</u> in the back of the book.

9. Steven Spielberg <u>has made</u> many movies.

10. A new theater <u>is being built</u> this year.

11. When <u>did</u> the first cartoon <u>made</u>?

12. Reagan <u>was elected</u> president in 1980.

13. The president <u>got shot</u> but he <u>wasn't get killed</u>.

14. The thief <u>was chased for</u> the police.

15. Arnold Schwarzenegger was an actor before he <u>was become</u> governor of California.

16. She <u>was arrived</u> in the U.S. three years ago.

17. The first animation <u>was created</u> by Winsor McCay. Mickey Mouse wasn't created by <u>he</u>.

PART 2 Fill in the blanks with the passive or active form of the verb in parentheses ( ). Use the tense indicated.

EXAMPLES   The movie _____*will be filmed*_____ in New York.
(future: film)

The movie director _____*has won*_____ many awards.
(present perfect: win)

1. Which actor _____ next year?
(future: choose)

Passive Voice; Participles Used as Adjectives; *Get* + Participles and Adjectives   **91**

2. Julia Roberts _____ in many movies.
   (present perfect: see)

3. My sister _____ popcorn during a movie.
   (simple present: not/eat)

4. A new movie _____ about World War II.
   (present continuous: make)

5. I _____ the Oscar presentation last year.
   (past: not/see)

6. The audience _____ the movie.
   (past: enjoy)

7. We _____ our tickets tomorrow.
   (future: buy)

8. Her parents _____ her to watch adult movies.
   (present: not/permit)

9. While the movie _____, one of the actors
   (past continuous: make)

   _____.
   (past: hurt)

10. *Star Wars* is a great movie. It _____ on a large
    (should/see)

    screen, not on a TV screen.

11. Today's animation _____ on a computer. It
    (simple present: do)

    _____ by hand.
    (simple present: not/draw)

12. Charlie Chaplin _____ interested in acting at
    (past: become)

    the age of five.

13. Chaplin _____ the U.S. in 1952 and
    (past: leave)

    _____ in 1972.
    (past: return)

14. President Lincoln _____ while he
    (past: shoot)

    _____ a play. He _____ a
    (past continuous: watch)   *(past: die)*

    few days later. The killer _____.
    (past: catch)

PART 3 Find the mistakes with the underlined words, and correct them. Not every sentence has a mistake. If the sentence is correct, write *C*.

EXAMPLES Are you ~~worry~~ *ied* about your children?
When did they get divorced?   **C**

1. You look like you don't understand the lesson. Are you confuse?

2. I very tired now. I just want to go to sleep.

3. I come form Miami. I'm not accustomed to cold weather.

4. Last week we saw a very boring movie.

5. My cousin was excited about coming to the U.S.

6. Do you have an interesting job?

7. I am surprised to find out that you don't like ice cream.

8. When did you get married?

9. I'm not satisfy with my grade in this course.

10. The teacher's office located on the second floor.

11. The library doesn't crowded at 8 a.m.

12. Do you disappointed with your grade?

PART 4 Fill in the blanks with the present participle or the past participle of the verb in parentheses ( ).

EXAMPLES The movie wasn't very good. In fact, it was ___*boring*___ ,
(bore)

I had a great meal. I feel very ___*satisfied*___ .
(satisfy)

1. We read an _____ story about Charlie Chaplin.
(interest)

2. He became _____ in acting when he was a child.
(interest)

3. He was well _____ all over the world.
(know)

4. When he left the U.S. in 1952, he was not _____ to re-enter.
(allow)

5. Chaplin was _____ four times.
(marry)

6. He was an _____ actor.
(entertain)

7. I am never _____ during one of his movies.
(bore)

8. There's an _____ new movie at the Fine Arts Theater.
(excite)

9. Are you _____ in seeing it with me?
(interest)

10. The movie theater is _____ on Saturday night.
(crowd)

11. I was _____ when I saw *Friday the Thirteenth*.
(frighten)

12. It was a very _____ movie.
(frighten)

13. I didn't like the movie I saw last week. I was very

_____ in it.
(disappoint)

14. My friend liked the movie. He thought it was a very

_____ movie.
(excite)

EXPANSION ACTIVITIES

Classroom Activities

1. Form a group of about five students. Match the event on the left with the name on the right. The answers can be found below.

a. The *Mona Lisa* was painted by	Alexander Fleming
b. Penicillin was discovered by	William Shakespeare
c. Mexico was conquered by	Steven Spielberg
d. DNA was discovered by	Hernán Cortéz
e. Cars were mass-produced by	Mark Twain
f. *MacBeth* was written by	Abraham Lincoln
g. *I Want to Hold Your Hand* was sung by	Leonardo Da Vinci
h. The slaves in the U.S. were freed by	The Beatles
i. *Bolero* was composed by	Crick and Watson
j. *Guernica* was painted by	Henry Ford
k. *Saving Private Ryan* was directed by	Maurice Ravel
l. *Tom Sawyer* was written by	Pablo Picasso

Answers:

a) Leonardo Da Vinci	g) The Beatles		
b) Alexander Fleming	h) Abraham Lincoln		
c) Hernán Cortéz	i) Maurice Ravel		
d) Crick and Watson	j) Pablo Picasso		
e) Henry Ford	k) Steven Spielberg		
f) William Shakespeare	l) Mark Twain		

2. Fill in the blanks. Then find a partner. Discuss your answers with your partner.

a. _____ is an interesting place in this city.

b. _____ is an interesting actress.

c. _____ is a boring topic in our grammar class.

d. A surprising fact about the U.S. is _____.

e. _____ is a relaxing activity.

f. I feel relaxed when _____.

g. I get bored when I _____.

h. I get angry when _____.

i. You know you're getting old when _____.

j. I get confused when _____.

k. People in my native country who _____ can get rich.

l. One of the main reasons people get divorced is _____.

3. In a small group of people give your opinions about the best actors and actresses.

Talk About it

1. Is it important to give awards to actors and actresses? Why or why not?

2. Have you ever seen an Academy Awards ceremony? What did you think of it?

3. How are American films different from films made in other countries?

4. What are some of your favorite movies? What movies have you seen lately?

5. Who are your favorite actors and actresses?

6. What American movies have been popular in your native country?

Write About it

Write about an entertainment event that you have recently attended (such as a movie in a theater, a concert, an art fair, a museum exhibit). Did you enjoy it? Why or why not? Was there anything surprising or unusual about it?

Outside Activities

1. Look for signs, headlines, and captions that use passive constructions. (Remember, sometimes the verb *be* is omitted in a sign.) Copy the passive sentences and bring them to class.

2. Rent and watch a Charlie Chaplin movie. Summarize the story.

Internet Activities

1. On the internet, find information about an actor or actress that interests you. Print out this information and bring it to class.

2. Find out who won the Oscars most recently in these categories: Best Actor, Best Actress, Best Picture, Best Director.

3. Check to see if your local newspaper has a Web site. If it does, are there movie listings?

4. At a search engine, type in *movies*. Find a summary of a movie that interests you. Print it and bring it to class.

5. Choose two of these famous actors. Find out when they were born and when they died.

Humphrey Bogart	Spencer Tracy	John Wayne
Marilyn Monroe	Henry Fonda	Gary Cooper
Clark Gable	Vivien Leigh	Audrey Hepburn
Cary Grant	Grace Kelly	Mary Pickford
Katherine Hepburn	Natalie Wood	Jack Lemmon

Additional Activities at **http://elt.thomson.com/gic**

LESSON

3

GRAMMAR

The Past Continuous[1]
The Past Perfect
The Past Perfect Continuous[2]
Comparison of Past Tenses

CONTEXT: Disasters and Tragedies

The Columbia Tragedy
The Titanic
Wildfires in Southern California
Survivors of the Titanic

[1] The past continuous is sometimes called the *past progressive*.
[2] The past perfect continuous is sometimes called the *past perfect progressive*.

3.1 | Overview of Past Tenses

In this lesson, we will be looking at all the past tenses.	
Simple Past Tense	She **drove** to her sister's house last night.
Past Continuous	She **was driving** when the accident happened.
Present Perfect	She **has driven** there many times.
Present Perfect Continuous	She **has been driving** since she was 18 years old.
Past Perfect	She knew the road well because she **had driven** it many times.
Past Perfect Continuous	She **had been driving** for three hours when the accident happened.

THE COLUMBIA TRAGEDY

Before You Read

1. What well-known accidents do you remember from history?
2. Do you remember what you were doing when a famous event occurred?

Read the following article. Pay special attention to the past continuous and the simple past-tense verbs.

Did You Know?

The Columbia was the first reusable space vehicle. Before the Columbia, manned space flight had been limited to rockets, which could only be used once, making the space program much more expensive.

On January 16, 2003, the Columbia space shuttle **left** on a science mission orbiting the Earth, with seven crew members aboard. It **stayed** in space for 16 days. On February 1, 2003, it **was traveling** back to Earth after completing its mission. NASA (the National Aeronautics and Space Administration) **received** its last communication from the Columbia on February 1, 2003, at 9 a.m. While the Columbia **was flying** over east Texas just 16 minutes from its landing in Florida, it **disintegrated**[3]. Families who **were** happily **waiting** for the return of their relatives at the Kennedy Space Center in Florida **received** the tragic news. People all over the world **were shocked** and **saddened** by this tragic loss of lives.

NASA **studied** the causes of this disaster. The investigation **concluded** that a piece of the left wing **fell** off as the Columbia **was lifting off.** This **created** a hole in the wing, and super-hot gases **entered** the wing's interior. As the Columbia **was approaching** its final destination, its left wing **burned.**

Even though the investigation is finished, farmers and hunters continue to find pieces of the rocket in their fields and nearby forests.

[3] *To disintegrate* means to break into small pieces.

The Columbia **was** the United States' second major disaster in space. The first one **was** in January 1986, when the space shuttle Challenger **exploded** 73 seconds after liftoff, killing all seven crew members.

NASA **was going to send** another rocket into space in March 2003, but this mission **was** postponed. Safety issues of future astronauts in space **needed** to be studied before another mission could take place.

1957	The USSR[4] puts the first satellite in space to orbit the Earth.
1961	The USSR puts the first man into space.
1966 (January)	The USSR lands a spacecraft on the moon.
1969	The first astronauts walk on the moon (Americans).
1970s and 1980s	The USSR and the U.S. explore Venus, Mars, Jupiter, and Saturn in fly-bys.
1986	The USSR launches the space station *Mir*.
1986	The U.S. spacecraft *Challenger* explodes shortly after liftoff. All seven crew members die.
1995	U.S. astronauts meet Russian cosmonauts at space station *Mir*.
2003	Seven U.S. astronauts are killed in the *Columbia* shuttle disaster.
2004	The U.S. lands a spacecraft on Mars.

[4] The USSR no longer exists as a country. In 1991, it broke up into 15 countries, the largest of which is Russia.

3.2 | The Past Continuous—Forms

Subject	*was / were*	Present Participle	Complement	Explanation
I She He It The rocket	was	traveling	fast.	To form the past continuous, use *was* or *were* + present participle (verb + *-ing*).
We You They The astronauts	were			

Language Notes:

1. To make the negative, put *not* between *was / were* and the present participle.

   I **was** *not* **living** in the U.S. in January 2003.

   Americans **were** *not* **expecting** this tragedy.

2. The contraction for *were not* is *weren't*. The contraction for *was not* is *wasn't*.

3. An adverb can be placed between *was / were* and the present participle.

   You **were** *probably* **watching** the news.

Questions and Short Answers

Question Word	*was / wasn't* *were / weren't*	Subject	Present Participle	Complement	Short Answer
	Was	the rocket	**traveling**	fast?	Yes, it was.
How fast	**was**	it	**traveling?**		
	Weren't	they	**flying**	over Florida?	No, they weren't.
Where	**were**	they	**flying?**		
	Were	you	**watching**	it on TV?	No, I wasn't.
Why	**weren't**	you	**watching**	it on TV?	
Who	**was**		**watching**	it on TV?	

Passive

Subject	*was / were*	*being*	Past Participle	Complement
The landing	**was**	**being**	**filmed.**	
Experiments	**were**	**being**	**done**	in space.

EXERCISE **1** Fill in the blanks with the correct form of the verb in parentheses ( ). Use the past continuous.

EXAMPLE The Columbia _____was approaching_____ Florida.
(approach)

1. Family members _____.
(wait)

2. The Columbia _____ over Texas.
(travel)

3. It _____ over Florida.
(not/travel)

4. It _____ to Earth after a successful mission.
(return)

5. The astronauts _____ forward to seeing their families.
(look)

6. Reporters _____ to interview the astronauts.
(prepare)

7. How many people _____?
(wait)

8. Where _____?
(they/wait)

9. Pieces of the Columbia _____ and
(passive: collect)

_____ together.
(put)

3.3 | The Past Continuous Tense—Uses

Examples	Explanation
What **were** you **doing** at 9 a.m. on February 1, 2003? 　I **was watching** TV. 　My brother **was sleeping.**	The past continuous is used to show that an action was in progress at a specific past time. It didn't begin at that time.
The Columbia **disintegrated** while it **was traveling** back to the Earth. Family members **were waiting** in Florida when the Columbia accident **happened.** The Columbia **was approaching** the Earth when it **lost** communication with NASA.	We use the past continuous together with the simple past tense to show the relationship of a longer past action to a shorter past action.
While the Columbia **was approaching** its Florida destination, family members **were waiting** for the astronauts. While the astronauts **were orbiting** the Earth, they **were doing** scientific studies.	The past continuous can be used in both clauses to show that two past actions were in progress at the same time.
Compare *when* and *while*. a. **While (When)** the Columbia *was flying* over Texas, it disintegrated. b. The Columbia was flying over Texas **when** it *disintegrated.*	The meaning of sentences (a) and (b) is basically the same. a. *While* is used with a past continuous verb (*was flying*). In conversation, many people use *when* in place of *while.* b. *When* is used with the simple past tense (*disintegrated*).
As the Columbia was approaching its final destination, its left wing burned. **While** the Columbia was approaching its final destination, its left wing burned.	*As* and *while* have the same meaning.
The astronauts **were going to** return with scientific data. Family members **were going to** celebrate with the astronauts. NASA **was going to** send astronauts into space in March 2003, but this mission was postponed.	*Was / were going to* means that a past plan was not carried out.

Punctuation Note:

If the time clause precedes the main clause, separate the two clauses with a comma.
　The Columbia was flying over Texas when it disintegrated. (No comma)
　When the Columbia disintegrated, it was flying over Texas. (Comma)

EXERCISE 2   ABOUT YOU Ask and answer. Ask the student next to you what he or she was doing at this particular time.

EXAMPLE   at 4 a.m.

A: What were you doing at 4 a.m.?
B: I was sleeping, of course.

1. at 10 p.m. last night

2. at 7 a.m. this morning

3. at 2 a.m. last night

4. when the teacher entered the classroom today

5. at _____ (*your choice of time*)

6. while the teacher was explaining the past continuous

EXERCISE 3   Fill in the blanks with the simple past or the past continuous form of the verb in parentheses ( ).

EXAMPLE   We __*were watching*__ cartoons on TV when we __*heard*__ the bad news.
                        (*watch*)   (*hear*)

1. While the Columbia _____ to Earth, it _____.
                                    (*return*)   (*disintegrate*)

2. My sister _____ when I _____ her up to tell
                      (*sleep*)   (*wake*)

    her about the accident.

3. A hunter _____ near the forest when he
                    (*walk*)

    _____ a piece of metal.
       (*find*)

4. When he _____ to pick up the piece of metal, his
                    (*go*)

    friend _____ him not to.
                  (*tell*)

5. When I _____ about the accident, I _____ to work.
                (*hear*)   (*drive*)

6. My sister _____ a TV program when the disaster
                      (*watch*)

    _____.
       (*happen*)

7. While the Columbia _____ to Earth, family
                                    (*return*)

    members _____ in Florida.
                      (*wait*)

8. What _____ when the accident _____ ?
              (*you/do*)   (*happen*)

9. The Challenger _____ off when it _____ in 1986.
                              (*lift*)   (*explode*)

3.4 | The Past Continuous or the Simple Past

Examples	Explanation

Compare:
a. What **were** you **doing** when you heard the news?
    I was watching TV.
b. What **did** you **do** when you heard the news?
    I called my sister.
 	
a. She **was driving** to work when she had an accident.
b. She **called** the police when she had an accident.
	a. Use the past continuous to show what was in progress *at* the time a specific action occurred.
	
	b. Use the simple past to show what happened *after* a specific action occurred.

a. On February 1, 2003, relatives **were waiting** in Florida for the astronauts. They **were getting** ready to celebrate. Camera crews **were preparing** to take pictures of the landing. Suddenly, at 9 a.m., just minutes before the landing, NASA lost communication with the Columbia. b. A NASA official **announced** the tragedy to the public. The president **went** on TV to express his sadness. NASA **began** an investigation of the accident. Investigators **went** to Texas to talk with witnesses.	a. Use the past continuous to show the events *leading up to* the main event of the story. b. Use the simple past tense to tell what happened *after* the main event of the story.

EXERCISE **4**   Fill in the blanks to complete these conversations.

1. *A reporter is interviewing a family in Texas after the Columbia disaster.*

   A: What <u>were you doing</u> at 9 a.m. on February 1, 2003?

             (example: you/do)

   B: I _____. A loud noise _____ me up. I

          (1 sleep)   *(2 wake)*

   _____ out of bed and _____ outside.

   (3 jump)   *(4 run)*

   I saw my husband outside. He _____ our car. We

                                  (5 fix)

   thought it was an earthquake. Then we _____ pieces

                                        (6 see)

   of metal on our property. I _____ to pick up a piece,

                            (7 go)

but my husband told me not to. Instead we _____ the
(8 call)

police. They told us not to touch anything.

2. *A reporter is interviewing a member of NASA after the Columbia
disaster.*

A: How fast _____ when the accident
(9 the Columbia/travel)

_____?
(10 happen)

B: It _____ at 12,500 m.p.h. We _____
(11 travel)   (12 communicate)

with the Columbia when, suddenly, communication _____.
(13 stop)

A: What _____ when you _____ that the crew
(14 you/do)   (15 realize)

members were lost?

B: We _____ the family members and the press. Many
(16 notify)

of the family members _____ at the Kennedy Space
(17 wait)

Center in Florida when the accident _____.
(18 happen)

A: What _____ after that?
(19 happen)

B: An investigation _____. We _____ to look
(20 begin)   (21 start)

for the pieces of the rocket and _____ to understand
(22 try)

the reason for the accident.

A: _____ all the pieces?
(23 you/find)

B: No, of course not. Many of the people of East Texas _____
(24 call)

to tell us about finding pieces on their land. Hunters _____
(25 call)

to tell us that while they _____ in forests, they _____
(26 hunt)   (27 find)

pieces of metal. We _____ enough pieces to come to
(28 find)

a conclusion about the cause of the accident.

EXERCISE 5 Fill in the blanks with the simple past or the past continuous of the verb in parentheses ( ).

EXAMPLES I _____was walking_____ to school when I ___saw___ a car accident.
_____(walk)_____(see)

The police ___came___ and ___gave___ a ticket to one of the drivers.
_____(come)_____(give)

1. I _____ ready for bed when someone _____
   _____(get)_____ to my door. I _____ the door and saw my neighbor.
   _____(open)_____

   He _____ in front of me with a video in his hand. He said,
   _____(stand)_____

   "I just rented a movie. Would you like to watch it with me?" I didn't

   want to be impolite, so I said yes. While we _____ the
   _____(watch)_____

   movie, I _____ asleep.
   _____(fall)_____

2. While the baby _____, the babysitter _____
   _____(sleep)_____ _____(watch)_____

   TV. Suddenly the baby _____ to cry, and the babysitter
   _____(start)_____

   _____ into the room to see what had happened. She
   _____(run)_____

   _____ up the baby and started to rock her. Then she
   _____(pick)_____

   _____ her back to bed.
   _____(put)_____

3. When I _____ home, my sister and brothers
   _____(get)_____

   _____ TV. I said, "I'm hungry. Let's eat." But they
   _____(watch)_____

   _____ off the TV. I _____ to cook dinner. They
   _____(not/turn)_____ _____(start)_____

   all _____ into the kitchen to see what I _____.
   _____(come)_____ _____(cook)_____

4. She _____ to the radio while she _____ on
   _____(listen)_____ _____(work)_____

   the computer. Suddenly she _____ the news of a terrible
   _____(hear)_____

   accident. She _____ to the TV to find out more information.
   _____(go)_____

5. While Sam _____ (drive), his cell phone _____ (ring). He

_____ (talk) on his phone when he _____ (have) a car

accident. He _____ (hit) a light post. Fortunately,

he _____ (wear) his seatbelt, so he wasn't hurt.

6. When the storm _____ (begin) last night, we _____ (watch)

a scary movie. The lights went out, so we _____ (have) to

use candles. While I _____ (look) for matches and candles,

my little brother suddenly _____ (enter) the room with a

flashlight and a scary mask. He really _____ (scare) me.

7. While I _____ (look) for my gloves in a drawer, I

_____ (find) an old photograph of me. In this photo, I

_____ (wear) a silly looking bathing suit. I can't even remember

who _____ (take) the picture.

8. I _____ (type) my composition on the computer when

suddenly we _____ (lose) electrical power. When the power

_____ (come) back on, I _____ (turn) on the computer,

but all my work was gone. I know how important it is to save my

work. I _____ (go) to save it on a disk, but I didn't have any.

So I _____ (lose) everything and _____ (have) to start

all over.

Before You Read

1. Have you ever traveled by ship? Where did you go? What was the trip like?

2. Did you see the 1997 movie *Titanic*? If so, did you enjoy it? Why or why not?

Read the following article. Pay special attention to the past perfect tense.

The year was 1912. The radio **had** already **been invented** in 1901. The Wright brothers **had** already **made** their first successful flight in 1903. The Titanic—the ship of dreams—**had** just **been built** and was ready to make its first voyage from England to America with its 2,200 passengers.

The Titanic was the most magnificent ship that **had** ever **been built.** It had luxuries that ships **had** never **had** before: electric light and heat, electric elevators, a swimming pool, a Turkish bath, libraries, and much more. It was built to give its first-class passengers all the comforts of the best hotels.

But rich passengers were not the only ones traveling on the Titanic. Most of the passengers in third class were emigrants who **had left** behind a complete way of life and were coming to America with hopes of a better life.

Did You
Know?

Only four female passengers in first-class died. (These women chose to stay with their husbands.) Almost half of the female passengers in third-class died.

The Titanic began to cross the Atlantic Ocean on April 10. The winter of 1912 **had been** unusually mild, and large blocks of ice **had broken** away from the Arctic region. By the fifth day at sea, the captain **had received** several warnings about ice, but he was not very worried; he didn't realize how much danger the ship was in. On April 14, at 11:40 p.m., an iceberg was spotted[5] straight ahead. The captain tried to reverse the direction of his ship, but he couldn't because the Titanic was traveling too fast and it was too big. It hit the iceberg and started to sink.

The Titanic **had** originally **had** 32 lifeboats, but 12 of them **had been removed** to make the ship look better. While the ship was sinking, rich people were put on lifeboats. Women and children were put on the lifeboats before men. By the time the third-class passengers were allowed to come up from their cabins, most of the lifeboats **had** already **left.**

Several hours later, another ship arrived to help, but the Titanic **had** already **gone** down. Only one-third of the passengers survived.

[5] To spot means to see suddenly.

The Past Continuous; The Past Perfect; The Past Perfect Continuous; Comparison of Past Tenses

3.5 | The Past Perfect Tense—Forms

Subject	*Had*	*Not /* Adverb	Past Participle	Complement	Explanation
The captain	**had**		**received**	several warnings.	To form the past perfect, use *had* + past participle.
He	**had**	not	**paid**	attention.	
The winter	**had**		**been**	unusually mild.	
The ship	**had**	originally	**had**	32 lifeboats.	
They	**had**	never	**been**	on a ship before.	

Language Notes:
1. The pronouns (except *it*) can be contracted with *had*: *I'd, you'd, she'd, he'd, we'd, they'd.*
   He'd received several warnings.
2. Apostrophe + *d* can be a contraction for both *had* or *would*. The word following the contraction will tell you what the contraction means.
   He'd spoken. = He *had* spoken.
   He'd speak. = He *would* speak.
3. For a negative contraction, use *hadn't*.
   He **hadn't** paid attention.
4. For an alphabetical list of irregular past tenses and past participles, see Appendix M.

Questions

Question Word	*Had*	Subject	Past Participle	Complement	Short Answer
	Had	the Titanic	**crossed**	the ocean before?	No, it **hadn't.**
How much experience	**had**	the captain	**had?**		
Who	**had**		**heard**	of the Titanic before?	

Passive

Subject	*Had*	Adverb	*Been*	Past Participle
Lifeboats	**had**		**been**	**removed.**
The survivors	**had**		**been**	**found.**
The airplane	**had**	already	**been**	**invented.**

EXERCISE **6**   Fill in the blanks with the past perfect of the verb in parentheses ( )
plus any other included words.

EXAMPLE   When we read about the Titanic, the story was not new to me because I
_____had seen_____ the movie.
           (see)

1. The captain of the Titanic _____ a serious mistake
                               (make)

   when he didn't listen to the warnings.

2. When the Titanic disaster occurred, how much experience

   _____?
        (the captain/have)

3. I didn't realize that airplanes _____ by the time
                                    (passive: invent)

   of the Titanic.

4. In 1912, World War I _____.
                        (not/yet/begin)

5. The story about the Titanic was new to me because I

   _____ an article about it before.
        (never/read)

6. _____ this story before we read
        (you/already/hear)

   about it in class?

7. How many lifeboats _____?
                       (have/the Titanic/originally)

   Why _____?
        (they/passive: remove)

3.6 | The Past Perfect—Use

The past perfect is used to show the relationship of two past events. We start at some time in the past (simple past) and then go back even more past (past perfect).

Examples	Explanation
By the time the rescue ship *arrived,* the Titanic **had** already **gone** down. By *1912,* the Wright brothers **had** already **invented** the airplane.	The past perfect is used to show that something happened before a specific date, time, or event.
When people got on the lifeboats, the rescue ship **hadn't** arrived **yet.** *When* the rescue ship arrived, many passengers **had** already **died.**	The past perfect is used to show that something happened or didn't happen before the verb in the *when* clause. *Yet* and *already* help show the time relationship.
There was a lot of ice in the water *because* the previous winter **had been** unusually mild. I knew about the Titanic *because* I **had seen** a movie about it.	The past perfect can be used after *because* to show a prior reason.
The captain *didn't realize* how close his ship **had come** to the iceberg. I *didn't know* that you **had seen** a movie about the Titanic.	The past perfect is used in a noun clause[6] when the main verb is past.
The passengers in third class were emigrants *who* **had left** behind their old way of life. The Titanic was the most magnificent ship **that had** *ever* **been built.**	The past perfect can be used in a *who / that / which* clause to show a prior action. The past perfect is sometimes used with *ever* + a superlative form.
Many emigrants on the Titanic **had** *never* **left** their homelands *before.*	The past perfect is used with *never . . . before* in relation to a past event (in this case, *they left their homelands*).
The ship **had been** at sea *for five days* when it hit an iceberg.	The past perfect is used with *for* + time period to show the duration of an earlier past action.
The year of the Titanic disaster was *1912.* The airplane **had** already **been invented.**	The simple past and the past perfect do not have to occur in the same sentence. We can start at some point in time (in this case, 1912) and then go back.

[6] For more about noun clauses, see Lesson 9.

Examples	Explanation
a. **Before** the Titanic hit the iceberg, the captain **tried** to turn the ship around. b. **Before** the Titanic hit the iceberg, the captain **had tried** to turn the ship around. a. The captain **realized** that he **made** a mistake. b. The captain **realized** that he **had made** a mistake. a. He failed the test **because** he **didn't study.** b. He failed the test **because** he **hadn't studied.**	In some cases, either the simple past (a) or the past perfect (b) can be used if the time relationship is clear. This is especially true with *before, after, because,* and in a noun clause (after *knew, realized, understood,* etc.).

EXERCISE 7 Fill in the blanks with the simple past or the past perfect of the verb in parentheses ( ).

EXAMPLE The Titanic had luxuries that ships ___had never had___ before.
          (never/have)

1. By 1912, the radio _____.
   (passive: already/invent)

2. The Titanic was the biggest ship that _____.
   (passive: ever/build)

3. The Titanic _____ 32 lifeboats.
   (originally/have)

4. When the Titanic _____ England, many of the
   (leave)
   lifeboats _____.
   (passive: remove)

5. By April 1912, pieces of ice _____ away from
   (break)
   the Arctic region.

6. The captain of the Titanic _____ attention
   (not/pay)
   to the warnings he _____.
   (receive)

7. When the Titanic _____ an iceberg, it _____
   (hit)   *(be)*
   at sea for four days.

8. By the time the poor immigrants _____ allowed to
   (be)
   come up from their cabins, most of the lifeboats _____.
   (already/leave)

9. By the time the rescue ship _____,
   (arrive)
   the Titanic _____.
   (already/sink)

EXERCISE 8 ABOUT YOU Tell if the following had already happened or hadn't happened yet by the time you got to class.

EXAMPLE the teacher / collect the homework
By the time I got to class, the teacher had already collected the homework.
OR
When I got to class, the teacher hadn't collected the homework yet.

1. the teacher / arrive

2. most of the students / arrive

3. the class / begin

4. the teacher / take attendance

5. I / do the homework

6. the teacher / hand back the last homework

7. the teacher / explain the past perfect

EXERCISE 9 Fill in the blanks with the simple past or the past perfect of the verb in parentheses ( ).

EXAMPLE By the time the U.S. ___*sent*___ a man into space (1962), the Russians
(send)

___*had already put*___ a man in space (1961).
(already/put)

1. When an American astronaut _____ on the moon in
(step)

1969, no person _____ on the moon before.
(ever/walk)

2. By 2003, NASA _____ hundreds of successful spaceflights.
(complete)

3. When the Columbia mission took off in 2003, NASA _____
(have)

only two serious accidents in its space program.

4. By the time the U.S. _____ a mission to Mars, the
(send)

reasons for the Columbia accident _____.
(already/discover)

5. By the time the 16 days were up, the Columbia crew

_____ all its scientific experiments.
(do)

6. Until 9 a.m. on February 1, NASA _____ good
(have)

communication with the Columbia.

7. At first, NASA couldn't understand what _____.
(happen)

8. When they lost communication with the Columbia, they were afraid that all of the astronauts _____.
   (die)

9. The original date for the Columbia mission was July 2002. The date was postponed until 2003 because cracks in the fuel line

   _____.
   (passive: find)

10. NASA _____ that the Columbia _____ a
    (know)   _(lose)_
    piece of its wing on liftoff, but they didn't think it would be a problem.

11. They _____ that this problem _____ a
    (not/realize)   _(create)_
    hole in the wing.

12. By the time the investigation _____ in April 2003, NASA
    (end)
    _____ 40 percent of pieces of the Columbia.
    (collected)

3.7 | *When* with the Simple Past or the Past Perfect

Sometimes *when* means *after*. Sometimes *when* means *before*.	
Examples	**Explanation**
a. When the captain saw the iceberg, he **tried** to turn the ship around. b. When the captain saw the iceberg, the ship **had been** at sea for five days.	If you use the simple past in the main clause (a), *when* means *after*. If you use the past perfect in the main clause (b), *when* means before.
a. When the Columbia lifted off, it **lost** a piece of its wing. b. When the Columbia lifted off on January 2003, it **had had** 27 successful missions.	

Compare	
***When* means *after*.**	***When* means *before*.**
When I came home, my wife and I **ate** dinner.	When I came home, my wife **had eaten** dinner.

EXERCISE 10 Write numbers to show which action happened first.

EXAMPLES

$\overset{1}{\text{When she got home,}}$ $\overset{2}{\text{she took an aspirin.}}$

$\overset{2}{\text{When she got home,}}$ she had $\overset{1}{\text{already taken an aspirin.}}$

1. When they came into the room, their son left.

2. When they came into the room, their son had just left.

3. When I got home from school, I did my homework.

4. When I got home from school, I had already done my homework.

5. When she got to my house, she had eaten dinner.

6. When she got to my house, she ate dinner.

7. The teacher gave a test when Linda arrived.

8. The teacher had already given a test when Linda arrived.

EXERCISE 11 Fill in the blanks with the verb in parentheses ( ). Use the simple past to show that *when* means *after*. Use the past perfect to show that *when* means *before*.

EXAMPLES

When I saw the movie *Titanic*, I ____*told*____ my friends about it.
(tell)

When I saw the movie *Titanic*, I _*had never heard*_ of this ship before.
(never/hear)

1. When the Titanic sank, a rescue ship _____ to pick
(come)

   up the survivors.

2. When the ship hit an iceberg, the captain _____
(receive)

   several warnings.

3. When the ship was built, people _____ amazed at how
(be)

   beautiful it was.

4. When the ship left England, 12 lifeboats _____.
(passive: *remove*)

5. When the passengers heard a loud noise, they _____
(run)

   to get on the lifeboats.

6. When the Arctic ice started to melt, pieces of ice _____
(break)

   away.

7. When people saw the Titanic for the first time, they _____

   _____ such a magnificent ship before.
(never/see)

8. When the rescue ship arrived, many passengers _____.
   (already/die)

9. When the Columbia accident happened, people _____
   (be)

   shocked.

10. When the Columbia accident happened, the astronauts

    _____ in space for 16 days.
    (be)

11. When relatives heard the news, they _____ to cry.
    (start)

12. When people in east Texas heard a loud sound, they

    _____ it was an earthquake.
    (think)

13. For months after the accident, farmers in east Texas found pieces

    of the Columbia that _____ in their fields.
    (fall)

WILDFIRES IN SOUTHERN CALIFORNIA

Before You Read

1. Do you know about any fires that burned for a long time?
2. Do you know anyone who has lost a home because of a natural disaster?

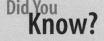

Read the following article. Pay special attention to the past perfect and the past perfect continuous tenses.

Did You Know?

San Francisco had a major earthquake in 1906. At least 1,000 people died.

In October 2003, wildfires in San Diego County burned out of control. Many residents had to leave their homes as they were warned of the approaching fire. They watched and waited as firefighters battled the fire.

One of the fires was started accidentally by a lost hunter in a forest, who **had been trying** to signal his location. Strong winds spread the fire quickly. The San Diego area **had had** very little rain or humidity, and there were millions of dry dead trees that caught fire quickly.

The fire **had been burning** for a week by the time firefighters got it under control. Many residents returned only to find that they **had lost** their homes and all their possessions. "We **had been living** in the same house for the past 26 years when we lost our home," said a San Diego woman, whose family went to stay with relatives nearby. "Now we have nothing, not even a photograph of our former lives."

(continued)

Many of the firefighters were exhausted because they **had been working** around the clock to get the fire under control. Firefighters from other areas in the U.S. came to help contain the fire. By the time the fire was brought under control, over 2,400 homes and businesses **had been destroyed** and 16 people **had died.**

3.8 | The Past Perfect Continuous—Forms

Subject	*Had*	*Not /* Adverb	*Been*	Present Participle	Complement	Explanation
We	**had**		**been**	**living**	in the same house.	To form the past perfect continuous, use: *had + been + verb –ing.*
Firefighters	**had**		**been**	**working**	around the clock.	
California	**had**	**not**	**been**	**getting**	much rain.	
A hunter	**had**	**probably**	**been**	**trying**	to send a signal.	

Questions and Short Answers

Question Word	*Had*	Subject	*Been*	Present Participle	Complement	Short Answer
	Had	it	**been**	**raining?**		No, it **hadn't.**
How long	**had**	the fire	**been**	**burning?**		
	Had	you	**been**	**living**	in the same house?	Yes, we **had.**
Who	**had**		**been**	**living**	in that house?	

EXERCISE 12 Fill in the blanks with the past perfect continuous tense.

EXAMPLE   I ___*had been driving*___ for two hours when I had an accident.
                    (drive)

1. The fire _____ for two days by the time firefighters
              (burn)
   put it out.

2. We _____ in a refugee camp for three months
        (live)
   when we got permission to come to the U.S.

3. He _____ the mountain for three hours when he fell.
       (climb)

4. The Titanic _____ for five days when it sank.
                 (travel)

5. By the time he retired, he _____ at the same job
                                (work)
   for 36 years.

6. Why _____ to send a signal?
      (the hunter/try)

The Past Continuous; The Past Perfect; The Past Perfect Continuous; Comparison of Past Tenses   **119**

3.9 | The Past Perfect Continuous—Uses

Examples	Explanation
The fire **had been burning** *for a week* by the time it was controlled. We **had been living** in the same house *for 26 years* when we lost our home. One of the fires was started by a lost hunter who **had been trying** to call attention to his location.	The past perfect continuous tense is used to show the connection of a continuous action that was completed before another past action. The amount of time of the continuous action is expressed with *for*.
Compare: a. By the time the fire was controlled, it **had been burning** for over a week. b. When the fire started, Southern California **had had** very little rain. c. When residents returned, they found out that their homes **had been destroyed.** d. By the time the fire ended, 16 people **had died.**	We use the past perfect continuous: a. When an action took place over a period of time, such as *over a week* We use the past perfect with: b. Nonaction verbs c. An action of no duration d. A multiple or repeated action

EXERCISE **13**   Fill in the blanks with the simple past tense or the past perfect continuous tense of the verb in parentheses ( ).

EXAMPLE   When I ___*came*___ to the U.S., I ___*had been studying*___ English for three
                        (come)   *(study)*
years.

1. I _____ for two years when I _____
         (wait)   *(get)*

    a chance to leave my country.

2. I _____ in the same house all my life when I
         (live)

    _____ my city.
              (leave)

3. I _____ very sad when I left my job because I
         (feel)

    _____ with the same people for ten years.
              (work)

4. I _____ to be a nurse for six months when a
(study)

war _____ in my country.
(break out)

5. When I _____ my country, the war
(leave)

_____ for three years.
(go on)

6. My family _____ in Germany for three months
(wait)

before we _____ permission to come to the U.S.
(get)

7. By the time I _____ to the U.S., I
(get)

_____ for four days.
(travel)

EXERCISE **14** Fill in the blanks with the past perfect continuous for a
continuous action. Fill in the blanks with the past perfect for a
one-time action, multiple or repeated actions, or a nonaction verb.

In the year 1800, the population of Chicago was only 5,000. But the

population _had been growing_ steadily since the beginning of the century.
(example: grow)

In 1871, Chicago _had recently passed_ St. Louis to become the fourth
(example: recently/pass)

largest city in the U.S. Chicago _____ a place of
(1 reach)

importance when the Great Chicago Fire began on October 8, 1871.

That October was especially dry because there _____
(2 be)

very little rain. At that time, most of the streets, sidewalks, bridges, and buildings were made of wood. On Sunday night, a fire broke out in a barn. The firefighters were exhausted that night because they

_____ a fire since the day before. Strong winds
(3 fight)

from the south quickly spread the fire to the center of the city. When the firefighters finally arrived at the fire, the fire

_____ out of control. It wasn't until two days later,
(4 spread)

when rain began to fall, that the fire finally died out. By this time, almost

300 people _____ and more than one hundred
(5 die)

thousand Chicagoans _____ their homes.
(6 lost)

Millionaires, who _____ in mansions,
(7 live)

as well as poor laborers, found themselves homeless. Chicagoans, rich

and poor, who _____ contact with each other,
(8 have/never)

gathered in parks and wondered how they would rebuild their lives.

Because of its great location for industry, Chicago remained strong

after the fire. By 1873, the city _____, this time
(9 passive: rebuild)

with brick instead of wood. Chicago continued to grow as a commercial

center, and, by 1890, its population _____ more
(10 reach)

than one million. Today Chicago is the third largest city in the U.S.

3.10 | The Past Perfect (Continuous) or the Present Perfect (Continuous)

Examples	Explanation
Have you ever **seen** a movie about the Titanic? I **have** never **been** on a ship. How many disasters **have** we **read** about so far?	The present perfect is used when we look back from the present time. 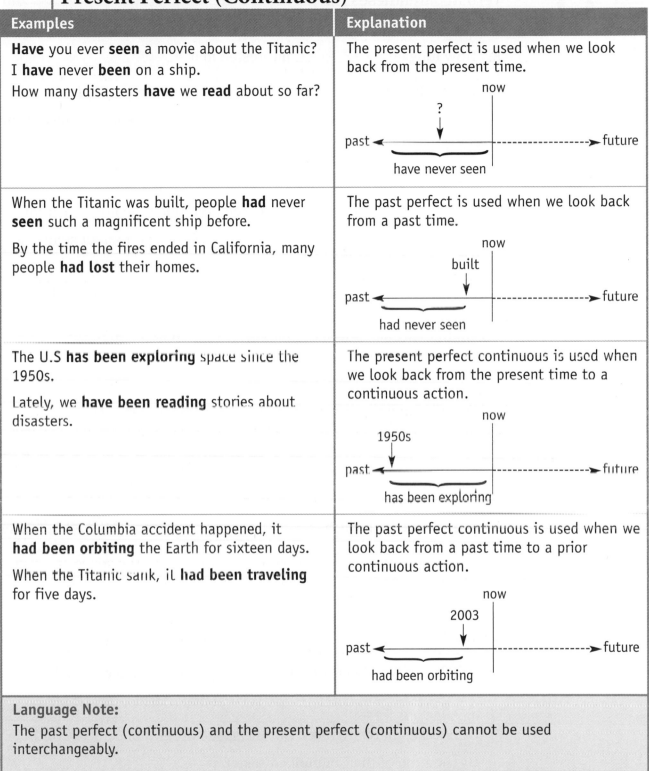
When the Titanic was built, people **had** never **seen** such a magnificent ship before. By the time the fires ended in California, many people **had lost** their homes.	The past perfect is used when we look back from a past time.
The U.S **has been exploring** space since the 1950s. Lately, we **have been reading** stories about disasters.	The present perfect continuous is used when we look back from the present time to a continuous action.
When the Columbia accident happened, it **had been orbiting** the Earth for sixteen days. When the Titanic sank, it **had been traveling** for five days.	The past perfect continuous is used when we look back from a past time to a prior continuous action.

Language Note:
The past perfect (continuous) and the present perfect (continuous) cannot be used interchangeably.

EXERCISE 15 Fill in the blanks with the present perfect, the present perfect continuous, the past perfect, or the past perfect continuous of the verb in parentheses ( ).

A: I'm really interested in space exploration.

B: How long _have you been_ interested in it?
(example: you/be)

A: Ever since I was a child. By the time I was ten years old, I

_____ to the space museum in
(1 go)

Washington, D.C. about five times.

B: Who took you?

A: My parents took me most of the time. But one time my fifth grade

class _____ all semester about space, and
(2 study)

our teacher took the class. Since that time, I _____
(3 always/dream)

about becoming an astronaut. I saw a film about the first moon

landing in 1969. It was so exciting to think that no man

_____ on the moon before.
(4 ever/walk)

B: Do you think it's possible for you to become an astronaut?

A: Sure. Why not? I _____ my bachelor's degree in
(5 already/get)

engineering. Lately I _____ a lot about the training that
(6 read)

astronauts go through. I _____ to NASA asking them
(7 already/write)

to send me more information on how to get into the space program.
And next semester I'm going to enter a master's program in physics.

B: Don't you have to be a pilot first?

A: Yes. I _____ 500 hours of flying lessons.
(8 already/take)

B: Aren't you worried about the risks of going into space? NASA

_____ several major disasters so far.
(9 have)

A: Of course, there are risks. But the space program needs to continue.

By the time of the Columbia disaster, it _____ 27
(10 already/have)

successful missions. And in general, there _____
(11 be)

more successes than failures up to now. Since the Columbia tragedy,

NASA _____ ways to improve the safety of its astronauts.
(12 study)

SURVIVORS OF THE TITANIC

Before You
Read

1. Why do you think the Titanic disaster is still interesting today?

2. If you could ask a survivor of the Titanic any question, what would you ask him or her?

Read the following article. Pay special attention to past tense verbs (simple past, past continuous, past perfect, past perfect continuous, and present perfect).

People **have been** fascinated with the Titanic disaster for about 100 years. Several movies **have been made** giving fictitious[7] stories of the passengers who died. But their real experiences are not known. However, approximately 700 people **survived** the Titanic disaster and **lived** to tell their stories to newspapers.

Philip Zanni, an Assyrian emigrant, **was traveling** to the U.S. in third class. He **was sleeping** when he **heard** a crash. He immediately **ran** to the upper deck[8] where he **saw** great confusion. Men **were lowering** the lifeboats, and Zanni **tried** to jump into one of them. But an officer with a gun **stopped** him, yelling, "Women and children first." Moments later, the officer **turned** away, and Zanni **jumped** on. He **was hiding** under one of the seats when the boat **pulled** away. There **were** 20 women and three men in the boat. They **had** to row quickly because the ship **was sinking.** When they were about two miles away, they **saw** the Titanic sink. It **wasn't** until five in the morning that they **saw** a rescue ship arrive. Zanni **reported** that while the survivors **were being raised** to the rescue ship, a woman **begged** Zanni to save her dog, which she **had been carrying** since leaving the Titanic.

Mary Davis, a second-class passenger, **was traveling** to visit her sister in New York. She **had saved** the money for the trip by working as a maid in London. She **was sleeping** when she **heard** a noise. She **was told** that there was no danger, and so she **returned** to bed. A few minutes later, she **was told** to go to the highest deck because the ship **was sinking.** Two men **helped** her get on a lifeboat, and then it **was lowered.** In the morning, the rescue ship **found** her boat and **pulled** the people aboard. When Ms. Davis **died** in 1987 at the age of 104, she **had lived** to be older than any other Titanic survivor.

[7] *Fictitious* means not real.
[8] A *deck* is a floor of a ship.

3.11 | Comparison of Past Tenses

Examples	Explanation
a. The Titanic **left** England on April 10, 1912. b. Mary Davis, a survivor of the Titanic, **lived** until she was 104 years old. c. I **saw** a movie about the Titanic last year. d. I **read** several articles about the space program last month.	The **simple past tense** shows an action that started and ended in the past. It does not show the relationship to another past action. It can be used for a short action (a) or a long action (b). It can be used for a single action (c) or repeated actions (d).
Many passengers **were sleeping** at 11:40 p.m. The Titanic **was crossing** the Atlantic when it sank. The Columbia **was returning** from its mission when the accident happened.	The **past continuous tense** shows that something was in progress at a specific time in the past.

a. When the rescue ship arrived, 1,500 passengers of the Titanic **had** already **died**.
b. When the Columbia accident happened, it **had** already **had** 27 successful missions.
	The **past perfect** shows the relationship of an earlier past action to a later past action.
	
	    a. earlier = *had died*; later = *arrived*
	    b. earlier = *had had*; later = *happened*

The Titanic **had been traveling** for five days when it sank. The fires in California **had been burning** for about a week when they were controlled.	The **past perfect continuous** is used with the amount of time of a continuous action that happened before another past action. *For* is used to show the amount of time.
People **have been** fascinated with the Titanic for about a hundred years. **Have** there **been** any space missions lately? California **has had** many disasters, including fires and earthquakes.	The **present perfect** uses the present time as the starting point and looks back.
We **have been talking** about the Titanic for several days. We **have been studying** past tenses for a few days. NASA **has been exploring** space since the 1950s.	The **present perfect continuous** uses the present time as the starting point and looks back at a continuous action that is still happening.
Compare: a. When my sister came home, I **ate** dinner. (simple past) b. When my sister came home, I **was eating** dinner. (past continuous) c. When my sister came home, I **had eaten** dinner. (past perfect)	Be especially careful with *when*. In sentence (a), I ate *after* my sister came home. In sentence (b), I was in the process of eating *when* my sister came home. In sentence (c), my dinner was finished *when* my sister came home.

Language Notes:

1. Sometimes the past continuous and the past perfect continuous can be used in the same case. The past perfect continuous is more common with a *for* phrase.

   The Titanic **was traveling** across the Atlantic when it hit an iceberg.

   The Titanic **had been traveling** *for five days* when it hit an iceberg.

2. Sometimes the simple past or the past perfect can be used in the same case.

   Some lifeboats **were** removed before the Titanic left.

   Some lifeboats **had been** removed before the Titanic left.

EXERCISE 16 Read a survivor's account of the night of the Titanic disaster.[9] Fill in the blanks with the simple past, the past perfect, or the past continuous of the verb in parentheses.

We ___had just fallen___ asleep when my wife _____ a noise. She
(example: just/fall)   (1 hear)

_____ me up and _____ that something _____ to the
(2 wake)   (3 say)   (4 happen)

ship. We _____ up on deck and everything _____ normal
(5 go)   (6 seem)

at first. The orchestra _____.
(7 still/play)

At first the officers _____ that the Titanic could not sink
(8 insist)

in less than ten hours. We were told that the Titanic _____
(9 communicate)

with other nearby ships and that help would reach us in an hour or two.

The crew _____ to lower the lifeboats. They _____ us that
(10 start)   (11 assure)

there _____ no danger, that they were just taking precautions.
(12 be)

After about six or seven lifeboats were lowered, people _____
(13 start)

to realize that they _____ in great danger. I saw an officer shoot
(14 be)

two passengers who _____ to get on a lifeboat.
(15 fight)

The thirteenth boat _____ with about 25 children
(16 passive: fill)

and a few women. While the boat _____, all of them
(17 passive: lower)

_____.
(18 scream)

[9] Adapted from *The Bulletin* San Francisco, April 19, 1912.

The Past Continuous; The Past Perfect; The Past Perfect Continuous; Comparison of Past Tenses **127**

I _____ one of the officers on the Titanic because I
(19 know)

_____ with him before on another ship. He _____ me into
(20 travel)   (21 push)

the thirteenth boat and _____ me to take care of the children.
(22 order)

As our boat _____, we _____ the orchestra
(23 leave)   (24 hear)

playing a religious song.

I will never forget the terrible scene as our boat _____ away.
(25 move)

Husbands and fathers _____ and _____ kisses to
(26 wave)   (27 throw)

their wives and children.

The ship _____ only three hours after it _____
(28 sink)   (29 hit)

the iceberg.

EXERCISE 17 Fill in the blanks with the correct past tense. Use the passive voice where indicated. In some cases, more than one answer is possible.

EXAMPLE The Titanic ___sank___ in 1912.
(sink)

1. The Titanic _____ in Ireland.
(passive: *build*)

2. When the captain _____ the iceberg, he
(see)

_____ to turn the ship around.
(try)

3. There was a lot of ice in the water in 1912 because the previous

winter _____ mild.
(be)

4. The Titanic _____ fast when it _____ an iceberg.
(travel)   (hit)

5. Many people _____ when they _____ a loud noise.
(sleep)   (hear)

6. When they _____ the noise, they _____ up.
(hear)   (wake)

7. When third-class passengers _____ to the top deck,
(go)

most of the lifeboats _____.
(already/leave)

8. A few hours later, another ship _____, but the Titanic
(arrive)

_____.
(already/sink)

9. The rescue ship _____ up the people in the lifeboats.
   (pick)

10. The Titanic _____ its first voyage when it _____.
    (make)   *(sink)*

11. In 1985, the ship _____ in the North Atlantic.
    (passive: finally/find)

12. People are still interested in the Titanic. People _____
    (be)

    interested in it for almost a hundred years.

13. Many articles and books _____ about the Titanic
    (passive: write)

    over the years.

14. Several movies _____ about the Titanic.
    (passive: make)

15. In 1912, the sinking of the Titanic was the worst tragedy that

    _____.
    (ever/occur)

16. I was going to invite my friends to come over and watch the video

    Titanic last month, but most of them _____ the movie.
    (already/see)

EXERCISE 18 Fill in the blanks with the correct past tense of the verb in parentheses ( ). In some cases, more than one answer is possible.

A: I loved the movie *Titanic*. I ___*saw*___ it for the first time when it
   (see)

   came out. Since then, I _____ it two more times.
   (1 rent)

   _____ it?
   (2 you/ever/see)

B: Do you mean the movie with Leonardo DiCaprio? Actually, I

   _____ it. But I _____ a 1950s
   (3 never/see)   *(4 see)*

   movie about the Titanic a few years ago.

A: The DiCaprio version was great. You should rent it.

B: You know, I _____ it about six months ago, but I only watched
   (5 rent)

   about 15 minutes of it. While I _____ it, there was a
   (6 watch)

   power failure in my area and the electricity _____
   (7 go)

   out for several hours. I _____ return the video that night.
   (8 have to)

   Up to now, I _____ all about it—until you mentioned it.
   (9 forget)

A: You should rent it again. It was a great story.

B: But everyone knows how the story _____. The ship
       (10 end)

_____ and a lot of people _____.
(11 sink)   *(12 die)*

A: But there was also a great love story. It's a story about a woman

named Rose. She _____ to marry a rich man when she
                  (13 plan)

_____ Jack and _____ in love with him. Jack was a poor
(14 meet)   *(15 fall)*

man who _____ in third class. When Rose was with Jack, she
        (16 travel)

_____ freer than she _____ before. But when
(17 feel)   *(18 ever/feel)*

Rose's fiancé _____ that Rose was in love with
              (19 find out)

was in love with another man, he _____ very angry.
                                  (20 become)

B: Stop! Don't tell me more. I think I'll rent the movie this weekend.

A: If you do, let me know. I'd like to watch it with you.

SUMMARY OF LESSON 3

1. Showing the relationship between two past actions

The Past Perfect

The reference point is past.	Another action is more past.
When the rescue ship **arrived,**	many people **had died.**
In **1912,**	the airplane **had** already **been invented.**

The Past Perfect Continuous

The reference point is past.	A continuous action preceded it.
A woman wanted to save the dog	that she **had been carrying** since she left the Titanic.
The captain couldn't turn the ship around	because it **had been traveling** so fast.

The Past Continuous

An action was in progress . . .	. . . at a specific time or when a shorter action occurred.
They **were sleeping**	at 11:40 p.m.
We **were watching** TV	when the Columbia accident occurred.

2. Relating the past to the present

The Present Perfect	The Present Perfect Continuous
Have you ever **seen** the movie *Titanic*? I **have** never **seen** it, but I'd like to. I **have seen** two movies so far this month. I**'ve** always **been** interested in space exploration.	She is watching the movie now. She **has been watching** it for 45 minutes. I**'ve been reading** a book about space exploration.

3. Describing the past without relating it to another past time

The Simple Past Tense
I **rented** a movie last week.   I **liked** the movie so much that I **watched** it twice.   Mary **lived** in England all her life.   The Columbia accident **happened** in 2003.

EDITING ADVICE

1. Don't use *be* to form the simple past tense.

   came
   He ~~was come~~ home at 6 o'clock last night.

2. Don't forget *be* in a past continuous sentence.

   was
   I ˄ walking on the icy sidewalk when I fell and broke my arm.

3. Do not use a present tense for an action that began in the past. Use the present perfect (continuous).

   have been
   I ~~am~~ married for ten years.

   has been
   She ~~is~~ working at her present job for seven months.

4. Don't forget *have* with perfect tenses.

   have
   I ˄ been living in the U.S. for six months.

5. Don't confuse the present perfect and the past perfect. The past perfect relates to a past event. The present perfect relates to a present situation.

   had
   When I started college, I ~~have~~ never used a computer before.

   has
   She's a teacher now. She ~~had~~ been a teacher for 15 years.

6. Use the simple past with *ago*.

came
He ~~was coming~~ to the U.S. four years ago.

7. Use *when*, not *while*, for an action that has no continuation.

when
I was washing the dishes ~~while~~ I dropped a plate.

8. Use the simple past, not the present perfect, in a *since* clause.

came
She has had her car ever since she ~~has come~~ to the U.S.

9. Don't use the continuous form for a repeated action.

drunk
By the time I got to work, I had ~~been drinking~~ four cups of coffee.

10. Don't confuse the *-ing* form with the past participle.

seen
When he moved to Chicago, he had never ~~seeing~~ a skyscraper before.

11. Be careful to choose the correct past tense in a sentence with *when*.

came
When I left my hometown, I ~~had come~~ to New York.

had begun
When I arrived in class, the test ~~began~~ already.

12. Don't confuse active and passive.

found
In 1985, the Titanic was ~~finding~~.

LESSON 3 TEST/REVIEW

PART 1 Find the mistakes with the underlined words, and correct them. Not every sentence has a mistake. If the sentence is correct, write *C*.

was taking
EXAMPLES I couldn't answer the phone when it rang because I ~~took~~ a shower.
She <u>found</u> a job last week.   **C**

1. I <u>was work</u> when the fire <u>started</u>.

2. How long <u>do you live</u> in this city?

3. They <u>were getting</u> married five years ago.

4. When he <u>came</u> to the U.S., he <u>had never studied</u> English before.

5. <u>Have you ever seeing</u> the mayor of this city?

6. By the time he got divorced, he <u>has been</u> married for ten years.

7. She <u>left</u> her dictionary in the library yesterday.

8. When she <u>came</u> to the U.S., she <u>had never spoken</u> English before.

9. My sister is in medical school. She <u>has wanted</u> to be a doctor ever since she <u>has been</u> a little girl.

10. My grandparents <u>were living</u> in Germany when World War II <u>started</u>.

11. I <u>been working</u> as a computer programmer for five years. I love my job.

12. My sister is a nurse. She <u>had been</u> a nurse for ten years.

13. When we <u>finished</u> dinner, we <u>washed</u> the dishes.

14. An accident <u>was happened</u> in front of my house early this morning.

15. Last year when the landlord <u>raised</u> my rent, I <u>decided</u> to move.

16. I wasn't injured in the car accident because I <u>had been wearing</u> my seat belt.

17. By the time my sister <u>came</u> to the U.S., our father <u>had already died</u>.

18. We <u>had been driven</u> for three hours when we had a flat tire.

19. When he came to the U.S., he <u>had</u> never <u>met</u> an American before.

20. Fifteen hundred people <u>died</u> on the Titanic.

21. <u>Have</u> you ever <u>traveled</u> by ship? No, I never <u>have</u>.

22. When they <u>came</u> to the U.S., they <u>saw</u> the Statue of Liberty for the first time.

23. She was eating lunch <u>while</u> the phone rang.

PART 2 Fill in the blanks with the simple past or the past perfect form of the verb in parentheses ( ).

EXAMPLE   When Mary Davis ___*came*___ to America, she
                                     (come)

___*had never left*___ England before.
        (never/leave)

1. I registered late for this class. The class _____
                                                    (already/have)

   a test on the review lesson by the time I ___ _____.
                                                  (register)

2. She _____ to go to Paris for vacation last year
        (want)

   because she _____ there before.
                    (never/go)

3. I got to class late. By the time I _____ to class, the
                                          (get)

   teacher _____ the homework.
              (already/explain)

The Past Continuous; The Past Perfect; The Past Perfect Continuous; Comparison of Past Tenses   **133**

4. When she got to work, she _____ that she

   _____ the stove on, so she had to go back home.
   (leave)

   (realize)

5. When my mother came to the U.S., she _____ afraid to speak
   _(be)_

   English because she _____ English with
   (never/speak)

   an American before.

6. When I _____ English lessons, I
   (start)

   _____ a foreign language before.
   (never/study)

7. Many people _____ when they
   (die)

   _____ into the water because the water was so cold.
   (jump)

8. Many of the survivors of the Titanic _____
   (already/die)

   of old age when the ship _____ in 1985.
   (passive: find)

9. He _____ the fire department
   (call)

   when the fire _____.
   (start)

10. When the fire department came, the house _____
    (already/burn)

    down.

PART 3 Fill in the blanks with one of the past tenses: simple past, past
continuous, present perfect (continuous), or past perfect
(continuous). In some cases, more than one answer is possible.

A: What _happened_ to your car?
(happen)

B: I _____ an accident yesterday.
(1 have)

A: How _____ it _____?
(2 happen)

B: I _____ to work when a dog _____ in front of my car.
(3 drive) _(4 run)_

I _____ my car suddenly, and the car behind me _____
(5 stop) _(6 hit)_

my car because the driver _____ me too closely.
(7 follow)

A: _____ a ticket?
(8 you/get)

B: No, but the driver who hit me did.

A: Who will pay to have your car fixed?

B: The other driver. When he _____ me, he _____ out of
(9 hit) *(10 get)*

his car and _____ me his insurance card. He's a new driver. He
(11 give)

_____ his driver's license for two months.
(12 only/have)

A: You're a new driver too, aren't you?

B: Oh, no. I _____ _____ for twenty years.
(13 drive)

A: I thought you _____ your driver's license a few months ago.
(14 get)

B: In this state, I have a new license. But I _____
(15 have)

a driver's license for many years before I _____ here.
(16 move)

A: _____ you ever _____ a ticket?
(17 get)

B: One time. I _____ about 65 miles an hour on the
(18 drive)

highway when a police officer _____ me. She said that the speed
(19 stop)

limit was only 55. She _____ me a ticket for speeding. She also
(20 give)

gave me a ticket because I _____ my seat belt.
(21 not/wear)

EXPANSION ACTIVITIES

Classroom
Activities

1. In a small group or with the entire class, turn to the person next to
   you and say a year. The person next to you has to tell a short story
   about his / her life at or before that time.

   EXAMPLES 1996
   I had just graduated from high school. I was living with
   my parents. I hadn't thought about coming to the U.S. at
   that time.

The Past Continuous; The Past Perfect; The Past Perfect Continuous; Comparison of Past Tenses **135**

1963
I hadn't been born yet.

1997
I had just had my second child. I was living with my wife's parents.

2. On an index card, write the following sentence, filling in the blank to make a **true** statement about yourself. The teacher will collect the cards and read the sentences. Try to guess who wrote the sentences.

EXAMPLE   When I came to this school, I had never _____ before.
When I came to this school, I had never paid so much for a textbook before.

Talk About it

1. Why do you think that women and children were put on lifeboats before men?

2. Do you think the space program should continue?

Write About it

Choose one of the following topics and write a short composition.

1. An accident or unusual experience that happened to you

2. How you met your spouse or a new friend

3. An important event in the history of your native country

4. A famous person who died in an accident, assassination, or another unusual way

5. Write about a tragedy in recent history. Tell what you *were doing* when you heard the news. Tell what you *did* when you heard the news.

Outside Activity

Rent the movie *Titanic* (1997) and/or *A Night to Remember* (1957). Write a summary of one of these movies.

Internet Activities

1. Find Web sites that tell about the Titanic. Find personal accounts of survivors. Report one of these to the class.

2. Find an article about the California fires of 2003. Bring it to class. Circle all the past tenses in the article.

3. Find an article about the Columbia tragedy of 2003. Bring it to class. Circle all the past tenses in the article.

4. Find an article about the Tsunami disaster of 2004. Bring it to class and report on a personal account.

Additional Activities at **http://elt.thomson.com/gic**

GRAMMAR

Modals—Present and Future
Related Expressions

CONTEXT: Consumer Warnings

Sweepstakes or Scam?
Telemarketing
Infomercials
My Elderly Neighbor

4.1 | Overview of Modals and Related Expressions

Modals = *can, could, shall, should, will, would, may, might, must*

Examples	Explanation
She **should** leave. (advice) She **must** leave. (necessity) She **might** leave. (possibility)	Modals add meaning to the verbs that follow them.

He **can help** you.
They **should eat** now.
You **must pay** your rent.
	The base form follows a modal.
	   Wrong: He can *helps* you.
	   Wrong: They should *eating* now.
	   Wrong: You must *to* pay.
	The modal never has an *-s* ending.
	   Wrong: He *cans* help you.

You **should not** leave now. He **cannot** speak English	To form the negative, put *not* after the modal. *Cannot* is written as one word.
A pen **should be used** for the test. The movie **can be seen** next week.	A modal can be used in the passive voice: modal + *be* + past participle
He **must** go to court. = He **has to** go to court. You **must** not park your car there. = You **are not supposed to** park your car there. He **can** speak English well. = He **is able to** speak English well.	The following expressions are like modals in meaning: *have to, have got to, be able to, be supposed to, be allowed to, had better*.
British: We **shall** study modals. **American:** We **will** study modals.	For the future tense, *shall* is more common in British English than in American English. Americans sometimes use *shall* in a question to make a suggestion or invitation. *Shall* we dance?

Language Note:
Observe statements and questions with modals:
  Affirmative: He *can* speak German.
  Negative: He *can't* speak French.
  ***Yes / No* Question:** *Can* he speak English?
  Short Answers: Yes, he *can*. / No, he *can't*.
  ***Wh-* Question:** Why *can't* he speak French?
  Subject Question: Who *can* speak French?

SWEEPSTAKES OR SCAM?

Before You Read

1. Do you get a lot of junk mail?

2. What do you do with these pieces of mail?

Read the following article. Pay special attention to *might, may, have to, must, should, be supposed to,* and *ought to.*

Jack Goldman
123 Lucky Drive
Anytown, NY 01234

Congratulations

Congratulations, Jack Goldman.
You're a winner!
Choose your prize of *$25,000,*
a new car, or an exotic vacation.
You can't afford to miss this offer!
Simply call 800-555-5555 today!

Did you ever get a letter with your name printed on it telling you that you have won a prize or a large amount of money? Most people in the U.S. get these letters.

We often get mail from sweepstakes companies. A sweepstakes is like a lottery. To enter a sweepstakes, you usually **have to** mail a postcard. Even though the chances of winning are very small, many people enter because they have nothing to lose and **might** even win something.

Are these offers of prizes real? Some of them are. Why would someone give you a prize for doing nothing? A sweepstakes is a chance for a company to promote its products, such as magazines. But some of these offers **might** be deceptive,[1] and you **should** read the offer carefully. The government estimates that Americans lose more than one billion dollars every year through "scams," or tricks to take your money. You **should** be careful of letters, e-mails, and phone calls that tell you:

- You **must** act now or the offer will expire.
- You **may** already be a winner. To claim your gift, you only **have to** pay postage and handling.
- You've won! You **must** call a 900 number to claim your prize.
- You've won a free vacation. All you **have to** do is pay a service fee.

You **shouldn't** give out your credit card number or Social Security number if you are not sure who is contacting you about the sweepstakes.

Senior citizens **should** be especially careful of scams. Eighty percent of the victims of scams are 65 or older. They often think that they **have to** buy something in order to win a prize and often spend thousands of dollars on useless items. Or they think that their chances of winning **might** increase if they buy the company's product. But in a legitimate sweepstakes, you **don't have to** buy anything or send any money. The law states that "no purchase necessary" **must** appear in big letters. In addition, the company **is supposed to** tell you your chances of winning.

How can you avoid becoming the victim of a scam? If you receive a letter saying you are a guaranteed winner, you **ought to** read it carefully. Most people just throw this mail in the garbage.

---

[1]Something that is deceptive tries to make you believe something that is not true.

4.2 | Possibilities—*May, Might, Could*

Examples	Explanation
You **may** already be a winner. You **might** win a prize. This **could** be your lucky day!	Use *may, might, could* to show possibilities about the present or future.
She **may not** know that she is a winner. I **might not** come to class tomorrow.	For negative possibility, use *may not* or *might not*. Don't use *could not*. It means *was / were not able to*. Do not make a contraction with *may not* or *might not*.
Do you think I might win? **Do you think I could** get lucky?	To make questions about possibility with *may, might, could,* say, "Do you think . . . *may, might, could* . . .?" The clause after *Do you think* uses statement word order.
Compare: a. **Maybe** you are right. b. You **may be** right. a. **Maybe** he is a winner. b. He **may be** a winner.	*Maybe,* written as one word (a), is an adverb. It is usually put before the subject. *May be,* written as two words (b), is a modal + verb. The meaning of (a) and (b) is the same, but notice that the word order is different.

EXERCISE 1 Fill in the blanks with appropriate verbs to complete this conversation.

A: What are you going to do this summer?

B: I haven't decided yet. I might ____*go*____ back to Peru, or I may
        (example)

_____ here and look for a summer job. What about you?
        (1)

A: I'm not sure either. My brother might _____ here. If he
                                                          (2)

does, we might _____ some interesting places in the U.S. I
                    (3)

received a letter a few days ago telling me that if I mail in a postcard,

I could _____ a trip for two to Hawaii.
              (4)

B: I don't believe those letters. When I get those kinds of letters, I just
throw them away.

A: How can you just throw them away? You could _____
                                                              (5)

a winner.

B: Who's going to give us a free trip to Hawaii for doing nothing?

A: Well, I suppose you're right. But someone has to win those prizes. It

could _____ me. And if I buy a lot of magazines from this
     (6)

company, my chances of winning might _____.
                                                    (7)

B: That's not true. Those letters always say, "No Purchase Necessary."

A: I really want to go to Hawaii with my brother.

B. Then I suggest you work hard and save your money.

A: I might _____ 90 years old by the time I have enough money.
                   (8)

EXERCISE 2 Answer these questions by using the word in parentheses ( ).

EXAMPLE Is the company legitimate? (*might*)
It might be legitimate.

1. Does the company give out prizes? (*may*)

2. Are the prizes cheap? (*could*)

3. Will I be chosen as a winner? (*might*)

4. Will this company take my money and give me nothing? (*might*)

5. Will I win a trip? (*could*)

EXERCISE 3 ABOUT YOU Fill in the blanks with possible results for the
following situations.

EXAMPLE If I pass this course, _*I might take a computer course next semester.*_

1. If I don't pay my rent, _____

2. If I save a lot of money, _____

3. If I drink a lot of coffee tonight, _____

4. If I eat a lot of sugar, _____

5. If I drive too fast, _____

6. If I exercise regularly, _____

7. If I increase my computer skills, _____

8. If I win a lot of money, _____

9. If I come late to class, _____

10. If I don't do my homework, _____

4.3 | Necessity and Urgency with *Must, Have To, Have Got To*

Modal	Explanation
Individuals and companies **must** (or **have to**) obey the law. Sweepstakes companies **must** (or **have to**) tell you the truth. "No Purchase Necessary" **must** (or **has to**) appear in big letters.	For legal obligation, use *must* and *have to*. *Must* has a very official tone. It is often used in court, in legal contracts (such as rental agreements), and in rules books.

You **must** act now! Don't wait or you will lose this fabulous offer!
 	
You**'ve got to** act now!
 	
You **have to** act now!
	Must, have to, and *have got to* express a sense of urgency. All three sentences to the left have the same meaning.
	
	Have got to is usually contracted:
	   I have got to = I've got to
	   He has got to = He's got to

I've got to help my sister on Saturday. She **has to** study for a test.	Avoid using *must* for personal obligations. It sounds very official or urgent and is too strong for most situations. Use *have to* or *have got to*.

Pronunciation Note:
In fast, informal speech,
- *have to* is often pronounced "hafta."
- *has to* is pronounced "hasta."
- *have got to* is often pronounced "gotta." (*Have* is often not pronounced before "gotta.")

EXERCISE 4 Fill in the blanks with an appropriate verb to talk about sweepstakes rules. Answers may vary.

EXAMPLE Sweepstakes companies must ____*obey*____ the law.

1. Sweepstakes companies must _____ "No Purchase Necessary" in big letters in the information they send to you.

2. Sweepstakes companies sometimes tell people that they must _____ a 900 number to win a prize.

3. Sweepstakes companies often tell people, "You must _____ now. Don't wait."

4. Companies must _____ the truth about the conditions of the contest.

5. If a sweepstakes company tells you that you must _____ something, it is not a legitimate sweepstakes.

EXERCISE 5 Fill in the blanks with an appropriate verb (phrase) to talk about driving rules. Answers may vary.

EXAMPLE Drivers must ___*stop*___ at a red light.

1. A driver must _____ a license.

2. In a car, you must _____ a baby in a special car seat.

3. You must _____ when you hear a fire truck siren.

4. In many cities, drivers must _____ a city sticker on their windshields.

5. A car must _____ a license plate.

EXERCISE 6 ABOUT YOU Fill in the blanks with words that describe personal obligations. Answers may vary.

EXAMPLE I have to ___*call my parents*___ once a week.

1. After class, I've got to _____ _____.

2. This weekend, I have to _____.

3. Before the next class, we've got to _____.

4. Every day I have to _____.

5. Once a month, I've got to _____.

6. When I'm not sure of the spelling of a word, I have to _____.

7. Before I go to sleep at night, I have to _____.

8. A few times a year, I've got to _____.

9. My English isn't perfect. I have to _____.

10. Before I take a test, I've got to _____.

EXERCISE 7 ABOUT YOU Make a list of personal obligations you have to do on the weekends.

EXAMPLE *On Saturdays, I have to take my sister to ballet lessons.*

_____

_____

_____

EXERCISE **8** ABOUT YOU Make a list of obligations you have at your job, at your school, or in your house.

EXAMPLE   *At work, I've got to answer the phone and fill out orders.*

_____

_____

_____

_____

_____

4.4 | Obligation with *Must* or *Be Supposed To*

Examples	Explanation
"No Purchase Necessary" **must** appear in big letters. This is the law. The sweepstakes company **must** tell you your chances of winning. People who win money **must** pay taxes on their winnings.	*Must* has an official tone.
Compare: a. Police officer to driver: "You **must** wear your seat belt." b. Driver to passenger: "You**'re supposed to** wear your seat belt." a. Teacher to student: "You **must** write your composition with a pen." b. Student to student: "You **are supposed to** write your composition with a pen."	a. A person in a position of authority (such as a police officer, parent, or teacher) can use *must*. The tone is very official. b. Avoid using *must* if you are not in a position of authority. Use *be supposed to* to remind someone of a rule.
Companies **are supposed to** follow the law, but some of them don't. Drivers **are supposed to** use a seat belt, but they sometimes don't. Students **are supposed to** be quiet in the library, but some talk.	*Be supposed to*, not *must*, is used when reporting on a law or rule that is broken.
Pronunciation Note: The *d* in *supposed to* is not pronounced.	

EXERCISE 9 A teenager is talking about rules his parents gave him and his sister. Fill in the blanks with *be supposed to* + an appropriate verb.

EXAMPLE I _'m supposed to babysit_ for my little sister when my parents aren't home.

1. I _____ my homework before I watch TV.

2. I (not) _____ on the phone with my friends for more than 30 minutes.

3. I _____ my room once a week. My mother gets mad when I leave it dirty.

4. If I go to a friend's house, I _____ my parents where I am so they won't worry.

5. I have a part-time job. I _____ some of my money in the bank. I (not) _____ my money on foolish things.

6. I _____ my parents with jobs around the house. For example, I _____ the dishes once a week. I _____ the garbage every day.

7. My sister _____ her toys away when she's finished playing.

8. She (not) _____ the stove.

9. She (not) _____ TV after 8 p.m.

10. She _____ to bed at 8:30.

EXERCISE 10 ABOUT YOU Report some rules in one of the following places: in your apartment, in court, in traffic, in a library, in class, on an airplane, or in the airport.

EXAMPLES _In my apartment, the landlord is supposed to provide heat in the winter._

I'm supposed to pay my rent by the fifth of the month.

_____

_____

_____

_____

EXERCISE 11 ABOUT YOU Tell about an obligation you or a member of your family has that is often not done.

EXAMPLE My sister is supposed to finish her homework before watching TV,

but she usually watches TV as soon as she gets home from school.

I'm supposed to wash the dishes in my house, but I often leave them

in the sink for the next day.

_____

_____

_____

4.5 | Advice with *Should, Ought To,* and *Had Better*

Examples	Explanation
Senior citizens **should** be careful of scams.	*Should* shows advisability. It is used to say that something is a good idea.
You **should** read the offer carefully to see what the conditions are.	
You **shouldn't** give your credit card number to people you don't know.	*Shouldn't* means that something is a bad idea. The action is not advisable.
You **shouldn't** believe every offer that comes in the mail.	
If you receive a letter saying you are a winner, you **ought to** throw it away.	*Ought to* has the same meaning as *should*. **Note:** *Ought* is the only modal followed by *to*. Don't use *ought to* for negatives and questions. Use *should*.
You **ought to** work hard and save your money. Don't expect to get rich from a sweepstakes.	
You **ought to** turn off the TV and do your homework.	*Ought to* is pronounced /ɔtə/.
I'm expecting an important phone call. I'**d better** leave my cell phone on so I won't miss it.	*Had better (not)* is used in conversation to show caution or give a warning. A negative consequence may result.
You'**d better not** give your credit card number to strange callers, or they might use it to make purchases in your name.	Use '*d* to contract *had* with a pronoun. In some fast speech, '*d* is omitted completely.
Compare: a. Companies and individuals **must** obey the law. b. You **should** read the letter carefully.	a. Use *must* for rules, laws, and urgent situations. b. Use *should* for advice.

EXERCISE 12   Give advice to people who are saying the following.

EXAMPLES   I'm lonely. I don't have any friends.

You should get a dog or a cat for companionship.

I'm so tired. I've been working hard all day.

You ought to get some rest.

1. I've had a headache all day.

   _____

2. The teacher wrote something on my paper, but I can't read it.

   _____

3. Every time I write a composition and the teacher finds mistakes, I have to write it all over again.

   _____

4. I got a letter telling me that I won a million dollars.

   _____

5. My old TV doesn't work well anymore. It's too expensive to repair.

   _____

6. I received an offer for a new job. It pays double what I get now.

   _____

7. My car is making a strange noise. I wonder what it is.

   _____

8. I sit at a desk all day. I don't get enough exercise. I'm gaining weight.

   _____

9. Whenever I tell my personal problems to my coworker, he tells other people.

   _____

10. I have to write a résumé, but I don't have any experience with this.

    _____

EXERCISE 13 ABOUT YOU Give advice about what people should do or say in the following social situations in your native culture. Share your answers with the class.

EXAMPLE   If you are invited to someone's house for dinner, _you should bring a_ _small gift._

1. If you invite a friend to eat in a restaurant, _____

_____

2. If you bump into someone, _____

_____

3. If you don't hear or understand what someone says, _____

_____

4. If someone asks, "How are you?" _____

_____

5. If you want to leave the dinner table while others are still eating,

_____

6. If a woman with a small child gets on a crowded bus, _____

_____

7. If you're invited to someone's house for dinner, _____

_____

8. If you meet someone for the first time, _____

_____

EXERCISE 14 Give a warning by using *you'd better (not)* in the following conversations.

EXAMPLE   **A:** Someone's at the door. I'll go and open it.

B: You_'d better not open it_____ if you don't know who it is.

1. **A:** The caller wants my Social Security number.

   B: Do you know who the caller is?

   A: No.

   B: You _____ him your Social Security number then.

2. A: I got a letter about a sweepstakes. Do you think I should enter?

B: You've probably got nothing to lose. But you _____ the letter carefully to make sure that it's legitimate.

3. A: This offer says the deadline for applying is Friday.

B: You _____. You don't have much time.

4. *(phone conversation)*

A: Hello?

B: Hello. I'd like to speak with Mrs. Green.

A: Speaking.

B: You are a winner! You _____ or you might lose this offer. You don't have much time.

A: You keep calling me and telling me the same thing. You

_____, or I'll report you.

5. A: You are the only person in the office who wears jeans.

B: What's wrong with that?

A: You _____ appropriately, or you might lose your job.

6. A: I don't like my supervisor's attitude. I'm going to tell her about it.

B: You _____. She might not like it.

7. A: I typed my composition on the computer, but I forgot to bring a disk to save it. I'll just print it.

B: Here. Use my disk. You _____ in case you have to revise it.

8. *(a driver and a passenger in a car)*

A: I'm getting sleepy. Can you drive for a while?

B: I can't. I don't have my driver's license yet. You _____

_____ for a while.

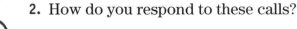

Before You Read

1. Do you ever get calls from people who are trying to sell you something?

2. How do you respond to these calls?

Read the following article. Pay special attention to *may, can, be permitted to, be allowed to*, and other modals.

You have just sat down to dinner when, suddenly, the phone rings. Someone is trying to sell you a magazine, a long-distance phone service, or a vacation. Has this ever happened to you?

Salespeople place about 100 million calls a year. They use an automatic dialer to call hundreds of homes at the same time. Some of these calls might offer you a better long-distance telephone service or let you know about a special rate for cable or DSL service. But sometimes these calls can be very annoying. Now there is something you can do about it.

In 2003, the U.S. government[2] created a "Do-Not-Call" registry. You can register your phone number online or by phone. If you do so, most telemarketers **are not permitted to** call you for five years. However, some telemarketers **can** still call you: political organizations and charities. Also, companies with which you do business, such as your bank, **may** call you to offer you a new product or service. However, when they call, you can ask them not to call you again. If you make this request, they **are not allowed to** call you again.

You **can** register up to three numbers on the "Do-Not-Call" national registry, including your cell phone number. It may take three months before the "do-not-call" order goes into effect. In the meantime, here are some suggestions for dealing with telemarketers:

- You could get a Caller ID to see who is calling. (About 40% of households have them.)
- You could ask your phone company if they have a "privacy manager," a service that screens unidentified phone calls. The phone will not even ring in your house unless the caller identifies himself.
- If you are not interested in the offer, you can try to end the phone call quickly. But you shouldn't get angry at the caller. He or she is just trying to make a living.
- If you do decide to buy a product or service, remember, you should never give out your credit card number if you are not sure who the caller is.

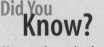

Did You Know?

Many telemarketing calls you receive come from call centers in India, Mexico, and other countries, where callers are paid much less than in the U.S.

---

[2] The Federal Trade Commission (FTC) is the government department that created this registry.

4.6 | Permission and Prohibition

Examples	Explanation
Political organizations **may** call you. (They **are permitted to** call you.) Charities **can** call you. (They **are allowed to** call you.)	Use *may* or *can* to show that something is permitted. Alternate forms are *be allowed to* and *be permitted to*.
If you put your phone number on a "Do-Not-Call" registry, companies **may not** call you for five years. If you ask a company to stop calling you, this company **cannot** call you again.	Use *may not* or *cannot* (*can't*) to show that something is prohibited. *Cannot* is written as one word. *May not* has no contraction form.
You **can** wear jeans to class. We **can** call our teacher by his first name.	In addition to legal permission, *can* also has the meaning of social acceptability.

Language Note:
The meaning of *cannot* or *may not* (not permitted) is very similar to the meaning of *must not* (prohibited).
Compare:
   a. You *can't* talk during a test.
   b. You *may not* talk during a test.
   c. You *must not* talk during a test.

   a. You *can't* bring food into the computer lab.
   b. You *may not* bring food into the computer lab.
   c. You *must not* bring food into the computer lab.

EXERCISE 15 Fill in the blanks to talk about what is and isn't permitted.

EXAMPLE We can ___talk___ in the hall, but we can't ___talk___ in the library.

1. If you put your name on a "Do-Not-Call" registry, companies may

   not _____.

2. In the library, you may not _____.

3. During a test, we can _____ but we cannot

   _____.

4. Books, CDs, and DVDs are protected by law. We are not permitted

   to _____.

5. In this building, we may not _____.

EXERCISE 16 ABOUT YOU Fill in the blanks with an appropriate permission word to talk about what is or isn't permitted in your native country.

EXAMPLES A man _____*isn't permitted*_____ to have more than one wife.

Teachers ____*can*____ talk about religion in public schools.

1. People _____ own a gun.

2. People under 18 _____ get married.

3. Children _____ work.

4. Children _____ see any movie they want.

5. A man _____ have more than one wife.

6. A married woman _____ get a passport without her husband's permission.

7. Teachers _____ talk about religion in public schools.

8. Teachers _____ hit children.

9. People _____ travel freely.

10. People _____ live anywhere they want.

EXERCISE 17   Write about what is or isn't permitted in these places. Use *can, may, be allowed to,* or *be permitted to.*

EXAMPLES   In the U.S., _____ *children may sue their parents.*

In a theater, _____ *you can't yell "fire."*

1. In the U.S., _____

2. In the computer lab, _____

3. In this classroom, _____

4. In a courtroom, _____

5. In my house / apartment building, _____

6. In an airplane, _____

7. In an airport, _____

8. In this city, _____

EXERCISE 18   ABOUT YOU Tell if these things are socially acceptable in your country or native culture.

EXAMPLE   Students can call their teachers by their first names.
In my country, students can't call their teachers by their first names. It's very impolite.

1. Parents can take small children to a party for adults.

2. If you are invited to a party, you can invite your friends.

3. Students can wear jeans to class.

4. Students can use a cell phone in class.

5. Students can remain seated when the teacher enters the room.

6. Students can call their teachers by their first names.

7. Students can talk to each other during a test.

8. Students can argue with a teacher about a grade.

9. Men and women can kiss in public.

10. Men and women can hold hands in public.

4.7 | Comparing Negative Modals

Examples	Explanation
You **must not** talk during the test. You **must not** bring food into the computer lab. If you are involved in a traffic accident, you **must not** leave.	It's prohibited. You have no choice in the matter. *Must not* has an official tone.
You **are not supposed to** talk during the test. You **are not supposed to** bring food into the lab. Shh! You**'re not supposed to** talk in the library.	*Be supposed to* is used as a reminder of a rule. It has an unofficial tone. Often the rule has already been broken.
Telemarketers **cannot** call you if you place your phone number on a "do-not-call" list. Telemarketers **may not** call you if you ask them to take you off their list.	It's prohibited. The meaning is similar to *must not*.
You **shouldn't** give strange callers your credit card number. You **shouldn't** buy products that you don't need.	It's a bad idea. This is advice.
You**'d better not** arrive late for the exam, or you won't have time to finish it. You**'d better not** call your friend late at night. She might be asleep. You might wake her up.	This is a warning. A negative consequence is stated or implied.
a. You **don't have to** buy magazines to enter a sweepstakes. b. I **don't have to** work on Saturday. It's my day off. c. We **don't have to** type our compositions. We can write them by hand.	a. It's not necessary. It is your choice to do it or not. b. It is not required. c. There are other choices or options.

Language Note:
Even though *must* and *have to* are similar in meaning in affirmative statements, they are completely different in meaning in negative statements.

You *must* obey the law. = You *have to* obey the law.

You *must not* talk during the test. = This is prohibited.

You *don't have to* use a pen for the test. = It is not necessary. You have a choice. You can use a pencil.

EXERCISE 19 ABOUT YOU Tell if students in this school or another school you have attended have to or don't have to do the following.

EXAMPLES wear a uniform
Students in my school don't have to wear a uniform.

take final exams
Students in my school have to take final exams.

1. stand up to answer a question
2. go to the chalkboard to answer a question
3. call the teacher by his or her title (for example, "Professor")
4. buy their own textbooks
5. pay tuition
6. attend classes every day
7. have a written excuse for an absence
8. get permission to leave the classroom
9. study a foreign language
10. attend graduation

EXERCISE 20 ABOUT YOU Tell if you have to or don't have to do the following.

EXAMPLES work on Saturdays
I have to work on Saturdays.

wear a suit to work
I don't have to wear a suit to work.

1. pay rent on the first of the month
2. study English
3. get up early on Sundays
4. cook every day
5. wear formal clothes (a suit, a dress, a uniform) to work / school
6. come to school on Saturdays

EXERCISE **21**   Fill in the blanks with *don't have to* or *must not.*

EXAMPLE   If you receive a sweepstakes postcard, you ___*don't have to*___ send it back.

1. You _____ buy something to win. No purchase is necessary.

2. Sweepstakes companies _____ break the law.

3. In a legitimate sweepstakes, you _____ call a 900 number to win a prize.

4. Passengers on an airplane _____ use a computer while the plane is taking off and landing.

5. Passengers on an airplane _____ carry a weapon.

6. Passengers on an airplane _____ walk around when the airplane is taking off or landing.

7. Passengers on an airplane _____ wear their seat belt after the seat belt sign is turned off.

8. Students _____ copy answers from each other during a test.

9. The students in this class _____ bring their dictionaries to class.

10. Teachers _____ teach in the summer if they don't want to.

11. Teachers in American schools _____ hit children. It is prohibited.

EXERCISE **22**   Fill in the blanks with *don't have to* or *must not* to describe situations in a public library.

EXAMPLES   You ___*must not*___ write in a library book.

You ___*don't have to*___ know the name of the author to find a book. You can find the book by the title.

Book Drop

1. You _____ wait until the due date to return a book. You can return it earlier.

2. You _____ return your books to the circulation desk. You can leave them in the book drop.

3. You _____ study in the library. You can study at home.

4. You _____ eat in the library.

5. You _____ tear a page out of a book.

6. You _____ make noise in the library.

EXERCISE 23 ABOUT YOU Work with a partner. Use *be (not) supposed to* to write a list of rules the teacher has for this class. Use affirmative and negative statements.

EXAMPLES *We're not supposed to use our books during a test.*

We're supposed to write five compositions this semester.

_____

_____

_____

_____

_____

_____

_____

EXERCISE 24 Write a list of driving rules. Use *must not* or *can't*. (Use *you* in the impersonal sense.)

EXAMPLE *You must not pass a car when you're going up a hill.*

_____

_____

_____

_____

_____

EXERCISE 25 Circle the correct words to complete these sentences.

EXAMPLES We (shouldn't, don't have to) talk loudly in the library.

We (shouldn't, don't have to) bring our dictionaries to class.

1. The teacher says we (can't, don't have to) use our books during a test.

2. The teacher says we (shouldn't, don't have to) sit in a specific seat in class. We can sit wherever we want.

3. We (can't, don't have to) talk to each other during a test. It's not permitted.

4. We (must not, don't have to) type our compositions. We can write them by hand.

5. We (shouldn't, can't) speak our native language in class. It's not a good idea.

6. We (don't have to, aren't supposed to) come back after the final exam, but we can in order to pick up our tests.

7. Parents often tell children, "You (shouldn't, don't have to) talk to strangers."

8. Parents (aren't supposed to, don't have to) send their kids to public schools. They can send them to private schools.

9. Teachers (aren't supposed to, don't have to) teach summer school if they don't want to.

10. English teachers (shouldn't, don't have to) talk fast to foreign students.

11. A driver who is involved in an accident must report it to the police. He (must not, doesn't have to) leave the scene of the accident.

12. I'm warning you. You (don't have to, 'd better not) spend so much time talking to your co-workers, or you might lose your job.

13. Drivers (don't have to, must not) go through red lights.

14. You (shouldn't, don't have to) make noise and disturb your neighbors.

15. Most American students (don't have to, had better not) study a foreign language in college. They have a choice.

16. I have a test tomorrow morning. I ('d better not, must not) stay out late tonight, or I won't be alert in the morning.

17. Some students (shouldn't, don't have to) pay tuition because they have a scholarship.

18. You (may not, don't have to) bring food into the computer lab. It's against the rules.

19. You (shouldn't, may not) talk on a cell phone while driving. Even though it's permitted, it's not a good idea.

20. You (don't have to, shouldn't) leave your cell phone on in class. It might disturb the class.

21. Those students are talking in the library. They should be quiet. They (must not, are not supposed to) talk in the library.

EXERCISE 26 Fill in the blanks to make true statements.

EXAMPLE I don't have to _make an appointment to see the teacher_____.

1. In this class, we aren't supposed to _____.

2. In this class, we don't have to _____.

3. The teacher doesn't have to _____,
   but he / she does it anyway.

4. In this building, we must not _____.

5. You'd better not _____,
   or the teacher will get angry.

6. We're going to have a test next week, so you'd better
   _____ the night before.

7. When another student doesn't know the answer, you shouldn't
   _____. You should let him try
   to find it himself.

8. You can't _____ _____ in the computer
   lab. It's not permitted.

9. Teachers should be patient. They shouldn't _____
   when students don't understand.

10. You don't have to _____ to win
    a sweepstakes prize.

EXERCISE 27 In your opinion, what laws should be changed? What new laws should be created? Fill in the blanks to complete these statements, using *must / must not, have to / don't have to, can / can't, should / shouldn't*. You may work with a partner or in small groups.

EXAMPLES There ought to be a law that says _you can't use your cell phone while_
driving.

There ought to be a law that says _that people who want to have a baby_
must take a course in parenting.

1. There ought to be a law that says _____

   _____

2. There ought to be a law that says _____

   _____

3. There ought to be a law that says _____

_____

4. There ought to be a law that says _____

_____

5. There ought to be a law that says _____

_____

4.8 | Making Suggestions

Examples	Explanation
How **can** I deal with telemarketing calls? You **could** use Caller ID to see who's calling. You **can** put your telephone number on a "do-not-call" list. You **could** end the call quickly.	*Can* and *could* are used to offer suggestions. More than one choice is acceptable. *Can* and *could* have the same meaning in offering suggestions. *Could* does not have a past meaning in offering suggestions.

Compare *can / could* and *should*:
 a. I'm having a problem with annoying telemarketing calls.
     You **could** get Caller ID. Or you **can** just hang up. Or you **can** put your phone number on a "Do-Not-Call" registry.
 b. A caller asked for my credit card number.
     You **should** be careful. You **shouldn't** give out your credit card number to strangers.
	a. Use *could* or *can* to offer one or more of several possibilities.
	
	 b. Use *should* or *shouldn't* when you feel that there is only one right way.

EXERCISE 28 Offer at least two suggestions to a person who says each of the following statements. You may work with a partner.

EXAMPLE I need to find a book about American history.

You could go to a bookstore. You can get one at the public library.

You could try an online bookstore.

1. I'm leaving for vacation tomorrow, and I need to find out about the weather in the city where I'm going.

_____

_____

2. I type very slowly. I need to learn to type faster.

_____

_____

3. My landlord is raising my rent by $50, and I can't afford the increase.

_____

_____

4. I'd like to learn English faster.

_____

_____

5. I want to know the price of an airline ticket to my country.

_____

_____

6. I need to buy a new computer, and I want to compare prices.

_____

_____

7. I'm going to a party. The hostess asked each guest to bring something to eat.

_____

_____

8. I need to lose ten pounds.

_____

_____

Before You Read

1. Do you think TV commercials are interesting?
2. Do you believe what you see in commercials?

Read the following conversation. Pay special attention to be supposed to.

We sometimes see "programs" on TV for products that **are supposed to** make our lives better. These look like real, informative TV shows, but they are not. They are called "infomercials" (*information* + *commercial*).

You**'re supposed to** think that you are watching an informative TV show and getting advice or information from experts and celebrities. These "shows" usually last 30 minutes, like regular TV shows. And they have commercial breaks, like regular TV shows, to make you believe they are real shows. These "shows" tell you that their products **are supposed to** make you thin, young, rich, or beautiful. For example, you may see smiling people with great bodies using exercise equipment. You**'re supposed to** believe that it's easy and fun to lose weight if you buy this equipment. But weight loss takes hard work and a lot of time.

Be careful when buying products from infomercials, because the results may not be what you see on TV.

4.9 | Expectations with *Be Supposed To*

Be supposed to is used to show that we have an expectation about something based on information we were given. In the examples on the left, we have an expectation because of a schedule.

Examples	Explanation
This diet pill **is supposed to** make you thinner in 30 days. This cream **is supposed to** grow hair in 30 days.	In the examples on the left, we expect something after watching an infomercial.
Let's rent *The Matrix* this weekend. It**'s supposed to** be a good movie. Let's go to Mabel's Restaurant. The food there **is supposed to** be very good. I was just listening to the radio. It**'s supposed to** rain this weekend, but tomorrow **is supposed to** be a nice day. I want to take Ms. King's class. She**'s supposed to** be a good teacher.	In the examples on the left, we expect something because we heard it or learned it from a friend, TV, radio, a newspaper, the Internet, etc.
The movie **is supposed to** begin at 8 p.m. The plane **is supposed to** arrive at 7:25.	

Be supposed to is used to show that something is expected of the subject of the sentence because of a rule, requirement, custom, or commitment (promise).

Examples	Explanation
Sweepstakes companies **are supposed to** tell you your chances of winning. Drivers **are supposed to** wear seat belts. We**'re not supposed to** talk during the test. You**'re not supposed to** talk in the library, but some students do anyway.	A person is expected to do something because of a law or rule. (See 4.4)
I**'m supposed to** write a paper for my class. I**'m supposed to** write about my favorite TV commercial.	A person is expected to meet a requirement (in these cases, by the teacher).
In many cultures, you**'re supposed to** take off your shoes before you enter a house. In the U.S., a bride and groom **are supposed to** send thank-you notes for their gifts.	A person is expected to behave in a certain way because of a custom.
I can't come to class tomorrow. I**'m supposed to** take my mom to the doctor. My friends are moving on Saturday. I**'m supposed to** help them.	A person is expected to do something because he has made a promise or commitment.

EXERCISE 29 Write a sentence telling what this new product is supposed to do.

EXAMPLE Are you starting to look old? Try Youth Cream.

It's supposed to make you look younger.

1. Are you bald? Use Hair Today, a new cream.

   _____

2. Do you look weak? Use Muscle Power, a new cream.

   _____

3. Do you forget things? Try Memory Builder, a new pill.

   _____

4. Is English hard for you? Try QuickEnglish, a new video.

   _____

5. Do you have stained teeth? Try WhiteBright Toothpaste.

   _____

6. Do you want to make money in 30 days? Try Fast Money, a new book.

   _____

7. Are you overweight? Try SlimTrim, a new diet drink.

   _____

8. Do you want to make your work in the kitchen easier? Buy Quick-Chop, a new device for chopping vegetables.

   _____

EXERCISE 30 Fill in the blanks with the correct form of *be* and *supposed to* and an appropriate verb.

W: What's that tube of cream I saw in the bathroom?

H: It's HairFast. It _'s supposed to grow_ a lot of hair on my head quickly.
      (example)

W: How often _____ it?
                    (1)

H: I _____ it three times a day.
          (2)

W: How much does it cost?

H: It's about ten dollars for each tube.

W: Ten dollars?

H: One tube _____ for a week.
 (3)

W: Just a week? How long will it take you to grow hair?

H: It _____ about six months before I
 (4)
start to see results.

W: Do you know how much money that's going to cost us?

H: I know it's expensive, but just imagine how much better I'll look with hair.

W: You know we want to buy a new house. We _____
 (5)
_____ our extra money into our house fund. But

you're wasting it on a product that may—or may not—bring results.

H: What about all the money you spend on skin products? All those stupid creams that _____ you look younger?
 (6)

W: Well, you want me to look young and beautiful, don't you?

H: Do you really think those products work?

W: This expensive cream I bought _____
the wrinkles around my eyes. (7)

H: You'll always be beautiful to me. I have an idea. Why don't you forget about the creams and I'll forget about the hair product. We can save our money, buy a house, and just get old together—in our new home.

EXERCISE 31 ABOUT YOU Work with a partner. Write a list of three things the teacher or this school expects from the students. Begin with *we*.

EXAMPLE _We're supposed to come to class every day._

1. _____

2. _____

3. _____

EXERCISE 32 Work with a partner. Write a list of three things that you expect from the teacher in this class. Begin with *he* or *she*.

EXAMPLE <u>She's supposed to correct us when we make a mistake.</u>

1. _____

2. _____

3. _____

MY ELDERLY NEIGHBOR

Before You Read

1. Why do you think elderly people enter so many sweepstakes?

2. What do you do when you get calls from telemarketers?

Read the following conversation. Pay special attention to *must*.

A: I'm worried about my elderly neighbor.

B: How old is she?

A: She **must be** about 80.

B: Why are you worried? Is her health bad?

A: No, she's fine. But she's all alone. Her children live far away. They don't call her very often.

B: She **must be** lonely.

A: I think she is. She enters sweepstakes and buys useless things all the time. She **must think** that if she buys things, she'll increase her chances of winning. I was in her garage yesterday, and she **must have** more than 50 boxes of things she doesn't use.

B: Doesn't she read the offers that are sent to her? Can't she see that her chances of winning are very small and that she doesn't have to buy anything to win?

A: She **must not read** those letters very carefully. In addition to these letters, she told me she gets about five or six calls from telemarketers every day. Her name **must be** on hundreds of lists.

B: Our family **must get** a lot of those calls too, but we're at work all day so we don't even know about them. Telemarketers don't usually leave a message.

A: Do you think I should warn my neighbor? I read an article that says that these companies take advantage of elderly people.

B: Why don't you talk to her about it? You can tell her to use Caller ID to see who's calling, or to put her name on a "Do-Not-Call" list.

A: I think I should.

4.10 | Logical Conclusions

Must has two completely different uses. In sections 4.3 and 4.4, we studied *must* as an expression of necessity. In the preceding reading and in the examples below, *must* shows a conclusion based on information we have or observations we make.

Examples	Explanation
My elderly neighbor lives alone. Her children are far away. She **must be** lonely. She **must think** that if she buys things, her chances of winning will increase.	We make a conclusion based on information we have or observations we make.
How old is she? She **must be** about 80. How many boxes does she have? She **must have** more than 50 boxes.	We can use *must* to make an estimate.
She **must not read** the letters carefully. She **must not understand** the conditions of the contest.	For a negative conclusion, use *must not*. Do not use a contraction.

Language Note:
Must, in the above cases, talks about the present only, not the future.

EXERCISE 33 In each of the conversations below, fill in the blanks with an appropriate verb to make a logical conclusion.

EXAMPLE **A:** Have you ever visited Japan?

B: I lived there when I was a child.

A: Then you must _____*know how to speak*_____ Japanese.

B: I used to, but I've forgotten it.

1. This is a conversation between two female students.

    A: Would you introduce me to Lee?

    B: Who's Lee?

    A: You must _____ who I'm talking about. He's in your speech class. He sits next to you.

    B: You mean Mr. Song?

    A: Yes, Lee Song. The tall handsome guy with glasses. He doesn't wear a wedding ring. He must _____ single.

    B: I'm not so sure about that. Not all married men wear a wedding ring.

2. This is a conversation between a married woman (M) and a single woman (S).

    M: My husband spends all his free time with our children.

    S: He must _____ kids very much.

    M: He does.

    S: How many kids do you have?

    M: We have four.

    S: Raising kids must _____ the hardest job in the world.

    M: It is, but it's also the most rewarding.

3. This is a conversation between a teacher (T) and a student (S).

    T: Take out the paper I gave you last Monday.

    S: I don't have it. Could you give me one, please?

    T: Were you in class last Monday?

    S: Yes, I was.

    T: Then you must _____ it.

    S: Oh, yes. You're right. Here it is.

4. This is a conversation between an American (A) and an immigrant (I).

   A: It must _____ hard to start your life in a new country.

   I: Yes, it is.

   A: You must _____ lonely at times.

   I: Yes. You must _____ how it feels. You went to live in Japan for a few years, didn't you?

   A: Yes, I did. It took me a long time to get used to it.

5. This is a conversation between two friends.

   A: I saw some experts on TV talking about a cure for baldness.

   They must _____ what they're talking about because they're experts.

   B: You must _____ that if you see it on TV it's true. But don't believe everything you see.

6. This is a conversation between two friends.

   A: I saw your uncle yesterday at the gym. How old is he?

   B: I'm not sure. My mother is 69 and he's her older brother. So he must _____ in his seventies. He goes to the gym four days a week to work out.

   A: He must _____ in great health.

   B: He is.

7. This is a conversation between two students in the school cafeteria.

   A: I see you're not eating your apple. In fact, you never eat fruit. You must not _____ fruit very much.

   B: You're right. I don't like fruit. Do you want my apple?

   A: Thanks. You're always eating potato chips. They're so fattening. They must _____ a million calories in them.

   B: Probably, but I never think about it.

   A: You should.

   B: You're always talking about calories. You must _____ about getting fat.

   A: I don't worry about it. I just try to eat well.

8. This is a conversation between two co-workers.

   A: Do you want to see a picture of my new baby?

   B: Yes.

   A: Here she is. She's about two months old now.

   B: She's so beautiful. You and your wife must _____ very happy.

   A: We are. But we don't get much sleep these days. You have a small baby. You must _____ what I'm talking about.

   B: I sure do.

9. This is a conversation between a young couple.

   A: Do you see that beautiful ring in the window? I really love it. Don't you?

   B: Yes, it's very beautiful. (*Thinking to himself*: This is an expensive jewelry shop. The ring must _____ over $5,000. She must _____ that I'm rich.)

10. This is a conversation between two strangers on the street.

    A: I see you're looking at a map. You must _____ a tourist. Are you lost?

    B: Please repeat.

    A: Are you lost?

    B: Speak slowly please.

    A: ARE YOU LOST? (*To herself:* He must not _____ any English.)

    B: (*To himself:* I asked her to speak more slowly and she's shouting instead. She must _____ that I'm deaf.)

4.11 | Probability vs. Possibility in the Present

Degrees of Certainty	Explanation
a. Who's calling? I have Caller ID. I see it **is** my sister.	a. We are certain that the information is true.
b. Who's calling? I don't know. I don't have Caller ID. It **might be** my sister. Or it **may be** my mother or it **could be** a telemarketer.	b. We have little or no evidence or information. There are many possibilities.
c. Who's calling? It **must be** my mother. It's 3 o'clock and she calls me every day at 3.	c. We conclude that something is true based on information we have or an estimate we make.
a. My elderly neighbor **has** no children.	
b. She **might have** nieces and nephews, but I'm not sure.	
c. She **must have** at least 50 boxes in her garage.	

EXERCISE 34   Decide if the situation is probable or possible. Fill in the blanks with *must* for probability or *may / might / could* for possibility.

EXAMPLES
A: Where is Linda Ramirez from?

B: Ramirez is a Spanish name. She ___*might*___ be from Mexico.

She ___*may*___ be from Colombia. There are so many countries where Spanish is spoken that it's hard to know for sure.

A: She ___*could*___ be from the Philippines. Filipinos have Spanish names, too.

B: Where is Tran Nguyen from?

A: I know that's a Vietnamese name. He ___*must*___ be from Vietnam.

1. A: What time is it?

   B: I don't have a watch. The sun is directly overhead, so it

     _____ be about noon.

2. A: Where's the teacher today?

   B: No one knows. She _____ be sick.

3. A: Does Yoko speak Japanese?

   B: She _____ speak Japanese. She's from Japan.

4. **A:** Where's Washington Avenue?

   B: I don't know. We're lost. There's a woman over there. Let's ask
   her. She _____ know.

5. **A:** Why is that student sneezing so much?

   B: I don't know. She _____ have a cold, or it
   _____ be an allergy.

6. **A:** Is Susan married?

   B: She _____ be married. She's wearing a wedding ring.

7. **A:** Why didn't Joe come to the party?

   B: Who knows? He _____ not like parties.

8. **A:** I need to make some copies, but don't have change for the copy
   machine.

   B: I _____ have some change. Let me look in my pocket.

9. **A:** I've never lived far from my parents before.

   B: You _____ miss them very much.

   A: I do.

10. **A:** Look at that young couple. They're always holding hands,
    smiling at each other, and kissing.

    B: They _____ be in love.

11. **A:** Linda never answers any questions in class.

    B: She _____ be shy or she _____ not know
    the answers to the questions.

12. **A:** I have a question about grammar.

    B: Let's ask the teacher. She _____ know the answer.

13. **A:** I have a question about American history.

    B: Why don't you ask our grammar teacher? He _____ know
    the answer.

4.12 | Modals with Continuous Verbs

Examples	Explanation
The child **should be sleeping.** She **shouldn't be watching** TV now.	Use modal + *be* + verb *–ing* for a present continuous meaning.
I can't reach my friend. His line is always busy. He **might be using** the Internet now.	
We **are supposed to be listening** to the teacher.	

EXERCISE 35 A student is home sick today. She looks at her watch and knows that her English class is going on right now. She knows what usually happens in class. Read the following statements and tell what *may*, *must*, or *should* be happening now.

EXAMPLE The teacher usually asks questions. (must)
He must be asking questions now.

1. The teacher sometimes sits at the desk. (may)

2. The teacher always does the exercises. (must)

3. The teacher explains the grammar. (should)

4. The teacher always helps the students. (must)

5. The teacher sometimes reviews the lesson. (might)

6. Sometimes the students don't pay attention. (be supposed to)

7. The students are probably wondering where I am. (must)

8. The teacher sometimes passes back papers. (might)

EXERCISE 36 *Combination Exercise.* Read this conversation. Choose the correct words in parentheses ( ) to complete the conversation. Sometimes both choices have the same meaning, so both answers are correct.

A: I received a letter about a sweepstakes. I think I
(may not, (am supposed to)) buy magazines in order to enter the contest.
   (example)

B: You're wrong. You (must not, (don't have to)) buy anything.
   (example)

A: But if I do, that (might not, may) increase my chances of winning.
   (1)

B: That's not true. I've read several articles on the Internet about sweepstakes and scams recently.

A: Then you (must, might) know a lot about this topic.
   (2)

B: I think I do. You (shouldn't, don't have to) believe everything you
   (3)
read on the Internet either.

A: How do I know what to believe?

B: You (must, should) use common sense. If an ad tells you that you are
   (4)
already a winner, you (shouldn't, must not) believe it.
   (5)

A: But if a letter tells me I've won a million dollars, I'd be crazy not to look into it further.

B: You'd be crazy if you did. Do you think someone is going to give you a million dollars for nothing?

A: No, but . . .

B: If you want to get rich, you (could, should) work hard and save your

                                                          (6)

  money.

A: But it (could, might) take years to get rich that way.

          (7)

B: That's the only way. Yes, you (could, can) buy lottery tickets and

                                       (8)

  enter sweepstakes, but you (should, might) lose a lot of money.

                                          (9)

A: I get offers by e-mail too. There are offers for products that

  (must, are supposed to) make me lose weight. I'm a bit overweight

       (10)

  and I (have to, have got to) lose 20 pounds.

            (11)

B: If you want to lose weight, you (might, ought to) eat a healthy diet

                                     (12)

  and exercise every day.

A: But that takes time. It (could, might) take months before I see a

                      (13)

  difference.

B: That's right. But it's the only way. All those ads tell you that problems

  (can, must) be fixed with easy solutions. But life isn't like that.

    (14)

A: You (must, should) think I'm stupid for believing all these things I

        (15)

  see and hear.

B: I don't think you're stupid. Some companies are very clever about
getting your interest. For example, infomercials often have celebrities
talking about a product. You (are expected to, are supposed to)

                                                        (16)

  trust the celebrity and believe what he or she says is true.

A: Perhaps the government (should, could) do something to stop these

                                      (17)

  ads from appearing in our e-mail, in our postal mailboxes, and on TV.

B: There are already laws telling companies what they

  (are allowed to, are permitted to) do or not. But it's up to you to be

       (18)

  informed, use your common sense, and protect yourself.

A: Well, thanks for your advice.

SUMMARY OF LESSON 4

Examples	Explanation
You **must** take a test to get a driver's license. You **must not** drive without a license.	Law or rule (official tone) Negative: Prohibition
You**'re supposed to** wear your seat belt. You**'re not supposed to** park here.	Law or rule (unofficial tone) Negative: Prohibition
I **have to** mail a letter. I**'ve got to** mail a letter. I **don't have to** go to the post office. I can put it in the mailbox.	Personal obligation Negative: Lack of necessity
You**'d better** study tonight, or you might fail the test. You**'d better not** stay up late tonight, or you won't be alert in the morning.	Warning; negative consequences statedor implied
You **should** exercise every day. You **ought to** exercise every day. You **shouldn't** eat so much ice cream.	Advice Negative: It's not advisable.
You **may / can** write the test with a pencil. You **cannot / may not** talk during a test.	Permission Negative: Prohibition
Students in the U.S. **can** wear jeans to class.	Social acceptability
I get annoying telemarketing calls. What **can** I do? You **could** be polite to the caller and listen, or you **can** say you're not interested and hang up.	Suggestions
You **may** win a prize. You **might** win a prize. You **could** win a prize.	Possibility about the future
It**'s supposed to** rain tomorrow. This face cream **is supposed to** make you look younger. My brother **is supposed to** call me this weekend. We**'re supposed to** write five compositions. You**'re supposed to** take your hat off in church. The movie **is supposed to** begin at 8 p.m.	Expectation because of information we receive or because of a promise, requirement, custom, or schedule.
She won a lot of money. She **must** be happy. She's eating very little. She **must not** be very hungry.	Deduction or logical conclusion about the present
I can't find my keys. They **might be** in your pocket. Did you look there? They **could be** on the table. Or they **may be** in your car. She looks confused. She **may not** know the answer. She **might not** understand the question.	Possibility about the present

1. Don't use *to* after a modal. (Exception: *ought to*)

   You should ~~to~~ buy a new car.

2. Use the base form after a modal.

   She can't ~~goes~~ go with you.

   You should ~~studying~~ study every day.

3. Don't forget ***d*** in *supposed to, permitted to, allowed to.*

   He's not suppose_d_ to drive. He's too young.

   You're not allow_ed_ to talk during the test.

4. Don't forget ***'d*** to express *had better.*

   You_'d_ better take the bus to work. Your car isn't working well.

5. Use *have / has* before *got to* in writing.

   We_'ve_ got to leave now.

6. Don't put two modals together.

   You must ~~can~~ be able to drive well before you can get your license.

7. Don't forget *be* or *to* in these expressions: *be supposed to, be able to, be permitted to, be allowed to.*

   They _are_ supposed to leave at 6 o'clock.

   I'm able _to_ work on Saturday.

8. Use correct word order in a question with a modal.

   What ~~I should~~ should I do?

PART 1   Find the mistakes with the underlined words, and correct them. Not every sentence has a mistake. If the sentence is correct, write *C*.

EXAMPLES   He ˈˢgot to talk to you.

You ought to come to class earlier.   **C**

1. You must to leave the building immediately.

2. We not allowed to use our books during a test.

3. To become a U.S. citizen, you must be able to speak simple English.

4. She can't find a job.

5. You're almost out of gas. You better fill up your gas tank.

6. The boss expects everyone to be on time. You'd better don't come late to the meeting.

7. She cans type very fast.

8. Where I can find information about museums in this city?

9. You're not allowed to talk during a test.

10. It's cold outside. You'd better take a sweater.

11. We're supposed to write a composition about our parents.

12. I got to buy a new car.

13. When is your brother supposed to arrive?

14. It's suppose to rain tomorrow.

PART 2 Look at the job application. Circle the best words to complete each sentence. The numbers on the application refer to each one of the sentences on the next page.

---

① Fill out the following form. Print in black ink or type. Bring it to the personnel office or mail it to:

Ms. Judy Lipton
P.O. Box 324
Tucson, Arizona 85744

Applications must be submitted by November 15.

② Name _____ _____ _____
   (last)   (first)   (middle initial)

Address _____

City _____ State _____ Zip Code _____

③ Telephone (   ) _____

④ Marital status (optional) _____   Sex _____   ⑤

⑥ Date of birth _____ _____ _____ (You must be at least 18.) ⑦
   (month)   (day)   (year)

⑧ Social Security number _____-_____-_____

⑨ Educational background

	Date graduated	Degree or major
High School	_____	_____
College	_____	_____
Graduate School	_____	_____

⑩ Employment History (Please start with your present or last job.)

Company	Position	Dates	Supervisor	Reason for leaving
_____	_____	_____	_____	_____
_____	_____	_____	_____	_____
_____	_____	_____	_____	_____
_____	_____	_____	_____	_____
_____	_____	_____	_____	_____

Do not write in the shaded box. For office use only.

⑪
Rec'd. by _____
Amer. cit. _____
Doc. checked _____
Transcripts received _____

⑫ The Immigration Act of 1986 requires all successful applicants to present documents to prove U.S. citizenship or permanent residence with permission to work in the U.S.

⑬ This company is an Equal Opportunity Employer. Race, religion, nationality, marital status, and physical disability will not influence our decision to hire.

⑭ I certify that these answers are true.

⑮ Signature: _____   Date: _____

EXAMPLE You (aren't supposed to, couldn't) use a red pen to fill out the application.

1. You (have to, might) submit the application to Ms. Lipton. Ms. Lipton (must, should) be the person in charge of hiring. She wants the application by November 15. Today is November 14. You ('d better not, mustn't) send it by regular mail. If you use regular mail, it (must not, might not) arrive on time. You (could, are supposed to) send it by overnight express mail, or you (might, can) take it to Ms. Lipton's office.

2. You (could, are supposed to) write your last name before your first name.

3. You (are supposed to, could) include your phone number.

4. You (shouldn't, don't have to) include your marital status.

5. For sex, you (might, are supposed to) write M for male or F for female.

6. To write the date of your birth in the U.S., you (should, can) write the month before the day (June 7, for example). You have several choices in writing the date. You (must, could) write June 7 or 6/7 or 6-7. If you put the day before the month, an American (might, should) think you mean July 6 instead of June 7.

7. To apply for the job, you (might, must) be over 18.

8. People who work in the U.S. (may, must) have a Social Security number.

9. You (may, are supposed to) include the schools you attended.

10. In the employment history section, you are asked why you left your last job. The employer (might, should) want to know if you were fired or if you left on your own.

11. You (can't, aren't supposed to) write in the shaded box. "Amer. cit." (must, should) mean American citizen.

12. You (must not, don't have to) be an American citizen to apply for the job. You can be a permanent resident. You (have to, should) prove your citizenship or residency. If you don't have permission to work in the U.S., you (might not, cannot) apply for this job.

13. The company (might not, may not) choose a worker based on race, religion, or nationality.

14. You (don't have to, must not) lie on the application form.

15. You (may, must) sign the application and include the date.

PART 3   Read the pairs of sentences. If the sentences have the same meaning, write *S*. If the sentences have a different meaning, write *D*.

EXAMPLES   You <u>have</u> to wear your seat belt. / You <u>must</u> wear your seat belt.   **S**

You <u>must</u> open the window. / You <u>should</u> open the window.   **D**

1. She <u>can</u> drive a car. / She <u>is able to</u> drive a car.

2. He <u>can't</u> speak Korean. / He <u>might not</u> speak Korean.

3. I'm <u>supposed to</u> help my sister on Friday. / I <u>might</u> help my sister on Friday.

4. You <u>don't have to</u> drive to work. / You <u>shouldn't</u> drive to work.

5. You're <u>not supposed to</u> write the answer. / You <u>don't have to</u> write the answer.

6. You're <u>not allowed to</u> use a pencil for the test. / You <u>may not</u> use a pencil for the test.

7. We <u>should</u> visit our mother. / We <u>ought to</u> visit our mother.

8. You <u>should</u> make a right turn here. / You <u>must</u> make a right turn here.

9. If you need more help, you <u>could</u> go to a tutor. / If you need more help, you <u>can</u> go to a tutor.

10. You <u>shouldn't</u> wear jeans. / You <u>must not</u> wear jeans.

11. You <u>must not</u> come back after the final exam. / You <u>don't have to</u> come back after the final exam.

12. I <u>have to</u> work tomorrow. / I've <u>got to</u> work tomorrow.

13. You <u>can't</u> eat in the computer lab. / You <u>are not allowed to</u> eat in the computer lab.

14. I <u>may</u> go to New York next week. / I <u>might</u> go to New York next week.

15. The final exam <u>could</u> be hard. / The final exam <u>might</u> be hard.

16. You <u>don't have to</u> call your teacher by her last name. / It is <u>not necessary to</u> call the teacher by her last name.

17. You <u>don't have to</u> fill out the application with a red pen. / You <u>aren't supposed to</u> fill out the application with a red pen.

18. You'd <u>better</u> wake up early tomorrow morning. / You <u>could</u> wake up early tomorrow morning.

Classroom Activities

1. Form a small group. Take something from your purse or pocket that says something about you. Show it to your group. Your group will make deductions about you.

   EXAMPLE car keys
   You must have a car.

2. On the left are some American customs. On the right, tell if there is a comparable custom in your native culture. Write what that custom is.

In the U.S.	In my native culture
When someone sneezes, you're supposed to say, "Bless you."	
If you're invited to a party, in most cases you're not supposed to take your children.	
Americans sometimes have potluck parties. Guests are supposed to bring food to the party.	
There are some foods you can eat with your hands. Fried chicken and pizza are examples.	
Students are not supposed to talk to each other during an exam.	
When you're too sick to go to work, you're supposed to call your employer and say you're not coming in that day.	

3. Bring in two copies of an application. It can be an application for a job, driver's license, license plate, apartment rental, address change, check cashing card, rebate, etc. Work with a partner. One person will give instructions. The other person will fill the application out. Use modals to help the other person fill it out correctly.

4. Find a partner and write some sentences to give advice for each of the following problems.

   a. I got permission to come to the U.S. I have a dog. I've had this dog for six years, since she was a puppy, but I can't take her with me. What should I do?
   b. I got a D in my biology class. I think I deserve a C. What should I do?

c. I need a new car, but I don't have enough money right now. What should I do?

d. I found an envelope with $100 in it in front of my apartment building. There is no name on it. What should I do?

e. My uncle came to live with us. He never cooks, cleans, or washes the dishes. I have to do everything. I'm very unhappy with the situation. What should I do?

Talk About it

1. Why do you think the elderly are often the victims of scams?

2. Have you ever seen a TV infomercial? For what kind of products? Do you believe the claims about the product?

3. How do you respond to telemarketing calls?

4. What do you think of TV commercials?

5. Did you ever win a prize in a contest, sweepstakes, or raffle? What did you win?

6. Did you ever buy a product that claims to do something but doesn't do it?

Outside Activities

1. Call your local phone company to find out how much it costs to order Caller ID service.

2. Watch an infomercial on TV. Write several sentences telling what the product is supposed to do.

3. If you have an apartment lease, make a copy of it and circle all the modals.

Internet Activities

1. Look for the Web sites of the Federal Trade Commission, the Better Business Bureau, or the National Fraud Information Center. Find some interesting consumer information to share with the class.

2. At a search engine, type in *do-not-call registry*. If you want to, add your phone number(s) to this registry.

3. At a search engine, type in *infomercial*. Find a report about TV infomercials. Print it and bring it to class.

4. At a search engine, type in *scam*. Print out an article about any type of scam you find and bring it to class. Circle all the modals in the article.

 Additional Activities at **http://elt.thomson.com/gic**

GRAMMAR
Modals in the Past

CONTEXT: The Kennedys and History in the Making

The Assassination of President John F. Kennedy
The Cuban Missile Crisis
John Kennedy, Jr.
The Media and Presidential Elections

President John F. Kennedy (1917–1963) and
son John, Jr. (1960–1999)

5.1 | Overview of Modals in the Past

You can express ideas about things that happened in the past by using a modal + *have* + past participle.

Active

Subject	Modal	*Not*	*Have*	Past Participle	Complement
You	must		have	heard	of the Kennedys.
I	should		have	read	the article.
We	might		have	seen	them on TV.
They	may	not	have	been	born yet.
John Junior	could		have	been	a politician.

Passive

Subject	Modal	*Not*	*Have Been*	Past Participle	Complement
Kennedy	might		have been	elected	again.
He	should		have been	protected	better.
He	could	not	have been	saved.	

THE ASSASSINATION OF PRESIDENT JOHN F. KENNEDY

Before You Read

1. Have you ever heard of President John F. Kennedy?

2. What political leaders have been assassinated?

Read the following article. Pay special attention to *must have*, *may have*, *might have*, and *could have*.

On November 22, 1963, Americans faced a great tragedy. President John F. Kennedy was assassinated in Dallas, Texas, while he was riding in an open car with the Governor of Texas. Who killed Kennedy, and why?

Immediately after the assassination, a suspect, Lee Harvey Oswald, 24 years old, was arrested. There was evidence showing that Oswald **must have shot** Kennedy from the sixth floor of a nearby building with a rifle. However, two days later, as Oswald was being transferred to a different jail, he was shot and killed by a man in the crowd. Why was he killed too? Because of Oswald's death, many questions remained unanswered.

An investigation took place to find out the truth behind the assassination. After examining a lot of evidence and questioning thousands of people, the investigating committee concluded that Oswald **must have been** the assassin and that he **must have acted** alone. But why did he do it? Some people think Oswald **might have been** an agent of the Soviet government. (In 1959, he gave up his American citizenship and moved to the Soviet Union.[1] He returned to the U.S. in 1962 with a Soviet wife.) Some think Oswald **may have been** a crazy man, just wanting to get attention. Others think the assassination **could have been ordered** by the Mafia.[2] Oswald's assassin, Jack Ruby, had connections with the Mafia. Did the Mafia want to prevent Oswald from talking?

Another question often asked is whether Oswald was the only gunman. Some witnesses report gunshots coming from two different directions. However, the investigating committee found no concrete evidence of this.

Even though the assassination occurred many years ago, people are still fascinated with this event. Books and movies have been made through the years offering new theories about this mysterious tragedy.

Did You Know?

John F. Kennedy was the fourth American president to be assassinated. The other three were Abraham Lincoln [1865], James Garfield [1881], and William McKinley [1901].

[1] In 1991, the country then called the Soviet Union broke up into 15 different countries, the largest of which is Russia. Other former Soviet countries are Ukraine, Belorus, Lithuania, Uzbekistan, and Georgia.
[2] The Mafia is a criminal organization.

5.2 | Past Probability (Deduction, Conclusion)

Examples	Explanation
After examining the evidence, the investigating committee concluded that Oswald **must have killed** Kennedy. Americans **must have felt** a great loss when their president died.	We use *must have* + past participle to make a statement of logical conclusion or deduction about a past event based on observations we make or information we have. We are saying that something is probably true.
When we were talking about Kennedy, Kim looked confused. She **must not have heard** of him.	For a negative probability, use *must not have* + past participle. Do not use a contraction for *must not* when it shows deduction or conclusion.

Language Note:
Compare:

Oswald *probably killed* Kennedy.
Oswald **must have killed** Kennedy.

You *probably saw* a film about the assassination.
You **must have seen** a film about the assassination.

EXERCISE 1 Fill in the blanks with an appropriate verb for past **probability**. Answers may vary.

1. **A:** Kennedy's death was such a tragedy.

   B: Who's Kennedy?

   A: You don't know who Kennedy was? He was so famous. You must
   ___have heard___ of him. Here's his picture in this book.
   (example)

   B: No, I've never heard of him. Wow. He was so handsome. He must
   _____ a movie star.

   A: No. He was an American president. He was assassinated in 1963 when he was only forty-six years old.

   B: That's terrible. It must _____ a hard time for Americans.

   A: Yes, it was. I remember my parents telling me about it. They were in high school when it happened. They must _____ about 15 or 16 years old. They really believed the Soviet government must _____ the assassination.

   B: Was Soviet involvement ever proven?

   A: No, but that's what my parents believed.

2. A: I followed your directions to go downtown yesterday. I took the number 60 bus, but it didn't take me downtown.

B: You must _____ me. I said, "16," not "60."

A: Really? I thought you said, "60."

B: It's hard to hear the difference between 16 and 60. Even native speakers misunderstand each other. Anyway, you must

_____ a terrible day.

A: Yes, I had an awful day. When I got off the bus, I was totally lost, so I took a taxi downtown.

B: A taxi must _____ you over $20!

A: In fact, it cost me $30. So I wasted a lot of time and money yesterday.

3. A: I called you a couple of times yesterday, but you didn't answer the phone.

B: You must _____ a wrong number. I always keep my cell phone on. What time did you call?

A: About 4 o'clock.

B: Oh. I must _____ at the hospital at that time visiting my sister. I had to turn off the phone when I was there. They don't allow cell phones in hospitals. Why did you call?

A: I forgot already

B: Then it must not _____ very important.

4. A. How did you like the party last Saturday, Terri?

B: I wasn't there.

A: What do you mean you weren't there? We talked for a few hours.

B: You must _____ with my twin sister, Sherri. We look alike.

A: She must _____ that I was crazy. I kept calling her Terri.

B: I'm sure she didn't think anything of it. She's used to it.

5. A: How did you do on the last test?

B: I didn't know about the test, so I didn't study. I failed it.

A: The teacher announced it last Thursday.

B: I must _____ absent that day.

A: I think Rona must _____ it too. When she got her paper, she started to cry.

B: Did you see Paula? She was so excited when she saw her exam. She must _____ an A.

6. A: Maria's relatives just went back to Mexico. They were here for a month.

B: She must _____ a wonderful time with them.

A: Yes, but she must _____ sad when she took them to the airport. She didn't want them to leave. She took them everywhere—to museums, to fancy restaurants, to concerts.

B: She must _____ a lot of money.

A: She knew she was going to spend a lot of money, so she saved a lot before they came.

A: I thought I was driving east, but now I think I'm driving north.

B: You must _____ a wrong turn somewhere. Let's take a look at the map. (*after looking in the glove compartment*). I can't find the map.

A: I must _____ it on the kitchen table. I was looking at it before we got in the car.

B: No problem. Let's just call our friends. They'll tell us how to get to their house. Let me use your cell phone.

A: Oh, no. The battery is dead. I must _____ the phone on all night last night.

B: I told you never to leave it on at night. Why don't we just stop at a gas station and get directions?

A: You know I don't like to ask for directions.

8. A: I said, "How are you?" to one of my classmates, and she answered, "I'm 58 years old." What was she thinking?

B: She must _____ that you said, "How *old* are you?"

A: She gave me a strange look. She must _____ that I was impolite asking about her age.

B: That's nothing. When I didn't speak much English, I went to a restaurant and asked the waitress for "soap" instead of "soup."

A: So did she bring you soap or soup?

B: Soup, of course.

A: Then she must _____ you in spite of your mistake.

9. A: I haven't seen Peter this semester. Have you?

B: He must _____.

A: Why would he drop out? He was close to getting his degree.

B: He said that he wouldn't come back if he didn't get financial aid.

He must not _____ financial aid this semester.

A: That's too bad.

10. **A:** You look tan. You must _____ out in the sun.

B: I was. I was in Florida for vacation.

A: That must _____ wonderful.

B: Actually, it was terrible. First, I lost our money and credit cards.

A: What did you do?

B: The credit card company cancelled our card and gave us a new one. We used the credit card to get cash.

A: So then the rest of your trip was fine, wasn't it?

B: Not really. We rented a car and it kept breaking down.

A: But it must _____ nice to get away from winter here and be in the sun.

B: We were there for two weeks. It must _____ for all but the last few days. Finally when the rain stopped, I got some sun.

5.3 | Past Possibility

Examples	Explanation
Why did Oswald kill Kennedy? There are several theories: The Mafia **may have ordered** the assassination. Oswald **might have been** crazy. He **could have been** the agent of another government.	To express possibility about the past, use *may have, might have*, or *could have* + past participle. The sentences on the left give theories about the past.
Oswald **may not have acted** alone. He **might not have been** the only assassin.	To show negative possibility, use *may not have* and *might not have*. Don't use *could not have* because it has a different meaning. (See Section 5.9.)

Language Note:
Compare:

Maybe the Mafia ordered the assassination.
The Mafia **may have ordered** the assassination.

Maybe Oswald was a Soviet agent.
Oswald **might have been** a Soviet agent.

EXERCISE 2 Change these *maybe* statements to statements with *may have, might have,* or *could have*. Situation: A student dropped out of the course after the first few weeks. These are some guesses about why he did it.

EXAMPLE Maybe he registered for the wrong section. (may)
He may have registered for the wrong section.

1. Maybe he preferred an earlier class. (could)

2. Maybe he wanted to be in his friend's class. (might)

3. Maybe the class was too hard for him. (may)

4. Maybe he got sick. (could)

5. Maybe he didn't like the teacher. (may)

6. Maybe he found a full-time job. (might)

7. Maybe he had a lot of problems at home. (could)

8. Maybe he left town. (might)

EXERCISE 3 Fill in the blanks with an appropriate verb for past **possibility**. Answers may vary.

1. **A:** I was trying to call you last night, but you didn't answer.

   B: What time did you call?

   A: After 8 p.m.

   B: Let's see. Where was I? I might _____*have been*_____ at the
   (example)
   library at that time.

   A: But I tried calling your cell phone too.

   B: I may _____ off. I often turn it off when I'm not expecting a call. Why didn't you leave a message?

   A: I did leave a message.

   B: Oh. I might _____ it by mistake.

   A: You deleted my message?

   B: Sorry.

2. **A:** Have you seen my keys?

   B: You're always losing your keys. You may _____ them in your pocket.

   A: No, they're not there. I already looked.

B: Well, you could _____ them as you were getting out of the car.

A: When I drop keys, I can hear them hit the ground, so I'm sure that's not it.

B: Well, you might _____ them in the door when you came in last night.

A: Oh, you're right! They're in the door. Thanks.

3. **A:** I'm so upset. I left my dictionary in class yesterday. Now I'll have to buy a new one.

   B: Why don't you ask the teacher? She might _____ _____ it.

   A: I already did. She didn't pick it up.

   B: Why don't you go to the "lost and found." Somebody may _____ _____ it and returned it there.

   A: Where's the "lost and found"?

   B: In front of the cafeteria.

4. **A:** I applied for a job three weeks ago, but so far I haven't heard anything. I probably didn't do well on the interview.

   B: You don't know that. They might _____ _____ hundreds of candidates for the job. Anyway, why don't you call and tell the company you're still interested.

   A: But they could _____ someone else already.

   B: You won't know if they hired someone else unless you ask.

5. **A:** I asked my boss for a raise last week, and she said she'd get back to me. But so far she hasn't mentioned anything.

   B: She might _____ about it. I'm sure she has a lot on her mind and can easily forget something. Why don't you ask her again?

6. **A:** I sent an e-mail to an old friend and I got a message saying it was undeliverable.

   B: You might _____ the address wrong.

   A: No. I checked. I wrote it correctly.

   B: Your friend may _____ his old account and opened a new one.

THE CUBAN MISSILE CRISIS

Before You Read

1. Has your native country ever been at war with another country? What started the war?

2. Do you think a nuclear war is possible today?

Read the following article. Pay special attention to *could have* + past participle.

In October 1962, the United States and the Soviet Union came close to war. The U.S. discovered that the Soviet Union was beginning to send nuclear missiles to Cuba, which is only about 90 miles from Florida. President John Kennedy saw this as a direct threat to national security; these weapons **could have been** used to destroy cities and military bases in the U.S. On October 22, President Kennedy announced on TV that any attack from Cuba would be considered an attack from the Soviet Union, and he would respond with a full

KASIMOV WITH IL-28 FUSELAGE CRATES ENROUTE TO CUBA
28 SEPTEMBER 1962

attack on the Soviets. He sent out the U.S. Navy to block Soviet ships from delivering weapons to Cuba. For 13 days, the world was at the edge of a major war. Finally, the Soviets agreed to send their missiles back and promised to stop building military bases in Cuba. In exchange, the U.S. promised to remove its missiles from Turkey.

In October of 2002, there was a reunion of many of the surviving players in this crisis. Cuban President Fidel Castro met with former Secretary of Defense Robert McNamara and other Americans, Cubans, and Russians involved in the decisions made 40 years earlier. Remembering their experiences, they all agreed that this was indeed a major crisis that **could have changed** the world as we know it. Discussing the viewpoints and experiences of the Americans, McNamara explained that a nuclear attack on a U.S. ship **could** easily **have grown** into a full nuclear war between the U.S. and the Soviet Union. A former CIA[3] analyst who studied spy photos told the group that at least 16 intermediate-range missiles in Cuba **could have reached** any point in the continental United States[4] except the northwest corner. He said at the conference, "October 27 is a day I'll never forget. The planet **could have been destroyed**." A former Kennedy aide added, "It **could have been** the end of the world, but here we are, 40 years later."

Fortunately, diplomacy[5] won over war. What **could have been** a tragic event is now only a chapter in history.

---

[3] The *CIA* is the Central Intelligence Agency, the U.S. agency that protects American secrets from other countries and gathers information about the secrets of other nations.

[4] The *continental* United States refers to all states except Hawaii and Alaska, which are not part of the U.S. mainland.

[5] *Diplomacy* is skillful negotiation between countries to try to work out problems without fighting.

5.4 | Past Direction Not Taken

We use *could have* + past participle to show that something did not happen.

Examples	Explanation
The Cuban Missile Crisis **could have been** the end of the world. An attack on a U.S. ship **could have grown** into a full nuclear war. Missiles **could have reached** almost any place in the U.S.	Use *could have* + past participle to show that something was possible in the past, but it didn't happen.
Kennedy and his advisors looked at several possibilities. They **could have attacked** immediately. They **could have invaded** Cuba. But they decided to give the Soviets a chance to remove the missiles and turn the ships around.	Use *could have* + past participle to show that a past opportunity was not taken. Several options were possible, but all but one were rejected.
I heard you moved last weekend. Why didn't you tell me? I **could have helped** you.	Use *could have* + past participle to show missed opportunities.
I was so hungry I **could have eaten** the whole pie by myself. I was so tired I **could have slept** all day. I was so happy when I got an A on the test I **could have kissed** the teacher. When the missiles were moved, we **could have jumped** for joy.	Use *could have* + past participle to show a desire to do something. Often an exaggeration is made in showing the desire.
Driver to pedestrian: Watch out, you idiot! I **could have killed** you. Father to son: Don't play baseball so close to the house. Your ball came within inches of the window. You **could have broken** the window. The 1962 crisis **could have been** the end of the world, but here we are, 40 years later.	Use *could have* + past participle to show that something came close to happening, but didn't.

EXERCISE **4**　Fill in the blanks with an appropriate verb for past **direction not taken.** Answers may vary.

EXAMPLE　**A:** Did you read about the Cuban Missile Crisis?
B: Yes. The U.S. almost went to war with the Soviet Union.

A: Those two big superpowers could _have destroyed_ the whole world!

Robert Kennedy

1. **A:** Did you read about Robert Kennedy?

   B: You mean John Kennedy, don't you?

   A: No, Robert, John's brother. He was running for president in 1968 when he was assassinated. He could _____ president of the U.S., but he was assassinated. He was only 42 years old.

2. **A:** I heard you bought a condo.

   B: We did.

   A: Why didn't you buy a house? Was it too expensive?

   B: We could _____ a house, but we don't have enough time for maintenance. So we thought a condo would be better. There's someone to take care of the grass in the summer and the snow in the winter.

3. **A:** What do you do for a living?

   B: I'm a waiter, but I could _____ a famous actor. Everyone says I've got a lot of talent. And my wife could

   _____ a career in modeling. She's so beautiful.

   A: It's not too late to follow your dream.

   B: We have small kids to support. So I think my acting days and her modeling days are over.

4. **A:** Do you want to see our new apartment? We moved last Saturday.

   B: Why did you move? You had a lovely apartment. I'm surprised you didn't stay there.

   A: We could _____ there. The rent wasn't too bad and the landlord was nice. But it was too far from school and work.

   B: Who helped you move?

A: We did it all ourselves.

B: Why didn't you let me know? I could _____ you.

A: We didn't want to bother our friends.

B: What are friends for?

A: Anyway, you have a small car. We needed to rent a van.

B: I could _____ my sister's van. She always lets me borrow it if I have to move stuff.

A: We appreciate your kindness, but everything worked out fine.

5. **A:** I can't believe you tried to fix the ceiling light without shutting off the electricity first. You could _____ yourself.

   B: But I didn't. I'm still alive and the light is fixed.

   A: You shouldn't take chances. And you got up on that tall ladder when you were home alone. You could _____, and no one would have been here to help you.

   B: But I didn't fall. You worry too much. Everything's okay. The light is fixed, and I didn't break a leg.

6. **A:** I bought stocks and sold them a few months later. Now they're worth four times as much as what I sold them for. I could _____ a lot of money.

   B: You never know with the stock market. You could _____ a lot of money too.

7. **A:** I'm so tired.

   B: What happened?

   A: I had to take three buses to get to a job interview in the suburbs. It took me almost two hours to get there.

   B: Why didn't you tell me? I could _____ you there in my car.

   A: I didn't want to bother you.

   B: You wasted a whole day today. You could _____ home hours ago.

   A: That's not a problem. I'm home now. And I did my homework while I was on the bus on the way there. On the way home, I slept most of the way. It's a good thing the person sitting next to me woke me up. I could _____ my bus stop.

EXERCISE 5 Fill in the blanks with the correct form of the verb in parentheses ( ) to show an exaggeration.

EXAMPLE The party was so wonderful that I could _have stayed_ all night.
(stay)

1. I was so tired that I could _____ for 12 hours yesterday.
(sleep)

2. I was so embarrassed when I made a mistake in my speech that I could _____ of shame.
(die)

3. She was so happy when she fell in love that she could _____ on air.
(walk)

4. I was so happy when my counselor told me about my scholarship that I could _____ him.
(kiss)

5. The movie was so good that I could _____ it again and again.
(watch)

6. Your cookies were so good that I could _____ all of them.
(eat)

7. I enjoyed dancing so much last night that I could _____ all night.
(dance)

8. It was so hot yesterday that we could _____ an egg on the street.
(fry)

EXERCISE 6 ABOUT YOU Fill in the blanks to tell about a missed opportunity that you did not take. Share your answers in a small group or with the entire class.

EXAMPLE _I could have gone to Germany instead of coming to the U.S., but it's_
easier to find a job in my profession in the U.S.

I could have _____ instead of

_____, but
(use verb + -ing)

_____

JOHN KENNEDY, JR.

Before You Read

1. Did you hear about the death of John Kennedy, Jr., in 1999? Where were you when you heard the news?

2. Do you know of any plane crashes in which someone famous died?

John Kennedy, Jr. (1960–1999)   John Kennedy, Jr. in 1963

Read the following article. Pay special attention to *was/were supposed to* and *should have* and other past modals.

The Kennedy family has seen more than its share of tragedies. President Kennedy was assassinated at the age of 46 in 1963. His brother, Robert, was assassinated at the age of 42 while he was running for president in 1968. Tragedy struck the Kennedy family again in 1999.

John Kennedy, Jr., could hardly remember his father. Born 17 days before his father was elected president of the U.S., he was three days short of his third birthday when his father was assassinated.

The president's son was handsome. Many people thought he could have been an actor, but his mother wanted him to be a lawyer. Some people expected him to follow in his father's and uncles' footsteps and go into politics. But after practicing law for a few years, he decided to publish a political magazine instead. Among the political leaders he interviewed was Fidel Castro, one of his father's political enemies.

Because he was so famous, Kennedy couldn't go out in public without being followed by photographers. He decided to learn to fly to avoid commercial airlines, where other passengers asked him questions, took his picture, and wanted his autograph.

On July 16, 1999, only 15 months after getting his pilot's license, he planned to fly to Massachusetts for his cousin's wedding. He took off with his wife and

(*continued*)

her sister as passengers at 8:30 p.m. They **were supposed to** arrive in Massachusetts a few hours later, but they never arrived. The next morning, searchers found their suitcases washed up on the shore. They concluded that Kennedy's plane must have crashed that night and that all three of them had died. The wedding that **was supposed to** take place was canceled as family members waited for more news. Six days later, the three bodies were found.

How or why did this accident occur? Experienced pilots believe that Kennedy made several deadly mistakes:

- He flew in darkness over water. As an inexperienced pilot, he **shouldn't have flown** in darkness.
- Because of the weather, visibility was very low that night, and he didn't have much experience using the instruments. He **shouldn't have flown** with such low visibility.
- He flew over water, where it is easy to become disoriented. He **should have stayed** close to the shoreline.
- He didn't leave a flight plan.[6] He **should have left** a flight plan.
- His plane was large and difficult to handle. He may not have been able to handle such a large plane in a difficult situation. As an inexperienced pilot, he **shouldn't have flown** such a big plane.
- He had broken his ankle a few months earlier and had to walk with a cane. Because of his injured ankle, he may not have been able to handle the foot pedals.

John Kennedy was only 39 years old when he died, seven years younger than his father was when he died. His wife was 33.

5.5 | Past Mistakes

Examples	Explanation
Kennedy **should have made** the trip in daylight. Kennedy **should have stayed** close to the shore. He **shouldn't have flown** in such bad weather conditions.	We use *should have* + past participle to comment on a mistake that was made. We are not really giving advice because it is impossible to change the past.
He **ought to have made** the trip in daylight.	Less frequently, we use *ought to have* + past participle. *Ought to* is not usually used for negatives.

Usage Note:
When a person receives an unexpected gift, he may be a little embarrassed. This person might say, *"You shouldn't have."* This means, "You shouldn't have gone to so much trouble or expense." or "You shouldn't have given me a gift. I don't deserve it." Saying this is considered polite, and an appropriate response might be, *"But it is my pleasure."*

[6] A *flight plan* gives information, such as the pilot's name, the speed of the airplane, the route, estimated flying time, fuel level, and registration of the airplane.

EXERCISE 7   Fill in the blanks with *have* and an appropriate past participle.

    EXAMPLE   Kennedy should _____*have flown*_____ before dark.

1. He didn't leave until after dark. He should _____ earlier.

2. He bought a large plane that was difficult to handle. He shouldn't

    _____ such a large plane

3. He chose to fly over water. He should _____ a better route.

4. He didn't pay much attention to the weather conditions. He should

    _____ attention to the weather conditions.

5. He didn't have much experience with the instrument panel. He

    should _____ more experience with the instrument panel if he wanted to fly at night.

6. When he realized it was getting dark, he should

    _____ until the next morning.

EXERCISE 8   Fill in the blanks with an appropriate verb for past mistakes.

    EXAMPLE   **A:** I didn't study for the last test, and I failed it

    B: You should _____*have studied*_____.

    A: I know, but there was a great party the night before, and I went with my friends.

    B: You shouldn't _____*have gone*_____ to a party the night

    before a test.

1. **A:** I'm so hungry. I didn't have time to eat breakfast this morning.

    B: You should _____ something before class.

    A: I know, but I was late.

    B: What time did you get up?

    A: About 45 minutes before class.

    B: You should _____ earlier. By the way, what topic did you use for your composition?

    A: Oh, my gosh! I forgot about the composition.

    B: You should _____ down the assignment.

    A: You're right. I'll get a calendar, and from now on, I'll write down all my assignments.

2. (*cell phone conversation*)

A: Hi. I'm at the supermarket now. Did you ask me to buy cereal?

B: Yes. Don't you remember? You should _____ the list.

A: I know, but I thought I'd remember everything so I didn't take the list.

B: This is what we need: a gallon of milk, a bag of dog food, and a watermelon.

A: Those things are heavy. How do you expect me to carry all of those things home?

B: In the car, of course.

A: Oh. I came here by bike. I should _____.

B: Yes, you should have.

3. A: How was your trip during spring break?

B: It was great. You should _____ with us.

A: I wanted to go with you, but I didn't have enough money.

B: You should _____ your money instead of spending it eating out in restaurants all the time.

A: You're right. And I shouldn't _____ so many CDs.

B: Did you get my postcard?

A: No. When did you send it?

B: Over two weeks ago. I should _____ to the post office instead of putting it in the hotel mailbox.

4. (*husband and wife*)

A: I washed my blue pants with my new white shirt and now my shirt looks blue.

B: You should _____ the clothes by color before putting them in the washing machine. I always separate mine.

A: I should _____ my clothes to you to wash.

B: I may be your wife, but I'm not your maid. So don't give me your dirty clothes.

5. (*wife and husband*)

A: This is a terrible trip. Why did you suggest going to the mountains? We should _____ to the coast. It's too cold here. I don't like cold weather.

B: You should _____ me that before we left.

A: I *did* tell you that, but you didn't pay attention. We didn't take jackets. We should _____ our jackets.

B: We can go and buy some.

A: I don't want to spend money on jackets when we've got perfectly good ones at home.

B: Maybe we should _____ at home instead of taking a trip.

6. (*student and teacher*)

A: Can you tell me my midterm grade?

B: Didn't you receive it by mail?

A: No. I moved right after the semester began.

B: You should _____ a change of address in the school office when you moved.

A: I'll report it today. So can you tell me my grade?

B: It's a C.

A: Why C? I got B's and A's on the tests.

B: But you didn't do all your homework. You should

_____ all your homework.

A: But I had to work full time.

B: You should _____ about that before you registered for four courses.

A: You're right. I didn't think much about homework when I registered.

7. **A:** I took a young woman from class out for dinner last week, but I didn't have enough money.

B: You should _____ enough money with you.

A: I took about $30 with me. I thought we were going to go to a fast-food place, but she chose a fancy restaurant.

B: You should _____ the restaurant.

A: I realized that later. She ordered appetizers, then dinner, then dessert and coffee. I thought she would pay for part of the dinner. But when the bill came, she just sat there.

B: You should _____ her that you wanted to split the bill.

A: I couldn't tell her that. I was trying to impress her.

B: So what did you do?

A: I went to the bathroom and called my brother on my cell phone. He rushed over to the restaurant and brought me some money. He pretended that our meeting there was an accident.

B: You should _____ her the truth. Lying to her is no way to start a relationship.

A: I don't think I'm going to go out with her again.

8. **A:** What happened to your car?

B: I had an accident. Someone hit me from behind.

A: What did the police say?

B: We didn't call the police. The other driver gave me his phone number and told me he would pay for the damage. But when I called, it was a disconnected number.

A: You should _____ the police.

B: And I should _____ information from his driver's license.

A: You mean you didn't even take information from his driver's license?

B: No. He looked honest.

A: You should _____ information about his insurance too.

B: I know. It's too late to get it now.

5.6 | *Be Supposed To* in the Past

Examples	Explanation
Kennedy and his wife **were supposed to** arrive in Massachusetts on Friday night, but they didn't.	*Was/were supposed to* is used to show that an expected action did not happen.
His cousin's wedding **was supposed to** take place the next day, but it didn't.	
We **were supposed to** have a test today, but the teacher was absent.	
You **were supposed to** stop at the stop sign, but you didn't.	*Was/were supposed to* is used for rules or promises that have been broken.
I **was supposed to** call my parents last night, but I forgot.	

EXERCISE 9 Fill in the blanks with a verb.

EXAMPLE She was supposed to _____*finish*_____ the report by Friday, but she didn't have enough time.

1. I was supposed to _____ my homework, but my printer wasn't working. So I wrote it by hand.

2. You were supposed to _____ me this morning. I waited all morning for your call.

3. Our plane was supposed to _____ at 9:45, but it was late. We had to wait in the airport for two more hours to start our trip.

4. The teacher was supposed to _____ our compositions yesterday, but he was sick and didn't do it.

5. It was supposed to _____ last weekend, so we cancelled our picnic. But it never rained.

6. I got a parking ticket yesterday. I wasn't supposed to

_____ on the east side of the street, but I didn't see the signs.

7. I couldn't get into the building. I was supposed to _____ my student ID, but I left it at home.

8. The kids weren't supposed to _____ the cookies before they ate dinner, but they did.

9. The play was supposed to _____ at 8 p.m., but it didn't begin until 8:10.

10. You were supposed to _____ out the application with a black pen, but you used a red pen.

THE MEDIA AND PRESIDENTIAL ELECTIONS

Before You Read

1. Have you ever voted in an election?

2. What do you know about the election process in the U.S.?

Harry Truman, President 1945–1953

Read the following article. Pay special attention to *must have* + past participle and *had to* + base form. Also pay attention to *couldn't have* + past participle and *couldn't* + base form.

Richard Nixon

John F. Kennedy

Did You Know?

Before 1951, a person **could be** president as many times as he wanted. Franklin Roosevelt was elected president four times (1932, 1936, 1940, and 1944). But in 1951, Congress passed a law limiting the presidency to two terms or a maximum of ten years. Truman **couldn't run** for re-election in 1952 because that would have given him 11 years as president.

The media—newspapers, magazines, radio, television, and now the Internet—play an important part in getting out information and often shaping public opinion. The media even played a historical role in two notable presidential elections.

When President Franklin Roosevelt died in 1945, Vice President Harry S. Truman became president. But in 1948, Truman **had to** campaign for re-election. He ran against Thomas Dewey. At that time, television was still new and most people did not own one. So candidates **had to** travel from city to city by train to meet the people. Truman traveled tirelessly, but Dewey was considered the stronger candidate.

Polls[7] were so sure of a Dewey victory that they stopped asking for public opinion a week before the election. The media, especially newspapers and the radio, thought that Truman **couldn't win.** When Truman went to bed the night of the election, he thought that he would lose.

The election results were coming in slowly and newspapers had to prepare the news of the election. On the basis of early opinion polls, the media concluded that Dewey **must have won** the election, and many newspapers showed Dewey's victory. However, they were wrong. Truman won by 2 million votes. When the votes were all counted, the newspapers **had to admit** their mistake.

Another example of how the media can influence results took place in the 1960 presidential race between John Kennedy and Richard Nixon. For the first time in history, the two candidates debated[8] each other on TV. They **had to** answer difficult questions. Many people who heard the Nixon-Kennedy debate on the radio thought that Nixon was the stronger candidate. But people who saw the debate on TV thought that the young, handsome Kennedy was the stronger candidate. Also Nixon was sweating under the hot lights, and people thought that he **must have been** nervous and uncomfortable with the questions. It was a close election, but Kennedy won. Many people think Kennedy **couldn't have won** without TV.

Today, presidential candidates know the power of television and other media in influencing public opinion. To enhance[9] their images, they wear clothes that make them look good on TV, practice their on-screen body language, and work hard to project a look that will result in victory.

[7] A *poll* is an analysis of public opinion on different matters compiled by special agencies. Statistics are made based on the answers to questions.

[8] In a debate, the candidates have to answer questions (on TV or radio) so that the public can judge who is the better candidate.

[9] *Enhance* means improve.

5.7 | *Must Have* vs. *Had To*

Must have + past participle and *had to* + base form have completely different meanings.

Examples	Explanation
Truman became president in 1945 when Franklin Roosevelt died. But he **had to** campaign for re-election in 1948. Truman **had to** travel by train to meet the people. During the debate, the candidates **had to** answer difficult questions.	To show necessity (personal or legal) in the past, we use *had to* + base form. We cannot use *must* in the past with this meaning.
Based on opinion polls, the newspapers concluded that Dewey **must have won.** Truman **must have been** surprised when he woke up in the morning and saw the newspapers. People thought that Nixon **must have been** nervous and uncomfortable during the debate.	When *must* shows a conclusion or deduction in the past, use *must have* + past participle.

EXERCISE 10 Below is a conversation between two American citizens about the 2000 presidential election. Write *had to* + base form for a past necessity. Write *must have* + past participle for a past deduction or conclusion.

A: The 2000 election between Al Gore, the Democratic candidate, and George W. Bush, the Republican candidate, was so strange.

B: It was?

A: Don't you remember? The election was close and they

  ___*had to count*___ the votes again to see who won. It took them five
  (example: count)

  weeks to figure out who won the election.

B: Bush and Gore ___*must have been*___ nervous that whole time waiting
  (example: be)

  to find out the results.

A: Yes, they probably were. And there were so many problems with the

  election that they _____ to the Supreme
  (1 go)

  Court to decide who won.

B: Did you vote in that election?

A: Of course.

B: You always vote for a Democrat, so you _____
  (2 vote)

  for Gore.

A: Yes, I did.

B: You _____ very disappointed when they finally
      (3 be)

announced that Gore lost.

A: Yes, I was. What about you? Who did you vote for?

B: I _____ overtime that day so I didn't vote.
      (4 work)

A: That's no excuse for not voting. Besides your boss is required to give
you time off to vote.

B: One person's vote doesn't matter much anyway.

A: It did in 2000. Every vote counted. The election was on November 7

and we _____ until December 13 to find out who
         (5 wait)

won the election because it was such a close race.

EXERCISE 11 Below is a conversation about John Kennedy, Jr.'s plane crash.
Write *had to* + base form for a past necessity. Write *must have* +
past participle for a past deduction or conclusion.

A: The Kennedy family has had so many tragedies. It

____*must have been*____ very sad for them when John Junior died.
   (example: be)

B: It _____ especially hard for John's wife's family.
        (1 be)

They lost two family members: John's wife, Carolyn, and her sister.

A: They were going to a wedding, and the family

_____ the wedding because of the tragedy.
      (2 cancel)

B: I heard that John had injured his ankle and _____
                                                        (3 walk)

with a cane. Maybe he couldn't control the plane because of it.

A: I don't think that was the problem. He didn't have enough

experience flying a big plane. It _____ hard for
                                     (4 be)

him to control a plane that size.

B: At least they didn't suffer. When the plane hit the water, the three of

them _____ immediately.
       (5 die)

A: John's poor uncle. He _____ and identify the bodies.
                              (6 go)

B: It _____ very hard for him.
        (7 be)

5.8 | *Could* + Base Form vs. *Could Have* + Past Participle

There are several ways to express *can* in the past, depending on the meaning you want to convey.

Examples	Explanation
John Kennedy, Jr. was rich. He **could buy** anything he wanted. (He **was able to buy** anything he wanted.) Now I can speak English well. A few years ago, I **could speak** only a few words of English. (I **was able to speak** only a few words of English.)	In affirmative statements, *could* + base form means *used to be able to*. The person had this ability over a period of time. *Was / were able to* can also be used for ability over a past period of time.
President Kennedy **was able to prevent** a war. He **was able to convince** the Soviets to send back their missiles. I looked on the Internet and **was able to find** more information about President Kennedy.	Use *was / were able to* for success in doing a single action. Do not use *could* for a single action.
John Kennedy, Jr. was a small child when his father died. He **couldn't remember** much about his father. He **wasn't able to remember** his father. The newspapers **weren't able to predict** the outcome of the 1948 election. The newspapers **couldn't predict** the outcome of the 1948 election.	In negative statements, *couldn't* and *wasn't / weren't able to* are used interchangeably.
John Junior **could have been** a politician, but he decided to publish a political magazine. The Cuban Missile Crisis **could have destroyed** the world.	Use *could have* + past participle for an action that didn't happen.
Some people thought that Kennedy **couldn't have won** the election without TV. When Kennedy was shot, some people thought they heard shots coming from two directions. If this is true, Oswald **couldn't have acted** alone.	Use *couldn't have* + past participle to show that something was impossible in the past.

EXERCISE 12   ABOUT YOU Fill in the blanks and discuss your answers. Answers will vary.

EXAMPLE   When I didn't know much English, I couldn't _talk to people on the phone._

1. When I was young, I could always count on
   _____.

2. When I was younger, I could _____ better than I can now.

3. When I was younger, I couldn't _____ as well as I can now.

4. One of my goals was to _____. I was / wasn't able (*choose one*) to achieve my goal.

5. I could never understand why _____.

6. When I didn't know much English, I couldn't
   _____.

7. I couldn't _____ because
   _____.

8. When I first came to the U.S., I was / wasn't (*choose one*) able to
   _____.

9. I could have _____, but I decided not to.

EXERCISE 13   John Kennedy, Jr. flew his own plane on the night of July 16, 1999. What are some other things he could have done that night? Write five sentences about opportunities he did not take.

EXAMPLE   _He could have stayed in a hotel that night._

1. _____
   _____

2. _____
   _____

3. _____
   _____

4. _____
   _____

5. _____
   _____

5.9 | More on *Couldn't Have*

Examples	Explanation
A: My parents voted for Kennedy in 1964. B: What? They **couldn't have voted** for him in 1964. He died in 1963. A: I think I saw your brother at the library yesterday. B: It **couldn't have been** him. He's in Europe on vacation.	*Couldn't have* + past participle is used to show disbelief or to show that someone's statement is absolutely impossible. We are saying that we can't believe this information because it is illogical.
Thanks so much for helping me paint my house. I **couldn't have done** it without you.	When we want to show gratitude or appreciation for someone's help, we often say, *"I couldn't have done it without you."*
Compare: a. I **couldn't vote** in the last election because I was out of town. b. You say you voted in the last election? You **couldn't have voted** because you weren't a citizen at that time. a. I **couldn't move** the refrigerator myself, so my brother helped me. b. You say you moved the piano by yourself? You **couldn't have moved** it by yourself. It's too heavy for one person.	In sentence (a), you know that something didn't happen in the past. In sentence (b), you are guessing that something didn't happen in the past. You are responding in disbelief to someone's statement.

EXERCISE 14 Fill in the blanks to make statements of disbelief.

EXAMPLE
A: When I was a child, I saw President Kennedy.

B: You ___couldn't have seen him!___ He died before you were born.

1. A: U.S. athletes won ten gold medals at the 1980 Olympics.

   B: They _____.
   The U.S. didn't participate in the 1980 Olympics.

2. A: We had an English test on December 25.

   B: You _____.
   The school was closed for Christmas Day.

3. A: President Kennedy ran for re-election in 1964.

   B: He _____.
   He died in 1963.

4. A: Oswald went to prison for many years for killing Kennedy.

   B: He _____.
   He was killed before he went to trial.

5. **A:** Look at the big fish I caught yesterday.

   B: You _____ that fish. It has a price on it. You must have bought it at the store.

6. **A:** I got an A on my math test.

   B: That's impossible. The teacher said that the highest grade was a

   B+. You _____ an A.

7. One student gave the teacher a perfect composition with no mistakes.

   The teacher thinks that the student _____ the composition by himself. Somebody must have helped him.

8. **A:** Somebody called me last night at midnight and didn't leave a message. Was it you?

   B: It _____ me. I was sleeping at midnight.

9. Teacher: You failed the test.

   Student: What? I _____ the test. I studied for it for five hours.

10. **A:** I can't find my house keys.

    B: Maybe you left them at work.

    A: I _____ them at work. I used them to open the door and get into the house a few minutes ago.

11. Thanks for helping me move last Saturday. I

    _____ without your help.

12. **A:** Hi. Don't you remember me?

    B: No, I'm sorry.

    A: We met in a math class last year.

    B: We _____ last year. I just started school two weeks ago.

13. **A:** Kennedy knew a lot about politics. Do you think he learned it from his dad?

    B: He couldn't _____ it from his dad. He was less than three years old when his dad died.

EXERCISE 15 *Combination Exercise.* A husband (H) and wife (W) are driving to a party and are lost. They are arguing in the car. Fill in the blanks to complete this conversation.

W: We're lost. And we don't even have a map. You should _*have taken*_
                                                              (example)

a map.

H: I didn't think we were going to need one. I must _____

_____ (1) a wrong turn.

W: I think you were supposed to make a right turn at the last

intersection, but you turned left. We should _____
_____ (2)

_____ for directions the last time we stopped for gas.

H: You know I don't like to ask for directions.

W: Let's use the cell phone and call the Allens and ask them how to get
to their house.

H: Let's see. I thought I had the cell phone in my pocket. I can't find it.

I must _____ _____ it at home.
(3)

W: No, you didn't leave it at home. I've got the phone here in my purse.
Oh, no. You forgot to recharge the battery. You should

_____ _____ it last night.
(4)

H: Why is it my fault? You could _____ it too.
(5)

W: Well, we'll just have to look for a pay phone. Do you have any change?

H: I only have dollar bills.

W: You should _____ some change with you.
(6)

H: Again, it's my fault.

W: Watch out! You could _____ that other car!
(7)

H: I wasn't going to hit that car. I didn't come anywhere close to it.

W: I don't know why we're going in our car anyway. The Petersons

offered us a ride. We could _____ with them.
(8)

H: You should _____ with the Petersons
(9)

and I should _____ home. I could
(10)

_____ the football game today
(11)

instead of listening to you complain!

5.10 | Continuous Forms of Past Modals

We use continuous modals in the past to talk about a specific time in the past.					
Subject	**Modal**	**Not**	**Have Been**	**Present Participle**	**Complement**
They	must		have been	waiting	at 8:30.
He	might		have been	sleeping	at 10:30 p.m.
You	could		have been	doing	your homework this morning.
I	should	not	have been	driving	so fast.

EXERCISE 16 Fill in the blanks with the continuous form of the modal.

EXAMPLE **A:** I was injured in a car accident. I wasn't wearing a seat belt.

B: You should _have been wearing_ your seat belt.

1. **A:** Why didn't you finish your homework?

   B: I was watching a movie on TV.

   A: You should _____ your homework instead.

2. **A:** I wasted so much time when I was young. I didn't take my studies seriously.

   B: But you had a good education.

   A: I know. But I could _____ English instead of playing soccer every day after school.

3. **A:** I tried to call you a few hours ago but there was no answer.

   B: I was home. I must _____ a shower when you called.

4. **A:** What do you think of last night's rainstorm?

   B: I didn't hear it. I must _____.

   A: How could you sleep through so much thunder?

   B: I'm a heavy sleeper.

5. **A:** I went to your house last Saturday, but you didn't answer the door. I thought you were going to be home.

   B: I often work on my car on Saturdays. I might _____ on my car when you arrived. Did you look in the garage?

   A: No. I didn't think about it.

6. (*teacher to student*)

    A: Peter, can you answer question number six?

    B: I'm sorry. I wasn't listening. I was thinking of something else. What was the question?

    A: You should _____.

SUMMARY OF LESSON 5

Must		
Meaning	**Present/Future**	**Past**
Legal obligation	I **must go** to court next week.	I **had to go** to court last week.
Urgency	I **must talk** to the doctor right now!	
Strong necessity	I **must study** for the test next week.	I **had to study** for the test last month.
Prohibition	You **must not tell** a lie in court.	
Deduction; conclusion	He's wearing a coat inside. He **must be** cold.	I can't find my keys. There's a hole in my pocket. I **must have lost** them.

Should		
Meaning	**Present/Future**	**Past**
Advice	You **should buy** a new car next year.	You **should have bought** a new car last year.
	You **shouldn't eat** fatty foods.	I **shouldn't have eaten** so many potato chips last night.

Can/Could

Meaning	Present/Future	Past
Ability	I **can speak** English now.	I **could speak** German when I was a child.
Acceptability	You **can wear** jeans to class every day.	You **could have worn** jeans to the party last week, but you didn't.
Permission/ prohibition	We **can use** a dictionary to write a composition. We **can't use** our books during a test.	We **could use** a dictionary to write the last composition. We **couldn't use** a dictionary during the last test.
Suggestion	How **can** I **learn** about computers? You **can take** a course, or you **could buy** a book and teach yourself.	
Possibility	Mary isn't here today. She **could be** sick.	Mary wasn't here yesterday. She **could have been** sick.
Direction not taken		I **could have gone** to Canada, but I decided to come to the U.S.
Impossibility; disbelief		A: I voted for President Clinton in 1996. B: You **couldn't have voted** for Clinton. You weren't a citizen in 1996.

May/Might

Meaning	Present/Future	Past
Permission	You **may use** a dictionary during the test.	
Possibility	I **may have** a job interview next week. I'm still not sure. The teacher isn't here. She **might be** sick.	Simon is wearing a suit to class. He **may have had** a job interview this morning. The teacher wasn't here yesterday. She **might have been** sick.

Ought To

Meaning	Present/Future	Past
Advice	She **ought to buy** a new car soon.	She **ought to have bought** a new car last year. (*rare*)

Related Expressions

Have To

Meaning	Present/Future	Past
Necessity (personal or legal)	I **have to study** now. I **have to go** to court next week.	I **had to study** yesterday. I **had to go** to court last week.
Lack of necessity	My job is close to my home. I **don't have to drive.** I can walk.	My last job was close to my home. I **didn't have to drive.** I could walk.

Have Got To

Meaning	Present/Future	Past
Necessity	I**'ve got to go** to court next week.	

Be Able To

Meaning	Present/Future	Past
Ability	She **is able to play** chess now.	She **was able to play** chess when she was a child.

Be Allowed To / Be Permitted To

Meaning	Present/Future	Past
Permission	We **are not allowed to talk** during a test. You **are not permitted to park** at a bus stop.	We **were not allowed to talk** during the last test. You **were not permitted to park** on this street yesterday because the city was cleaning the streets.

Be Supposed To

Meaning	Present/Future	Past
Expectation	My brother **is supposed to arrive** at 10 p.m. The weatherman said it **is supposed to rain** tomorrow. I**'m supposed to help** my brother move on Saturday.	My brother **was supposed to arrive** at 10 p.m., but his plane was delayed. The weatherman said it **was supposed to rain** yesterday, but it didn't. I **was supposed to help** my brother move on Saturday, but I got sick.
Reporting rules and customs	You **are supposed to wear** your seat belt. You **are not supposed to talk** during a test.	He **was supposed to wear** his seat belt, but he didn't. They **weren't supposed to talk** during the test, but they did.

Had Better		
Meaning	Present / Future	Past
Warning	You'**d better take** an umbrella, or you'll get wet.	

EDITING ADVICE

1. After a modal, always use a base form.

   have
   He could ~~has~~ gone to the party.

2. To form the past of a modal, use *have* + past participle.

   have eaten
   I shouldn't ~~ate~~ so much before I went to bed last night.

3. Don't confuse *must have* + past participle and *had to* + base form.

   had to take
   I was absent last week and ~~must have taken~~ the test in the teacher's office.

4. Don't confuse *couldn't have* + past participle and *couldn't* + base form.

   find
   Last night when I got home I couldn't ~~have found~~ a parking space.

5. Use the correct form for the past participle.

   gone
   He should have ~~went~~ to the doctor when he felt the pain in his chest.

6. Don't forget the **d** in *supposed to*. Don't forget the verb *be*.

   d
   You were suppose to meet me after class yesterday.
            ^
   was
   I supposed to work last Saturday, but I got sick.
   ^

7. *Can* is never used for the past.

   couldn't drive
   He ~~can't drove~~ his car this morning because the battery was dead.

LESSON 5 TEST/REVIEW

PART 1 Find the mistakes with the underlined words, and correct them. Not every sentence has a mistake. If the sentence is correct, write *C*.

EXAMPLES When he heard the good news about his scholarship, he

      have
  must ~~has~~ been excited.

  I <u>had to go</u> to court last week. **C**

1. I <u>was supposed to go</u> on vacation last week, but I got sick.

2. You <u>should have seen</u> the movie with us last week. We had a great time.

3. When your son graduated from college last year, you <u>must be</u> proud.

4. Why did you take the bus to work this morning? You <u>could have driven</u> your car.

5. He looked so tired when he got home from work. He <u>must had</u> a hard day today.

6. I <u>could have went</u> to the University of Illinois, but I decided to go to Truman College instead.

7. My wife is angry because I was late. I <u>should had called</u> her to tell her I was going to be late.

8. I didn't have time to call you yesterday because I <u>had to worked</u> all day yesterday.

9. Last week, he <u>should told</u> his mother the truth about his car accident, but he lied to her.

10. Thanks for helping me find a job. I <u>couldn't have found</u> it without your help.

11. Her daughter was sick yesterday, so she <u>had to leave</u> work early.

12. I <u>should studied</u> English when I was a child.

13. I had to work last Saturday, so I <u>couldn't go</u> to the party.

14. Everyone left the party early. They <u>must not have had</u> a very good time.

15. There wasn't enough food at the party. The host <u>should has bought</u> more food.

16. I <u>can't called</u> you last night because I lost your phone number.

PART 2 Fill in the blanks with the correct form of an appropriate verb. Answers may vary.

EXAMPLE The report on President Kennedy's death said that Oswald

  must _____*have killed*_____ Kennedy.

1. President Kennedy might _____ by the government of another country.

2. John Kennedy, Jr. grew up without a father. It must

_____ hard to grow up without a father.

3. John Kennedy, Jr. flew in the dark. He shouldn't

_____ in the dark.

4. He got lost and couldn't _____ his way
because he was flying over water.

5. He must _____ confused because of
poor visibility.

6. He went to the airport late that day. He should

_____ to the airport earlier.

7. Carolyn Bessette's parents must _____ very
sad when they heard that two of their daughters had died.

8. Kennedy and his wife could _____ on a
commercial airplane, but Kennedy decided to use his own airplane.

9. The search teams couldn't _____ the
bodies for six days.

10. Some experts believe Kennedy didn't have enough experience flying.

They think he should _____ more experience.

11. **A:** I think Kennedy, his wife, and sister-in-law probably survived for
a few days.

B: They couldn't _____ at all. The airplane hit the

water with great force. They must _____ instantly.

12. Kennedy's cousin had to _____ her
wedding because of the sad news.

PART 3 Look at the job application. Complete each sentence.

EXAMPLE His didn't print the application. He should ___*have printed*___

___*or typed*___ the application.

1. He wrote his application with a pencil. He was supposed to

_____ .

2. He didn't write his zip code. He should _____
his zip code.

3. He forgot to include his area code. He should

_____ it.

4. He included his marital status. He didn't have to

_____ it.

5. He wrote the day (18) before the month (2). He should

_____ .

Fill out the following form. Print in black ink or type. Bring it to the personnel office or mail it to:

Ms. Judy Lipton
P.O. Box 324
Tucson, Arizona 85744

Applications must be submitted by November 15.

Name ___Wilson___ ___Jack___ ___N___
        (last)   (first)   (middle initial)

Address ___5040 N. Albany Ave.___

City ___Chicago___ State ___Ill___ Zip Code _____

Telephone ( ) ___539-2756___

Marital status (optional) ___divorced___ Sex ___M___

Date of birth ___18___ ___2___ ___69___ (You must be at least 18.)
         (month) (day) (year)

Social Security number ___549___-___62___-___7149___

Educational background:

		Date graduated	Degree or major
High School	Roosevelt	1897	
College			
Graduate School			

Employment History (Please start with your present or last job.)

Company	Position	Dates	Supervisor	Reason for leaving
Apex	stockboy	5/88–3/90	R. Wilinot	personal
Smith, Inc.		5/90–12/94	M Smith	pay
Olson Co.	loading dock	1/95-present	B. Adams	

Do not write in the shaded box. For office use only.

Rec'd. by ___J.W.___
Amer. cit. ___yes___
Doc. checked ___?___
Transcripts received ___yes___

The Immigration Act of 1986 requires all successful applicants to present documents to prove U.S. citizenship or permanent residence with permission to work in the U.S.

This company is an Equal Opportunity Employer. Race, religion, nationality, marital status, and physical disability will not influence our decision to hire. ___Catholic___

I certify that these answers are true.

Signature: ___Jack N. Wilson___ Date: ___13/11/04___

6. He wrote that he graduated from high school in 1897. He couldn't

_____ in 1897. That's more than 100

years ago! He must _____ 1987.

7. He didn't fill in any college attended. He might not _____

_____ college.

8. He said that he left his first job for personal reasons. He might

_____ because he didn't like his boss. Or he

could _____ because the salary wasn't
high enough.

9. He didn't fill in his reason for leaving his last job. He should

_____.

10. He wrote in the shaded box. He wasn't supposed to

_____. He must not _____

_____ the directions very carefully.

11. He included his religion. He wasn't supposed to

_____ it. He must not _____
the sentence about religion.

12. He printed his name on the bottom line. He was supposed to

_____.

13. He mailed the application by regular mail on November 14. He

should _____. It might not _____ on time.

PART 4   Fill in the blanks with the past of the modal or expression in parentheses ( ).

After Alan (A) has waited for two hours for his friend Bill (B) to arrive for dinner, Bill finally arrives.

A: Why are you so late? You ___*were supposed to*___ be here two hours ago.
                                                    (example: be supposed to)

B: I'm sorry. I got lost and I _____ your house.
                                               (1 can't/find)

A: You _____ a road map.
                      (2 should/take)

B: I did, but I _____ it while I was driving. I
                              (3 can/not/read)

_____ a wrong turn.
       (4 must/make)

A: Where did you get off the highway?

B: At Madison Street.

A: That's impossible. You _____ off at Madison
                                     (5 can/not/get)

Street. There's no exit there.

B: Oh. It _____ Adams Street, then.
(6 must/be)

A: But Adams Street is not so far from here.

B: I know. But I had a flat tire after I got off the highway.

A: Did you call for a tow truck?

B: I _____ for a tow truck because I'm a
(7 can/call)

member of a motor club. But I thought it would take too long. So I
changed the tire myself.

A: But you're over two hours late. How long did it take you to change
the tire?

B: It _____ about 15 minutes, but then I
(8 might/take)

_____ home, take a shower, and change clothes.
(9 have to/go)

I was so dirty.

A: You _____ _____ _____ me.
(10 should/call)

B: I wanted to, but I _____ the paper where
(11 can/not/find)

I had your phone number. I _____ it while I was
(12 must/lose)

changing the tire.

A: Well, thank goodness you're here now. But you'll have to eat dinner
alone. I got hungry and ____ _____ for you.
(13 can/not/wait)

EXPANSION ACTIVITIES

Classroom Activities

1. A student will read one of the following problems out loud to the
class. The student will pretend that this is his or her problem. Other
students will ask for more information and give advice about the
problem. Try to use past and present modals.

Problem A My mother-in-law came to the U.S. last May. She stayed
with us for three months. I told my husband that he had to find
another apartment for her. He didn't want to. I finally said to my
husband, "Tell her to leave, or I'm leaving." So he helped her move
into her own apartment. Now my husband is mad at me. Do you
think I did the right thing?

Problem B I had a beautiful piano. I got if from my grandmother,
who bought it many years ago. When I moved into my new apartment, I couldn't take the piano because it was too big for the
entrance. So I sold it. Do you think I did the right thing?

Problem C My wife gave me a beautiful watch last Christmas. While I was on a business trip in New York last month, I left my watch in my hotel room. A few days later, I called the hotel, but they said that no one reported finding a watch. So far, I haven't told my wife that I lost the watch. What should I do?

Problem D A very nice American family invited me to dinner last night. The wife worked very hard to make a beautiful dinner. But I'm not used to eating American food and thought it tasted awful. But I ate it so I wouldn't hurt their feelings. They invited me to dinner again next week. What can I do about the food?

Problem E *Write your own problem, real or imaginary.*

2. Fill out the application on page 178 of Lesson Four. Make some mistakes on purpose. Find a partner and exchange books with him or her. Tell each other about the mistakes using modals.

   EXAMPLE For "sex" you wrote *M*. You're a woman, so you should have written *F*.

Talk About it

The following excerpt from a poem by John Greenleaf Whittier is about regret. Discuss the meaning of the poem.

> For all sad words of tongue or pen,
> The saddest are these: "It might have been!"

Write About it

1. Write about a mistake you once made. Tell about what you should have done to avoid the problem.

2. Write a short composition about another direction your life could have taken. What made you decide not to go in that direction?

3. Write about a famous person who died tragically. What could this person have done differently to prevent his or her death?

Internet Activities

1. Look for information about President John F. Kennedy and his son, John Kennedy, Jr. Bring an article about one of these two men to class.

2. At a search engine, type in *Kennedy assassination*. Look at the different assassination theories. Summarize the theories.

3. Find an article about the Cuban Missile Crisis and bring it to class. Circle all the modals in the article.

4. Find out more information about the U.S. presidential election in 2000. What were some of the problems in counting the votes?

Additional Activities at **http://elt.thomson.com/gic**

LESSON 6

6.1 | Adjective Clauses—An Overview

An adjective clause is a group of words that describes or identifies the noun before it.

Examples	Explanation
I have a friend **who is a computer programmer.**	Here the adjective clause tells you about the friend.
You should buy a computer **that has a big memory.**	Here the adjective clause tells you about the computer.
People **who send e-mail** usually write letters **that are short.**	The adjective clause can describe any noun in the sentence. In the sentence to the left, an adjective clause describes both the subject (*people*) and the object (*letters*).

SPAM

Before You Read

1. Do you get unwanted e-mail asking you to buy products or order services?

2. What do you do with this e-mail?

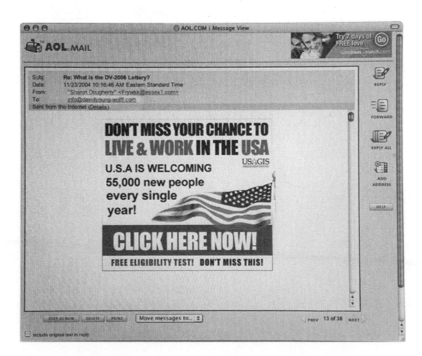

Did You Know?

Even Bill Gates, one of the richest men in the world, gets spam asking him if he wants to get rich or get out of debt.

Do you ever get e-mail **that promises to make you rich or thin?** Do you get e-mail **that tries to sell you a mortgage or a vacation package?** Do you ever receive an offer **that will give you a college diploma in a year?** This kind of advertising through e-mail is called "spam." Spam is e-mail **that you haven't asked for.** It is the electronic equivalent of junk mail or telemarketing calls. About half of the e-mail sent today is spam. In 2002, 260 billion spam e-mails were sent. A year later, in 2003, this number rose to 4.9 trillion. Bill Gates, the founder of Microsoft, calls spam "pollution of the e-mail ecosystem."

How do spammers get your e-mail address? They use several methods. When you buy something online, you are often asked for an e-mail address when you place an order. Spammers buy addresses from online companies. In addition, spammers search chat rooms, bulletin boards, and newsgroups for e-mail addresses. Spammers regularly sell lists of e-mail addresses to other spammers.

Where does spam come from? It comes from companies **that want your money.** Many of these companies try to take your money by making false claims ("Lose 50 pounds in 10 days!"). But most people delete this kind of e-mail without even reading it. So why do spammers send e-mail **that nobody wants to read?** The answer is simple: Some people *do* read this mail and a very small percentage even buy the product or order the service **that is offered.** And a small percentage of trillions of e-mails means money. One spammer **who lives in Florida** made so much money that he sold his business for $135 million dollars and retired at the age of 37.

What can you do to eliminate spam?

- You could simply delete it.
- You could get anti-spam software. (Some software is free, offered by the Internet service provider **you use.**)
- You can get a separate e-mail address to give to retailers **who require an e-mail address,** and use your primary e-mail address just for people **you know.**
- On a Web site, when you see a box **that asks you if you want more information,** make sure to uncheck the box.

Many people **who are unhappy with the amount of spam they receive** are asking their lawmakers to enact laws **that would stop spam.**

6.2 | Relative Pronoun as Subject

The relative pronouns *who, that,* and *which* can be the subject of an adjective clause.

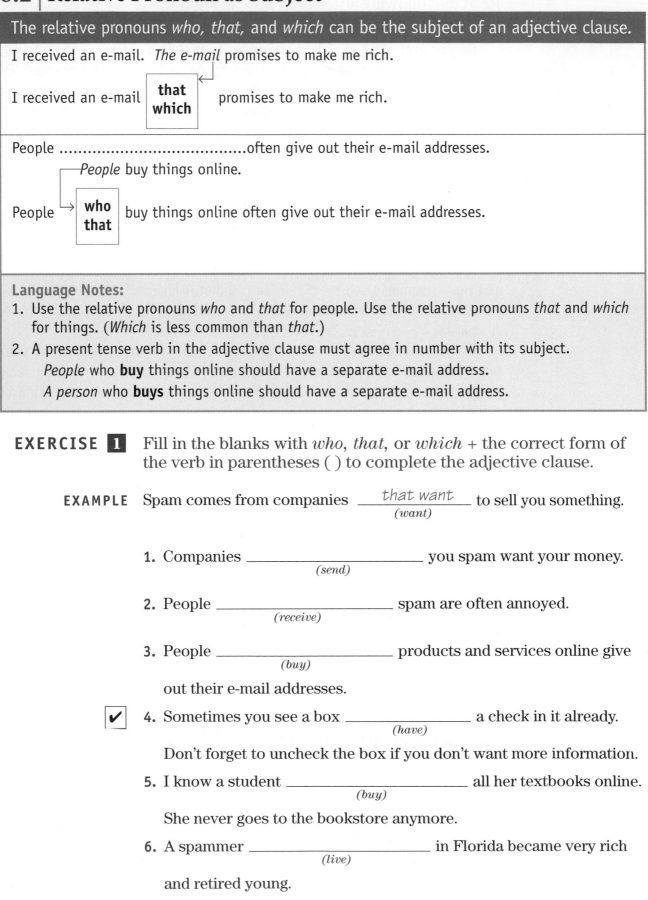

I received an e-mail. *The e-mail* promises to make me rich.

I received an e-mail | **that** **which** | promises to make me rich.

People ....often give out their e-mail addresses.

People buy things online.

People → | **who** **that** | buy things online often give out their e-mail addresses.

Language Notes:
1. Use the relative pronouns *who* and *that* for people. Use the relative pronouns *that* and *which* for things. (*Which* is less common than *that*.)
2. A present tense verb in the adjective clause must agree in number with its subject.
   People who **buy** things online should have a separate e-mail address.
   A person who **buys** things online should have a separate e-mail address.

EXERCISE **1**   Fill in the blanks with *who, that,* or *which* + the correct form of the verb in parentheses ( ) to complete the adjective clause.

EXAMPLE   Spam comes from companies ___*that want*___ to sell you something.

                               (want)

1. Companies _____ you spam want your money.

             (send)

2. People _____ spam are often annoyed.

       (receive)

3. People _____ products and services online give

      (buy)

out their e-mail addresses.

✔ 4. Sometimes you see a box _____ a check in it already.

             (have)

Don't forget to uncheck the box if you don't want more information.

5. I know a student _____ all her textbooks online.

       (buy)

She never goes to the bookstore anymore.

6. A spammer _____ in Florida became very rich

      (live)

and retired young.

7. You shouldn't believe an offer _____ you that

(promise)

you will lose 50 pounds in a week.

EXERCISE **2** Use the phrase below to write a complete sentence.

EXAMPLES a computer that has a small memory

A computer that has a small memory is not very useful today.

a company that promises to make me rich in three weeks

I wouldn't want to do business with a company that promises

to make me rich in three weeks.

1. e-mail that comes from friends and relatives

_____

2. companies that send spam

_____

3. students who don't have a computer

_____

4. children who spend all their time on the computer

_____

5. people who have a high-speed Internet connection

_____

6. Web sites that offer free music downloads

_____

7. "colleges" that offer a four-year diploma in six months

_____

8. people who don't know anything about computers

_____

EXERCISE **3** ABOUT YOU Fill in the blanks with an adjective clause.
Discuss your answers.

EXAMPLE I don't like people ___*who say one thing but do something else.*___

1. I don't like people _____

2. I don't like apartments _____

3. I don't like movies _____

4. I like movies _____

5. I don't like teachers _____

6. I like teachers _____

7. I don't like teenagers _____

8. I like to have neighbors _____

9. I don't like to have neighbors _____

10. I like to receive mail _____

11. I have never met a person _____

12. I can't understand people _____

13. I like classes _____

14. I like to be around people _____

15. I don't like to be around people _____

16. A good friend is a person _____

17. I have a good friend _____

18. I once had a car _____

EXERCISE 4   Work with a partner. Write a sentence with each of the words given to describe the ideal situation for learning English. You may use singular or plural.

EXAMPLES   class   *Classes that have fewer than 20 students are better than large classes.*

teacher   *I prefer to have a teacher who doesn't explain things in my language.*

1. teacher _____

2. college / school _____

3. textbook _____

4. class _____

5. classroom _____

6. computer lab _____

7. school library _____

8. classmate _____

9. dictionary _____

10. study group _____

6.3 | Relative Pronoun as Object

The relative pronouns *who(m)*, *that*, and *which* can be the object of an adjective clause.

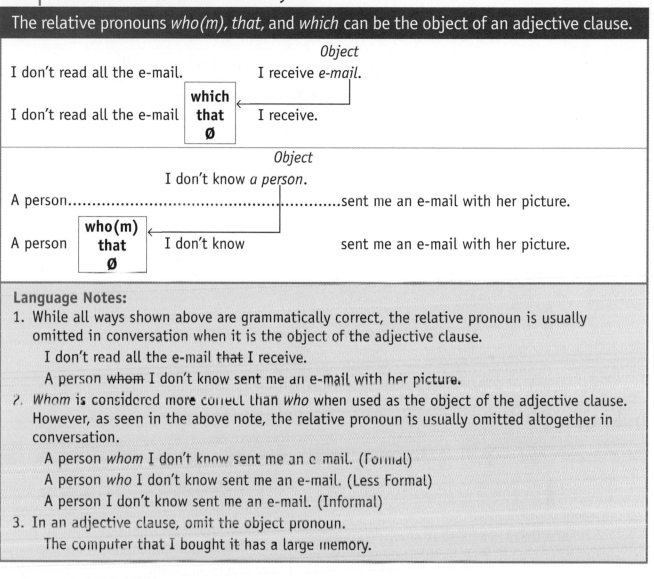

Language Notes:

1. While all ways shown above are grammatically correct, the relative pronoun is usually omitted in conversation when it is the object of the adjective clause.

   I don't read all the e-mail ~~that~~ I receive.

   A person ~~whom~~ I don't know sent me an e-mail with her picture.

2. *Whom* is considered more correct than *who* when used as the object of the adjective clause. However, as seen in the above note, the relative pronoun is usually omitted altogether in conversation.

   A person *whom* I don't know sent me an e-mail. (Formal)

   A person *who* I don't know sent me an e-mail. (Less Formal)

   A person I don't know sent me an e-mail. (Informal)

3. In an adjective clause, omit the object pronoun.

   The computer that I bought ~~it~~ has a large memory.

EXERCISE 5 Fill in the blanks to make an appropriate adjective clause.

EXAMPLE My friend just bought a new dog. The last dog ___*he had*___ died a few weeks ago.

1. I have a hard teacher this semester. The teacher _____ last semester was much easier.

2. I studied British English in my native country. The English _____ now is American English.

3. The teacher gave a test last week. Almost everyone failed the test _____.

4. When I read English, there are many new words for me. I use my

   dictionary to look up the words I _____ .

5. I had a big apartment last year. The apartment _____

   _____ now is very small.

6. Did you contact the owner of the wallet _____
   on the street?

7. I write poetry. One of the poems _____
   won a prize.

8. The last book _____ was very sad. It
   made me cry.

9. She has met a lot of people at school, but she hasn't made any

   friends. The people _____ are all
   too busy to spend time with her.

6.4 | Comparing Pronoun as Subject and Object

Examples	Explanation
Compare: a. I receive a lot of e-mail **(that)** I delete without reading. b. I receive a lot of e-mail **that** promises to make me rich.	In sentences (a), the relative pronoun is the object of the adjective clause. It is often omitted, especially in conversation. The new subject introduced (*I*) indicates that the relative pronoun is an object and can be omitted.
a. A student **(whom)** I met in my math class doesn't want to own a computer. b. A student **who** has good grades can get a scholarship.	In sentences (b), the relative pronoun is the subject of the adjective clause. It cannot be omitted. The fact that there is no new subject after *that* or *who* indicates that the relative pronoun is the subject. *Wrong:* A student has good grades can get a scholarship.

EXERCISE 6   Fill in the blanks with an adjective clause.

A: I'm so tired of all the spam _____*I get*_____.
                                    (example)

B: Do you get a lot?

A: Of course, I do. Doesn't everyone?

B: I don't.

A: How is that possible?

B: I have an e-mail address _____ ,just
                                        (1)
for shopping online. I don't use it for anything else. The e-mail

address _____ to my friends is private.
                    (2)
I don't give it to anyone else.

A: I never thought about having different e-mail addresses for different
things. Don't you have to pay for each e-mail account?

B: There are a lot of e-mail providers _____
                                                    (3)
_____ for free.

For example, you can use Hotmail™ or Yahoo™ for free. But they have
limited space and aren't good for everything. I like to send a lot of

photos. The photos _____ are often
                                (4)
too big for my free Hotmail account, but it's perfect for the shopping

_____ _____ online.
                (5)

A: Do you do a lot of shopping online?

B: Yes. For example, I buy a lot of textbooks online. The textbooks

_____ online are often cheaper than
                (6)
the ones in the bookstore.

A: How can I get one of these free accounts?

B: You just go to their Web site and sign up. Choose a username and password. If the username _____ has

(7)
already been chosen by someone else, you can choose another one or simply add some numbers to it. For example, I chose SlyFox, but it was already taken, so I added the year of my birth, 1986. So I'm SlyFox1986.

B: Why did you choose that name?

A: That's the name _____ when I was a

(8)
child. My older brother was always giving people nicknames. After you choose a username, choose a password. Make sure it's a number or word _____ easily. If you forget your

(9)
password, you won't be able to use your account. The password
_____ should never be obvious.

(10)
Never, for example, use your birth date, address, phone number, or Social Security number.

B: What password did you choose?

A: The password _____ is a secret.

(11)
I will never tell it to anyone.

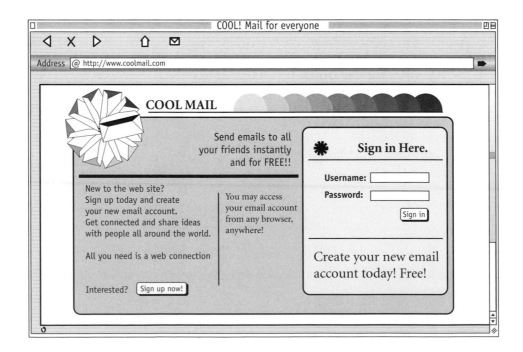

6.5 | Relative Pronoun as Object of Preposition

The relative pronouns can be the object of a preposition (*to, about, with, of, for,* etc.).

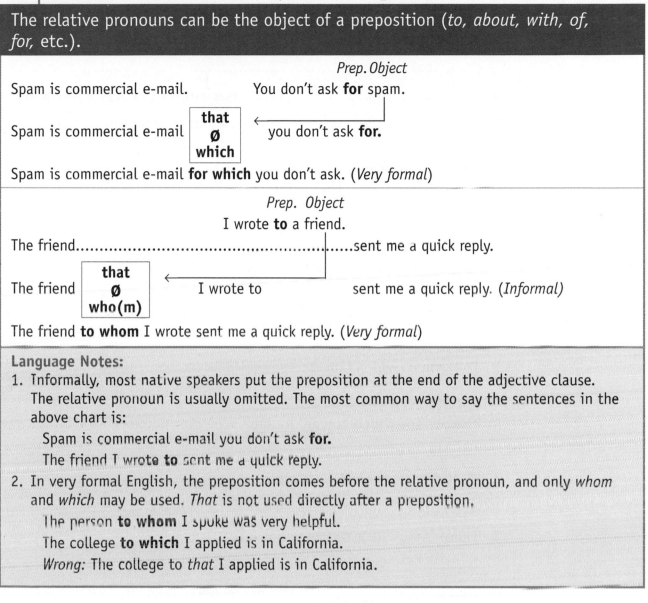

Prep. Object

Spam is commercial e-mail.   You don't ask **for** spam.

Spam is commercial e-mail **that / Ø / which** ← you don't ask **for.**

Spam is commercial e-mail **for which** you don't ask. (*Very formal*)

Prep. Object

I wrote **to** a friend.

The friend..sent me a quick reply.

The friend **that / Ø / who(m)** ← I wrote to   sent me a quick reply. (*Informal*)

The friend **to whom** I wrote sent me a quick reply. (*Very formal*)

Language Notes:
1. Informally, most native speakers put the preposition at the end of the adjective clause. The relative pronoun is usually omitted. The most common way to say the sentences in the above chart is:

    Spam is commercial e-mail you don't ask **for.**

    The friend I wrote **to** sent me a quick reply.

2. In very formal English, the preposition comes before the relative pronoun, and only *whom* and *which* may be used. *That* is not used directly after a preposition.

    The person **to whom** I spoke was very helpful.

    The college **to which** I applied is in California.

    Wrong: The college to *that* I applied is in California.

EXERCISE 7 ABOUT YOU Complete each statement.

EXAMPLE The class I was in last semester _____ *was very crowded.* _____

1. The city I come from _____

2. The school I graduated from _____

3. The house / apartment I used to live in _____

4. The elementary school I went to _____

5. The teacher I studied beginning grammar with _____

_____

6. Most of the people I went to elementary school with _____

_____

7. _____ is a subject I'm very interested in.

8. _____ is a topic I don't like to talk about.

EXERCISE 8 Make these sentences more informal by taking out the relative pronoun and putting the preposition at the end of the adjective clause.

EXAMPLE He applied to several colleges in which he was interested.

He applied to several colleges he was interested in. _____

1. I don't understand a word about which you are talking.

_____

2. The gym to which I used to go raised its fee.

_____

3. The pen for which you are looking is in your pocket.

_____

4. Those are the children for whom the babysitter is responsible.

_____

5. There is very little of which I'm sure.

_____

6. That is the counselor with whom you need to speak.

_____

EXERCISE 9 This is a conversation between two friends. One just came back from an island vacation where he had a terrible time. Fill in each blank with an adjective clause. Answers may vary.

A: How was your trip?

B: Terrible.

A: What happened? Didn't your travel agent give you good advice?

B: I didn't use a travel agent. I asked some friends for cheap ways to

take a vacation. One friend I ____*talked to*____ told me to look for
                                    (example)

vacations online. So I did. There was a choice of hotels. The name of

the hotel _____ was "Ocean View," so I thought I would
                (1)

see the ocean from my window. The view _____ from my
                                              (2)

window was of a brick wall. I didn't see any water at all. The only

water _____ was in the bathroom sink.
           (3)

A: What kind of food did they serve?

B: The food _____ made me sick.
                      (4)

A: Did you meet any interesting travelers?

B: I didn't like the other travelers _____. They were
                                              (5)

unfriendly.

A: Did you travel with an interesting companion?

B: The person _____ was boring. We weren't
                        (6)

interested in the same things. The things _____
                                                  (7)

were different from the things _____.
                                      (8)

A: Did you take pictures?

B: The pictures _____ didn't come out.
                          (9)

A: Did you find any interesting souvenirs?

B: The souvenirs _____ were cheaply made.
                            (10)

I didn't buy any.

A: Could you communicate with the people on the island? Do they
speak English?

B: No. I don't understand the language _____.
                                                  (11)

A: Did you spend a lot of money?

B: Yes, but the money _____ was wasted.
                                (12)

A: Why didn't you change your ticket and come home early?

B: The ticket _____ couldn't be changed.
                        (13)

A: Are you going to have another vacation soon?

B: The next vacation _____ will be in
                                (14)

December. I think I'll just stay home.

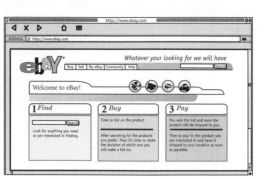

Before You Read

1. What do you do with old things of yours that you no longer want? Do you sell them or throw them away?

2. Do you collect anything (coins, stamps, dolls, etc.)? Where can you buy your collectibles?

Read the following article. Pay special attention to *when* and *where*.

Did You Know?

Pierre Omidyar was ranked the second richest man under 40 years old in 2002. His wealth was estimated to be $3.82 billion dollars. (The richest man under 40 in the same year was Michael Dell, the founder of Dell Computer.)

Did you ever want to sell an ugly lamp that your aunt gave you for your birthday? Or an old toy that is taking up space in your closet? Or are you trying to buy another train for your toy train collection? In the old days, buyers and sellers were limited to newspapers, garage sales, and flea markets[1] in their area to buy and sell unusual things. But since 1995, eBay has provided an online global community **where** people buy and sell almost anything. People are no longer limited to finding buyers and sellers in the local area **where** they live.

The creator of eBay, Pierre Omidyar, graduated from Tufts University in 1988 with a degree in computer science. He got his idea of an online trading community in 1995, **when** his wife, a collector of plastic candy dispensers, was trying to buy a piece for her unusual collection. From his California home, Omidyar developed an online trading site, and, within a short period of time, his wife was able to find what she was looking for, and Omidyar made a little money on the trade.

Using this idea, Omidyar created eBay, a Web site **where** people can put a photo of the object they want to sell, and give a starting price for an auction. In an auction, the person who makes the highest offer within a

Pierre Omidyar

[1] A *flea market* is a large area where individuals rent a space to sell used goods. It is usually outdoors.

certain period of time gets to buy the item. Not everything on eBay is sold by auction. Some items have fixed prices too. eBay makes its money by charging the seller a small percentage of the final price.

Meg Whitman

By 1998, eBay had become so big that Omidyar and his partner could no longer handle it without expert help. They brought in Meg Whitman, whose knowledge of business helped make eBay the success it is today. She changed eBay from a company that sold several categories of used things to a large marketplace of 11 million items in 18,000 categories of both new and used merchandise. Every day more than half a million items are sold. In the year 2001 alone, over $9 billion worth of merchandise changed hands on eBay, including cars, jewelry, toys, computers—and anything else you can imagine.

Not only can you buy and sell on eBay, you can also meet people whose interests you share. Whitman is proud of the online communities she has created. For example, doll collectors all over the world can "meet" each other and exchange information on bulletin boards and in chat rooms. Friendships are formed on eBay among people who share an interest in the same collectibles.

eBay is now among the top 10 Web sites visited.

6.6 | *Where* and *When* in Adjective Clauses

Examples	Explanation
eBay is a Web site **where people can buy and sell things.** eBay is a community **where you can meet people who share your hobby.**	*Where* means "in that place." *Where* cannot be omitted.
There was a time **(when) collectors were limited to their local areas.** Do you remember the day **(when) you saw a computer for the first time?**	*When* means "at that time." *When* can be omitted.

EXERCISE 10 Tell what information you can find on certain Web sites. If you're not sure, go to the Web site. Or you can take a guess and check it out later.

EXAMPLE WhiteHouse.gov is a Web site _____*where you can read about*_____
the White House and the president.

1. Weather.com is a Web site _____

2. Mapquest.com is a Web site _____

3. CNN.com is a Web site _____

4. USPS.gov is a Web site _____

5. Hotmail.com is a Web site _____

6. Travelocity.com is a Web site _____

7. Newsweek.com is a Web site _____

8. IRS.gov is a Web site _____

9. Redcross.org is a Web site _____

10. Harvard.edu is a Web site _____

EXERCISE 11 Fill in the blanks.

EXAMPLE I like to use the computer lab at a time _____*when it isn't crowded.*_____

1. The teacher shouldn't give a test on a day when _____

2. I like to study at a time when _____

3. Saturday is the day when _____

4. _____ is the season when _____

5. Between 7 and 9 a.m. is the time when _____

6. _____ was the year when _____

EXERCISE 12 ABOUT YOU Fill in the blanks to tell about yourself.

EXAMPLE _____*June*_____ is the month when I was born.

1. _____ is a place where I can relax.

2. _____ is a place where I can have fun.

3. _____ is a place where I can be alone and think.

4. _____ is a place where I can meet my friends.

5. _____ is a place where I can study undisturbed.

6. _____ is a time when I can relax.

7. _____ is a time when I like to watch TV.

8. _____ is a day when I have almost no free time.

9. _____ is a time when I like to use the Internet.

6.7 | *Where, When, That,* or *Which* in Adjective Clauses

Examples	Explanation
a. In 2002, Pierre gave the graduation speech at the college **where he had gotten his degree.** b. In 2002, Pierre gave the graduation speech at the college *from* **which he had gotten his degree.** c. In 2002, Pierre gave the graduation speech at the college **(that) he had gotten his degree** *from*.	Instead of *where* (a), the adjective clause can have preposition + *which* (b) or *that* + preposition (c). If you use *where*, don't use a preposition (in this case, *from*). The meaning of (a), (b), and (c) is essentially the same.
a. 1995 is the year **when eBay got its start.** b. 1995 is the year *in* **which eBay got its start.** c. 1995 is the year **(that) eBay got started** *in*.	Instead of *when* (a), the adjective clause can have preposition + *which* (b) or *that* + preposition (c). If you use *when*, don't use a preposition. The meaning of (a), (b), and (c) is essentially the same.

Compare:
a. She lives in a home **where** people use the computer a lot.
b. She lives in a home **that** has three computers.
	In sentence (a), *where* means *there* or *in that place*.
	   People use the computer a lot *there*.
	In sentence (b), *that* means *home*.
	   The *home* has three computers.

a. February is the month **when** I was born.
b. February is the month **that** has only 28 days.
	In sentence (a), *when* means *then* or *in that month*.
	   I was born *then*.
	In sentence (b), *that* means *the month*.
	   The *month* has only 28 days.

EXERCISE 13 Fill in the blanks with *where*, *that*, or *which*.

EXAMPLE The home ———*where*——— I grew up had a beautiful fireplace.

1. The store —————— I bought my computer is having a sale now.

2. Do you bookmark the Web sites —————— you visit often?

3. The box at the top of your browser is the place in —————— you write the Web address.

4. There are Web sites —————— you can compare prices of electronics.

5. The city —————— I was born has a lot of parks.

6. I don't like cities —————— have a lot of factories.

7. I like to shop at stores —————— have products from different countries.

8. I like to shop at stores —————— I can find products from different countries.

9. A department store is a store in —————— you can find all kinds of goods—clothing, furniture, toys, etc.

10. I have a photograph of the home —————— I grew up.

11. The office —————— you can get your transcripts is closed now.

12. She wants to rent the apartment —————— she saw last Sunday.

13. I would like to visit the city —————— I grew up.

14. The town in —————— she grew up was destroyed by the war.

EXERCISE 14 Fill in the blanks with *when* or *that* or nothing.

EXAMPLE December 31, 1999 was a time ———*when*——— people celebrated the beginning of the new century.

1. Six o'clock is the time at —————— the auction stops.

2. Do you remember the year —————— Meg Whitman started to work for eBay?

3. 2004 was a year —————— had 366 days.

4. New Year's Eve is a time —————— I love.

5. February is the only month —————— has fewer than 30 days.

6. My birthday is a day ——————— I think about my past.

7. December is a time ——————— a lot of Americans buy gifts.

8. My parents' anniversary is a date ——————— has a lot of meaning for them.

9. Do you give yourself the time ——————— you need to write a good composition?

10. She wrote about a time ——————— she couldn't speak English well.

11. Our vacation to Paris was the best time ——————— we had ever had.

Before You Read

1. What are some differences between a handwritten letter and an e-mail?

2. Do you ever use instant messages?

Part 1: Read the following handwritten letter, instant message, and e-mail.

May 14, 2005

Dear Fran,

   I was so happy to receive the letter you sent me with the photos of your adorable children. They've grown so big since the last time I saw them. How do they like their new school?

   As you know, our wedding is planned for September 12. We hope you'll be able to come. I've been so busy planning for the wedding, working, and studying that I haven't had much time to write lately. I hope you can understand.

   I'm enclosing a picture of my fiancé. He has a sister **whose daughter goes to the same school as your son in Oakland**. I wonder if they know each other. Her name is Wanda Chen. Ask your son if he knows her.

   I'm working now as a babysitter. The family **whose daughter I take care of** is from Japan. I'm even learning a few words in Japanese.

   I'm also taking math classes at City College. The teacher **whose class I'm taking this semester** is very young. She just graduated from college, but she teaches very well.

(continued)

```
JoeP:   how r u
NetSan: fine. i have a joke 4 u
JoeP:   dont have time now. brb
JoeP:   back
NetSan: wanna hear the joke now?
JoeP:   e-mail it 2 me. dont 4-get gotta go now
NetSan: y?
JoeP:   gotta talk 2 a co-worker whose laptop I fixed
NetSan: k. i'll send my joke 2 u later 2-day. g'bye 4 now
```

```
From:    jill
Subject: attachment

  fran,
  attached <attachment> r the pics i promised u. wanna
  see more? i'll call u tomorrow nite will u b home?
  jill
```

Part 2: Read the following article. Pay special attention to
adjective clauses beginning with *whose*.

When was the last time you received a handwritten letter in your mailbox? Are there people **whose letters you've saved for years?** The art of letter writing seems to be dying for many people as more and more of us are using e-mail, instant messages, and text messages for fast, easy communication.

You might think the United States is a country of serious Internet users. But there are many people **whose only online activity** is sending and receiving e-mail and chatting. When people send e-mail and instant messages, they often don't give much thought to how they write; many people use abbreviations and omit punctuation and capital letters. They  simply write the first thing that comes into their head, click, and send it. There are people **whose only experience with writing letters** is by e-mail.

Letter writing usually takes longer, but people love to receive handwritten letters that are long and full of news. The paper is often attractive, the handwriting is personal, and the contents are interesting and detailed.

On the other hand, writing quick, short e-mail notes is a great way to keep in touch with distant friends and relatives. But e-mail exposes us to the danger of viruses. There are people **whose enjoyment seems to come from creating viruses that cause problems for the rest of us.** Some viruses have shut down hundreds of thousands of computers in one day. You should never

Did You Know?

Postal mail is often called "snail mail" becase it is much slower than e-mail.

open an attachment from a sender **whose name you don't recognize.** Postal letters never contain viruses. And they provide a personal, intimate connection with a friend or relative.

Regardless of whether you prefer to send and receive handwritten letters or e-mails, it is important and fun to stay connected with friends and family.

6.8 | *Whose* + Noun in an Adjective Clause

Whose is the possessive form of *who*. It stands for *his, her, its, their,* or the possessive form of the noun.

Whose + noun can be the subject of the adjective clause

                         Subject
There are people. *Their enjoyment* comes from creating viruses.
                    ↓
There are people **whose enjoyment comes from creating viruses.**

                                      Subject
Companies can lose a lot of money. *Their computers* are infected with a virus

Companies **whose computers are infected with a virus** can lose a lot of money.

Whose + noun can be the object of the adjective clause

                                                          Object
Don't open an attachment from a sender. You don't recognize *the sender's name.*

Don't open an attachment from a sender **whose name you don't recognize.**

         Object
I've saved *my friends' letters* for years. They are amazed that I still have their mail.

Friends **whose** letters I've saved for years are amazed that I still have their mail.

EXERCISE 15   Underline the adjective clause in each sentence.

EXAMPLE   Companies <u>whose sites you visit may sell your e-mail</u> address to spammers.

1. Spammers send e-mail to all the people whose names are on their lists.

2. On eBay you can meet people whose interests you share.

3. I sent an e-mail to all the people whose e-mail addresses are in my address book.

4. I only open attachments of senders whose names I recognize.

5. The person whose e-mail I forwarded to you got angry at me for not asking her permission first.

6. A company whose Web site I visit often sends me coupons by e-mail.

7. Companies whose computers are affected with a virus can lose all their data.

8. I have to talk to a co-worker whose laptop I borrowed.

EXERCISE 16   Use the sentence in parentheses to form an adjective clause.

EXAMPLE   eBay is a company _____ *whose customers buy and sell thousands* _____ *of items a day* _____. (Its customers buy and sell thousands of items a day.)

1. Pierre Omidyar is a creative person _____. (His idea for eBay made him a very wealthy man.)

2. My friend has a sister _____. (Her daughter is studying to be a computer programmer.)

3. The teacher _____ uses a computer in the classroom. (I'm taking his class.)

4. There are some people _____. (Their idea of fun is to infect other people's computers with a virus.)

5. The police have arrested people _____. (Their viruses have infected thousands of computers.)

6. The person _____ got angry with me. (I forwarded her letter to everyone in my address book.)

7. I received a letter with an attachment from a sender _____

_____. (I don't recognize his or her name.)

8. The family _____ has three computers in their house. (I babysit for their daughter).

6.9 | Adjective Clauses After Indefinite Pronouns

An adjective clause can follow an indefinite pronoun: *someone, something, everyone, everything, no one, nothing, anything*.

Examples	Explanation
IP RP Everyone **who received my e-mail** knows about the party. IP RP I don't know anyone **who has never used e-mail.**	The relative pronoun (RP) after an indefinite pronoun (IP) can be the subject of the adjective clause. The relative pronoun cannot be omitted.
IP RP Something **(that) he wrote** made me angry. IP RP I didn't read anything **(that) I received** today.	The relative pronoun (RP) after an indefinite pronoun (IP) can be the object of the adjective clause. In this case, it is usually omitted.

Language Notes:

1. An indefinite pronoun takes a singular verb (the *-s* form).

   Everyone who **uses** e-mail has an e-mail address.

   I don't know anyone who **doesn't** have a computer.

2. An adjective clause does not usually follow a personal pronoun, except in very formal language and in some proverbs.

   He who laughs last laughs best.

   He who hesitates is lost.

EXERCISE 17 Fill in the blanks with an adjective clause. Use information from nearby sentences to help you. Answers may vary.

A woman (W) is trying to break up with a man (M).

M: I heard you want to talk to me.

W: Yes. There's something ___*I want to tell you*___
   (example)

M: What do you want to tell me?

W: I want to break up.

M: Are you angry at me? What did I say?

W: Nothing _____ made me angry.
   (1)

M: Did I do something wrong?

W: Nothing _____ made me mad.
   (2)

M: Then what's the problem?

W: I just don't love you anymore.

M: But I can buy you anything _____.
(3)

W: I don't want anything from you. In fact, I'm going to return

everything _____.
(4)

M: But I can take you anywhere _____.
(5)

W: I don't want to go anywhere with you.

M: What about all the love letters I sent you by e-mail?

W: I deleted everything _____.
(6)

M: Didn't you believe anything _____?
(7)

W: I found out that you said the same thing to three other women.

M: That's not true. Everything _____ was sincere.
(8)

W: How can it be sincere? You wrote the same thing to my cousin's best friend, my neighbor, and my classmate. The only thing you changed

was the name after "Dear." Everything else _____
(9)

was the same. So goodbye!

EXERCISE 18 Fill in the blanks with an adjective clause. Answers may vary.

EXAMPLE I don't send e-mail to everyone ____*I know*____.

1. You should read everything _____ in an e-mail before sending it.

2. When sending an e-mail, you shouldn't write anything

_____.

3. I received 20 e-mails today. Nothing _____ was important. It was all spam.

4. Some people delete everything _____ after they read it.

5. If you have a buddy list, you can send an instant message to

someone _____.

6. People you don't know may send you attachments. You shouldn't

open an attachment from anyone _____.
It may contain a virus.

EXERCISE 19   Fill in the blanks with an adjective clause.

EXAMPLE   I know someone _____ *who can help you with your car problem* _____ .

1. I don't know anyone _____ .

2. I know someone _____ .

3. Everyone _____ can go to the next level.

4. Anyone _____ should ask the teacher.

5. Everything _____ is useful.

EXERCISE 20   *Combination Exercise.* Circle the correct word in parentheses ( ) to complete the sentences. Ø means no word is necessary.

EXAMPLE   What is a computer virus? A virus is a computer code (what, (that,) who, whose) attaches itself to other programs and causes harm to programs, data, or hardware.

1. Viruses are written by people (they, who, whom, whose) enjoy causing problems for the rest of us.

2. What is spam? Spam is commercial e-mail (who, where, what, Ø) you haven't asked for.

3. Who is Bill Gates? Bill Gates is the man (who, whom, which, what) created Microsoft.

4. Bill Gates was born at a time (when, that, which, then) personal computers were not even in people's imaginations.

5. Who is Meg Whitman? She is the woman (to who, whom, to whom, to which) Pierre Omidyar turned over the operation of eBay in 1998.

6. Omidyar needed to bring in someone (who, whose, who's, who his) knowledge of business was greater than his own.

7. A computer is a tool (Ø, whom, about which, whose) most of us use today for fast access to information.

8. The Internet is a tool (that, what, when, Ø) has been around since the 1970s.

9. What is eBay? eBay is a Web site (that, where, there, which) you can buy and sell items.

10. The Internet can be slow at times (where, when, that, which) there is a lot of traffic.

11. The people (Ø, which, whose, where) you meet in chat rooms are sometimes very rude.

12. I have all the letters (that, what, where, whose) my parents have sent to me.

13. The computer lab is never open at a time (which, then, where, when) I need it.

14. I always delete the spam (who, that, when, whose) I receive.

15. On eBay, you can meet people (who, whom, who they, they) have the same interests as you do.

16. You can create an address book (when, that, where, whose) you can keep the e-mail addresses of all your friends.

17. You can create an address book (which, in which, there, in that) you can keep the e-mail addresses of all your friends.

18. There are chat rooms (there, where, which, that) people with the same interests can meet each other.

19. A virus writer is a person (his, whose, who, whom) enjoyment comes from creating problems for computer users.

20. Do you know anyone (Ø, who, whom, which) doesn't own a computer?

21. A man (who, whom, whose, who's) in my math class doesn't own a computer.

22. Don't believe everything (what, who, whom, Ø) you read on the Internet.

EXERCISE 21 *Combination Exercise.* Fill in the blanks with an adjective clause by using the sentences in parentheses or the context to give you clues.

A: How was your move last month?

B: It was terrible.

A: Didn't you use the moving company ___*I recommended*___?
    (example)

   (I recommended a company.)

B: The company _____ was not available on
    (1)

   the day _____. *(I had to move on*
    (2)

   this day.) I used a company _____.
    (3)

   (I found the name on the Internet.)

A: What happened?

B: First of all, it was raining on the day _____.
(4)

That made the move take longer, so it was more expensive than I thought it would be.

A: It's not the company's fault that it rained.

B: I know. But there are many other things _____.
(5)

(Things were their fault.) The movers broke the mirror

_____ _____. *(I had just bought the mirror.)* And
(6)

they left muddy footprints on the carpet _____.
(7)

(I had just cleaned the carpet.) I thought I was getting professional

movers. But the men *(They sent these men to my home.)* _____

_____ _____ were college students. They
(8)

didn't have much experience moving. Because the move took them so long, they charged me much more than I expected to pay. The

information *(They have information.)* _____
(9)

on their Web site says $100 an hour. But they charged me $800 for six hours of work.

A: You should talk to the owner of the company.

B: I called the company several times. The woman *(I talked to a*

woman.) ___ _____ _____ said that the owner would
(10)

call me back, but he never has.

A: You should keep trying. Make a list of everything _____

_____. *(They broke or ruined things.)*
(11)

Their insurance will probably pay for these things.

B: I don't know if they have insurance.

A: You should never use a company _____.
(12)

B: Everyone _____ *(I've talked to people.)*
(13)

tells me the same thing.

A: Don't feel so bad. Everyone makes mistakes. We learn from the

mistakes _____. Why didn't you ask
(14)

your friends to help you move?

B: Everyone _____ *(I know people.)* is so
(15)

busy. I didn't want to bother anyone.

A: By the way, why did you move? You had a lovely apartment.

B: It wasn't mine. The person *(I was renting her apartment.)*

_____ spent a year in China,
(16)

but when she came back last month, I had to leave.

A: How do you like your new place?

B: It's fine. It's across the street from the building

_____. *(My sister lives in that*
(17)

building.) So now we get to see each other more often. Why don't
you come over sometime and see my new place?

A: I'd love to. How about Saturday after 4 p.m.? That's the only time

_____. *(I don't have too much to do at that time.)*
(18)

B: Saturday would be great.

CREATING THE WORLD WIDE WEB

Before You **Read** 1. Besides computers, what other inventions have changed the way people communicate with each other?

2. When you think about computers and the Internet, what famous names come to mind?

Tim Berners-Lee

Read the following article. Notice that some adjective clauses are separated from the main clause with a comma.

Most people have never heard of Tim Berners-Lee. He is not rich or famous like Bill Gates.

Berners-Lee, who works in a small office at the Massachusetts Institute of Technology, is the creator of the World Wide Web. The creation of the Web is so important that some people compare Berners-Lee to Johann Gutenberg, who invented printing by moveable type in the fifteenth century.

Berners-Lee was born in England in 1955. His parents, who helped design the world's first commercially available computer, gave him a great love of mathematics and learning.

In 1980, Berners-Lee went to work at CERN, a physics laboratory in Geneva, Switzerland, where he had a lot of material to learn quickly. He had a poor memory for facts and wanted to find a way to keep track of things he couldn't remember. He devised a software program that allowed him to create a document that had links to other documents. He continued to develop his idea through the 1980s. He wanted to find a way to connect the knowledge and creativity of people all over the world.

In 1991, his project became known as the World Wide Web. The number of Internet users started to grow quickly. However, Berners-Lee is not completely happy with the way the Web has developed. He thinks it has become a passive tool for so many people, not the tool for creativity that he had imagined.

In 1999, Berners-Lee published a book called *Weaving the Web,* in which he answers questions he is often asked: "What were you thinking when you invented the Web?" "What do you think of it now?" "Where is the Web going to take us in the future?"

Did You Know?

What is the difference between the Web and the Internet? In 1989, Berners-Lee created a system of hyperlinks (words or pictures you can click on to take you to other information), making the 15-year-old Internet easy for everyone to use. This system of hyperlinks is known as the (World Wide) Web.

6.10 | Nonessential Adjective Clauses

Examples	Explanation
Berners-Lee, **who was born in England**, now lives in the U.S.	Some adjective clauses are not essential to the meaning of the sentence. A nonessential adjective clause adds extra information. The sentence is complete without it.
Berners-Lee's parents, **who helped design the first computer**, gave their son a love of learning.	
Berners-Lee went to work at CERN, **which is a physics laboratory in Geneva.**	A nonessential adjective clause is separated by commas from the main part of the sentence.
Berners-Lee was born in 1955, **when personal computers were beyond people's imagination.**	
Pierre Omidyar, **who created eBay**, was born in France.	A nonessential adjective clause begins with *who, whom, which, where, when,* or *whose. That* is not used in a nonessential adjective clause.
Pierre Omidyar, **whose wife is a collector**, got his idea for eBay in 1995.	
Pierre brought in Meg Whitman, **whose knowledge of business helped make eBay the success it is today.**	

EXERCISE 22 Put commas in the following sentences to separate the adjective clause from the main part of the sentence.

EXAMPLE The abacus, which is a wooden rack with beads, was probably the first computer.

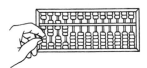

1. The abacus which was created about 2,000 years ago helped people solve arithmetic problems.

2. The first modern computer which was called ENIAC took up a lot of space (1,800 square feet).

3. ENIAC was created in 1942 when the U.S. was involved in World War II.

4. ENIAC which helped the government store important data was built at the University of Pennsylvania.

5. Personal computers which were introduced in the 1970s are much smaller and faster than previous computers.

6. Bill Gates went to Harvard University where he developed the programming language BASIC.

7. Bill Gates dropped out of Harvard to work with Paul Allen who was his old high school friend.

8. Together Gates and Allen founded Microsoft which has made both of them very rich.

9. In 1984, Apple produced the first Macintosh computer which was easier to use than earlier computers.

10. In 1990, Bill Gates introduced Windows which was Microsoft's version of the popular Macintosh operating system.

11. Berners-Lee whose name is not widely recognized made a great contribution to the world.

12. The Internet which has been around since the 1970s was not available to most people until the Web was created.

Bill Gates

6.11 | Essential vs. Nonessential Adjective Clauses[2]

Examples	Explanation
Bill Gates, **who created Microsoft**, never finished college. Berners-Lee, **whose parents helped design the first computer**, loved mathematics. Berners-Lee works at MIT, **where he has a small office**. eBay was in Omidyar's hands until 1998, **when he turned over the operation of the company to Meg Whitman**.	In the examples to the left, the adjective clause is **nonessential** because, without it, we can still identify the noun in the main clause. Try reading the sentences without the adjective clause. The sentences are complete. The adjective clause adds extra information to the sentence. A nonessential adjective clause is set off from the rest of the sentence by commas.
The people **who built the first computers** worked at the engineering department of the University of Pennsylvania. There are many people **whose only online activity is sending and receiving e-mail**.	In the examples to the left, the adjective clause is **essential** because, without it, we can't identify the noun. Try reading the sentences without the adjective clause. If we take it out, the noun isn't properly identified and the idea isn't complete.
Compare: a. The computer, **which was invented in the 1940s,** has become part of our everyday lives. (Nonessential)	Example (a) refers to the whole class of computers as an invention.
b. The computer **(that, which) I bought two years ago** is slow compared to today's computers. (Essential)	Example (b) refers to only one computer, which is identified by the adjective clause.
Compare: a. A person who invents something is very creative and intelligent. (Essential)	In sentence (a), the adjective clause is essential in order to explain which person is creative and intelligent.
b. Berners-Lee, who invented the Web, is not rich. (Nonessential)	In sentence (b), the adjective clause is nonessential because it provides extra information. Berners-Lee is unique and does not need to be identified. The adjective clause is nonessential.
Compare: a. The computer **(which or that)** she just bought has a big memory. (Essential)	In an essential adjective clause (a), the relative pronouns *which* or *that* can be used or omitted.
b. Microsoft, **which** Bill Gates helped create, is a billion-dollar company. (Nonessential)	In a nonessential adjective clause (b), only the relative pronoun *which* can be used. It cannot be omitted.

[2] Nonessential adjective clauses are often called nonrestrictive adjective clauses.

Language Note: Here are some questions to help you decide if the adjective clause needs commas or not. If the answer to any of these questions is *yes*, then the adjective clause is set off by commas.

- Can I put the adjective clause in parentheses?

  Bill Gates **(who created Microsoft)** never finished college.

- Can I write the adjective clause as a separate sentence?

  Bill Gates created Microsoft. **He never finished college.**

- If the adjective clause is deleted, does the sentence still make sense?

  Bill Gates never finished college.

- Is the noun a unique person or place?

  Berners-Lee, who works at MIT, invented the Web.

- If the noun is plural, am I including all members of a group (all my cousins, all my friends, all Americans, all computers)?

  My friends, who are wonderful people, always help me. (All of my friends are wonderful people.)

  Compare:

  I send e-mail to my friends **who have home computers and Internet service.**
  (Not all of my friends have home computers and Internet service.)

EXERCISE 23 Decide which of the following sentences contains a nonessential adjective clause. Put commas in those sentences. If the sentence doesn't need commas, write *NC*.

EXAMPLES People who send e-mail often use abbreviations. **NC**

My father, who sent me an e-mail yesterday, is sick.

1. Kids who spend a lot of time on the computer don't get much exercise.

2. My grammar teacher who has been teaching here for 20 years knows a lot about computers.

3. Viruses which can be sent in attachments can destroy your hard drive.

4. People who get spam every day can get very annoyed.

5. My best friend who gets at least 30 pieces of spam a day wrote a letter to his senator to complain.

6. Berners-Lee whose parents were very educated loves learning new things.

7. Marc Andreesseon created Netscape which is a popular Web browser.

8. Berners-Lee worked in Switzerland where the CERN physics laboratory is located.

9. The Instant Message which was a creation of America Online is available to many e-mail users.

10. Did you like the story that we read about Berners-Lee?

11. The computer you bought three years ago doesn't have enough memory.

12. The computer which is one of the most important inventions of the twentieth century has changed the way people process information.

13. Bill Gates who created Microsoft with his friend became a billionaire.

14. My best friend whose name is on my buddy list contacts me every day through an instant message.

EXERCISE 24 Combine the two sentences into one. The sentence in parentheses ( ) is not essential to the main idea of the sentence. It is extra information.

EXAMPLE eBay is now a large corporation. (It was started in Pierre Omidyar's house.)

eBay, which was started in Pierre Omidyar's house, is now

a large corporation.

1. Marc Andreessen was only 24 when he became rich. (He founded Netscape.)

   _____

   _____

2. The World Wide Web is used by millions of people around the world. (It was created by Tim Berners-Lee.)

   _____

   _____

3. Tim Berners-Lee was born in England. (We saw his picture on page 250 and 251.)

   _____

   _____

4. The book *Weaving the Web* answers a lot of questions about the creation of the Web. (It was written by Berners-Lee in 1999.)

   _____

   _____

5. Berners-Lee knew about computers from an early age. (His parents helped design one of the first computers.)

_____

_____

6. Tim Berners-Lee works at MIT. (He has a small office there.)

_____

_____

7. Pierre Omidyar got his idea for eBay in 1995. (His wife couldn't find one of her favorite collectibles at that time.)

_____

_____

8. eBay hired Meg Whitman in 1998. (More expert business knowledge was needed at that time to run the company.)

_____

_____

9. E-mail did not become popular until the 1990s. (It was first created in 1972.)

_____

_____

10. Bill Gates often gets spam asking him if he wants to become rich. (He's the richest man in the U.S.)

_____

_____

11. Pierre Omidyar came to the U.S. when he was a child. (His father was a professor of medicine.)

_____

_____

6.12 | Descriptive Phrases

Some adjective clauses can be shortened to descriptive phrases. We can shorten an adjective clause in which the relative pronoun is followed by the verb *be*.

Examples	Explanation
Compare: a. People **who are unhappy with the amount of spam they receive** should write to their lawmakers. b. People **unhappy with the amount of spam they receive** should write to their lawmakers. a. Pierre Omidyar, **who is the founder of eBay,** is one of the richest men in the world. b. Pierre Omidyar, **the founder of eBay,** is one of the richest men in the world.	Sentences (a) have an adjective clause. Sentences (b) have a descriptive phrase.
a. One-half of all of the e-mail **that is sent today** is spam. b. One-half of all the e-mail *sent* **today** is spam. a. There are about 11 million items **that are listed on eBay.** b. There are about 11 million items *listed* **on eBay.**	A descriptive phrase can begin with a **past participle.** Compare sentences (a) with an adjective clause to sentences (b) with a descriptive phrase.
a. A man **who is living in Florida** retired at the age of 37 after making millions in the spam business. b. A man *living* **in Florida** retired at the age of 37 after making millions in the spam business. a. Shoppers **who are using eBay** can locate a hard-to-find item. b. Shoppers *using* **eBay** can locate a hard-to-find item.	A descriptive phrase can begin with a **present participle** (verb -*ing*). Compare sentences (a) with an adjective clause to sentences (b) with a descriptive phrase.
a. Spam, **which is unwanted commercial e-mail,** is an annoying problem. b. Spam, **unwanted commercial e-mail,** is an annoying problem. a. eBay, **which is an auction Web site,** is very popular. b. eBay, **an auction Web site,** is very popular.	A descriptive phrase can give a definition or more information about the noun it follows. This kind of descriptive phrase is called an **appositive.** Compare sentences (a) with an adjective clause to sentences (b) with an appositive.
a. A man **who is in Florida** retired at the age of 37. b. A man *in* **Florida** retired at the age of 37. a. Pierre, **who is from France,** created eBay. b. Pierre, *from* **France,** created eBay.	A descriptive phrase can begin with a preposition (*with, in, from, of,* etc.) Compare sentences (a) with an adjective clause to sentences (b) with a prepositional phrase.

Language Notes:

1. A descriptive phrase can be essential or nonessential. A nonessential phrase is set off by commas.

   People **unhappy** with the amount of spam they receive should write to their lawmakers. (*Essential*)

   Pierre Omidyar, **the founder of eBay,** is one of the richest men in the world. (*Nonessential*)

2. An appositive is always nonessential.

   Amazon.com, **an online store,** is a very popular Web site.

EXERCISE **25** Shorten the adjective clauses by crossing out the unnecessary words.

EXAMPLE On eBay, people ~~who are~~ living in California can sell to people ~~who are~~ living in New York.

1. Netscape is a popular Web browser which is used by millions.

2. Bill Gates, who is one of the richest people in the world, gets spam asking him if he wants to become rich.

3. There are a lot of dishonest companies which are trying to take your money.

4. eBay takes a percentage of each sale that is made on its Web site.

5. A virus is a harmful program which is passed from computer to computer.

6. Tim Berners-Lee, who was born in England, now works at M.I.T.

7. M.I.T., which is located in Cambridge, Massachusetts, is an excellent university.

8. Berners-Lee developed the idea for the Web when he was working at CERN, which is a physics lab in Switzerland.

9. Berners-Lee's parents worked on the first computer that was sold commercially.

10. People who are using the Web can shop from their homes.

11. People who are interested in reading newspapers from other cities can find them on the Web.

12. The World Wide Web, which is abbreviated WWW, was first introduced on the Internet in 1991.

13. Computers which are sold today have much more memory and speed than computers which were sold 10 years ago.

14. Marc Andreessen, who was the creator of Netscape, quickly became a billionaire.

15. You can download Netscape, which is a popular Internet browser.

Combine the two sentences. Use a phrase for the sentence in parentheses ( ).

EXAMPLE Microsoft Windows made personal computers easy to use. (Windows was created by Bill Gates.)

> *Microsoft Windows, created by Bill Gates, made personal computers*
>
> *easy to use.*

1. Google is very easy to use. (It is a popular search engine.)

   _____

   _____

2. Have you ever used Mapquest? (It is a Web site that gives maps and driving directions.)

   _____

   _____

3. "Melissa" infected a lot of computers in 1999. (It is a virus.)

   _____

   _____

4. Tim Berners-Lee was born in 1955. (This is the same year Bill Gates was born.)

   _____

   _____

5. Marc Andreessen quickly became a billionaire. (He is the creator of Netscape.)

   _____

   _____

Marc Andreessen

EXERCISE 27   *Combination Exercise.* Combine these short sentences into longer sentences using adjective clauses or descriptive phrases.

EXAMPLE   Pierre Omidyar came to the U.S. when he was a child. His father was a professor of medicine.

> *Pierre Omidyar, whose father was a professor of medicine, came to*
>
> *the U.S. when he was a child.*

1. Pierre Omidyar was born in France. He wrote his first computer program at age 14.

   _____

   _____

2. *Business Week* named Meg Whitman among the 25 most powerful business managers. *Business Week* is a popular business magazine.

   _____

   _____

3. Bill Gates was born in 1955. His father was a lawyer.

   _____

   _____

4. Bill Gates wrote his first computer program in 1967. He was only 12 years old at that time.

   _____

   _____

5. Bill Gates has three children. His wife was a marketing executive at Microsoft.

   _____

   _____

6. Marc Andreessen is the co-founder of Netscape. He taught himself BASIC programming at the age of nine.

   _____

   _____

7. Andreessen and James Clark created Netscape. It was originally called "Mosaic."

_____

_____

8. Netscape went public in 1995. Andreessen was only 24 years old.

_____

_____

9. Michael Dell created Dell computers. He dropped out of college after his first year.

_____

_____

10. Dell's parents were worried about Michael. His grades were dropping.

_____

_____

11. Dell's business started to perform well at the end of his first year of college. At that time, his business was making over $50,000 a month.

_____

_____

12. Dell Computers was one of the first companies to sell computers online. It was selling about $18 million of computers a day by the late 1990s.

_____

_____

13. In 2000, *Forbes* named Dell Computers the third most admired company in the U.S. (*Forbes* is a business magazine.)

_____

_____

	Essential	Nonessential
Pronoun as subject	People (**who** or **that**) **write e-mail** aren't careful about spelling. I just bought a computer **that (or which) has a very big memory.**	Bill Gates, **who created Microsoft,** is one of the richest people in the world. eBay was created in San Jose, **which is a city near San Francisco.**
Pronoun as object	The first computer **(that or which) I bought** didn't have a mouse. The people **(who, whom, that) you meet in chat rooms** are sometimes very silly.	My first computer, **which I bought in 1996,** is much slower than my new computer. My father, **whom you met at the party,** is a programmer.
Pronoun as object of preposition	The person **to whom I sent an e-mail** never answered me. (Formal) The person **(whom, who, that) I sent an e-mail to** didn't answer me. (Informal)	Berners-Lee, **about whom we read,** is an interesting person. (Formal) Berners-Lee, **whom we read about,** is an interesting person. (Informal)
Where	The store **where I bought my computer** has good prices.	Berners-Lee works at the Massachusetts Institute of Technology, **where he has a small office.**
When	I'll never forget the day **(when) I saw a personal computer for the first time.**	The Web was created in 1991, **when most people did not have home computers.**
Whose + noun as subject	Children **whose parents are poor** often don't have a home computer.	Berners-Lee, **whose parents worked on computers,** learned a lot in his home.
Whose + noun as object	There are friends **whose letters I've saved for years.**	My mother, **whose letters I've saved,** died two years ago.
Adjective clause after indefinite compound	I don't know anyone **who has a Macintosh computer.** Everything **I learned about computers** is useful.	——————
Descriptive phrase	Home computers **made 20 years ago** didn't have a big memory.	Bill Gates, **the founder of Microsoft,** became a billionaire.

1. Never use *what* as a relative pronoun.

   who
   She married a man ~~what~~ has a lot of money.

   that
   Everything ~~what~~ you did was unnecessary.

2. You can't omit a relative pronoun that is the subject of the adjective clause.

   who
   I know a man ˄ speaks five languages.

3. If the relative pronoun is the object of the adjective clause, don't put an object after the verb.

   The car that I bought ~~it~~ has a stick shift.

4. Make sure you use subject-verb agreement.

   I know several English teachers who speak~~s~~ Spanish.

   has
   A car that ~~have~~ a big engine is not economical.

5. Put a noun before an adjective clause.

   The student w
   ~~W~~ho wants to leave early should sit in the back.

6. Put the adjective clause near the noun it describes.

   The teacher ˄ speaks Spanish (whose class I am taking).

7. Don't confuse *whose* with *who's*.

   whose
   A student ~~who's~~ grades are good may get a scholarship.

8. Put the subject before the verb in an adjective clause.

   my cousin bought
   The house that ~~bought my cousin~~ is very beautiful.

9. Use *whose*, not *his*, *her*, or *their*, to show possession in an adjective clause.

   whose
   I have a friend ~~who his~~ knowledge of computers is very great.

PART 1 Find the mistakes with the underlined words, and correct them. Not every sentence has a mistake. If the sentence is correct, write *C*.

EXAMPLES The students should correct the mistakes <u>that they make them</u>.

The students <u>about whom we were speaking</u> entered the room.   **C**

1. The teacher <u>what we have</u> is from Canada.

2. Five students were absent on the day when <u>was given the final test</u>.

3. The room <u>where we took</u> the test was not air-conditioned.

4. <u>Who</u> missed the test can take it next Friday.

5. Students <u>who knows</u> a lot of English grammar can take a composition course.

6. The teacher <u>whose class</u> I'm taking speaks English clearly.

7. A tutor is a person <u>whom helps students</u> individually.

8. Everyone wants to have a teacher <u>whose pronunciation is clear</u>.

9. The student <u>whose sitting</u> next to me is trying to copy my answers.

10. A teacher helped me at registration <u>who speaks my native language</u>.

11. The teacher gave a test <u>had 25 questions</u>.

12. The student <u>which</u> sits near the door always leaves early.

13. I have a neighbor <u>who his</u> son plays with my son.

14. Do you know anyone <u>who has</u> a German car?

15. The textbook <u>we are using</u> has a lot of exercises.

16. The people <u>who lives</u> upstairs make a lot of noise in the morning.

PART 2 Fill in the blanks to complete the adjective clause. Answers may vary.

EXAMPLES **A:** Do you like your new roommate?

B: Not really. The roommate *I had last year* was much nicer.

A: Are there any teachers at this school *who speak Spanish*?

B: Yes. Ms. Lopez speaks Spanish.

1. **A:** I heard you had a car accident. You hit another car.

   B: Yes. The woman whose ————————————————————
   wants me to pay her $700.

2. **A:** I bought a laptop for $1,500.

   B: That's a lot of money. The laptop ————————————
   only cost $1,000.

3. **A:** Did you buy your textbooks at Berk's Bookstore?

   B: No. The store ———————————————————————— is
   about ten blocks from school. Books are cheaper there.

4. **A:** My husband's mother always interferes in our married life.

   B: That's terrible. I wouldn't want to be married to a man whose

   ————————————————————————————————.

5. **A:** What did the teacher say about registration?

   B: I don't know. She spoke very fast. I didn't understand everything

   ————————————————————————————————.

6. **A:** Do you remember your first day in the U.S.?

   B: Of course. I'll always remember the day ———————————
   in my new country.

7. **A:** The teacher is talking about a very famous American, but I
   didn't hear his name.

   B: The man ——————————————————— is John Kennedy.

8. **A:** Did you buy the dictionary I recommended to you?

   B: No. The dictionary ————————————————— is just as
   good as the one you recommended.

9. **A:** Do you remember the names of all the students?

   B: No. There are some students ————————————————.

PART 3 Complete each statement. Every sentence should have an
adjective clause.

EXAMPLE   The library is a place ——— *where you can read* ———.

1. The teacher ————————————————————————— doesn't
   teach here anymore.

2. Everything ————————————————————————— is
   important to me.

3. Teachers ——————————————————————— aren't good
   for foreign students.

4. The teacher will not pass a student whose ————————————.

5. I would like to live in a house _____.

6. The classroom _____ is clean and pleasant.

7. I will never forget the day _____.

8. I never got an answer to the question _____ about the test.

9. Everyone _____ had a great time.

10. I don't like the dictionary _____, so I'm going to buy a better one.

11. Computers _____ ten years ago are slow compared to today's computers.

12. A laboratory is a place where _____.

13. There's so much noise in my house. I need to find a place

    _____.

14. Small children whose _____ learn to read faster than children who sit in front of the TV all day.

PART 4 Combine each pair of sentences into one sentence. Use the words in parentheses ( ) to add a nonessential adjective clause to the first sentence.

EXAMPLE Pierre Omidyar got the idea for eBay in 1995. (His wife is a collector.)

Pierre Omidyar, whose wife is a collector, got the idea

for eBay in 1995.

1. Berners-Lee was born in 1955. (Most people knew nothing about computers in 1955.)

    _____

2. The Internet changed the way people get their information. (It became popular in the 1990s.)

    _____

3. Berners-Lee studied physics in college. (His parents were programmers.)

    _____

4. Berners-Lee is not a well-known person. (We read about him in this lesson.)

    _____

5. Berners-Lee works at MIT. (He has a small office there.)

    _____

PART 5 Some of these adjective clauses can be shortened. Shorten them by crossing out unnecessary words. Some of the adjective clauses cannot be shortened. Do not change them. Write "no change" (*NC*).

EXAMPLES Thanksgiving, ~~which is~~ an American holiday, is in November.

Everyone who came to dinner enjoyed the food.   **NC**

1. The English that is spoken in the U.S. is different from British English.

2. A lot of people like to shop on eBay, which is an auction Web site.

3. Do not disturb the students who are studying in the library.

4. In the U.S. there are many immigrants who are from Mexico.

5. The computer that you bought has a very big memory.

6. She doesn't like the music that her daughter listens to.

7. Everyone who saw the movie liked it a lot.

8. Everyone whom I met at the party was very interesting.

9. Children who watch TV all day don't get enough exercise.

10. Parents whose children are small should control the TV programs that their kids watch.

11. The teacher with whom I studied beginning grammar comes from Canada.

12. The Web, which was introduced in 1991, has changed the way many companies do business.

PART 6 Some of the following sentences need commas. Put them in. If the sentence doesn't need commas, write "no commas."

EXAMPLES The last article we read was about the Internet.

no commas

Alaska, which is the largest state, has a very small population.

1. Ms. Thomson who was my English teacher last semester will retire next year.

2. I don't like teachers who give a lot of homework.

3. I studied engineering at the University of Michigan which is located in Ann Arbor, Michigan.

4. The computer I bought last month has a very big memory.

5. The computer which is one of the most important inventions of the twentieth century can be found in many American homes.

6. eBay is a Web site where people can buy and sell items.

7. My mother who lives in Miami has a degree in engineering.

8. I have two sisters. My sister who lives in New Jersey has three children.

9. Our parents who live with us now are beginning to study English.

10. The American flag which has 13 stripes and 50 stars is red, white, and blue.

11. The city where I was born has beautiful museums.

12. St. Petersburg where I was born has beautiful museums.

EXPANSION ACTIVITIES

Classroom Activities

1. **Game. Yes, but . . .** Work with a partner. One person will finish the sentence giving a point of view. The other person will contradict the first person by saying, "Yes, but . . ." and giving a different point of view.

   EXAMPLE   People who get married when they are young . . .
   A: People who get married when they are young have a lot of energy to raise their children.
   B: Yes, but people who get married when they are young are not very responsible.

   a. Couples who have a lot of children . . .

   b. People who immigrate to the U.S. . . .

   c. English books that have the answers in the back . . .

   d. People who have a lot of money . . .

   e. People who have a car . . .

   f. People who live in the same place all their lives . . .

   g. Teachers who speak fast . . .

   h. People who use credit cards . . .

   i. Cities that have a lot of factories . . .

   j. Movies that have a lot of violence . . .

   k. Parents who do everything for their children . . .

   l. Couples who have children when they're in their 40s . . .

   m. People who use the Internet a lot . . .

2. Fill in the blanks and discuss your answers in a small group.

   a. People ————————————————— have an easy life.

   b. No one likes or respects people ————————————————

   c. People who ————————————————— want to come to the U.S.

   d. There are a lot of people who ————————————————

3. **Dictionary Game.** Form a small group. One student in the group will look for a hard word in the dictionary. (Choose a noun. Find a word that you think no one will know.) Other students will write definitions of the word. Students can think of funny definitions or serious ones. The student with the dictionary will write the real definition. Students put all the definitions in a box. The student with the dictionary will read the definitions. The others have to guess which is the real definition.

   EXAMPLE nonagenarian
   Sample definition: A nonagenarian is a person who has none of the characteristics of his generation.
   Real definition: A nonagenarian is a person who is between 90 and 99 years old.

   (**Alternate:** The teacher can provide a list of words and definitions beforehand, writing them on small pieces of paper. A student can choose one of the papers that the teacher has prepared.)

Talk About it

1. In what ways does the computer make life better? In what ways does it make life worse?

2. Discuss the differences between using e-mail and postal mail. In what cases is it better to use e-mail? In what cases is it better to write a letter, put it in an envelope, and mail it?

Write About it

1. Write a paragraph telling the different ways you use your computer (or the computers at this school).

2. Write about an important person you know about who didn't receive much attention or money for his or her work.

3. Write about an important invention. How did this invention change society?

1. Find Tim Berners-Lee's Web site. What kind of information can you get from his Web site?

2. Go to a Web site that sells books. Find Berners-Lee's book, *Weaving the Web.* How much is it? Find a review of his book and print it out.

3. If you don't use AOL, type in *AOL Instant Messenger* at a search engine. Find out how to use this service.

4. Bring in a copy of a spam e-mail you received. Talk about the offers. Are they believable?

5. Go to eBay and find an item you might be interested in buying. Find the starting price.

6. At a search engine, type in *How Stuff Works.* Look up an article about spam. Circle all the adjective clauses in the article.

Additional Activities at **http://elt.thomson.com/gic**

LESSON

7

GRAMMAR

Infinitives
Gerunds

CONTEXT: Helping Others

Andrew Carnegie, Philanthropist
Charity and Volunteering
Bicycling to Raise Money for AIDS
Helping Others Get an Education
Mimi's Bike Ride
Global Volunteers

7.1 | Infinitives—An Overview

An infinitive is *to* + base form: *to go*, *to be*, *to see*.	
Examples	**Explanation**
I want **to help.**	An infinitive is used after certain verbs.
I want him **to help.**	An object can be added before an infinitive.
I'm happy **to help.**	An infinitive can follow certain adjectives.
It's important **to help** others.	An infinitive follows certain expressions with *it*.
Do you volunteer your time in order **to help** others?	An infinitive is used to show purpose.
He's old enough **to help.** She's too young **to help.**	An infinitive is used after expressions with *too* and *enough*.

ANDREW CARNEGIE, PHILANTHROPIST[1]

Before You Read

1. Who are some of the richest people today?

2. Should rich people help others?

Andrew Carnegie, 1835–1919

 Read the following article. Pay special attention to infinitives.

Andrew Carnegie was one of the world's richest men. He made a fortune in the oil and steel industries but spent most of his life giving his money away.

Carnegie was born in Scotland in 1835. When he was 13 years old, his family immigrated to the United States. A year later, he started **to work** for $1.20 a week. He was intelligent and hardworking, and it didn't take him long **to become** rich. But he always remembered the day he wanted **to use** a library in Pittsburgh but was not permitted **to enter.** He was disappointed **to learn** that the library was for members only.

[1] A *philanthropist* is a person who gives away money to help other people.

As Carnegie's fortunes grew, he started **to give** his money away. One of his biggest desires was **to build** free public libraries. He wanted everyone **to have** access to libraries and education. He believed that education was the key to a successful life. In 1881, there were only a few public libraries. Carnegie started to build free libraries for the people. Over the doors of the Carnegie Library of Pittsburgh, carved in stone, are his own words, "Free to the People." By the time Carnegie died, there were more than 2,500 public libraries in the English-speaking world.

But building libraries was not his only contribution. In his book, *The Gospel of Wealth*, he tried **to persuade** other wealthy people **to give** away their money. These are some of the ideas he wrote about in his book:

- **To give** away money is the best thing rich people can do.
- It is the moral obligation of the wealthy **to help** others.
- It is important for a rich person **to set** an example for others.
- It is not good **to have** money if your spirit is poor.
- It is the mind that makes the body rich.
- It is a disgrace[2] **to die** rich.

By the time he died in 1919, Carnegie had given away more than $350 million.

Did You **Know?**

$350 million in 1919 would be equivalent to $3.7 billion today.

[2] A *disgrace* is something that brings shame or dishonor.

7.2 | Verbs Followed by an Infinitive

Examples	Explanation
Carnegie wanted **to build** libraries. He started **to work** when he was 14. He decided **to give** away money. Everyone deserves **to have** an education.	Some verbs are followed by an infinitive.
I want **to make** money and **help** others.	In a sentence with two infinitives connected by *and*, the second *to* is usually omitted.
Everyone wants **to be given** an opportunity to succeed.	To make an infinitive passive, use *to be* + past participle.

Language Note:
The verbs below can be followed by an infinitive.

agree	deserve	love*	seem
appear	expect	manage	start*
attempt	forget	need	try*
begin*	hate*	offer	want
can('t) afford	hope	plan	wish
can't stand*	intend	prefer*	would like
choose	know how	prepare	refuse
continue*	learn	pretend	
decide	like*	promise	

* These verbs can also be followed by a gerund with little or no change in meaning. See Section 7.14.

EXERCISE 1 Fill in the blanks with an infinitive based on the story you just read.

EXAMPLE Andrew Carnegie started _____ *to work* _____ when he was very young.

1. He tried _____ a library when he was young, but he wasn't allowed inside.

2. He wanted _____ free public libraries.

3. He thought it was important for rich people _____ poor people.

4. He thought it was better _____ a rich spirit than a big bank account.

5. He thought that rich people needed _____ an example for others.

6. He decided _____ a lot of money to help others.

7. He thought it was a terrible thing _____ rich.

EXERCISE 2 ABOUT YOU Fill in the blanks with an infinitive. Share your answers with the class.

EXAMPLE I like ___*to eat Chinese food*___.

1. I don't like _____, but I have to do it anyway.

2. I can't afford _____.

3. I've decided _____.

4. I want _____, but I don't have enough time.

5. I don't want _____, but I have to do it.

6. I sometimes forget _____.

7. I love _____.

8. I need _____ and _____ every day.

9. I don't know how _____, but I'd like to learn.

10. I would like _____.

EXERCISE 3 ABOUT YOU Answer these questions. You may discuss your answers.

EXAMPLE Why did you decide to come to this city?
I decided to come here because I wanted to go to this school.

1. Why did you decide to come to this school?

2. What did you need to do to get into this school?

3. When did you start to study English?

4. What do you expect to have five years from now (that you don't have now)?

5. What do you hope to accomplish in your lifetime?

6. Do you want to learn any other languages? Which ones? Why?

7. Do you plan to get a college degree? In what field?

8. Do you plan to transfer to a different school?

9. What do you plan to do after you graduate?

EXERCISE 4 Fill in the blanks with the passive form of the verb in parentheses ( ).

EXAMPLE Children like ___to be given___ toys.
                        (give)

1. Children have _____ about giving, not just taking.
                        (teach)

2. My elderly neighbor needs _____ to the hospital
                                            (drive)
   because he can't drive. I'm going to offer to drive him.

3. Some people who make donations don't want their names

   _____.
        (know)

4. Money for a charity needs _____.
                                    (collect)

5. There are many ways to help. Parks need _____.
                                                    (clean)

6. There are many ways of helping children. Children need

   _____ and _____.
        (love)   *(respect)*

7. Carnegie thought that libraries needed _____ for
                                                (build)
   the public.

8. Everyone wants _____ a chance to succeed in life.
                        (give)

7.3 | Object Before Infinitive

After the verb, we can use an object + an infinitive.

Example	Explanation
a. Carnegie wanted **everyone to have** educational opportunities. b. He encouraged **rich people to help** others. c. He wanted **them to donate** money. d. Our parents want **us to help** others.	The object can be a noun (a and b) or a pronoun (c and d).
Carnegie encouraged people **not** to be selfish. The teacher advised us **not** to talk during an exam.	Put *not* before an infinitive to make a negative.

Language Note:
The verbs below can be followed by a noun or object pronoun + an infinitive.

advise	expect	persuade
allow	forbid	remind
appoint	force	teach*
ask	invite	tell
beg	need	urge
convince	order	want
encourage	permit	would like

*After *teach*, *how* is sometimes used: He taught me *how to ski*.

EXERCISE 5 ABOUT YOU Tell if you want or don't want the teacher to do the following.

EXAMPLES speak fast
I don't want the teacher to speak fast.

answer my questions
I want him to answer my questions.

1. explain the grammar

2. review modals

3. give us a lot of homework

4. give us a test on gerunds and infinitives

5. give a lot of examples

6. speak slowly

7. correct my pronunciation

8. teach us idioms

EXERCISE 6 Tell if the teacher expects or doesn't expect you to do the following.

EXAMPLES come on time
The teacher expects us to come on time.

wear a suit to class
The teacher doesn't expect us to wear a suit to class.

1. write perfect compositions
2. learn English in six months
3. do the homework
4. stand up to answer a question
5. raise our hands to answer a question

6. ask questions
7. study on Saturdays
8. practice English every day
9. speak English without an accent
10. use the Internet

EXERCISE 7 Change the following imperative statements to statements with an object pronoun plus an infinitive.

EXAMPLE A woman says to her husband, "Teach the children good values."
She wants him to teach the children good values.

1. My parents always said to me, "Help others."

   My parents expected _____

2. A mother says to her children, "Be kind to others."

   She wants _____

3. The father said to his children, "Give to charity."

   The father advised _____

4. Parents say to their children, "Study hard."

   Parents want _____

5. I said to you, "Work hard."

   I would like _____

6. My parents said to us, "Give money to the poor."

   My parents reminded _____

7. A father says to his daughter, "Be generous."

   He wants _____

8. My parents said to me, "Don't be selfish."

   My parents encouraged _____

9. Parents say to their children, "Be polite."

   They expect _____

EXERCISE 8   ABOUT YOU Use the words given to tell what your family wanted from you when you were growing up.

EXAMPLES   want / move away
My parents didn't want me to move away.

expect / get married
My mother expected me to get married when I graduated from college.

1. expect / respect older people
2. allow / stay out late at night
3. want / help them financially
4. expect / get good grades in school
5. encourage / have a lot of friends
6. want / be obedient
7. want / be independent
8. permit / choose my own friends
9. expect / get married
10. encourage / save money
11. advise / be honest
12. encourage / go to college

CHARITY AND VOLUNTEERING

Before You **Read**

1. Do you ever receive address labels in the mail with your name and address printed on them?

2. Do you ever watch a TV channel that asks you to send money to support it?

Read the following article. Pay special attention to verbs followed by infinitives and base forms.

There are more than 600,000 charities in the U.S. that you can give to. In addition, there are thousands of volunteer organizations. But it isn't always easy to **get** people **to give** willingly.

One way charities **get** people **to contribute** is by offering a payroll deduction at work. An employee can have a certain amount of each paycheck deducted, so the money goes to charity before the employee even sees it. If you are asked to give at your job, keep in mind that it is voluntary; no one can **make** you **give.**

Another way to **get** you **to give** is to send you something free in the mail, such as address labels with your name and address printed on them. Some people feel guilty about accepting the gift without giving something. Also some charities **have** volunteers **stand** at intersections with a can or box, asking passing drivers for donations. Often they give you something, such as candy, for your donation.

Public TV and radio stations have fundraisers. Several days out of the year, they ask for your money to support the programs you like. The station **has** volunteers **answer** phones to take your credit card number.

Besides giving money, people can volunteer their time. Some volunteers **help** kids **learn** to read; others help feed the homeless; others **help** elderly people **get** meals.

Helping others **makes** us **feel** good. To encourage us to give, the government **lets** us **deduct** our contribution, which lowers our taxes.

7.4 | Causative Verbs

Some verbs are often called *causative* verbs because one person causes, enables, or allows another to do something.

Examples	Explanation
Carnegie **persuaded** wealthy people **to give** away their money. You **convinced** me **to help** the poor. They **got** us **to contribute** to charity.	*Get, persuade, convince* are followed by an object + infinitive. *Get*, in the example on the left, means persuade.
Carnegie **helped** people **to get** an education. Volunteers **help** kids **learn** to read.	After *help* + object, either the infinitive or the base form can be used. The base form is more common.
The government **lets** you **deduct** your contribution to charity. The teacher doesn't **let** us **talk** during a test.	*Let* means permit. *Let* is followed by an object + base form. (*Permit* and *allow* are followed by an infinitive.) **Compare:** The teacher doesn't **let** us **talk**. The teacher doesn't **permit** us **to talk**.
a. No one can **make** you **give** to charity. b. Volunteering my time **makes** me **feel** good. c. A sad movie **makes** me **cry**.	*Make* is followed by an object + base form. In sentence (a), *make* means force. In sentences (b) and (c), *make* means to cause something to happen.
Public TV stations **have** volunteers **answer** the phones and take donations. The teacher **had** us **write** a composition about charity.	*Have* means to give a job or task to someone. *Have*, in this case, is followed by an object + base form.

EXERCISE 9   Fill in the blanks with the base form or the complete infinitive of the verb in parentheses ( ).

I volunteer for my local public radio station. Several times a year the station tries to persuade listeners ___*to give*___ money to the station.
(example: give)

Without listener support, the radio station could not exist. The station managers have us _____ the phones when listeners
(1 answer)

call to contribute. We let callers _____ by check or
(2 pay)

credit card. To get listeners _____, the station offers
(3 contribute)

some prizes. For example, for a $60 contribution, you can get a coffee mug. For a $100 contribution, you can get a book. Everyone can listen to public radio for free. No one makes you _____ for it.
(4 pay)

But listeners should pay for this service, if they can. They should help the station _____ for its excellent programming.
(5 pay)

EXERCISE 10 ABOUT YOU Fill in the blanks with the base form and finish the sentence.

EXAMPLE The teacher lets us ___*talk in groups when we work on a problem.*___

1. When I was a child, my parents didn't let me _____

   _____

2. When I was a child, my parents made me _____

   _____

3. During a test, the teacher doesn't let us _____

   _____

4. The teacher often has us _____

5. My parents helped me _____

7.5 | Adjective Plus Infinitive

Certain adjectives can be followed by an infinitive.

Examples	Explanation
Some people are happy **to help** others. Are you willing **to donate** your time? I am proud **to be** a volunteer. I am sad **to see** so many needy people in the world. We are pleased to be able **to help.**	Certain adjectives can be followed by an infinitive. Many of these adjectives describe a person's emotional or mental state.

Language Note:
The following adjectives can be followed by an infinitive.

afraid	eager	pleased*	sad
ashamed*	glad	prepared*	sorry
delighted*	happy	proud	surprised*
disappointed*	lucky	ready	willing

*Note: Many -ed words are adjectives.

EXERCISE 11 ABOUT YOU Fill in the blanks with an infinitive (phrase).

EXAMPLE Before I came here, I was afraid ___ *to speak English.*

1. When I left my parents' house, I was eager _____

   _____

2. When I started college or high school, I was surprised (to see, learn, find out) _____

3. When I was a child, I was afraid _____

   _____

4. Now I'm afraid _____

5. I'm happy _____

6. I'm lucky _____

7. When I left my hometown, I was sorry _____

   _____

8. When I was _____ years old, I was ready _____

   _____

EXERCISE  *Combination Exercise.* Fill in the blanks with an infinitive or a base form in this conversation between an uncle (U) and his nephew (N). Answers may vary.

U: What do you plan ___*to do*___ this summer?
  (example)

N: I wanted _____ a summer job, but I couldn't find
  (1)

one. It's going to be boring. I'm ready _____, but
  (2)

no one wants _____ me. And my parents expect me
  (3)

_____ a job. My mom won't let me
  (4)

_____ home all day and watch TV or hang out with
  (5)

my friends at the swimming pool.

U: Are you trying _____ money for your college
  (6)

education?

N: Not really. I haven't even thought about saving for college yet. I want

a job because I'm planning _____ a car.
  (7)

U: You need _____ about college too. You're going to
  (8)

graduate next year.

N: I'm planning _____ to a community college, so it
  (9)

won't be so expensive. And my parents are willing

_____ for my college tuition.
  (10)

U: Have you thought about volunteering your time this summer?

N: Not really. I just want _____ money.
  (11)

U: Don't just think about money. Try _____ about how
  (12)

you can help other people. You can help little kids

_____ to read. Or you can help
  (13)

_____ the parks by picking up garbage.
  (14)

N: I keep telling you. I just want _____ money. What
  (15)

will I get if I do those things? I won't get my car.

U: You'll get satisfaction. Helping others will make you

_____ good. And you will learn
(16)

_____ responsible. After you finish community
(17)
college and go to a four-year college, it will look good on your
application if you say you volunteered. It will help you

_____ into a good college.
(18)

A: Why are you trying so hard to get me _____ a
(19)
volunteer?

B: I volunteered when I was your age, and I found that it was more
valuable than money.

A: OK. I'll volunteer if you're willing _____ me the
(20)
money for the car.

BICYCLING TO RAISE MONEY FOR AIDS

Before You Read

1. How can one person help solve a big problem like AIDS or cancer?

2. Can you imagine riding a bike over 500 miles?

Read the following article.* Pay special attention to *in order to*
and *to*.

San Francisco

Los Angeles

California

Since the early 1980s, more than 25 million people have died of AIDS worldwide and more than 40 million people are now infected. How can one person do his or her part **to help** fight this deadly disease? Dan Pallotta decided to try. In 1994, at the age of 32, he organized a bike ride from San Francisco to Los Angeles **in order to call** attention to the AIDS epidemic. He found 471 people willing to bike the 525 miles (845 km) in seven days. **To raise** money, each rider asked friends and relatives to give donations in support of the ride. Since 1994, more than 124,000 people have taken part in the rides and more than $222 million have been raised for AIDS research.

*Statistics are as of May 2003.

(*continued*)

These rides take place in many locations in the U.S. (Alaska, Minneapolis to Chicago, Boston to New York, San Francisco to Los Angeles). Of course, **to ride** such a long distance, a rider has to be in good shape. Many riders prepare for months ahead **in order to be** ready for the ride. But even riders in good shape sometimes need a break. Vans ride along with the cyclists **in order to pick up** anyone who needs to rest for a while.

At the end of the ride, cyclists are tired, but they have the satisfaction of having finished the ride and of raising money **to fight** the problem of AIDS.

7.6 | Using the Infinitive to Show Purpose

Example	Explanation
Dan organized the bike ride **in order to** raise money for AIDS. Vans ride along with the cyclists **in order to** pick up tired riders. **In order to** ride a long distance, you have to be in good shape.	*In order to* shows purpose. It answers the question "Why?" or "What for?"
Dan organized the bike ride **to** raise money for AIDS. Vans ride along with the cyclists **to** pick up tired riders. **To** ride a long distance, you have to be in good shape.	*In order to* can be shortened. We can simply use *to*.
a. **In order to help others,** Carnegie gave away his money. b. Carnegie gave away his money **in order to help others.**	a. The purpose clause can precede the main clause. Use a comma to separate the two clauses. b. The purpose clause can follow the main clause. Don't use a comma.

EXERCISE 13 Fill in the blanks to complete the sentences. Answers may vary.

EXAMPLE In order to <u>*learn more about volunteering*</u>, you can use the Internet. You can find lots of information there.

1. Carnegie donated his money to _____ libraries.

2. You can volunteer in order to _____ job experience. But in order to _____ money, you need a paying job.

3. To _____ a job, you need experience. To _____ experience, you need a job.

4. You can volunteer your time in order to _____ people. There are many people who need help.

5. Dan Pallotta organized bike rides in order to _____.

EXERCISE 14 Complete each sentence. Answers may vary.

EXAMPLE Many students have jobs in order ___*to pay for their education*___.

1. I want to learn English in order to _____.
2. I came to this school to _____.
3. We're studying this lesson to _____.
4. I use my dictionary to _____.
5. Many people use spell-check in order to _____.
6. Many people use Caller ID to _____.
7. I _____ in order to relax.
8. I _____ to learn new words.
9. You should register early to _____.
10. Many students apply for financial aid to _____.
11. If you aren't satisfied with your score on the TOEFL test, you can take it a second time in order to _____ your score.
12. If you're absent, you can call a classmate to _____.
13. You need a password in order to _____.
14. You can use the Web site "weather.com" to _____.
15. Many people use e-mail to _____.

7.7 | Infinitive as Subject

Examples	Explanation
It's good **to help** other people. **It** was Carnegie's dream **to build** libraries. **It**'s hard **to ride** a bike 500 miles.	An infinitive phrase can be the subject of a sentence. We usually begin the sentence with *it* and put the infinitive phrase at the end of the sentence.
It is important **for rich people** to set an example. It is necessary **for bike riders** to train for the long ride.	*For* + an object can give the infinitive a specific subject.
It costs a lot of money **to build** a library. **It takes** many days **to ride** from Los Angeles to San Francisco.	An infinitive is often used after *cost* + money and *take* + time.
Carnegie was a poor immigrant, but it didn't take **him** long **to become** rich. How much did it cost **him to build** a library?	An indirect object can follow *take* and *cost*.
To build libraries was Carnegie's dream. **To give** money away is the best thing rich people can do. **To help** others gives a person satisfaction.	Sometimes we begin a sentence with an infinitive phrase. A sentence that begins with an infinitive is very formal.

EXERCISE 15 Complete each statement with an infinitive phrase.

EXAMPLE It isn't polite _____*to interrupt a conversation.*_____

1. It's dangerous _____

2. It isn't healthy _____

3. It isn't polite _____

4. It's illegal _____

5. It's a good idea _____

6. It's the teacher's responsibility _____

7. It costs a lot of money _____

8. It's important for me _____

9. It's boring for the students _____

10. It's fun for children _____

11. It's easy for Americans _____

12. It took me a long time _____

13. It cost me a lot of money _____

14. It will probably take me a long time _____

EXERCISE 16 Make sentences with the words given.

EXAMPLE dangerous / children
It's dangerous for children to play with matches. _____

1. fun / children

_____

2. necessary / children

_____

3. important / a family

_____

4. difficult / a large family

_____

5. necessary / working parents

_____

6. difficult / women in my native culture

_____

7. hard / single parents

_____

8. difficult / the teacher

_____

EXERCISE 17 Complete each statement. Begin with *it*.

EXAMPLES   _It's impossible_____ to be perfect.

It costs me 30¢ a minute to make a long-distance phone call to my hometown.

1. _____to work hard.

2. _____ to fall in love.

3. _____ to get married.

4. _____ to make a mistake in English.

5. _____ to be lonely.

6. _____ to help other people.

7. _____ to take a taxi from this school to my house.

8. _____ to eat lunch in a restaurant.

9. _____ to go to college.

10. _____ to buy my textbooks.

11. _____ to learn English.

12. _____ to give away money.

13. _____ to have a lot of friends.

14. _____ to travel.

15. _____ to ride your bike from New York to Boston.

EXERCISE 18 Change these statements to make them less formal by starting them with *it*.

EXAMPLE   To raise money for charity is a good thing.

_____It's a good thing to raise money for charity._____

1. To ride a bike 500 miles is not easy.

_____

2. To fight disease takes a lot of money.

_____

3. To give away money is the responsibility of the rich.

_____

4. To produce high quality public radio takes a lot of money.

_____

5. To build libraries was Carnegie's dream.

6. To raise money for AIDS was Dan Pallotta's goal.

7.8 | Infinitive with *Too* and *Enough*

Too shows that the adjective or adverb is excessive for a specific purpose. *Enough* shows that an adjective, adverb, or noun is sufficient for a specific purpose.

Examples	Explanation
Young Carnegie was **too poor to enter** the library. You drive **too slowly to drive** on the highway. She's **too old to cook** for herself. A volunteer delivers her meals.	Word Order: *too* + adjective / adverb + infinitive
I have **too much work to do,** so I have no time to volunteer. There are **too many problems** in the world **to solve** in one day.	Word Order: *too much* + noncount noun + infinitive *too many* + plural count noun + infinitive
Are you **strong enough to ride** a bike for 500 miles? She trained **hard enough to finish** the AIDS ride.	Word Order: Adjective / adverb + *enough* + infinitive
Carnegie had **enough money to build** libraries. I don't have **enough time to volunteer** this summer.	Word Order: *enough* + noun + infinitive
There is enough volunteer work **for everyone** to do. The bike ride is too hard **for me** to do.	The infinitive phrase can be preceded by *for* + object.
a. I can't volunteer this summer because I'm **too busy.** b. Carnegie could build libraries because he had **enough money.**	Sometimes the infinitive phrase can be omitted. It is understood from the context. a. too busy to volunteer b. enough money to build libraries

EXERCISE 19 Fill in the blanks with *too* + adjective or adverb, or *too many /
much* + noun. Answers may vary.

EXAMPLE It's ___*too late*___ for a student to register for this semester.

1. This lesson is _____ to finish in one class period.

2. The cafeteria is _____ for me to study there.

3. Some Americans speak English _____ for me to
understand.

4. The bus is sometimes _____ for me to get a seat.

5. It's _____ to go swimming today.

6. It's _____ to predict next week's weather.

7. She earns _____ to qualify for a scholarship.

8. I can't go out with you. I have _____ to do this
afternoon.

EXERCISE 20 Fill in the blanks with *enough* + noun, or adjective / adverb +
enough. Answers may vary.

EXAMPLE I don't speak English ___*well enough*___ to be in a college-credit writing
course.

1. This exercise is _____ to finish in a few minutes.

2. I don't type _____ to write my compositions by
computer.

3. He doesn't have _____ to do all the things he
wants to do.

4. She's only 16 years old. She's not _____ to get
married.

5. You didn't run _____ to win the race.

6. He doesn't have _____ to buy new computer.

7.9 | Gerunds—An Overview

To form a gerund, put an *-ing* ending on a verb. A gerund is used as a noun (subject or object).

Examples	Explanation
Subject a. **Tennis** is fun. b. **Swimming** is fun. *Object* a. I enjoy **summer.** b. I enjoy **helping** people.	You can use a gerund in the same place you use any subject or object.
Contributing money is one way to help. **Volunteering** can give you a lot of satisfaction.	A gerund (phrase) can be used as the subject of a sentence.
I enjoy **volunteering my time.** I can't imagine **riding a bike** for 500 miles.	A gerund (phrase) can be used as the object of a sentence.
I'm excited *about* **going on a bike trip.** Let's volunteer this summer instead *of* **wasting our time at the beach.**	A gerund (phrase) can be used as the object of a preposition.
Carnegie accused rich people of **not helping** others. **Not being** able to enter a library made Carnegie feel bad.	To make a gerund negative, put *not* before the gerund.
I appreciate **being corrected** when I make a mistake. She enjoys **being treated** like a queen.	A gerund can be passive: *being* + past participle.

HELPING OTHERS GET AN EDUCATION

Before You Read

1. Do you think that all rich people like to live in luxury?
2. Do you know anyone who is very generous?

🎧 Read the following article. Pay special attention to gerunds.

When we think of philanthropists, we usually think of the very rich and famous, like Andrew Carnegie. However, Matel Dawson, who was a forklift driver in Michigan, was an ordinary man who did extraordinary things.

Dawson started **working** at Ford Motor Company in 1940 for $1.15 an hour. By **working** hard, **saving** carefully, and **investing** his money wisely, he became rich. But he didn't care about **owning** expensive cars or **taking** fancy vacations. Instead of **spending** his money on himself, he enjoyed **giving** it away. Since 1995, he donated more than $1 million for college scholarships to help poor students who want to get an education.

Matel Dawson, 1921–2002

Why did Dawson insist on **giving** his money away to college students? One reason was that he did not have the opportunity to finish school. He had to drop out of school after the seventh grade to help support his poor family. He realized the importance of **having** an education and regretted not **having** the opportunity. Also, he learned about **giving** from his parents. He watched them work hard, save their money, and help others less fortunate. His mother made Dawson promise to always give something back. He was grateful to his parents for **teaching** him the importance of **helping** others.

When he became rich, he didn't change his lifestyle. He continued **driving** his old car and **living** in a one-bedroom apartment. And he didn't stop **working** until shortly before he died at the age of 81. When asked why he worked long past the time when most people retire, he replied, "It keeps me **going**, **knowing** I'm helping somebody."

7.10 | Gerund as Subject

Examples	Explanation
Working gave Dawson satisfaction. **Giving away money** made Dawson feel good.	A gerund or a gerund phrase can be the subject of the sentence.
Helping others *gives* a person pleasure.	A gerund subject takes a singular verb.
Not finishing school can affect your whole life.	To make a gerund negative, put *not* before the gerund.

EXERCISE 21 Fill in the blanks with a gerund.

EXAMPLE ____*Helping*____ others made Dawson feel good.

1. _____ in a factory was not an easy job.

2. Not _____ an education always bothered Dawson.

3. _____ an education is expensive in the U.S.

4. _____ money didn't give Dawson satisfaction.

5. _____ an old car was not a problem for Dawson.

6. _____ a vacation wasn't important for Dawson.

7. _____ that he was helping people was very important to Dawson.

EXERCISE 22 Complete each statement.

EXAMPLE Leaving home ____*was the most difficult decision I have ever made.*____

1. Making new friends _____ _____

2. Changing old habits _____

3. Finding an apartment _____

4. Thinking about my future _____

5. Getting a job _____

EXERCISE 23 Complete each statement with a gerund (phrase) as the subject.

EXAMPLE ____*Taking a warm bath*____ relaxes me at the end of the day.

1. _____ is difficult for people who don't speak English.

2. _____ is an important decision in a person's life.

3. _____ is a healthy activity.

4. _____ isn't good for you (is an unhealthy activity).

5. _____ makes me feel proud.

7.11 | Gerund After Prepositions and Nouns

Examples	Pattern
Dawson **didn't care about owning** fancy things. He **believed in helping** others.	Verb + preposition + gerund
Carnegie was **famous for building** libraries. Dawson was **concerned about helping** poor college students. Dan Pallotta was **successful at raising** money for AIDS.	Adjective + preposition + gerund
Dawson **thanked his parents for teaching** him to save money.	Verb + object + preposition + gerund
Dawson didn't **spend money going** on vacations or **eating** in expensive restaurants. He didn't **have a hard time saving** money.	A gerund is used directly after the noun in the following expressions: *have a difficult time, have difficulty, have experience, have fun, have a good time, have a hard time, have a problem, have trouble, spend time, spend money*

EXERCISE 24 Complete the questions with a gerund (phrase). Then ask another student these questions.

EXAMPLE Are you lazy about _____ *writing compositions?* _____

1. Are you worried about _____
2. Are you interested in _____
3. Do you ever think about _____
4. Were you excited about _____
5. Do you ever dream about _____

EXERCISE 25 ABOUT YOU Fill in the blanks with a gerund phrase.

EXAMPLE I had problems _____ *getting a student loan.* _____

1. I had a hard time _____
2. I have a lot of experience _____
3. I don't have much experience _____
4. I spent a lot of money _____
5. I don't like to spend my time _____

6. I have a lot of fun _____

7. I don't have a good time _____

8. I don't have a problem _____

7.12 | Using the Correct Preposition

It is important to choose the correct preposition after a verb, adjective, or noun.

Preposition Combinations		Common Phrases	Examples
Verb + Preposition	verb + *about*	care about complain about dream about forget about talk about think about worry about	I **care about helping** people. Carnegie **dreamed about opening** public libraries.
	verb + *to*	adjust to look forward to object to	I am **looking forward to volunteering.**
	verb + *on*	depend on insist on plan on	I **insist on helping** my grandmother.
	verb + *in*	believe in succeed in	Does he **believe in giving** to those in need?
Verb + Object + Preposition	verb + object + *of*	accuse . . . of suspect . . . of	He **accused me of leaving** work early.
	verb + object + *for*	apologize to . . . for blame . . . for forgive . . . for thank . . . for	They **thanked me for taking** care of their children.
	verb + object + *from*	keep . . . from prevent . . . from prohibit . . . from stop . . . from	Don't let him **keep you from getting** to your job.
	verb + object + *about*	warn . . . about	The teacher **warned the students about talking** in the library.

(*continued*)

Preposition Combinations		Common Phrases	Examples
Adjective + Preposition	adjective + *of*	afraid of capable of guilty of proud of tired of	I'm **afraid of going** out at night.
	adjective + *about*	concerned about excited about upset about worried about	The students are **worried about passing** the exam.
	adjective + *for*	responsible for famous for grateful . . . to . . . for	The victims are **grateful to the** volunteers **for helping.**
	adjective + *at*	good at successful at	Bill Gates is very **good at giving** a lot of money away.
	adjective + *to*	accustomed to used to	I'm not **accustomed to wearing** glasses.
	adjective + *in*	interested in	Are you **interested in getting** a volunteer job?
Noun + Preposition	noun + *of*	in danger of in favor of the purpose of	The students are all **in favor of having** class outside.
	noun + *for*	a need for a reason for an excuse for technique for	What is your **reason for going** home early?

Language Notes:

1. *Plan, afraid,* and *proud* can be followed by an infinitive too.

    I plan **on buying** a laptop. / I plan **to buy** a laptop.

    I'm afraid **of going** out at night. / I'm afraid **to go** out at night.

    He's proud **of being** a volunteer. / He's proud **to be** a volunteer.

2. Notice that in some expressions, *to* is a preposition followed by a gerund, not part of an infinitive.

    Compare:

    I need *to wear* glasses. (infinitive)

    I'm not accustomed *to wearing* glasses. (*to* + gerund)

EXERCISE 26 Fill in the blanks with a preposition (if necessary) and the gerund of the verb in parentheses ( ). In some cases, no preposition is necessary.

A: My father's going to retire next month. He's worried _about having_
(example: have)

nothing to do.

B: I don't blame him _____ worried. For a lot of people,
(1 be)

their self-worth depends _____, and when they
(2 work)

retire, they feel worthless.

A: My mother is afraid that he'll spend all his time _____
(3 watch)

TV. Besides, she's not accustomed _____ him home
(4 have)

all day.

B: Doesn't he have any interests?

A: Well, he's interested _____, but he lives in an apartment
(5 garden)

now so he doesn't have a garden. When he had a house, he was always

proud _____ the nicest garden on the block.
(6 have)

B: Has he thought _____ at the Botanical Gardens?
(7 volunteer)

A: Do they use volunteers?

B: I think so. He would have a great time _____ there.
(8 work)

A: You're right. He would be good _____ tours because
(9 give)

he knows so much about flowers. This would give him a reason

_____ up in the morning. I'm grateful to you
(10 get)

_____ me this idea. I can't wait to tell him.
(11 give)

B: I'm sure your mother will be grateful too.

EXERCISE 27 ABOUT YOU Ask a question with the words given. Use the correct preposition (if necessary) and a gerund. Another student will answer.

EXAMPLES fond / read

A: Are you fond of reading?
B: Yes, I am.

care / get a good grade

A: Do you care about getting a good grade?
B: Of course I do.

1. have trouble / understand spoken English

2. lazy / do the homework

3. have a technique / learn new words

4. afraid / fail this course

5. good / spell English words

6. interested / study computer programming

7. have experience / work with computers

8. think / buy a house some day

7.13 | Verbs Followed by Gerunds

Examples	Explanation
Dawson enjoyed **giving** money away. He couldn't imagine not **helping** others. Students appreciate **receiving** financial aid.	Many verbs are followed by a gerund.

The following verbs take a gerund.

admit	delay	finish	permit	recommend
advise	deny	imagine	postpone	resent
appreciate	discuss	keep (on)	practice	risk
avoid	dislike	mind[2]	put off[3]	stop
can't help[1]	enjoy	miss	quit	suggest
consider				

Do you **go shopping** every day? Do you like to **go fishing**?	*Go* + gerund is used in many idiomatic expressions of sport and recreation.

Below are expressions with *go* + gerund.

go boating	go fishing	go sailing	go skiing
go bowling	go hiking	go shopping	go swimming
go camping	go hunting	go sightseeing	
go dancing	go jogging	go skating	

Language Notes:
[1] *Can't help* means to have no control: When I see a sad movie, I *can't help* crying.
[2] I *mind* means that something bothers me. I *don't mind* means that something is OK with me; it doesn't bother me: Do you *mind* living with your parents? No, I don't *mind*.
[3] *Put off* means postpone: I can't *put off* buying a car. I need one now.

EXERCISE 28 Fill in the blanks to complete these statements about the reading on Matel Dawson. Answers may vary.

EXAMPLE Matel Dawson liked _____*helping students.*_____

1. He regretted not _____

2. Students appreciated _____ from Dawson.

3. He didn't mind _____ an old car.

4. He couldn't imagine not _____, so he didn't retire.

5. He didn't mind _____ in a small apartment.

6. He kept on _____ until shortly before he died at the age of 81.

EXERCISE 29 ABOUT YOU Complete the sentences with a gerund (phrase).

EXAMPLE I avoid _____*walking alone at night.*_____

1. The teacher doesn't permit _____

2. I don't mind _____

3. It's difficult to quit _____

4. I enjoy _____

5. I don't enjoy _____

6. I can't imagine _____

7. I don't like to go _____

8. I avoid _____

9. I appreciate _____

10. I often put off _____

7.14 | Verbs Followed by Gerund or Infinitive

Examples	Explanation
Dawson liked **giving** money away. He liked **to give** money away. He started **working** in 1940. He started **to work** in 1940.	Some verbs can be followed by either a gerund or an infinitive with no difference in meaning.

Language Note:
The verbs below can be followed by either a gerund or an infinitive with no difference in meaning.

begin	continue	like	prefer
can't stand*	hate	love	start

* *Can't stand* means can't tolerate: I *can't stand* living in a cold climate.

EXERCISE 30 In the following sentences, change gerunds to infinitives and infinitives to gerunds.

EXAMPLES He began to work at 4:30.
He began working at 4:30.

I love sleeping on the beach.
I love to sleep on the beach.

1. Do you prefer to study in the morning?

2. She hates washing the dishes.

3. When did you begin studying English?

4. If you continue talking about politics, I'm going to leave.

5. They can't stand to watch violent movies.

6. I love to get letters, don't you?

EXERCISE 31 This is a conversation between a teenager and his older brother. Fill in the blanks with an appropriate gerund or infinitive. It doesn't matter which one you use.

A: I want to work this summer, but I can't decide what to do.

B: How about volunteering in a museum?

A: I can't stand _____*being*_____ indoors all day. I prefer
        (example)

_____ outdoors.
        (1)

B: You're a great swimmer. Why don't you volunteer to teach kids how to swim?

A: I hate _____ with kids. It's hard work.
        (2)

B: Well, what do you like?

A: I love _____ at the beach.
  (3)

B: Maybe you should get a job as a lifeguard.

A: Great idea! I'll start _____ for a job tomorrow.
  (4)

B: That's what you said yesterday.

A: I guess I'm lazy. I just don't like _____.
  (5)

7.15 | Infinitive and Gerund as Subject

Examples	Explanation
It is expensive **to go** to college. **It** is important **to have** a college education. **It** makes me feel good **to give** money to poor people.	An infinitive phrase can be the subject of a sentence. We usually begin the sentence with *it* and put the infinitive phrase at the end of the sentence.
Going to college is expensive. **Having** a college education is important. **Giving** money to poor people makes me feel good.	A gerund phrase can be used as the subject.
To pay for college is difficult for most families. **To build** libraries was Carnegie's dream. **To give** money away is the best thing rich people can do, according to Carnegie.	Sometimes we begin a sentence with an infinitive phrase. A sentence that begins with an infinitive is very formal.

EXERCISE **32** Change these statements. Change the subject to a gerund form.

EXAMPLE It is wonderful to help others.

Helping others is wonderful. _____

1. It costs a lot of money to go to college.

    _____

2. It is hard to work and study at the same time.

    _____

3. It is important to invest your money wisely.

    _____

4. It is difficult to work in a factory.

    _____

5. It can be boring to do the same thing every day.

    _____

6. It is satisfying to help others.

_____

7. It is a challenge to ride a bike for 500 miles.

_____

8. It is necessary to ask viewers to contribute to public TV.

_____

7.16 | Gerund or Infinitive After a Verb: Differences in Meaning

After *stop, remember,* and *try,* the meaning of the sentence depends on whether you follow the verb with a gerund or an infinitive.

Examples	Explanation
a. Dawson loved to work. He didn't **stop working** until he was 80. b. Dawson wanted to finish school, but he **stopped to get** a job.	a. *Stop* + gerund = Quit or discontinue an activity b. *Stop* + infinitive = Quit one activity in order to start another activity
a. Do you **remember reading** about Carnegie? b. Dawson's mother said, "Always **remember to help** other people."	a. *Remember* + gerund = Remember that something happened earlier b. *Remember* + infinitive = Remember something and then do it
a. Dawson has always had a simple lifestyle. When he became rich, he **tried living** a fancier lifestyle, but it didn't bring him satisfaction. a. I always write my compositions by hand. I **tried writing** them on a computer, but I don't type fast enough. b. Carnegie **tried to enter** a library when he was young, but he was told it was for members only. b. Mary **tried to ride** her bike 500 miles, but she couldn't.	a. *Try* + gerund = Experiment with something new. You do something one way, and then, if that doesn't work, you try a different method. b. *Try* + infinitive = Make an effort or an attempt

EXERCISE 33 Fill in the blanks with the gerund or infinitive of the verb in parentheses ( ).

EXAMPLES Stop ___*bothering*___ me. I'm trying to study.
                                (bother)

The teacher always says, "Remember ___*to do*___ your homework."
                                           (do)

1. When the teacher came in, the students stopped _____.
                                                                    (talk)

2. When you learn more English, you will stop _____ your
                                                                (use)

   dictionary so much.

3. When you're tired of studying, stop _____ a break.
                                                          (take)

4. I saw my friend in the hall, and I stopped _____ to her.
   (speak)

5. My sister and I had a fight, and we stopped _____
   (speak)
   to each other. We haven't spoken to each other for two weeks.

6. Cyclists in the AIDS ride often stop _____.
   (rest)

7. If they are tired, they can stop _____ their bicycles.
   (ride)

8. There's a van that will stop _____ up tired cyclists.
   (pick)

9. The teacher usually remembers _____ the homework papers.
   (return)

10. You should remember _____ an infinitive after certain verbs.
    (use)

11. Will you remember _____ the homework during spring break?
    (do)

12. Do you remember _____ the passive voice last month?
    (learn)

13. Remember _____ the passive voice when the subject does
    (use)
    not perform the action of the verb.

14. I remember not _____ much English a few years ago.
    (understand)

15. I remember _____ the present perfect tense even
    (study)
    though I don't always use it correctly.

16. I always try _____ a few new words every day.
    (learn)

17. I need more money. I'm going to try _____ a part-time job.
    (find)

18. Susan tried _____ her bike 100 miles, but she couldn't
    (ride)
    because she was out of shape.

19. I need to find out information about a new bike. I went to the
    company's Web site, but I couldn't find the information I needed. I
    tried _____ the Webmaster, but I got no answer. I tried
    (e-mail)
    _____ the phone number on the Web site, but I didn't get a
    (call)
    person to talk to. I tried _____ a letter by postal mail. I'm
    (send)
    still waiting for an answer.

EXERCISE 34  Read the following conversation between a son (S) and his mother (M). Fill in the blanks with the gerund or infinitive of the word in parentheses ( ).

S: Hi, Mom. I'm calling to say good-bye. I'm leaving tomorrow.

M: Where are you going?

S: To California.

M: You didn't tell me.

S: Of course, I did. I remember ___telling___ you about it when I was at
(example: tell)

your house for dinner last week.

M: Oh, yes. Now I remember _____ you say something about it.
(1 hear)

Why are you going?

S: I have a good friend there, and I'm going to do an AIDS ride with

him. We're going to try _____ it together.
(2 finish)

M: Have I met your friend?

S: He was here last year at my birthday party. You met him then.

M: I don't remember _____ him. Anyway, how are you
(3 meet)

getting to California?

S: I'm driving.

M: Alone?

S: Yes.

M: If you get tired, you should stop _____ at a rest area.
(4 rest)

And you can stop _____ a cup of coffee every few hours.
(5 get)

S: I will.

M: Don't stop _____ strangers. It could be dangerous.
(6 pick up)

S: Of course, I won't.

M: And remember _____ your cell phone on in case
(7 leave)

I want to call you.

S: I will. Mom, stop _____ so much. And stop
(8 worry)

_____ me so much advice. I'm 24 years old!
(9 give)

M: Try _____. I'm your mother. Of course, I worry.
(10 understand)

Before You Read

1. After reading the articles in this lesson, can you think of ways you'd like to volunteer to help others?

2. What do you think motivates people to volunteer?

Read the following personal account of Mimi, a woman who went on several AIDS rides. Pay special attention to *used to*, *be used to*, and *get used to*.

Alaska

Before I went on my AIDS ride, I **used to think** that one person's contribution is not very important. But I was wrong. In 1998, I went on my first AIDS ride in California, from San Francisco to Los Angeles.

Even though I bike to and from work every day (20 miles round trip), I **wasn't used to riding** long distances. Also, I live in Chicago, where the land is flat so I **wasn't used to riding** in hills and mountains. I trained for about six months before the ride, riding at least 150 miles a week.

I **used to own** a ten-speed road bike, but I realized that I would need something better for the long, hilly ride. I bought a new 24-speed mountain bike. This new bicycle helped me a lot in the California trip. It was so satisfying to complete the ride. I raised almost $5,000 for AIDS research. I felt so good about it that I started looking for more rides to do.

In 2001, I did the Alaska ride, which was especially difficult. It was much colder than expected. Some of the riders **couldn't get used to** the cold and had to quit. But I'm proud to say that I finished it and went on to do four more AIDS rides.

7.17 | *Used To / Be Used To / Get Used To*

Used to + base form and *be used to* + gerund have completely different meanings.

Examples	Explanation
Mimi **used to** own a ten-speed bike. Now she owns a 24-speed bike.	*Used to* + base form shows that an activity was repeated or habitual in the past. This activity has been discontinued.
She **used to** think that one person couldn't make a difference. Now she knows that every person's contribution counts.	For the negative, use *didn't use to*. **Note:** Omit the *d* in the negative.
Libraries **used to be** for rich people only. Now anyone can use the library.	
I didn't **use to** speak English at all. Now I speak it fairly well.	
Mimi **is used to riding** her bike in Chicago, which is flat.	*Be used to* + gerund or noun means "be accustomed to." The sentences to the left describe a person's habits. They show what is normal and comfortable.
She **is used to riding** in nice weather.	
She **isn't used to** cold wind in August.	For the negative, use *be + not + use**d** to*.
Some of the riders **couldn't get used to** the cold and wind and had to quit.	*Get used to* + gerund or noun means "become accustomed to." Often we use *can, can't, could,* or *couldn't* before *get used to*.
Dawson **couldn't get used to spending** money on himself.	For the negative, use *can't* or *couldn't + get used to*.
I'm from Arizona. I **can't get used to** the cold Chicago winters.	**Note:** Do not omit the *d* in the negative.
My friend comes from India, where they drive on the left side of the street. He had to **get used to driving** on the right side in the U.S.	

Pronunciation Note:
The *d* in *used to* is not pronounced.

EXERCISE 35 Finish these statements. Answers may vary.

EXAMPLE I used to ___*go everywhere by bus*___, but now I have a car and drive everywhere.

1. My uncle used to _____, but now he's rich.

2. I used to _____ a stick shift car, but now I drive an automatic.

3. They used to _____ an apartment, but now they have a house.

4. When she was younger, she used to _____, but now she stays home on Saturday nights.

5. He used to _____ money on foolish things, but now he saves his money.

6. My college used to _____ Northeast College, but they changed the name. Now it's called Kennedy College.

EXERCISE 36 ABOUT YOU Write sentences comparing the way you used to live with the way you live now.

EXAMPLES *I used to live with my whole family. Now I live alone.*

I used to work in a restaurant. Now I'm a full-time student.

I didn't use to speak English at all. Now I speak English pretty well.

Ideas for sentences:

school	job	hobbies	fashions
apartment / house	family life	friends	

1. _____

2. _____

3. _____

4. _____

5. _____

EXERCISE 37 A student wrote about things that are new for her in the U.S. Fill in the blanks with a gerund or a noun.

EXAMPLE I'm not used to _shopping in large supermarkets_. In my native country, I shopped in small stores.

1. I'm not used to _____ a small apartment. In my native country, we lived in a big house.

2. I'm not used to _____. In my native country, it's warm all year round.

3. I'm not used to _____ a student. I'm 35 years old, and I've been out of school for 15 years.

4. I'm not used to _____. I studied British English in my native country.

5. I'm not used to _____ on Sundays. In my native country, Sunday is a day when people rest, not shop and do laundry.

6. I'm not used to _____ in class. In my native country, the teacher talks and the students only listen and write.

7. I'm not used to _____ on the right side of the road. In my native country, we drive on the left side of the road.

EXERCISE 38   ABOUT YOU Fill in the blanks to make three different sentences beginning with "I'm not used to . . . "

EXAMPLE   *I'm not used to wearing a coat in the winter.*

1. _____

2. _____

3. _____

EXERCISE 39   ABOUT YOU Fill in the blanks with three different answers.

EXAMPLES   When I came to this city, it was hard for me to get used to:

living in a small apartment. _____

American pronunciation. _____

When I came to this city, it was hard for me to get used to:

1. _____

2. _____

3. _____

EXERCISE 40   Here is a story of a San Francisco woman who did the Alaska AIDS ride. Circle the correct words in parentheses ( ) to complete the story.

    In 2000 I went on the AIDS bike ride in Alaska. My friends told me about it and asked me to join them. At first I was afraid. My friends are good bike riders. They (*used to / are used to*) (*ride / riding*) long
                                    (1)   *(2)*
distances because they do it all the time. They persuaded me to try it because it was for such a good cause.

    To get ready for the ride, I had to make some lifestyle changes. (*I'm / I*) used to be a little overweight, so I had to slim down and get in
    (3)
shape. First, I went on a diet. (*I / I'm*) used to a lot of meat, but now I
                            (4)
try to eat mostly vegetables and fish. Also, I decided to get more exercise. I used to (*take / taking*) the bus to work every day, but I
                    (5)
decided to start riding my bike to work. I work ten miles from home, so it was hard for me at first. But little by little, I (*got used to / used to*) it.
                                              (6)
On the weekends, I started to take longer rides. Eventually I got used to (*ride / riding*) about 45–50 miles a day.
    (7)

When the time came for the AIDS ride, I thought I was prepared. I live in San Francisco, which is hilly, so I was used to (*ride / riding*) up
(8)
and down hills. But it's not cold in San Francisco. On some days the temperature in Alaska was only 25 degrees (F) with strong winds. At first I (*wasn't / couldn't*) get used to the cold and sometimes had to ride
(9)
in the van. It was especially hard to (*used / get used*) to the strong winds.
(10)
But little by little, I got (*use / used*) to it.
(11)

I am proud to say I was one of the 1,600 riders who finished the ride. I didn't (*use / used*) to think that one person could make a difference,
(12)
but I raised close to $4,000. As a group we raised $4 million. And I've become a much healthier person because of this experience.

GLOBAL VOLUNTEERS

Before You Read

1. Do you ever think about all the poor people in the world?

2. How can we help poor people in other countries?

Read the following article. Pay special attention to base forms and *-ing* forms after sense-perception verbs (*see*, *listen*, *hear*, etc.).

When Michele Gran and Bud Philbrook were planning to get married in 1979, they were planning to take a relaxing honeymoon cruise. But whenever Michele turned on the world news, she **saw** people **living** in poverty. She **saw** children **go** without proper nutrition and education. Instead of their planned honeymoon, Michele suggested that they spend a week helping poor people in Guatemala.

When their friends and relatives **listened** to them **tell** about their unusual honeymoon, they became interested in how they could also help. In 1984, Bud and Michele established Global Volunteers, an organization that helps people throughout the world. Since then, they have sent almost 13,000 volunteers to 25 countries. Volunteers work together with the local people on projects, such as building schools in Ghana or taking care of orphans in Romania.

Bud used to practice law and Michele used to work in state government, but in the early '90s, they quit their jobs to spend all their time with Global Volunteers.

7.18 | Sense-Perception Verbs

After sense-perception verbs (*hear, listen to, feel, smell, see, watch, observe*), we can use either the *-ing* form or the base form with only a slight difference in meaning.

a. Their friends **listened to** them **tell** about their unusual honeymoon. b. Matel Dawson **saw** his mother **work** hard.	The base form shows that a person sensed (*saw, heard,* etc.) something from start to finish. a. They listened to Bud and Michele tell the whole story. b. All his life, Dawson saw his mother's work habits.
a. Michele **saw** people **living** in poverty. b. When I entered the classroom, I **heard** the teacher **talking** about volunteer programs.	The *-ing* form shows that something is sensed while it is in progress. a. Michele saw people while they were living in poverty. b. I heard the teacher while she was talking about volunteer programs.

EXERCISE 41 Fill in the blanks with the base form or *-ing* form of the verb in parentheses ( ). In many cases, both forms are possible.

By their example, my parents always taught me to help others. One time when I was a child going to a birthday party with my father, we saw a

small boy ___walking___ alone on the street. As we approached him, we
    (example: walk)

heard him _____. My father went up to him and asked him
    (1 cry)

what was wrong. The boy said that he was lost. I saw my father

_____ his hand and heard him _____ the boy
    (2 take)   *(3 tell)*

that he would help him find his parents. My father called the police on his cell phone. Even though we were in a hurry to go to the party, my father insisted on staying with the boy until the police arrived. I really wanted to go to the party and started to cry. I felt my father

_____ my hand and talk to me softly. He said, "We
    (4 take)

can't enjoy the party while this little boy is alone and helpless." Before

the police arrived, I saw a woman _____ frantically in
                     (5 run)

our direction. It was the boy's mother. She was so grateful to my father for helping her son that she offered to give him money. I heard my father

_____ her, "I can't take money from you. I'm happy to
    (6 tell)

be of help to your son."

Another time we saw new neighbors _____ into
(7 move)
the house next door. We saw them _____ to move a piano
(8 struggle)
into the apartment. We had planned a picnic that day, but my parents
suggested that we help them. I heard my mother _____
(9 tell)
my father, "We can have a picnic another day. But these people need to
move in today. Let's offer them a hand." There are many other cases
where I saw my parents _____ their own pleasure to
(10 sacrifice)
help others.

I hear so many children today _____, "I want" or
(11 say)
"Buy me" or "Give me." I think it's important to teach children to think
of others before they think of themselves. If they see their parents

_____ others, they will probably grow up to be
(12 help)
charitable people.

EXERCISE 42

Combination Exercise. Read the true story of a young woman,
Charity Bell, who became a foster mother (a person who gives
temporary care to a child in her home). Fill in the blanks with the
correct form of the verb in parentheses ( ) and add prepositions
to complete the story.

It's difficult _____*for*_____ a college student _____*to have*_____ time for
(example)   (example; have)
anything else but studying. But Charity Bell, a student at Harvard, made

time in her busy schedule _____ babies in need. Bell, a single
(1 help)
woman, became a foster mother.

Bell became interested in _____ needy babies when she was 23
(2 help)
years old. At that time, she volunteered at a hospital for very sick

children. The volunteer organization wanted her _____ to the kids
(3 read)
and _____ games with them. The parents of these very sick
(4 play)
children were there too, but they were often too tired _____ or
(5 read)
_____ with their kids. They were grateful to her _____
(6 play)   (7 help)
them. One day she went to the hospital and heard a baby _____
(8 cry)
so loudly in the next room. She went into that room and picked up the

baby; the baby immediately stopped _____. She stayed with the
(9 cry)

baby for a few hours. When she began _____ (10 leave), the baby started

_____ (11 cry) again. Bell asked the nurse about this baby, and the nurse told her that the baby was taken away from her parents and they couldn't find a temporary home for her.

The next day, Bell made some phone calls and started _____ (12 learn) about how to be a foster parent. She made herself available to help on

nights and weekends. Her phone started _____ (13 ring) immediately.

She got used to _____ (14 pick) up the phone in the middle of the night.

She became accustomed _____ (15 take) in children that

no one else wanted. Before she started taking care of babies, she used

_____ (16 sleep) seven or eight hours a night. Now she sometimes gets as little as three or four hours of sleep a night.

By the time she was 28 years old and in graduate school, Bell had

been foster mother to 50 children. _____ (17) order _____ (18)

complete her studies, she had _____ (19) take "her" babies to class

with her. Her professors let her _____ (20 do) this. They understood that it

was necessary _____ (21) her _____ (22 study) and _____ (23 take) care

of the babies at the same time. And her classmates didn't complain

_____ (24 have) a baby crying in the back of the class.

Everyone understood how important it was _____ (25) her

_____ (26 help) these babies.

Usually, she takes in babies for a few days, but one time she had a baby for six months. Even though she is sometimes tired, she is never

too tired _____ (27 take) in a child that needs her. Incredibly, she only

gets $12 a day for _____ (28 take) care of these children. However, she

gets great satisfaction watching a baby _____ (29 grow). Bell has had

as many as eight children at a time. It is hard _____ her
(30)

_____ "her babies" _____, but there are more babies
(31 see)   (32 leave)

waiting for her. _____ love to an unwanted child is her
(33 bring)

greatest joy.

SUMMARY OF LESSON 7

Infinitives and Base Forms

Examples	Explanation
Dawson wanted **to help** others.	An infinitive is used after certain verbs.
His mother wanted him **to help** others.	An object can be added before an infinitive.
He was happy **to give** away his money.	An infinitive can follow certain adjectives.
Public TV stations have fundraisers **in order to get** money. Matel Dawson gave his money **to help** students get an education.	An infinitive is used to show purpose.
It's important **to help** others. **To help** others is our moral obligation.	*It* can introduce an infinitive subject. (INFORMAL) The infinitive can be in the subject position. (FORMAL)
It's important **for rich people to help** others. It's fun **for me to volunteer**.	*For* + noun or object pronoun is used to give the infinitive a subject.
Carnegie had enough money **to build** libraries. Dawson was too poor **to finish** school.	An infinitive can be used with *too* and *enough*.
Dawson heard his mother **talk** about helping others. I hear a baby **crying**.	After the sense perception verbs, a base form or an *-ing* form is used.
It is important **to be loved**.	An infinitive can be used in the passive voice.
She let me **work**. She made me **work**. She had me **work**.	After causative verbs *let, make,* and *have,* use the base form.
She got me **to work**. She convinced me **to work**. She persuaded me **to work**.	After causative verbs *get, convince,* and *persuade,* use the infinitive.
Dawson helped students **to get** an education. He helped them **pay** their tuition.	After *help*, either the infinitive or the base form can be used.

Gerunds

Examples	Explanation
Going to college is expensive in the U.S.	A gerund can be the subject of the sentence.
Dawson enjoyed **giving** money away.	A gerund follows certain verbs.
Dawson learned about **giving** from his parents.	A gerund is used after a preposition.
He had a hard time **supporting** his family.	A gerund is used after certain nouns.
He doesn't like to **go shopping**.	A gerund is used in many idiomatic expressions with *go*.
I dislike **being told** a lie.	A gerund can be used in the passive voice.

Gerund or Infinitive—Differences in Meaning

Examples	Explanation
My father **used to be** a lawyer. Now he is retired. I **used to be** overweight. Now I'm in great shape.	Discontinued past habit
She has six children. She **is used to being** around kids. I ride my bike to work every day. I **am used to riding** my bike in all kinds of weather.	Present custom
I have never lived alone before and it's hard for me. I can't **get used to living** alone.	Change of custom
I met a friend at the library, and I **stopped to talk** to her.	Stop one activity in order to do something else
I had a fight with my neighbor, and we **stopped talking** to each other.	Stop something completely
I **try to give** a little money to charity each year. Mimi **tries to ride** her bike to work a few times a week.	*Try* = make an attempt or effort
I put 85¢ in the soda machine and nothing came out. I **tried hitting** the machine, but still nothing happened.	*Try* = experiment with a different method
You must **remember to turn off** the stove before you leave the house.	Remember and then do
My grandmother repeats herself a lot. She didn't **remember telling** the story, so she told it again.	Remember something about the past

For a list of words followed by gerunds or infinitives, see Appendix D.

1. Don't forget *to* when introducing an infinitive.

   He needs ⌃*to* leave.

   It's necessary ⌃*to* have a job.

2. Don't omit *it* when introducing an infinitive.

   ~~Is~~ *It's* important to know a second language.

   It c ~~C~~osts a lot of money to get a college education.

3. With a compound infinitive, use the base form after *and*.

   He needed to finish the letter and ~~went~~ *go* to the post office.

4. After *want*, *need*, and *expect*, use the object pronoun, not the subject pronoun, before the infinitive.

   She wants ~~that I~~ *me to* speak English all the time.

5. Don't use *to* between *cost* or *take* and the indirect object.

   It cost ~~to~~ me $500 to fly to Puerto Rico.

   It took ~~to~~ him three months to find a job.

6. Use *for*, not *to*, when you give a subject to the infinitive.

   It is easy ~~to~~ *for* me to speak Spanish.

7. Use *to* + base form, not *for*, to show purpose.

   He exercises every day ~~for~~ *to* improve his health.

8. Use a gerund or an infinitive, not a base form as a subject.

   Find⌃*ing* a good job takes time. **OR** *It takes time to find a good job.*

9. Be careful with *used to* and *be used to*.

My brother ~~is~~ used to live in New York. Now he lives in Boston.

'm   living
I've lived alone all my life and I love it. I‸used to ~~live~~ alone.

10. Be careful to use the correct form after *stop*.

ing
She told her son to stop ~~to~~ watch‸TV and go to bed.

11. Use a gerund, not an infinitive, after a preposition.

ing
I thought about ~~to~~ return‸to my hometown.

12. Make sure to choose a gerund after certain verbs and an infinitive after others.

ing
I enjoy ~~to~~ walk‸in the park.

I like to walk in the park. *Correct*

13. Use *not* to make the negative of a gerund.

not
He's worried about ~~don't~~ finding a job.

14. Use a base form or an *-ing* form after a sense-perception verb.

I saw the accident ~~to~~ happen.

ing
I can smell the soup ~~to~~ cook‸.

15. Use a gerund, not the infinitive, with *go* + a recreational activity.

ing
I like to go ~~to~~ fish‸at the river.

16. Use the base form, not the infinitive, after causative verbs *let*, *make*, and *have*.

He let me ~~to~~ borrow his car.

The teacher made me ~~to~~ rewrite my composition.

PART 1 Find the mistakes with the underlined words, and correct them. Not every sentence has a mistake. If the sentence is correct, write C.

EXAMPLES   He was surprised ^to get the job.

                To help other people is our moral obligation.   **C**

1. She let me to use her cell phone.

2. My daughter is out of town. I want that she call me.

3. Do you like to watch TV?

4. She's old enough get married.

5. She wanted me to help her with her homework.

6. He decided to rent a car and drove to San Francisco.

7. It took me five minutes finish the job.

8. My friend helped me move the piano.

9. Live in a foreign country is difficult.

10. The teacher had us come to her office to discuss our grades.

11. It will cost to me a lot of money to replace my old computer.

12. She needs speak with you.

13. She got me to tell her the secret.

14. The teacher made the student take the test a second time.

15. It was hard to me to find a job.

16. She persuaded her son to wash the dishes.

17. Costs a lot of money to buy a house.

18. He turned on the TV for watch the news.

19. He stopped to work at 4:30 and went home.

20. I met my friend in the cafeteria, and I stopped to talk to her for a few minutes.

21. I like to cook, but I dislike to wash the dishes.

22. I had a good time talking with my friends.

23. Do you go shop for groceries every week?

24. I used to living with my parents, but now I live alone.

25. My sister couldn't get used to live in the U.S., so she went back to our native country.

26. When I came into the room, I heard the teacher <u>talking</u> about the final exam.

27. The walls of my apartment are thin, and I can hear my neighbors <u>to fight</u>.

28. I can smell my neighbors' dinner <u>cooking</u>.

29. She thanked me <u>for take</u> care of her dog while she was on vacation.

30. Did you have trouble <u>to find</u> my apartment?

31. Please remember <u>to turn</u> off the lights before you go to bed.

32. I started <u>learning</u> English when I was a child.

33. I thought about <u>don't coming</u> back to this school next semester.

34. She complained about <u>being disturbed</u> while she was trying to study.

35. Your dress needs <u>to be cleaned</u> before you can use it again.

36. He tried <u>to repair</u> the car by himself, but he couldn't.

37. Did you see the boy <u>fell</u> from the tree?

PART 2 Fill in the blanks with the gerund, the infinitive, or the base form of the verb in parentheses ( ). In some cases, more than one answer is possible.

EXAMPLE <u> Answering </u> the phone during dinner really bothers me.
(answer)

1. I started _____ dinner last night and the phone rang.
(eat)

2. Someone was trying _____ me something.
(sell)

3. I don't enjoy _____ during dinner.
(passive: interrupt)

4. Sometimes they want me _____ money to charity, but I
(donate)

   don't like _____ my credit card number to strangers on
(give)

   the phone.

5. I tell them I'm not interested in _____ their product.
(buy)

6. _____ them you're not interested doesn't stop them.
(tell)

   They don't let you _____ their sales pitch.
(interrupt)

7. I used to _____ to the caller politely, but I don't do it
(listen)

   anymore.

8. I've told them politely that I don't want to _____,
(passive: bother)

but they don't listen.

9. I keep _____ these phone calls.
(get)

10. I've thought about _____ my phone number, but I
(change)

heard that they'll get my new number.

11. _____ my phone number is not the answer to the
(change)

problem.

12. It's impossible _____ them from _____ you.
(stop)   (call)

13. I finally decided _____ Caller ID.
(get)

14. It's better _____ who's calling before you pick up the
(see)

phone.

15. Now I have the choice of _____ ___ up or
(pick)

_____ up the phone when it rings.
(not pick)

PART **3** Fill in the blanks with the correct preposition.

EXAMPLE We must concentrate ___on___ learning English.

1. What is the reason _____ doing this exercise?

2. Your grade in this course depends _____ passing the tests and doing the homework.

3. I dreamed _____ climbing a mountain.

4. The teacher insists _____ giving tests.

5. The Wright brothers are famous _____ inventing the airplane.

6. I hope I succeed _____ passing this course.

7. Most students care _____ getting good grades.

8. I'm not accustomed _____ wearing jeans to school.

9. Students are interested _____ improving their pronunciation.

10. Are you afraid _____ getting a bad grade?

11. Are you worried _____ getting a bad grade?

12. I'm not used _____ speaking English all the time.

PART 4   Tell if these pairs of sentences mean about the same thing or have completely different meanings. Write *same* or *different*.

EXAMPLES   It's important to spell correctly.
To spell correctly is important.   _____*same*_____

I used to live in New York.
I'm used to living in New York.   _____*different*_____

1. I can't remember to brush my teeth.
I can't remember brushing my teeth.   _____

2. I like to cook.
I like cooking.   _____

3. Going to college is expensive.
It's expensive to go to college.   _____

4. I plan to buy a computer.
I plan on buying a computer.   _____

5. I stopped watching TV.
I stopped to watch TV.   _____

6. She started to lose weight.
She started losing weight.   _____

EXPANSION ACTIVITIES

Classroom Activities

1. Tell about teachers and students in your school. What do students expect from teachers? What do teachers expect from students? Find a partner, and compare your lists.

Teachers (don't) expect students to:	Students (don't) expect teachers to:
Teachers expect students to come to class on time.	Students don't expect teachers to be friendly.

2. Fill in the blanks. Discuss your answers in a small group.

a. I used to worry about _____

b. Now I worry about _____

c. I used to have difficulty _____

d. Now I have difficulty _____

e. People in my family are not used to _____

f. Americans are not used to _____

g. I'm used to _____ because I've done it all my life.

h. I'm not used to _____

because _____

i. I often used to _____,
but I don't do it anymore. (OR I rarely do it.)

Talk About it

1. These words are written on Andrew Carnegie's tombstone: "Here lies a man who was able to surround himself with men far cleverer than himself." What do you think this means?

2. In your native culture, do rich people help poor people?

3. Do you ever give money to people on the street who collect money for charity? Why or why not?

4. If a homeless person asks you for money, do you help this person? Why or why not? Are there a lot of homeless people or beggars in your hometown? Do other people help them?

5. Would you like to volunteer your time to help a cause? What would you like to do?

Write About it

1. Write a paragraph telling if you agree or disagree with the following statements by Andrew Carnegie:

- It is not good to have money if your spirit is poor.
- It is the mind that makes the body rich.
- It is a disgrace to die rich.

2. Write about a belief you used to have that you no longer have. What made you change your belief?

3. Write a paragraph or short essay telling how your lifestyle or habits have changed over the last ten years.

4. Write about an expectation that your parents had for you that you did not meet. Explain why you did not do what they expected.

5. Write about an expectation you have for your children (or future children).

Outside Activities

1. Ask a friend or neighbor to fill in the blanks in these statements. Report this person's answers to the class.

   - I'm worried about _____

   - I'm grateful to my parents for _____

   - I have a good time _____

   - I used to _____, but I don't do it anymore.

2. Rent the movie *Pay It Forward*. Write a summary of the movie.

Internet Activities

1. At a search engine, type in *charity*. Find the names of charitable organizations. What do these organizations do to help people?

2. Type in *volunteer*. Find the names of volunteer organizations. Write down three ways people can volunteer to help others.

3. Find the name of a volunteer organization near you. What kind of volunteers are needed?

4. At a search engine, type in *AIDS bike ride*. Print an article about someone's personal account of a specific ride.

Additional Activities at **http://elt.thomson.com/gic**

LESSON

8

GRAMMAR

Adverbial Clauses and Phrases
Sentence Connectors
So / Such . . . That

CONTEXT: Coming to America

A Nation of Immigrants
New Immigrants: The Lost Boys of Sudan
Slavery—An American Paradox
The Changing Face of America
Adopting a Baby from Abroad

8.1 | Adverbial Clauses—An Overview

An adverbial clause gives more information about the main clause. It is also called a *dependent clause*.

Main clause	*Dependent clause*
I like living in the U.S.	even though I miss my country.

Example	Type of Clause
She went to Canada **before she came to the U.S.**	Time clause
She went to Canada first **because she couldn't get a visa for the U.S.**	Reason clause
She came to the U.S. **so that she could be with her relatives.**	Purpose clause
She came to the U.S. **even though she didn't know English.**	Contrast clause
She will go back to her country **if she saves enough money.**	Condition clause

Language Notes:

1. An adverbial clause is dependent on the main clause for its meaning. It must be attached to the main clause.

   Wrong: She came to America. Because she wanted to study English.

   Right: She came to America because she wanted to study English.

2. The dependent clause can come before or after the main clause. If it comes before, it is usually separated from the main clause with a comma.

   Compare:

   I went to Canada before I came to the United States. (No comma)

   Before I came to the United States, I went to Canada. (Comma)

A NATION OF IMMIGRANTS

Before You Read

1. Why do many people leave one country and move to another?

2. What do immigrants have to give up? What do they gain?

Read the following article. Pay special attention to different ways of giving reasons.

Did You
Know?
Over the last decade, 52.2 percent of foreign-born immigrants were born in Latin America, 25.5 percent in Asia, 14.0 percent in Europe, and the remaining 8.3 percent in other regions of the world.

The United States is unique in that it is a nation of immigrants, old and new. The U.S. takes in more immigrants than the rest of the world combined, about 1.3 million a year. In 2003, 32.5 million people, or 11.5 percent of the population, was foreign born. Between 1995 and 1998, three million immigrants entered the U.S. legally. Why have so many people from other countries left family and friends, jobs, and traditions to start life in a new country? The answer to that question is as diverse as the people who have come to America.

Between 1820 and 1840, many Germans came **because of** political unrest and economic problems. Between 1840 and 1860, many Irish people came **because of** famine.[1] The potato crop, which they depended on, had failed. Between 1850 and 1882, many Chinese people came to America **because of** famine.

The early group of immigrants came from Northern and Western Europe. In 1881, a large group started arriving from Eastern and Southern Europe. Jews from Eastern Europe came **to** escape religious persecution; Italians came **for** work. Most came **to** find freedom and a better life. The number of immigrants grew; between 1881 and 1920, more than 23.4 million immigrants came. In 1910, 15 percent of the population was foreign born.

In 1924, Congress passed a law restricting the number of immigrants, and immigration slowed. In 1965, Congress opened the doors again and immigration started to rise. In the 1960s and 1970s, Cubans and Vietnamese people came **to** escape communism. In the 1980s, Jews from the former Soviet Union came **because of** anti-Semitism,[2] and in the 1990s, Bosnians came **because of** war. Many people came **so that** they could be reunited with their families who had come before.

In addition to legal immigration, about 300,000 come to the U.S. each year illegally. **Since** the U.S. Census cannot count these people, this number is only an estimate.

---

[1] *Famine* means extreme hunger because of a shortage of food.
[2] *Anti-Semitism* means prejudice or discrimination against Jews.

8.2 | Reason and Purpose

There are several ways to show reason and purpose.

Examples	Explanation
We came to the U.S. *because* **our relatives are here.** *Because* **he couldn't find a job in his country,** he came to the U.S.	*Because* introduces a clause of reason.
Many Irish immigrants came to the U.S. *because of* **hunger.** *Because of* **war in their country,** many people left Ethiopia.	*Because of* introduces a noun (phrase).
Since **the U.S. Census cannot count illegal immigrants,** their number is only an estimate. *Since* **the U.S. limits the number of immigrants it will accept,** many people cannot get an immigrant visa.	*Since* means *because*. It is used to introduce a fact. The main clause is the result of this fact. Remember: *Since* can also be used to show time. **Example:** He has been in the U.S. *since* 2003. The context tells you the meaning of *since*.
In order to **make money,** my family came to the U.S. Many people come to America *to* **escape economic hardship.**	*In order to* shows purpose. The short form is *to*. We follow *to* with the base form of the verb.
Many people come to the U.S. *so that* **they** *can* **be reunited with family members.** Many people come to the U.S. *so* **they** *can* **be reunited with family members.** *So that* **I** *would* **learn English,** I came to the U.S. *So* **I** *would* **learn English,** I came to the U.S.	*So that* shows purpose. The short form is *so*. The purpose clause usually contains a modal: *can, will,* or *may* for future; *could, would,* or *might* for past.
People come to America *for* **freedom.** Some people come to America *for* **better jobs.**	*For* + noun or noun phrase shows purpose.
Compare: a. She came here **to** be with her family. b. They came here **for** a better life.	a. Use *to* before a verb. b. Use *for* before a noun.
Compare: a. He came to the U.S. **because he wanted to be** reunited with his brother. b. He came to the U.S. **so that he could be** reunited with his brother.	a. **Because** can be followed with **want.** b. Do not follow *so that* with *want*. *Wrong:* He came to the U.S. *so that he wanted to be* reunited with his brother.

> **Language Note:**
>
> *So* is also used to show result.
>
> **Compare:**
> **Purpose:** I came to the U.S. alone **so** I could get an education.
> **Result:** I came to the U.S. alone, **so** I miss my family.
> Notice that in the above sentences, a comma is used for result but not for purpose.

EXERCISE 1 Fill in the blanks with *because, because of, since, for, (in order) to,* or *so (that)*.

EXAMPLE Many immigrants came to America ___*to*___ escape famine.

1. Many immigrants came _____ they didn't have enough to eat.

2. Many immigrants came _____ they could feed their families.

3. Many immigrants came _____ they could escape religious persecution.

4. Many immigrants came _____ the political situation was unstable in their countries.

5. Many immigrants came _____ the poor economy in their countries.

6. Many immigrants came _____ be reunited with their relatives.

7. _____ war destroyed many of their homes and towns, many people had to leave their countries.

8. Many immigrants came _____ escape poverty.

9. Many immigrants came _____ freedom.

10. Often immigrants come _____ they can make more money.

11. Often immigrants come _____ make more money.

12. Often immigrants come _____ they see a better future for their children here.

13. Most immigrants come to America _____ a better life.

EXERCISE 2 Fill in the blanks with a reason or purpose. Answers will vary.

EXAMPLE Some immigrants come to the U.S. because ____*their native country*____
*has an unstable government.*_____

1. Some immigrants come to the U.S. because _____

   _____

2. Some immigrants come to the U.S. so that _____

   _____

3. Some immigrants come to the U.S. for _____

   _____

4. Since _____, many
   immigrants choose not to return to their country of origin.

5. Life in the U.S. is sometimes difficult because of _____

   _____

6. I chose to live in this city because _____

7. I chose to study at this school because _____

8. I come to this school for _____

9. I use my dictionary to _____

10. I'm saving my money because _____

11. I'm saving my money so that _____

12. I'm saving my money for _____

13. I'm saving my money in order to _____

14. Since _____, many
    immigrants go to big cities.

EXERCISE 3 Fill in the blanks with *because, because of, since, so (that),* or
(in order) to. Answers may vary.

Two women are talking.

A: I heard you moved.

B: Yes. We moved last month. We bought a big house

____*so that*____ we would have room for my parents. They're
(example)

coming to the U.S. next month _____ they want to be
(1)

near their children and grandchildren.

A: Don't you mind having your parents live with you?

B: Not at all. It'll be good for them and good for us.

_____ our jobs, we don't get home until after 6 p.m.
(2)

A: Aren't your parents going to work?

B: No. They're not coming here _____ jobs. They're in
(3)

their late 60s and are both retired. They just want to be grandparents.

A: It's great for kids to be near their grandparents.

B: I agree. Grandparents are the best babysitters. We want the kids

to stay with their grandparents _____ they won't
(4)

forget our language. Also, we want them to learn about our native

culture _____ they have never been to our country.
(5)

Our son, who's five, is already starting to speak more English than

Spanish. He prefers English ___ _____ all his friends in
(6)

kindergarten speak English.

A: That's how kids are in America. They don't want to speak their

native language _____ they want to be just like
(7)

their friends. Do your parents speak English?

D: Just a little. When we get home after work, we hope they'll take

classes at a nearby college _____ improve their
(8)

English. What about your parents? Where do they live?

A: They live a few blocks away from me.

B: That's great! You can see them any time.

A: Yes, but we almost never see each other _____ we
(9)

don't have time. _____ they work in the
(10)

day and I work in the evening, it's hard for us to get together.

Before You Read

1. Was your trip to America difficult? In what ways?

2. Was there anything that surprised you about life in America?

🎧 Read the following article. Pay special attention to time words: *when, while, until, during, for,* and *whenever.*

Africa

The Lost Boys of Sudan are new immigrants in America, eager to start a new life. They are called "the Lost Boys" because, after their families were killed in war, they went from country to country until some of them found a home in America.

The Lost Boys were just children living in southern Sudan **when** their long journey to America began in the late 1980s. **While** these young boys were in the field taking care of their cattle, their villages were bombed. These boys, mostly between the ages of 4 and 12 years old, ran for their lives. **For** three months, they walked hundreds of miles **until** they reached Ethiopia. They survived by eating leaves, roots, and wild fruit. **During** that time, many died of starvation and disease or were eaten by lions. They finally reached Ethiopia, where they stayed in refugee camps **until** 1991, **when** a war started in Ethiopia and the camps were closed. They ran again, back to Sudan and then to Kenya, where they stayed in a refugee camp **for** almost ten years. Of the approximately 27,000 boys who left Sudan, only 11,000 of them survived.

During their time in the refugee camp, they got some schooling and learned basic English. In 1999, the United Nations and the U.S. government agreed to resettle 3,700 lost boys in the U.S. **As** they were coming to America, they were thinking about the new and uncertain life ahead. Things in the U.S. would certainly be different.

Now in their twenties and early thirties, the Lost Boys living in America have had to learn a completely new way of life. **When** they moved to their new homes, they had to learn about new foods, different appliances, and new technologies. They had not even seen a refrigerator or stove or telephone **until** they came to America. In addition to their home surroundings, their world around them was completely different. **When** John Bol of Chicago saw an American supermarket for the first time, he was amazed at the amount of food. He asked if it was the palace of a king.

Agencies helped them with money for food and rent for a short time **until** they found jobs. Most of them have been studying English and working full time **since** they arrived. Although their future in the U.S. looks bright, **whenever** they think about their homeland, they are sad because so many of their family members and friends have died.

8.3 | Time Expressions

Examples	Explanation
When their villages were bombed, the Lost Boys ran. Some Sudanese boys think they will go home **when** their country *is* at peace.	*When* means "at that time" or "immediately after that time." In a future sentence, use the present tense in the time clause.
Whenever they think about their country, they are sad. **Whenever** they tell their story, Americans are amazed.	*Whenever* means "any time" or "every time."
They walked **until** they reached Ethiopia. They received money for a short time **until** they got jobs.	*Until* means "up to that time."
Some of them have had no news of their families **since** they left Sudan. They have been studying English **ever since** they came to the U.S.	*Since* or *ever since* means "from that time in the past to the present." Use the present perfect or present perfect continuous in the main clause.
They walked **for** three months. They stayed in a refugee camp **for** many years.	Use *for* with the amount of time.
During the day, they walked. **During** their time in the refugee camp, they studied English.	Use *during* with a time such as *day, night, summer* or a specific time period (*the time they were in Ethiopia, the month of August, the week of March 2*) or an event (*the class, the trip, the movie, the meeting*).
While they were taking care of their cattle, their villages were bombed. **As** they were coming to America, they were thinking about their new life ahead.	Use *while* or *as* with a continuous action.
Compare: a. They walked **for** three months. b. They walked **during** the day. They lived in refugee camps **during** their childhood.	a. Use *for* with the amount of time. b. Use *during* with a named period of time (such as *the day, their childhood, the class, the month of May*).
Compare: a. They were taking care of their cattle **when** their villages were bombed. b. **While** they were taking care of their cattle, their villages were bombed.	a. Use *when* with a simple past action. b. Use *while* with a continuous action.

EXERCISE 4 Fill in the blanks with *since, until, while, when, as, during, for,* or *whenever.* In some cases, more than one answer is possible.

EXAMPLE The Lost Boys were very young _____*when*_____ they left Sudan.

1. They had never seen a gas stove _____ they came to the U.S.

2. Some of them have not heard anything about their families _____ they left Sudan.

3. _____ they were traveling to the U.S., they were wondering about their future.

4. _____ their march to Ethiopia, many of them died.

5. _____ they came to the U.S., they saw modern appliances for the first time.

6. They walked _____ many months.

7. They crossed the river _____ the rainy season.

8. Some died _____ they were marching to Ethiopia.

9. They studied English _____ they were living in Kenya.

10. _____ they came to the U.S., they have been studying English.

11. _____ they think about their families, they feel sad.

12. In the U.S. many of them work _____ they are going to school.

13. They lived in Ethiopia _____ about four years.

14. They had very little to eat _____ they came to America.

EXERCISE 5 Fill in the blanks with an appropriate time word. In some cases, more than one answer is possible.

_____*When*_____ I was a child, I had heard many stories about life in
(example)

America. _____ I saw American movies, I imagined that
(1)

one day I would be in a place like the one I saw. My uncle had lived in

the U.S. _____ many years, and he often came back to
(2)

visit. _____(3)_____ he came back, he used to tell me stories and

show me pictures of the U.S. _____(4)_____ I was a teenager, I

asked my mother if she would let me visit my uncle _____(5)_____

my summer vacation, but she said I was too young and the trip was too

expensive. _____(6)_____ I was 20, I finally decided to come to the

U.S. _____(7)_____ I was traveling to the U.S., I thought about all

the stories my uncle had told me. But I really knew nothing about the

U.S. _____(8)_____ I came here.

_____(9)_____ I came to the U.S., I've been working hard and

trying to learn English. I haven't had time to meet Americans or have

much fun _____(10)_____ I started my job. I've been here

_____(11)_____ five months now, and I just work and go to

school. _____(12)_____ I'm at school, I talk to my classmates

_____(13)_____ our break, but on the weekends I'm alone most of

the time. I won't be able to make American friends _____(14)_____

I learn more English.

The American movies I had seen showed me beautiful places, but I
never imagined how much I would miss my family and friends.

EXERCISE 6 Fill in the blanks with an appropriate expression.

EXAMPLES For _____many years_____, she has been living in the U.S.

Since _____1997_____, she has been living in the U.S.

1. During _____, she lived in Poland.

2. For _____, she lived in Poland.

3. Since _____, she has been working in the U.S.

4. While _____, she met her future husband.

5. When _____, she was living in Poland.

6. Until _____, she lived with her parents.

7. Whenever _____, she visits her parents.

EXERCISE 7 ABOUT YOU Complete the statements that apply to you. If the time expression is at the beginning of the sentence, add a comma before the main clause.

EXAMPLES Whenever I have a job interview *, I feel nervous.* _____

Ever since I found a job *, I haven't had much time to study.* _____

1. Ever since I was a child _____

2. When I was a child _____

3. _____ ever since I started attending this school.

4. _____ when I started attending this school.

5. _____ until I started attending this school.

6. When the semester began _____

7. Since the semester began _____

8. _____ when I was _____ years old.

9. _____ until I was _____ years old.

10. _____ ever since I was _____ years old.

11. When I graduated _____

12. Since I graduated _____

13. Until I graduated _____

14. _____ when I found a job.

15. _____ since I found a job.

16. _____ until I found a job.

17. When I bought my car _____

18. Until I bought my car _____

19. Since I bought my car _____

20. Whenever I drive _____

8.4 | Using the *-ing* Form After Time Words

If the subject of a time clause and the subject of the main clause are the same, the time clause can be changed to a participle phrase. The subject is omitted, and the present participle (*-ing* form) is used.

Examples

Subject   *Subject*

a. The Lost Boys went to Ethiopia after **they left** Sudan.

b. The Lost Boys went to Ethiopia after **leaving** Sudan.

     Subject   *Subject*

a. While **they were crossing** the river, some of the Lost Boys drowned.

b. While **crossing** the river, some of the Lost Boys drowned.

In sentences (a), the subject of the main clause and the subject of the time clause are the same.

In sentences (b), we delete the subject after the time word (*after, while*) and use a present participle (*-ing*).

EXERCISE 8   Change the time clause to a participle phrase.

EXAMPLE   While they were crossing a river, many boys drowned.

While crossing a river, many boys drowned.

1. The Lost Boys went to Kenya before they came to America.

   _____

2. While they were living in Kenya, they studied English.

   _____

3. Before they came to America, the Lost Boys had never used electricity before.

   _____

4. Santino learned how to use a computer after he came to America.

   _____

5. Until he found a job, Daniel got help from the U.S. government.

   _____

6. Peter wants to go back to Sudan after he graduates from college.

   _____

Before You Read

1. What do you know about the history of slavery in the U.S.?

2. Do you think everyone is equal in the U.S. today?

Read the following article. Pay special attention to *even though*, *although*, and *in spite of (the fact that)*.

Did You Know?

African-Americans make up about 12.3 percent of the U.S. population today.

For the first three centuries after Columbus came to America in 1492, the largest group of immigrants arrived in America—unwillingly. Ten to twelve million Africans were brought to work as slaves in the rice, sugar, tobacco, and cotton fields of the agricultural south.

In 1776, when America declared its independence from England, Thomas Jefferson, one of the founding fathers of the United States, wrote, "All men are created equal" and that every person has a right to "life, liberty, and the pursuit of happiness." **In spite of** these great words, Jefferson owned 200 slaves at that time.

Even though the importation of slaves finally ended in 1808, the slave population continued to grow as children were born to slave mothers. The country became divided over the issue of slavery. The North wanted to end slavery; the South wanted to continue it. In 1861, civil war broke out between the North and the South. In 1865, when the North won, slavery was ended. **In spite of the fact that** African-Americans were freed, it took another 100 years for Congress to pass a law prohibiting discrimination because of race, color, religion, sex, or national origin.

Although many new arrivals see the U.S. as the land of equality, it is important to remember this dark period of American history.

[3] A *paradox* is a situation that has contradictory aspects.

8.5 | Contrast

Examples	Explanation
Even though slavery ended, African-Americans did not get equality. **Although** life in the refugee camps was hard, the Lost Boys learned English. **In spite of the fact that** Jefferson wrote about equality for everyone, he owned 200 slaves.	For an unexpected result or contrast of ideas, use a clause beginning with *even though, although,* and *in spite of the fact that*. A clause has a subject and a verb.
In spite of Jefferson's declaration of liberty for all, he owned slaves. **In spite of** their hard lives, the Lost Boys are hopeful about their future.	Use *in spite of* + noun or noun phrase to show contrast. A clause doesn't follow *in spite of*.
Even though the Lost Boys are happy in the U.S., they **still** miss their families in Sudan. Even though it's hard for an immigrant to work and go to school, they have to do it **anyway.**	*Still* and *anyway* can be used in the main clause to emphasize the contrast.

EXERCISE 9 Fill in the blanks with *in spite of* or *in spite of the fact that*.

EXAMPLES _____*In spite of the fact that*_____ the law says everyone has equal rights, some people are still suffering.

The Sudanese boys have not lost their hopes for a bright future, _____*in spite of their hard lives*_____.

1. _____ slavery ended in 1865, African-Americans did not receive equal treatment under the law.

2. The slave population continued to grow _____ Americans stopped importing slaves from Africa.

3. _____ Thomas Jefferson's belief in equality for all, he owned slaves.

4. Many immigrants come to America _____ the difficulty of starting a new life.

5. _____ their busy work schedules, the Sudanese boys go to school.

6. _____ everything in America is new for them, the Sudanese boys are adapting to American life.

7. _____ life is not perfect in the U.S., many immigrants want to come here.

EXERCISE 10   Complete each statement with an unexpected result.

EXAMPLE   I like the teacher even though   *he gives a lot of homework.*

1. I like my apartment even though _____

2. I like this city even though _____

3. I like this country even though _____

4. I like this school even though _____

5. I have to study even though _____

6. I like my job in spite of (the fact that) _____

7. Some students fail tests in spite of (the fact that) _____

8. My uncle passed the citizenship test even though _____

9. The U.S. is a great country in spite of (the fact that) _____

10. Many people want to come to the U.S. even though _____

11. There are many poor people in the U.S. in spite of (the fact that)

_____

EXERCISE 11 Complete each statement by making a contrast.

EXAMPLE Even though many students have jobs, _they manage to come to class_ _and do their homework._

1. Even though the U.S. is a rich country, _____

   _____

2. In spite of the fact that Thomas Jefferson wrote "All men are created

   equal," _____

3. Even though I don't speak English perfectly, _____

   _____

4. In spite of the fact that my teacher doesn't speak my language, ____

   _____

5. Even though I miss my friends and family, _____

   _____

6. In spite of my accent, _____

THE CHANGING FACE OF AMERICA

1. What do you think is the largest ethnic minority in the U.S.?

2. Do you ever see signs in public places in Spanish or any other language?

Read the following article. Pay special attention to condition clauses beginning with *if, even if,* and *unless.*

Did You Know?

Two Mexican-American sisters, Linda Sanchez and Loretta Sanchez, made history when both were elected to the U.S. Congress in 2002 to represent California.

The U.S. population is over 295 million. This number is expected to rise to more than 400 million by 2050. **Unless** there are changes in immigration patterns, 80 million new immigrants will enter the U.S. in the next 50 years.

For most of the nineteenth and twentieth centuries, the majority of immigrants to the U.S. were Europeans. However, since 1970, this trend has changed dramatically. Today most immigrants are Hispanics.[4] In 2003, Hispanics passed African-Americans as the largest minority. The Hispanic population increased more than 50% between 1990 and 2000. **If** current patterns of immigration continue and **if** the birth rate remains the same, Hispanics, who are now 13% of the total population, will be 24% of the population by 2050. Hispanics are already about 32% of the population of California and Texas. More than 50% of the people who have arrived since 1970 are Spanish speakers. The largest group of Hispanic immigrants comes from Mexico.

Because of their large numbers, Hispanic voters will have political power. **If** they vote as a group, they will have a great influence on the choice of our nation's leaders.

There are many questions about the future of America. One thing is certain: the face of America is changing and will continue to change.

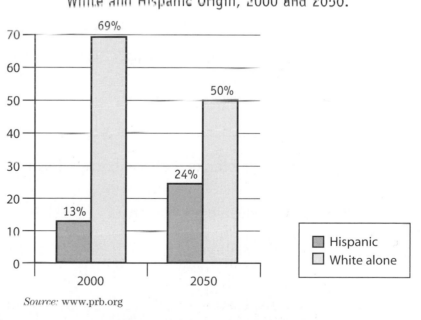

Estimated and Projected U.S. Population, White and Hispanic Origin, 2000 and 2050.

Source: www.prb.org

---

[4] A *Hispanic* is an American whose origin is a Spanish-speaking country, such as Mexico or Cuba.

8.6 | Condition

If, even if, and **unless** are used to show that a condition is needed for something to happen.

If current immigration patterns and birth rates **remain** the same, Hispanics **will be** 25 percent of the population by 2050. **If** Hispanics **vote** together, they **will have** a lot of political power. **If** my brother **comes** to the U.S., he **will live** with me.	Use *if* to show that the condition affects the result. In a future sentence, use the simple present tense in the condition clause.
Even if the immigration of Hispanics **slows** down, their number **will increase** because of their present birth rate. **Even if** the economy of my country **improves**, I **won't go** back.	Use *even if* to show that the condition doesn't affect the result.

Unless immigration laws **change**, 80 million new immigrants **will come** here in the next 50 years.
 	
 My brother **won't come** to the U.S. **unless** he **gets** a scholarship at an American university.
 	
 I **won't go** back to my country **unless** my parents **need** me.
	Use *unless* to mean *if not*.
	 Compare:
	    I won't go **unless** you **go.**
	    I won't go **if** you **don't go.**

a. *If* I **think** about my native country, I **get** homesick. b. *Whenever* I **think** about my native country, I **get** homesick. c. Children in America **learn** English *even if* their parents **speak** another language at home. d. You **can't come** to the U.S. *unless* you **have** a visa.	Sentences with *if, even if,* and *unless* can also be about the general **present.** In that case, the present tense is used in both clauses. **Note:** Sentences (a) and (b) have the same meaning.

EXERCISE 12   Fill in the blanks with the correct form of the verb in parentheses ( ).

EXAMPLE   If the Hispanic population _____*continues*_____ to grow, 24% of the
                                         (continue)

U.S. population _____*will be*_____ Hispanic by the year 2050.
                       (be)

1. If the U.S. _____ almost 80 million people
                     (add)

to the population in the next 50 years, it _____
                                                        (have to)

build 30 million more housing units.

2. Even if the number of immigrants _____ down, (go)

   the population _____ because of the high birth (increase)

   rates of immigrants.

3. If more children _____ born in the next 50 years, (be)

   more schools _____. (passive: need)

4. The class size _____ if the number of school-age (increase)

   children _____. (grow)

5. The U.S. population _____ over 400 million by (be)

   2050 if immigration _____ at the same rate. (continue)

6. Immigrants _____ to come to the U.S. unless (continue)

   there _____ a change in immigration policy. (be)

7. Children of immigrants _____ their native (forget)

   language unless their parents _____ them to (encourage)

   speak, read, and write it.

8. If immigrant parents _____ their children about (not/educate)

   their former country, their children _____ about (not/know)

   their family history.

EXERCISE 13 ABOUT YOU Complete each statement.

EXAMPLE If I speak my native language all the time, ___*I won't learn English.*___

1. If I make a lot of long distance calls, _____

2. I'll get a good grade if _____

3. If I don't pass this course, _____

4. My English will improve if _____

5. I'll go back to my native country if _____

6. I will become a citizen if _____

7. If I can't come to class next week, _____

EXERCISE 14 Change the *if* clause in the sentences below to an *unless* clause.

EXAMPLE You can't get on an airplane if you don't have a photo ID. _You can't get_
on an airplane unless you have a photo ID.

1. You can't enter the U.S. if you don't have a passport. _____

_____

2. Children of immigrants will forget their language if they don't use it.

_____

3. Immigrants will continue to come to the U.S. if conditions in their
native countries don't improve. _____

_____

4. An American citizen can't be president of the U.S. if he or she was
not born in the U.S. _____

_____

5. If the increase in the Hispanic population doesn't change, Hispanics
will be 24% of the U.S. population by the middle of the century. _____

_____

_____

EXERCISE 15 ABOUT YOU Complete each statement.

EXAMPLE I don't usually eat fast food _____ _unless I'm in a hurry._ _____

1. I work / study every day unless _____

2. I'm usually in a good mood unless _____

3. I usually answer the phone unless _____

4. I'm going to stay in this city unless _____

5. I will continue to study at this school unless _____

_____

6. I can't afford to go to college / school unless _____

_____

7. I won't be able to take the next course unless _____

_____

EXERCISE 16 Complete each statement. Answers will vary.

EXAMPLE Coffee doesn't affect me. I can sleep even if ___*I drink a cup of coffee*___
*at night.*_____

1. Cold weather doesn't bother me. I go out even if _____

_____

2. Making grammar mistakes is OK. People will understand you even if

_____

3. A lot of people in the U.S. have a foreign accent. People will

understand you even if _____ _____

4. Will they call off the football game for bad weather? No. They will

play football even if _____ _____

5. He will fail the course because he never does his homework and he's

absent a lot. Even if _____ _____ _____, he will
fail the course.

6. I always do my homework. I may be absent next week, but I'll do my

homework even if _____ _____

7. I may move to a suburb. I will continue to study in the city even if

_____

8. Children of immigrants learn English even if _____ _____

_____

EXERCISE 17 Fill in the blanks in this conversation between two Hispanic
mothers.

A: My youngest daughter is seven years old, and she doesn't speak

Spanish anymore. _____*If*_____ I say something to
(*example*)

her in Spanish, she understands, but she answers in English.

B: _____ all her friends speak English, of course she's
(1)

going to speak English.

A: My mother lives with us. She doesn't speak English. She can't understand what my daughter is saying _____ (2) I translate it for her.

B: I have the same problem. My son is 14 and he won't speak Spanish _____ (3) he has to. Last month he had to because my parents came to visit from Guatemala. But he mixes Spanish with English. My parents had a hard time understanding him. There are a lot of Spanish words he doesn't remember _____ (4) I remind him.

A: We can't fight it. Our kids won't speak Spanish well _____ (5) we go back to live in our native countries. And we're not going to do that. We came to the U.S. as immigrants.

ADOPTING A BABY FROM ABROAD

Before You Read

1. Do you know anyone who has adopted a baby?

2. Is it important for parents to teach their children about their ancestors?

Read the following article. Pay special attention to sentence connectors: *however, in addition, furthermore,* and *as a result*.

Many American couples want to adopt children. **However,** there is such a long waiting list and there are so few babies available that people often have to wait years for a child. **In addition,** the process has become so complicated and slow that people often get discouraged with American adoptions. **As a result,** many Americans are turning to foreign countries for adoption. Americans bring home babies from countries such as China, Russia, Ukraine, South Korea, Guatemala, and the Philippines. In 2002, 20,000 foreign babies were adopted by American families.

However, the process of foreign adoption is not easy or cheap. First, it can cost from $10,000 to $25,000. **In addition,** the Immigration and Naturalization Service (INS) often takes six weeks to four months to process the paperwork. **Furthermore,** parents usually have to travel to the country for a one- to four week stay.

In spite of all these difficulties, these tiny immigrants bring joy to many American families.

8.7 | Sentence Connectors

Ideas can be connected by sentence connectors. These connectors show the relationship between ideas.

Examples	Explanation
Many couples want to adopt American children. **However,** there are very few babies available. The U.S. is not a perfect country. **Nevertheless,** many people want to immigrate to this country.	Sentence connectors that show contrast are *however* and *nevertheless*. These words are similar in meaning to *but*.
Foreign adoption is not for everyone. It can be expensive. **In addition,** it can take a long time. My sister came to the U.S. to earn more money. **Furthermore,** she wanted to be reunited with our family.	Sentence connectors that add more information to the same idea are *in addition, furthermore,* and *moreover*. These words are similar in meaning to *and*.
The Hispanic population is growing for several reasons. **First,** immigration brings in a large number. **In addition,** the birth rate among Hispanics is high.	Sometimes people order their thoughts using *first, second, third*, etc. These ordinal numbers can be substituted with *in addition, furthermore,* and *moreover*.
Many couples are frustrated with the adoption process in the U.S. **Therefore,** they go to other countries to adopt. Many couples in China prefer sons. **As a result,** the majority of adoptions from China are girls.	Sentence connectors that show result or conclusion are *therefore, as a result,* and *for this reason*. These words are similar in meaning to *so*.

Punctuation Note:
Use either a period or a semicolon (;) before a sentence connector. Use a comma after a sentence connector.

   My friends couldn't adopt a baby here. **Therefore,** they went to another country to adopt.
   My friends couldn't adopt a baby here; **therefore,** they went to another country to adopt.

EXERCISE 18   Fill in the blanks with an appropriate connecting word.

EXAMPLE   The Lost Boys were happy living with their families in Sudan. _However_, a war forced them to leave.

1. The Lost Boys faced many problems when they left Sudan. They

   didn't know where to go. _____, they didn't have enough to eat.

2. Some of them couldn't swim. _____, some drowned when they had to cross a river in their escape.

3. Finally they found safety in a refugee camp in Kenya. _____,
   conditions in the camp were very poor.

4. Many of the boys had never seen a gas stove before they came to the U.S. _____, they did not understand how to cook at first.

5. They faced problems in the U.S. They had to find jobs quickly. _____, they had to go to school to improve their English.

6. They are happy that they came to the U.S. _____, they still miss their family and friends back home.

7. Many immigrants came to America at the beginning of the twentieth century. _____, immigration slowed down during World War I.

8. Jews had a hard life in Russia and Poland. Many lived in poor conditions. _____, they were the victims of anti-Semitism.

9. My grandfather immigrated to the U.S. to find a job and make more money. _____, he wanted to be reunited with his relatives.

10. There was a big famine in Ireland. _____, many Irish people left and came to America.

11. In 1924, Congress passed a law restricting the number of immigrants. _____, many people who wanted to come here couldn't.

12. Many Cubans wanted to escape communism in the 1960s. _____, many of them couldn't get permission to leave Cuba.

13. Many Cubans tried to get permission to leave Cuba legally but couldn't. _____, many people found other ways of leaving. Some built or bought small boats and tried to reach Florida by sea.

14. More than a million legal immigrants came to the U.S. in 2001. _____, about 400,000 illegal immigrants came that year.

15. A war broke out in Yugoslavia in 1992. _____, many people died or lost their homes.

16. Most immigrants came to the U.S. because they wanted to. _____, Africans were brought here against their will to work as slaves.

17. In 1776, Thomas Jefferson wrote, "All men are created equal."

_____, Jefferson had 200 slaves at the time he wrote these words.

18. Africans were brought to the U.S. to work as slaves in different areas of the U.S. _____, many African families were destroyed.

19. Slavery officially ended in 1865. _____, many African-Americans continued to suffer.

20. African-Americans had been the largest minority for many years. _____, this changed in 2003 when the Hispanic population became the largest minority.

21. Adopting a foreign baby is complicated. People have to pay a lot of money. _____, they have to travel to the foreign country to fill out forms and pick up the baby.

EXERCISE 19 Complete each statement. Answers will vary.

EXAMPLE The U.S. is a rich country. However, _____*it has many poor people.*_____

1. It is important for me to learn English. Therefore, _____

_____

2. It is important for me to learn English. However, _____

_____

3. Living in another country is difficult. Immigrants have to adjust to a new language. In addition, _____

_____

4. Some children speak one language at home and another at school. As a result, _____

5. To learn a new language, you must master the grammar. In addition,

_____

6. No one wants to leave friends and family. However, _____

_____

7. If someone wants to come to the U.S. to visit, he or she must have a passport. In addition, _____

_____

8. It's important for a new immigrant to know English. Therefore,

_____

9. I wanted to study English when I was young. However, _____

_____

10. I may not speak English perfectly. However, _____

_____

EXERCISE 20 *Combination Exercise.* Circle the correct words to complete this story.

Many people have come to America (*because* / *for*) freedom. But Africans lost their freedom and were brought to America against their will *(for* / *to)* work in the fields. Africans were taken from their homes
(1)
and put on slave ships (*for* / *to*) cross the Atlantic. (*Because of* / *Since*)
(2)   (3)
hard conditions, many died along the way.

(*In spite of* / *In spite of the fact that*) they worked hard from morning
(4)
till night, they received no money. In fact, they were often beaten if they didn't obey. They were forced to work hard (*so that* / *in order to*) white
(5)
plantation owners could become rich. (*Although* / *Unless*) many people
(6)
in the North were against slavery, slavery continued in the South
(*because of* / *since*) Southern slave owners did not want to give up their
(7)
cheap labor supply.

(*Even though* / *However,*) the law prohibited the importation of slaves,
(8)
slavery continued to increase. (*In spite of* / *In spite of the fact that*) the
(9)
difficulties of living under slavery, slaves formed strong communities. They tried to keep their African cultural practices, which included music and dance. (*Because* / *For*) people from the same regions in Africa
(10)
were separated from each other, they lost their native languages, used English, and were given biblical names rather than African names.

Most of the African-Americans in the North were free. (*In addition* / *However*), they didn't have an easy life. They couldn't
(11)
attend public schools. (*Furthermore* / *However*), they weren't allowed
(12)
to vote. Many slaves from the South tried to run away to the North. (*However,* / *Although*) some were caught and sent back to their "owners."
(13)

(*Unless / Until*) the slaves were finally freed in 1865, they
(14)

faced many difficulties. (*In spite of the fact that / In spite of*) the
(15)

majority of Africans by that time were born in America, they suffered

discrimination (*because / because of*) the color of their skin.
(16)

Discrimination was still legal (*when / until*) 1965, when Congress
(17)

passed a law prohibiting discrimination in jobs and education.

(*Although / In spite of*) there has been progress toward equality for
(18)

all, there are still many inequalities in American life.

8.8 | So . . . That / Such . . . That

We can show result with *so . . . that* and *such (a) . . . that*.	
Examples	**Explanation**
Americans have to wait **such a long time** to adopt an American baby **that** many are turning to foreign adoptions. The Sudanese Boys had **such an awful trip that** many of them died along the way.	We use: *Such* + adjective + noun + *that* **Note:** Use *a* or *an* before a singular count noun.

Foreign adoption is **so expensive that** many people cannot afford it.
Small children learn English **so easily that** they become fluent in a short time.
	We use:
	   So + adjective + *that*
	   So + adverb + *that*

There are **so many** Spanish-speaking people in Miami **that** you can hear Spanish wherever you go.
There are **so few** babies available for adoption in the U.S. **that** many Americans adopt foreign babies.
	We use:
	   So many + plural count noun + *that*
	   So few + plural count noun + *that*

There was **so much** poverty in Ireland in the 1800s **that** Irish people were forced to leave.
The Sudanese Boys had **so little** to eat **that** many of them died.
	We use:
	   So much + noncount noun + *that*
	   So little + noncount noun + *that*

Language Note:
That is often omitted in informal speech.
   John works **so hard** (*that*) he doesn't have time to rest.
   American life is **so strange** for him (*that*) it will take him time to understand it.

EXERCISE 21 Fill in the blanks with *so*, *so much*, *so many*, *so few*, *so little*, or *such (a / an)*.

EXAMPLE We had __so many__ problems in our country that we decided to leave.

1. I waited _____ long time that I thought I would never get permission.

2. When I got to the Miami airport, the security lines were

   _____ long that I had to wait for almost two hours.

   There were _____ people arriving at the same time.

3. I came to the U.S. by winning the Green Card Lottery. I was

   _____ happy when I got my letter that I started to cry.

4. The U.S. is _____ rich and powerful country that people from all over the world want to come here.

5. I come from Mexico. There is _____ unemployment in Mexico that many people try to come to the U.S. for jobs.

6. Before I got my visa, I had to fill out _____ papers and

   answer _____ questions that I thought I would never be able to do it.

7. Our family has been in the U.S. for _____ long time that we hardly even speak our native language anymore.

8. My neighbor's baby was _____ young when she arrived from China that she doesn't remember anything about China at all.

9. There are _____ American babies to adopt that many families adopt babies from China, Russia, and other countries.

10. My uncle earned _____ money in Guatemala that he couldn't support his family, so he came to the U.S.

EXERCISE **22**   Fill in the blanks with *so, so much / many / little / few,* or *such (a / an).* Then complete each statement with a result.

EXAMPLES   Michael is __such a__ good student __that he gets 100% on all his tests.__

Learning another language is __so__ hard __it can take a lifetime to do it.__

1. My math class is _____ easy _____

   _____

2. Peter is taking _____ classes this semester

   _____

3. The teacher gives _____ homework _____

   _____

4. Sometimes the teacher talks _____ fast _____

   _____

5. My roommate is from India. She speaks English _____ well

   _____

6. My biology class is _____ boring _____

   _____

7. Ms. Stevens is _____ good teacher _____

   _____

8. English has _____ irregular verbs _____

   _____

9. We had _____ long test _____

   _____

10. I had _____ mistakes on my test _____

    _____

11. The teacher gave _____ confusing explanation

    _____

12. I was _____ tired in class yesterday _____

    _____

Abbreviations: C = Clause
NP = Noun Phrase
VP = Verb Phrase

1.

Words that connect a dependent clause or phrase to an independent clause:		
Function	**Connectors**	**Examples**
Reason	*because* + C *since* + C *because of* + NP	**Because** he doesn't understand English, he can't find a job. **Since** he doesn't understand English, he can't find a job. **Because of** his poor English, he can't find a job.
Time	*when* *whenever* *until* *while* *for* *during* *since*	**When** I find a job, I'll buy a car. **Whenever** I work overtime, I make extra money. I worked **until** 8 p.m. I worked **until** the store closed. **While** I was slicing the bread, I cut my finger. I've been working **for** three hours. I worked **during** my summer vacation. I've been working **since** 9 a.m. I've been working **since** I woke up this morning.
Purpose	*(in order) to* + VP *so (that)* + C *for* + NP	He exercises **(in order) to** lose weight. He exercises **so (that)** he can lose weight. He exercises **for** his health.
Contrast	*even though* + C *although* + C *in spite of the fact that* + C *in spite of* + NP	**Even though** he's rich, he's not happy. **Although** he's rich, he's not happy. **In spite of the fact that** he's rich, he's not happy. **In spite of** his wealth, he's not happy.
Condition	*if* *even if* *unless*	**If** it snows, we won't drive. We'll drive **even if** it rains. I won't go **unless** you go with me. I don't want to go alone.

2.

Words that connect two independent clauses:		
Function	**Connectors**	**Examples**
To add more to the same idea	*in addition* *furthermore* *moreover*	Adopting a baby from another country is not easy. Parents have to pay a lot of money. **In addition,** they have to get permission from the INS.
To add a contrasting idea	*however* *nevertheless*	The law says that everyone is equal. **However,** inequalities still exist.
To show a result	*therefore* *as a result* *for this reason*	It is difficult for an uneducated person to find a job that pays well. **Therefore,** I've decided to educate myself and get a degree. There was a war in Sudan. **For this reason,** many people left.

3.

Words that introduce result clauses:		
Function	**Connectors**	**Examples**
Result with adjectives and adverbs	*so* + adjective + *that* *so* + adverb + *that*	I was **so tired that** I fell asleep in front of the TV. She speaks English **so fluently that** everyone thinks it's her first language.
Result with quantity words	*so many* + plural noun + *that* *so much* + noncount noun + *that* *so few* + plural noun + *that* *so little* + noncount noun + *that*	I received **so many letters that** I didn't have time to read them all. I received **so much mail that** I didn't have time to read it all. He has **so few friends that** he's lonely. She has **so little time that** she rarely takes a vacation.
Result with nouns	*such (a)* + adjective + noun + *that*	It was **such a good movie that** I watched it three times. These are **such good grapes that** I can't stop eating them.

Punctuation Note:
Compare:

He went home from work early because he was sick. (No comma)

Because he was sick, he went home from work early. (Comma)

He was sick. Therefore, he went home from work early. (Period before the connecting word, comma after *therefore*)

He had such a bad headache that he had to go to bed. (No comma)

1. Use *to*, not *for*, with a verb when showing purpose.

   She went to the doctor ~~for~~ *to* get a checkup.

2. Don't combine *so* with *because*, or *but* with *even though*.

   Because he was late, ~~so~~ he didn't hear the explanation.

   Even though she speaks English well, ~~but~~ she can't write it.

3. Use *because of* when a noun phrase follows.

   He came late because ^*of* bad traffic.

4. Don't use *even* without *though* or *if* to introduce a clause.

   Even ^*though* he's a poor man, he's happy.

   I won't call you even ^*if* I need your help.

5. Use the *-ing* form, not the base form, after a time word if the subject is deleted.

   Before ~~go~~ *going* home, he bought some groceries.

6. Don't confuse *so that* with *because*.

   He came to the U.S. so ~~that~~ *because* he wanted freedom.

7. After *so that*, use a modal before the verb.

   I bought a DVD player so that I ^*could* watch all my favorite movies at home.

8. Always follow a sentence connector with a complete sentence.

   He came to the U.S. because he wanted more freedom. In addition, ^*he wanted to get a better* education.

9. In a future sentence, use the simple present tense in the *if* clause or time clause.

   If I ~~will~~ go back to my hometown, I will visit my best friend.

10. *However* connects two sentences. *Although* connects two parts of the same sentence.

                                            However,
    She was absent for three weeks. ~~Although~~ she did all the homework.

11. Use *so* + adjective / adverb. Use *such* when you include a noun.

                     such a
    My grandfather is ~~so~~ wise person that everyone goes to him for advice.

LESSON 8 TEST/REVIEW

PART 1   Find the mistakes with the underlined words, and correct them. Not every sentence has a mistake. If the sentence is correct, write *C*. Do not look for punctuation mistakes.

                                  could be
EXAMPLES I came here so that I <u>am</u> with my family.

              <u>After leaving</u> Greece, I went to Turkey.   **C**

1. <u>Even</u> he is a rich man, he isn't very happy.

2. <u>Since</u> she came to the U.S., she has been living with her sister.

3. She can't go to the party <u>unless</u> she gets a babysitter for her baby.

4. Because he can't find a job, <u>so</u> he doesn't have much money.

5. If I <u>will go</u> to the library today, I'll return your books for you.

6. Even though she has good qualifications and speaks English well, <u>but</u> she can't find a job.

7. I'm saving my money <u>for buy</u> a new car.

8. <u>Because</u> her health is bad, she is going to quit her job.

9. The children couldn't go out and play <u>because</u> the rain.

10. <u>In spite of</u> she has a big family, she feels lonely.

11. The weather won't stop me. I'll drive to New York <u>even</u> it rains.

12. Before <u>prepare</u> dinner, she washed her hands.

13. <u>Since</u> the stores are very crowded on the weekends, I like to shop during the week.

14. He's going to buy a digital camera <u>so that he can</u> take pictures of his children.

15. He sent his mother a picture of his children <u>so that she sees</u> her grandchildren.

16. Alex left his country <u>so that</u> he didn't like the political situation there.

17. You shouldn't open the door <u>unless</u> you know who's there.

18. He uses spell-check <u>to</u> check the spelling on his compositions.

19. She is <u>so a bad cook</u> that no one wants to eat dinner at her house.

20. I have <u>so much</u> homework that I don't have time for my family and friends.

21. I use e-mail <u>for stay</u> in touch with my friends.

22. I need to get some credits before I enter the university. In addition, <u>the TOEFL test.</u>

PART 2 Punctuate the following sentences. Some sentences are already complete and need no more punctuation. If the sentence is correct, write *C*.

EXAMPLES When he met her, he fell in love with her immediately.

I'll help you if you need me. **C**

1. The teacher will help you if you go to her office.

2. She always gets good grades because she studies hard.

3. Even though owning a dog has some disadvantages there are more advantages.

4. Because he didn't study he failed the test.

5. Before he got married his friends made a party for him.

6. She did all the homework and wrote all the compositions however she didn't pass the course.

7. Although I didn't do the homework I understood everything that the teacher said.

8. Even though he worked hard all weekend he wasn't tired.

9. I stayed home last night so that I wouldn't miss a call from my parents.

10. I am unhappy with my job because I don't get paid enough furthermore my boss is an unpleasant person.

11. She was so emotional at her daughter's wedding that she started to cry.

12. My boss never showed any respect for the workers as a result many people quit.

PART 3 Fill in the blanks with an appropriate time word: *when, whenever, while, for, during, since,* or *until.*

EXAMPLE My friends were talking _during_ the whole movie. Everyone around them was annoyed.

1. They talk _____ they go to the movies. This happens every time.

2. They were talking _____ everyone else was trying to watch the movie.

3. They started talking _____ they sat down at the beginning of the movie.

4. They talked _____ two hours.

5. They didn't stop talking _____ they left.

6. _____ the movie was over, they left and went their separate ways.

7. I haven't seen them _____ we went to the movies last week.

8. I hate it when people talk to each other _____ a movie.

PART 4 Fill in the blanks with *because, because of, since, for, so that, in order to,* or *therefore.* In some cases, more than one answer is possible.

EXAMPLE I came to this school _in order to_ learn English.

1. He came to the U.S. _____ he could learn English.

2. He came to the U.S. _____ find a better job.

3. He came to the U.S. _____ economic problems in his country.

4. He came to the U.S. _____ be with his family.

5. He came to the U.S. _____ a better future.

6. _____ the U.S. is a land of opportunity, many immigrants want to come here.

7. The U.S. is a land of opportunity. _____, many people from other countries want to immigrate here.

8. Irish people came to America in the 1800s _____ they didn't have enough to eat.

PART 5 Fill in the blanks with *even though*, *in spite of the fact that*, *in spite of*, or *however*. In some cases, more than one answer is possible.

EXAMPLE _____Even though_____ there are many opportunities in the U.S., my cousin can't find a job.

1. _____ his fluency in English, he can't find a job.

2. He's fluent in English. _____, he can't find a job.

3. _____ he has lived here all his life, he can't find a job.

4. He can't find a job _____ he has good job skills.

PART 6 Fill in the blanks with *if*, *unless*, or *even if*.

EXAMPLE _____*If*_____ you're absent, you should call the teacher to let him know.

1. You must do the homework _____ you're absent. Absence is no excuse for not doing the homework.

2. You should come to every class _____ you're sick. If you're sick, stay home.

3. _____ can't come to class, you need to call the teacher.

4. Some people go to work _____ they have a cold. They don't want to lose a day's pay.

PART 7 Fill in the blanks with *so*, *so many*, *so much*, or *such*.

EXAMPLE I was _____*so*_____ late that I missed the meeting.

1. There were _____ people at the party that there wasn't anywhere to sit down.

2. The food was _____ delicious that I didn't want to stop eating.

3. I had _____ a hard day at work yesterday that I didn't have time for lunch.

4. My son is _____ intelligent that he graduated from high school at the age of 15.

5. She spent _____ a long time on her composition that she didn't have time to do the grammar exercises.

PART 8 Complete each sentence.

EXAMPLE I didn't learn to drive until _____ *I was 25 years old.* _____

1. I come to this school for _____

2. I come to this school so that _____

3. People sometimes don't understand me because of _____

   _____

4. Since _____, it is necessary for immigrants to learn it.

5. She came to the U.S. to _____

6. I don't watch much TV because _____

7. I like to watch movies even though _____

8. Many people like to live in big cities in spite of the fact that _____

   _____

9. Please don't call me after midnight unless _____

10. I can usually understand the general meaning of a movie even if __

    _____

11. I didn't speak much English until _____

12. I fell asleep during _____

13. Some students didn't study for the last test. As a result, _____

    _____

14. The teacher expects us to study before a test. However, _____

    _____

15. When applying for a job, you need to write a good résumé. In

    addition, _____

16. My mother has such a hard job that _____

17. There are so many opportunities in the U.S. that _____

    _____

18. It was so cold outside last night that _____

Classroom Activities

1. Write the following sentence on a card, filling in the blank with one of your good qualities. The teacher will collect the cards and read them one by one. Other students will guess who wrote the card.

   My friends like me because _____

2. Form a small group. Tell which one of each pair you think is better and why. Practice reason and contrast words.

   - owning a dog or owning a cat
   - driving a big car or driving a small sports car
   - sending an e-mail or writing a letter by hand
   - watching a movie at home on a DVD player or watching a movie in a theater
   - writing your compositions by hand or writing them on a computer
   - studying at a small community college or studying at a large university
   - living in the city or living in a suburb

3. For each of the categories listed below, write a sentence with *even though* in the following pattern:

   I like _____ _____ even though _____.

   Categories: food, exercise, movies, people, places, restaurants, hobbies, or animals

   EXAMPLES   I like to travel even though it's expensive.
   I like to eat fast food even though I know it's not good for me.

   Find a partner and compare your answers to your partner's answers.

4. Write three sentences to complain about this city. Work with a small group. Practice *so / such . . . that*.

   EXAMPLE   There is so much traffic in the morning that it takes me over an hour to get to work.

5. Write three sentences about this school. Try to convince someone that this is a good school.

   EXAMPLE   The teachers are so friendly that you can go to them whenever you need help.

Talk About it

1. Frederick Douglass was an ex-slave who became a leader against slavery. In 1852, at a celebration of American Independence Day, Frederick Douglass gave a speech. He said, "This Fourth of July is yours, not mine. You may rejoice, I must mourn." Look up the words *rejoice* and *mourn.* Then tell what you think he meant by this.

2. In what ways will the U.S. be different when Hispanics make up 25 percent of the population?

3. What are the major reasons people immigrate to the U.S. from your native country?

4. Do you think the U.S. is richer or poorer because of its immigrant population?

5. Besides the U.S., what other countries have large numbers of immigrants? Is the immigrant population accepted by the native population?

6. When American parents adopt babies from other countries, should they try to teach them about their native countries? Why or why not?

Write About it

1. Write about how an agency or people have helped you and your family since you came to the U.S.

2. Do you think a country is richer or poorer if it has a large number of immigrants? Write a short composition to explain your point of view.

Outside Activities

1. Interview an African-American. Ask him to tell you how slavery has affected his life today. Ask him to tell you about discrimination in America today. Tell the class what you learned about this person.

2. Interview a Hispanic who has been in the U.S. for a long time. Ask him to tell you if Spanish is still used in the home. Ask him if he feels discrimination as a Hispanic-American. Tell the class what you learned about this person.

3. Interview an American-born person. Tell him or her some of the facts you learned in this lesson about immigration. Ask this person to tell you his or her opinion about immigration.

4. Ask an American-born person where his ancestors were originally from. How many generations of his family have lived in the U.S.? Does he have any desire to visit his family's country of origin?

Internet Activities

1. The following people came to America as immigrants. Find information about one of them on the Internet. Who is this person? What country did he / she come from? Print out a page about one of these people.

Madeleine Albright	David Ho	Carlos Santana
Mario Andretti	Henry Kissinger	Sammy Sosa
Liz Claiborne	Yo-Yo Ma	Arnold Schwarzenegger
Gloria Estefan	Zubin Mehta	Elizabeth Taylor
Andy Garcia	Martina Navratilova	Elie Wiesel

2. Type in *Ellis Island* at a search engine. What is Ellis Island and why is it important in the history of immigration? Where is it?

3. Find information about one of the following African-Americans: Frederick Douglass, Harriet Tubman, John Brown, Martin Luther King, Jr. Write a summary of an article you found on the Internet.

4. Find the Declaration of Independence on the Internet. Print it out and read it.

5. Type in *Lost Boys of Sudan* at a search engine. Print an article and bring it to class. Write a short summary of the article.

6. Type in *Foreign Adoption* or *International Adoption* at a search engine. Find a Web site that gives information about adopting a baby abroad. Find out the costs, where the babies come from, how long a family has to wait to get a baby, or any other interesting information. Report your information to the class.

7. Go to About.com. Type in *Immigration Policies* or *Immigration Affairs* or *Immigration 9/11*. Find an article about pre- and post-9/11 immigration guidelines. Did the events of September 11, 2001, change immigration policies? If so, how?

 Additional Activities at **http://elt.thomson.com/gic**

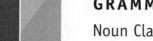

LESSON

9

GRAMMAR: Noun Clauses

Noun Clauses After Verbs and Adjectives
Noun Clauses as Included Questions
Noun Clauses as Direct Quotes
Noun Clauses in Reported Speech

CONTEXT: Caring for Children

Bringing Up Baby
Pediatricians' Recommendations
Day Care
Dr. Benjamin Spock
A Folk Tale
Being an Au Pair

9.1 | Noun Clauses—An Overview

A **clause** is a group of words that has a subject and verb. A **noun clause** functions as a noun in a sentence.

Compare:

noun

He said hello.

noun clause

He said that **he wanted to see the baby.**

Examples	Explanation
I think **that babies are cute.** It's important **that children get a good education.** She didn't realize **that the baby was sick.**	We use a noun clause to include a *statement* within a statement.
I don't know **how old the child is.** I don't remember **if I had a babysitter when I was a child.**	We use a noun clause to include a *question* within a statement.
She said, **"I will pick up my son at 4:30."** I asked, **"Where will you pick him up?"**	We use a noun clause to *repeat* someone's exact words.
She said **that she would pick up her son at 4:30.** I asked her **where she would pick him up.**	We use a noun clause to *report* what someone has said or asked.

BRINGING UP BABY

Before You Read

1. Should employers provide maternity leave for new mothers? Why or why not?

2. Do you think grandparents should have a big part in raising children? Why or why not?

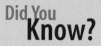

Read the following article. Pay special attention to noun clauses.

Research shows **that a baby's early experiences influence his brain development.** What happens in the first three years of a baby's life affects his emotional development and learning abilities for the rest of his life. It is a well-known fact **that talking to infants increases their language ability** and **that reading to them is the most important thing parents can do to raise a good reader.** Some parents even think **that it's important to play Mozart to babies and show them famous works of art.** However, there is no scientific evidence to support this. It is known, however, **that babies whose parents rarely talk to them or hold them can be damaged for life.** One study shows **that kids who hardly play or who aren't touched very much develop brains 20 to 50 percent smaller than normal.**

Educators have known for a long time **that kids raised in poverty enter school at a disadvantage.** To prevent a gap[1] between the rich and the poor, they recommend early childhood education. A recent study at the University of North Carolina followed children from preschool to young adulthood. The results showed **that children who got high quality preschool education from the time they were infants benefited in later life.** In this study, 35 percent of children who had preschool education graduated from college, compared with only 14 percent of children who did not have preschool education.

While it is important to give babies stimulating activities, experts warn **that parents shouldn't overstimulate them.**

Did You Know?

In 1970, fewer than 8 percent of kids were enrolled in preschool. In 1998, more than 28 percent were enrolled.

[1]A *gap*, in this case, means a difference.

9.2 | Noun Clauses After Verbs and Adjectives

Examples	Explanation
Parents know **(that) kids need a lot of attention.** Some parents think **(that) babies should listen to Mozart.** Studies show **(that) early childhood education is important.**	A noun clause can follow certain **verbs.** *That* introduces a noun clause. *That* is often omitted, especially in conversation.

A noun clause often follows one of these verbs:
 	
    believe   find out   notice   remember
    complain   forget   predict   show
    decide   hope   pretend   suppose
    dream   know   realize   think
    expect   learn   regret   understand
    feel*
 	
Feel followed by a noun clause means "believe" or "think." I *feel* that it's important for a mother to stay home with her baby. = I *believe / think* that it's important for a mother to stay home with her baby.	

I am sure **(that) children need a lot of attention.** Are you surprised **(that) some parents read to babies?** Parents are worried **(that) they don't spend enough time with their kids.**	A noun clause can be the complement of the sentence after certain **adjectives.**

A noun clause often follows *be* + an adjective:
 	
    be afraid   be clear   be obvious
    be amazed   be disappointed   be sure
    be aware   be glad   be surprised
    be certain be happy be worried	

It has been said **that it takes a village to raise a child.**	A noun clause can be used after certain verbs in the passive voice.
A: I hope **that our children will be successful.** **B:** I hope **so** too. **A:** Do you think **that the children are learning something?** **B:** Yes, I think **so.**	Noun clauses can be replaced by *so* after *think, hope, believe, suppose, expect,* and *know.* Do not include *so* if you include the noun clause. *Wrong:* I think **so** the children are learning something.
I realize that the child is tired **and that** he hasn't eaten lunch. I know that you are a loving parent **but that** you can't spend much time with your child.	Connect two noun clauses in the same sentence with *and that* or *but that.*

EXERCISE 1  Underline the noun clauses in the conversation below between two mothers.

EXAMPLE **A:** Do you know <u>that it's good to read to children when they're very young?</u>

B: Yes, I do. But I didn't realize that playing music was important too.

A: I'm not so sure that music is beneficial, but I suppose it can't hurt.

B: I think that it's good to give kids as much education as possible before they go to school.

A: I'm sure that's a good idea. But don't forget that they're just kids. They need to play too.

B: Of course they do. I hope my children will be successful one day.

A: I predict they will be very successful and happy.

EXERCISE 2 Fill in the blanks to complete the noun clause. Answers may vary.

EXAMPLE Research shows that _____*a baby's early experiences*_____ influence his brain development.

1. Educators know that _____ _____
   enter school at a disadvantage.

2. Some parents think that _____ _____
   classical music for babies.

3. We all know that _____ _____
   to babies increases their language ability.

4. A study shows that _____
   have smaller brains.

EXERCISE 3 Respond to each statistic about American families by beginning with "*I'm surprised that . . .*" or "*I'm not surprised that. . .*"

EXAMPLE Fifty percent of marriages in the U.S. end in divorce.
I'm not surprised that 50 percent of marriages end in divorce.

1. Only 26 percent of American households are made up of a mother, a father, and children.

2. About 7 million American children are home alone after school.

3. About 12 percent of American children don't have health insurance.

4. About 20 percent of American children live in poverty.

5. Sixty-eight percent of married mothers work outside the home.

6. In families where both parents work, women do most of the housework and child care.

7. Thirty-two percent of working wives with full-time jobs earn more than their husbands.

8. Fifty-six percent of adults are married.

9. About ten percent of adults live alone.

10. Sixty-five percent of families own their homes.

11. The average size of new American homes has increased as the size of the American family has decreased.

12. Twenty-five percent of households have only one person.

13. Twenty-seven percent of kids live in single-parent families.

EXERCISE 4 ABOUT YOU Fill in the blanks with a noun clause to talk about your knowledge and impressions of the U.S.

EXAMPLES I know *that there are fifty states in the U.S.*

I'm surprised that *so many people live alone.*

1. I think _____

2. I'm disappointed _____

3. I know _____

4. I'm afraid _____

5. It's unfortunate _____

6. I'm surprised _____

7. I've noticed _____

8. Many people think _____

EXERCISE 5 What's your opinion? Answer the questions using *I think* and a noun clause. Discuss your answers.

EXAMPLE Should mothers of small kids stay home to raise them?

I think mothers of small kids should stay home if their husbands can make enough money. But if they need the money, I think they should work.

1. Should the government pay for child care for all children?

2. Can children get the care and attention they need in day care?

3. Should fathers take a greater part in raising their kids?

4. Should grandparents help more in raising their grandchildren?

5. Should the government give new mothers maternity leave? For how long?

6. Should parents read books to babies before they learn to talk?

7. Should parents buy a lot of toys for their children?

PEDIATRICIANS' RECOMMENDATIONS

Before You Read

1. What are some good habits that children should develop? How can their parents encourage these habits?

2. Is television a bad influence on children? Why or why not?

Read the following article. Pay special attention to noun clauses.

Did You Know?

The average American child spends an average of 5.5 hours a day using some form of media (TV, computer, CD player, radio, etc.). More than nine out of ten food ads on Saturday morning TV are for unhealthy foods, such as candy and fast food.

The American Academy of Pediatrics (AAP) is worried that American children spend too much time in front of the TV. The AAP suggests **that pediatricians help parents evaluate their children's entertainment habits.** Doctors are concerned that children who spend too much time in front of the TV don't get enough exercise. At least one in five children is overweight. In the last 20 years, this number has increased more than 50 percent.

The AAP recommends **that children under two not watch any TV at all.** It is essential **that small children have direct interactions with parents for healthy brain growth.** The AAP advises **that parents offer children stimulating activities.**

The AAP recommends **that pediatricians be good role models** by not having TVs in their waiting rooms.

9.3 | Noun Clauses After Expressions of Importance

Examples	Explanation
The AAP *recommends* **that pediatricians be good role models.** The pediatrician *suggested* **that she read to her kids.**	A noun clause is used after verbs that show importance or urgency. The base form is used in the noun clause. The subject pronoun is used before the base form. **Compare Pronouns:** 　　He wants *her* to read. 　　He suggested that *she* read.
Some verbs that express importance or urgency are: 　　advise*　　　　　forbid*　　　　　request 　　ask*　　　　　　insist　　　　　　require* 　　beg*　　　　　　order*　　　　　suggest 　　demand　　　　recommend　　　urge* 　　*The starred verbs can also be followed by an object + infinitive. 　　I advise *that she stay* home with her small children. 　　I advise *her to stay* home with her small children.	
It is essential **that a baby have stimulation.** *It is important* **that parents spend time with their children.**	A noun clause is used after expressions of importance beginning with *it*. The base form is used in the noun clause.
Some expressions that show importance or urgency are: 　　　　　　　It is advisable　　　　　　　　It is important 　　　　　　　It is essential　　　　　　　　It is necessary 　　　　　　　It is imperative　　　　　　　It is urgent The above expressions can also be followed by *for* + object + infinitive. 　　It is essential *that they play* with their children. = 　　It is essential *for them to play* with their children.	
The AAP advises that children under two **not watch** any TV at all.	For negatives, put *not* before the base form.

EXERCISE 6　　Rewrite these sentences as noun clauses.

EXAMPLE　　Kids should see a doctor regularly.

It is important that <u>kids see a doctor regularly.</u>

1. Kids should eat a healthy diet.

   It is essential that _____

2. A child should exercise regularly.

   It is important that _____

3. A child must receive love.

It is essential that _____

4. Children shouldn't watch a lot of TV.

Doctors recommend that _____

5. Doctors want parents to give their children a healthy diet.

Doctors suggest that _____

6. Parents should talk to their babies and hold them.

It is essential that _____

7. Some parents tell their children to turn off the TV.

Some parents insist that _____

8. Children shouldn't eat a lot of candy.

Dentists recommend that _____

9. Parents should be good role models.

It is essential that _____

DAY CARE

1. Do you think it's OK for mothers of small babies to work outside the home?

2. In your native culture, do women with babies work outside the home? Who takes care of the children?

Read the following article. Pay special attention to noun clauses.

Working parents often put their children in day care. While most parents interviewed say they are satisfied with the day care they use, experts believe that only about 12 percent of children receive high quality care. Many parents really don't know **how good their day care service is.**

When choosing a day care center, of course parents want to know **how much it costs.** But there are many other questions parents should ask and observations they should make. Parents need to know **if the caregiver is loving and responds to the child's needs.** Does the caregiver hug the child, talk to the child, smile at the child, play with the child?

It is also important to know **if the day care center is clean and safe.** A parent should find out **how the caregiver takes care of sick children.** Is there a nurse or doctor available to help with medical care? Do caregivers know first aid?

Parents should ask **how many children there are per caregiver.** One caregiver for a group of eight four- or five-year-olds may be enough, but babies need much more attention; one caregiver for three babies is recommended.

Experts believe that parents should not put their babies in child care for the first four months. During this time, it is important for babies to form an attachment to their mothers.

Did You Know?

Twenty percent of preschoolers in married families are cared for by fathers, up from 17% in 1997.

9.4 | Noun Clauses as Included Questions

A noun clause is used to include a question in a statement or another question.

Examples	Explanation
Wh- Questions with auxiliaries or be	
Where is the mother? I don't know **where the mother is**. What should she do? I'm not sure **what she should do**. When will the children go home? Do you know **when the children will go home?**	Use statement word order in an included question—put the subject before the verb.
Wh- Questions with do / does / did	
When do the children go home? I don't know **when the children go home**. What does the child want? Do you know **what the child wants?** Where did the child go? I wonder **where the child went**.	Remove *do / does / did* in the noun clause. The verb will show the *-s* ending or the past tense.
Wh- Questions About the subject	
Who takes care of the kids? I'd like to know **who takes care of the kids**. How many teachers work there? Please tell me **how many teachers work there**.	There is no change in word order in questions about the subject.
Yes / No Questions with auxiliaries or be	
Will the children be safe? I don't know **if the children will be safe**. Is the center clean? I'd like to know **if the center is clean or not**. Can the child play outside? I'm not sure **whether the child can play outside or not**.	Add the word *if* or *whether* before including a *yes / no* question. You can add *or not* at the end. Use statement word order—put the subject before the verb.
Yes / No Questions with do / does / did	
Do the kids like their teacher? Can you tell me **whether the kids like their teacher?** Does the child want to go home? I don't know **if the child wants to go home**. Did your parents give you toys? I can't remember **if my parents gave me toys or not**.	Remove *do / does / did* in the included question. Add *if* or *whether* (. . . *or not*). The verb in the included question will show the *-s* ending or the past tense.

(continued)

An included question is used after phrases such as these:	
I don't know	Do you remember
Please tell me	Do you know
I have no idea	Can you tell me
I wonder	Are you sure
I don't remember	Do you understand
You need to decide	Would you like to know
It's important to ask	Does anyone know
I'm not sure	
Nobody knows	
I can't understand	
I'd like to know	
I can't tell you	

Punctuation Note: Use a period at the end of the included question if the sentence is a statement. Use a question mark if the sentence begins with a question.

   I don't know what time it is.

   Do you know what time it is?

Usage Note: When asking for information, especially from a stranger, an included question sounds more polite than a direct question.

   Direct Question: Who is the director of the day care center?

   More Polite: Can you tell me who the director of the day care center is?

EXERCISE 7 Fill in the blanks with an appropriate question word or phrase (*who, what, where, when, why, how, how many,* or *how much*) or *if* or *whether.*

EXAMPLE   Can you tell me _how much_ time the children spend watching TV?

   I'd like to know _____if_____ the day care center is expensive.

1. I don't know _____ my child's teacher's name is.

2. I can't remember _____ the class begins at seven o'clock or eight o'clock.

3. You should ask _____ people take care of the children. It's good to have a lot of teachers.

4. I would like to know _____ the day care center is clean or not.

5. I would like to know _____ the day care center is expensive.

6. I would like to know _____ the caregivers do if the child gets sick.

7. Can you tell me _____ the director of the program is? I've never met her.

8. I have no idea _____ the day care center costs.

9. Please tell me _____ the day care center is located.

EXERCISE 8 Circle the correct words to complete the statement or question.

EXAMPLE Please tell me how old (*is your child /* (*your child is*)).

1. I'd like to know when (*I have to / do I have to*) pick my child up.

2. Do you know what (*is the teacher's name / the teacher's name is*)?

3. Do you know (*is the center open / if the center is open*) on Saturday?

4. Can you tell me how much (*you paid / did you pay*) for the service?

5. I don't know where (*the day care center is located / is located the day care center*).

6. I want to know how old (*your son is / is your son*).

7. I'd like to know how much (*the service costs / does the service cost / costs the service*).

8. Can you tell me when (*the center closes / closes the center*)?

9. I'd like to know (*the children watch TV / do the children watch TV / if the children watch TV*) at the center.

10. Please tell me (*if works a nurse / whether a nurse works / does a nurse work*) at the center.

11. I'd like to know (*the center has / has the center / whether the center has*) an outdoor playground or not.

12. I wonder (*if the teacher loves / does the teacher love / if loves the teacher*) small children.

EXERCISE 9   Write these questions as included questions. (These are questions about the subject.)

EXAMPLE   Who wants to leave now?

I don't know *who wants to leave now.*

1. How many students in this class come from South America?

I don't know _____

2. Who read the article about working mothers?

I'd like to know _____

3. What happened in the last class?

Can you tell me _____

4. Who brought a dictionary today?

I don't know _____

5. Who failed the test?

I wonder _____

EXERCISE 10   Write these questions as included questions. (These are *wh-* questions with *be* or an auxiliary verb.)

EXAMPLE   How many tests have we had?

I don't remember *how many tests we have had.*

1. When will we have the final exam?

I need to know _____

2. How many lessons are we going to finish?

Can you tell me _____

3. Where is the teacher from?

I wonder _____

4. Where will the final exam be?

You should ask _____

5. When can the teacher see me?

I need to know _____

EXERCISE 11 Write these questions as included questions. (These are *wh-* questions with *do, does,* or *did.*)

EXAMPLE   Where did you buy your books?

Can you tell me *where you bought your books?*

1. When does the class begin?

   Can you tell me _____

2. What grade did I get on the last test?

   Can you tell me _____

3. How many mistakes did I make?

   I'd like to know _____

4. How many questions does the test have?

   It's not important to know _____

5. How many compositions does the teacher want?

   You should ask the teacher _____ _____

EXERCISE 12 Write these questions as included questions. (These are *yes / no* questions with an auxiliary verb or *be.*)

EXAMPLE   Is the teacher American?

I'd like to know *if the teacher is American.*

1. Is the test going to be hard?

   I don't know _____

2. Will you be our teacher next semester?

   I'd like to know _____

3. Can you help us with registration?

   I'd like to know _____

4. Have you been teaching here for a long time?

   Can you tell me _____

5. Are the students confused?

   I have no idea _____

EXERCISE 13   Write these questions as included questions. (These are *yes / no* questions with *do, does,* or *did.*)

EXAMPLE   Does your teacher give a lot of homework?

Can you tell me *if your teacher gives a lot of homework?*

1. Does the school have a cafeteria?

    You should ask _____

2. Did everyone pass the last test?

    I don't know _____

3. Did you buy a used book?

    Please tell me _____

4. Does the teacher speak Spanish?

    I'm not sure _____

5. Do I need to write a composition?

    Can you tell me _____

EXERCISE 14   These are some questions parents can ask before choosing day care for their children. Include each question after "I'd like to know."

EXAMPLE   How much does it cost?

I'd like to know *how much it costs.*

1. Do the caregivers have a lot of experience?

    I'd like to know _____

2. How does the caregiver discipline the children?

    I'd like to know _____

3. Can the caregiver handle problems without getting angry or impatient?

    I'd like to know _____

4. Am I welcome to drop in and visit?

    I'd like to know _____

5. How does the caregiver take care of sick children?

    I'd like to know _____

6. Is there a nurse or doctor to help with medical care?

    I'd like to know _____

7. Are there smoke alarms in the building?

I'd like to know _____

8. How many caregivers are there?

I'd like to know _____

9. Does the caregiver hug the children?

I'd like to know _____

10. How many children are there for each caregiver?

I'd like to know _____

11. Are the toys clean?

I'd like to know _____

12. Is the day care center licensed by the state?

I'd like to know _____

13. Do the children have stimulating activities?

I'd like to know _____

9.5 | Question Words Followed by an Infinitive

Examples	Explanation
What should I do? a. I don't know **what I should do.** b. I don't know **what to do.** Where can I find information? a. Please tell me **where I can find information.** b. Please tell me **where to find information.**	Some noun clauses with *can, could,* and *should* can be shortened to an infinitive phrase. Sentences (a) use a noun clause. Sentences (b) use an infinitive.
Should she work or stay home with her children? a. She can't decide **if she should work or stay home with her children.** b. She can't decide **whether to work or stay home with her children.**	Sentence (a) uses a noun clause. Sentence (b) uses an infinitive. Use *whether,* not *if,* to introduce an infinitive. *Wrong:* She can't decide *if* to work or stay home with her children.
How can I find a good day care center? I don't know **how to find a good day care center.**	An infinitive is used after *know how.*

EXERCISE 15 Complete these sentences with an infinitive phrase.

EXAMPLE What should I do about my problem?

I don't know _what to do about my problem._

1. Where can I buy textbooks?

   I don't know _____

2. What classes should I register for?

   I can't decide _____

3. Should I take morning classes or evening classes?

   I don't know _____

4. What else should I do?

   I don't know _____

5. How can I use the computer in the library?

   I don't know _____

6. What can I do about cancelled classes?

   I don't know _____

7. Should I take biology or physics?

   I can't decide _____

8. Should I buy new textbooks or used books?

   I'm not sure _____

EXERCISE 16 ABOUT YOU Complete each statement with an infinitive phrase. Discuss your answers in a small group or with the entire class.

EXAMPLE I can't decide _whether to stay in this city or move to another city._

1. When I came to this school, I didn't know _____

   _____

2. I can't decide _____

3. When I came to this city, I had to decide _____

   _____

4. A new student at this college needs to know _____

   _____

5. There are so many choices of products in the stores. Sometimes I

   can't decide _____

EXERCISE 🎧 **17** Two students are talking. Fill in the blanks to complete the included questions. Use correct punctuation (period or question mark). Answers may vary.

A: Hi. Where are you going in such a hurry?

B: I need to get to the library before it closes. What time does it close?

A: I'm not sure what time _____*it closes*_____.
(example)

B: What time is it now?

A: I don't have my watch, so I don't know what time _____.
(1)

But I'm sure it must be after six. Why do you need to use the library?

B: The teacher told us to write a paper. She told us to choose a topic.

I don't know what topic _____.
(2)

A: You have small children. Why don't you write about child development?

B: That's a good topic. But I have to start somewhere. I don't even

know where _____.
(3)

A: Try going to the Internet. Use a search engine and type in *child development*.

B: I don't know how _____ the Internet.
(4)

And I don't have a computer at home.

A: You don't? Let's go to the library and use the computers there.

B: I don't know where _____.
(5)

A: They're in the back. Come. I'll show you.

(Later)

B: Uh-oh. The library is closed. I wonder what time

_____ tomorrow.
(6)

A: The sign says, "Open 9 a.m. to 6 p.m."

B: Can you meet me at the library at 10 o'clock tomorrow and help me?

A: I'm not sure _____ or not. I have an appointment
(7)

at 8:30, and I don't know _____
(8)

by 10 o'clock or not. But don't worry; the librarian can show you how
to do a search.

Before You Read

1. Have you ever heard of Dr. Benjamin Spock? What do you know about him?

2. What are some differences in the ways that children are raised in different cultures?

Dr. Benjamin Spock, 1903–1998

Read the following article. Pay special attention to the words in quotation marks ("...") and other noun clauses.

Did You Know?

Dr. Spock's book has been translated into 40 different languages.

New parents are always worried that they might be making a mistake with their new baby. The baby cries, and they don't know if they should let him cry or pick him up. The baby is sick, and they don't know what to do. **"Trust yourself. You know more than you think you do,"** wrote Benjamin Spock in his famous book *Dr. Spock's Baby and Child Care,* which first appeared in 1946. This book has sold over 50 million copies, making it the biggest-selling book after the Bible. In fact, many parents say **that it is the parents' bible for raising children.**

Before Dr. Spock's book appeared, John Watson was the leading child-care expert in the 1920s and 1930s. He wrote, **"Never hug or kiss your children; never let them sit in your lap."** He continued, **"If you must, kiss them once on the forehead when they say good night. Shake hands with them in the morning."** Also, he told parents **that it was necessary to feed children on a rigid schedule.** Dr. Spock disagreed with this strict manner of raising children and decided **that he would write a book. "I wanted to be supportive of parents rather than scold them,"** Dr. Spock said. **"Every baby needs to be smiled at, talked to, played with . . . gently and lovingly. Be natural and enjoy your baby."**

Dr. Spock never imagined **that his book would become so popular.** The last edition came out in 1998, a few months after his death at age 94. He will be remembered for his common-sense advice. **"Respect children because they deserve respect, and they'll grow up to be better people."**

9.6 | Noun Clauses as Exact Quotes of Notable Words

Dr. Spock said, **"Trust yourself."** John Watson said, **"Never hug or kiss your children."** Parents ask, **"What is the right way to take care of a baby?"**	An exact quote is used when the exact words are worth repeating and they are remembered because: • they have been recorded on video or audio. OR • they are a quote from a book, newspaper, or magazine.
a. **Dr. Spock said,** "Every baby needs to be smiled at." b. "Every baby needs to be smiled at," **Dr. Spock said.** c. "Every baby needs to be smiled at," **said Dr. Spock.**	The *said* or *asked* phrase can come at the beginning (a) or the end of a quote (b and c). If it comes at the end, the subject and the verb can be inverted (c).
"More than anything else," **said Dr. Spock,** "children want to help."	An exact quote can be split, with the *said* or *asked* phrase in the middle, separated from the quote by commas.

Language Note:
Study the punctuation of sentences that contain an exact quote. Note that the first letter of an exact quote is a capital.

Dr. Spock said, "Trust yourself."

The mother asked, "Why is the baby crying?"

"Why is he crying?" asked the father.

"I'm going to feed him," said the mother.

"More than anything else," said Spock, "children want love."

EXERCISE 18 Read these quotes by Dr. Spock and Dr. Watson. Add quotation marks and capital letters where they are needed.

EXAMPLE Watson said, **"N**~~n~~ever kiss your child.**"**

1. Spock said you know more than you think you do.

2. Spock said what good mothers and fathers instinctively feel like doing for their babies is usually best.

3. I wanted to be supportive of parents said Spock.

4. Watson said treat your children like small adults.

5. Too much love will harm your baby said Watson.

6. The most important value is to bring up children to help others, first in their family, and then other people said Spock.

7. To reduce violence in our society said Spock we must eliminate violence in the home and on television.

8. If children worship material success rather than truth or compassion Spock said it is because they have absorbed those values from others.

A FOLK TALE

Before You Read

1. What kinds of stories or folk tales are popular for children in your native culture?

2. What stories do you remember your parents telling you when you were a child?

Nasreddin is a character in many folk tales throughout the world. Read this story about Nasreddin. Pay special attention to exact quotes.

One day a neighbor passed Nasreddin's house and saw him outside his barn on his hands and knees. He appeared to be looking for something.

"What are you doing?" the neighbor asked.

"I'm looking for something," answered Nasreddin.

"What are you looking for?" the neighbor asked.

"I'm looking for my ring. It's very valuable," Nasreddin replied.

"I'll help you," said his neighbor. The neighbor got down on his hands and knees and started to help Nasreddin look for his ring. After searching for several hours, the neighbor finally asked, "Do you remember where you were when you lost it?"

"Of course," replied Nasreddin. "I was in the barn milking my cow."

"If you lost your ring inside the barn, then why are we looking for it outside the barn?" asked the neighbor.

"Don't be a fool," said Nasreddin. "It's too dark in the barn. But out here we have light."

9.7 | Exact Quotes in Telling a Story

Examples	Explanation
"What are you doing?" the neighbor asked. **"I'm looking for my ring,"** said Nasreddin.	Exact quotes are used in story telling to give words to the characters. Follow the same punctuation and word order rules as in Section 9.6.
"I will help you," said the neighbor, **"as soon as I can."**	An exact quote can be split, with the *said / asked* phrase in the middle.

EXERCISE 19   Read the following fable[2] by Aesop. Insert quotation marks and correct punctuation.

A hungry wolf was looking for food when he met a house dog that was passing by. Cousin said the dog. Your life is much harder than mine. Why don't you come to work with me and get your food given to you regularly?

I would like that said the wolf. Do you know where I can find such a job?

I will easily arrange that for you said the dog. Come with me to my master's house and we will share my work.

So the wolf and the dog went towards the town together. On the way there, the wolf noticed that the hair on a certain part of the dog's neck was very much worn away, so he asked him how that had come about.

Oh, it is nothing said the dog. That is only the place where the collar is put on me every night to keep me chained up. It hurts a bit at first, but you will soon get used to it.

Then good-bye to you said the wolf. I would rather starve than be a fat slave.

[2] A *fable* is a short story that teaches a lesson. Usually the characters of a fable are animals.

9.8 | Noun Clauses as Reported Speech

We use an **exact quote** when we want to write exactly what someone has said. The exact words are important. We use **reported speech** when we want to paraphrase what someone has said. The exact words are not important or not remembered. The idea is more important than the exact words.

Exact Quote	Reported Speech
Dr. Spock said, **"You know more than you think you do."**	Dr. Spock told parents that they should trust their own instincts.
The dog said to the wolf, **"I will take you to my master's house."**	The dog told the wolf that he **would** show him his way of life.
John Watson said, **"It is necessary to feed children on a rigid schedule."**	John Watson told parents that it **was** necessary to control their children's eating.
Nasreddin said, **"I lost my ring."**	Nasreddin told his neighbor that he **couldn't find** his ring.

EXERCISE **20** In the paragraph below, underline the noun clauses that show reported speech. Circle the verbs in the noun clauses. What tenses are used?

Last week my daughter's day care teacher called me at work and told me that my daughter had a fever and was resting in the nurse's office. I told my boss that I needed to leave work immediately. He said that it would be fine. As I was driving my car on the expressway to the school, a police officer stopped me. She said that I had been driving too fast. She said that I had been driving 10 miles per hour over the limit. I told her that I was in a hurry because my daughter was sick. I said I needed to get to her school quickly. I told the police officer that I was sorry, that I hadn't realized I had been driving so fast. She said she wouldn't give me a ticket that time, but that I should be more careful in the future, whether my daughter was sick or not.

9.9 | The Rule of Sequence of Tenses

After a past tense verb in the main clause (such as *said, told, reported,* etc.), the tense of the verb in the noun clause moves back one tense. This change in tense is called the **rule of sequence of tenses.** Observe the difference in verb tenses in the exact quotes on the left and the reported speech on the right.

Exact Quote	Reported Speech
He said, "I **know** you." (present)	He said (that) he **knew** me. (simple past)
He said, "I **am studying**." (present continuous)	He said (that) he **was studying.** (past continuous)
He said, "She **saw** me yesterday." (simple past)	He said (that) she **had seen** him the day before. (past perfect)
He said, "She **was helping** me." (past continuous)	He said (that) she **had been helping** him. (past perfect continuous)
He said, "I **have taken** the test." (present perfect)	He said (that) he **had taken** the test. (past perfect)
He said, "I **had** never **done** that." (past perfect)	He said (that) he **had** never **done** that. (past perfect) Note: There is no change for the past perfect.
Modals	
He said, "I **can** help you tomorrow."	He said (that) he **could** help me the next day.
He said, "She **may** leave early." (*may* = possibility)	He said (that) she **might** leave early.
He said, "You **may** go." (*may* = permission)	He said (that) I **could** go.
He said, "I **must** go."	He said (that) he **had to** go.
He said, "I **will** stay."	He said (that) he **would** stay.
Modals That Do Not Change Their Forms in Reported Speech	
He said, "You **should** leave."	He said (that) I **should** leave.
He said, "You **should have** left this morning."	He said (that) I **should have** left that morning.
He said, "You **could have** come."	He said (that) I **could have** come.
He said, "You **must have** known."	He said (that) I **must have** known.

Language Note:
We even change the tense in the following sentence:

The teacher asked me what my name **was.**

Even though your name is still the same, the tense shows that the conversation took place at a different time and place.

(continued)

Observe all the differences between a sentence that has an exact quote and a sentence that uses reported speech.

Sentence with Exact Quote:	Sentence with Reported Speech:
She said, "I will help you tomorrow."	She said *that she would* help *me the next day*.
• quotation marks • comma after *said* • doesn't contain *that* • pronouns = *I, you* • verb = *will help* • time = *tomorrow*	• no quotation marks • no comma after *said* • contains *that* (optional) • pronouns = *she, me* • verb = *would help* • time = *the next day*

Language Note:
Time words change in reported speech.

today → that day

yesterday → the day before; the previous day

tomorrow → the next day; the following day

this morning → that morning

tonight → that night

now → at that time

EXERCISE 21 An adult is talking about things her parents and grandparents used to tell her when she was a little girl. Change to reported speech. Follow the rule of sequence of tenses.

EXAMPLE You are the love of my life.
My grandmother told me that ___*I was the love of her life.*___

1. You will always be my baby.

   My mother told me that _____

2. You have an easy life compared to mine.

   My father told me that _____

3. We had a much harder life.

   My grandparents told me that _____

4. We want you to be happy.

   My parents told me that _____

5. You don't understand life.

   My mother told me that _____

6. You have to listen to your teacher.

My father told me that _____

7. You can be anything you want if you study hard.

My parents told me that _____

8. We don't like to punish you, but sometimes it's necessary.

My parents told me that _____

9. Punishing you hurts me more than it hurts you.

My father told me that _____

10. We will always love you.

My grandparents told me that _____

11. You should wash your hands before meals.

My mother told me that _____

12. We will take you to the circus if your grades are good.

My grandparents promised me that _____

9.10 | Say vs. Tell

Examples	Explanation
a. She **said that** the children were happy.	a. In reported speech, we **say** that . . . .
b. She **told me that** the children were happy.	b. In reported speech, we **tell** someone that . . . . Tell is followed by an indirect object, but said is not.
c. She **added that** the day care had 15 staff members.	c. Other common verbs used in reported speech that *do not* have an indirect object are: add answer explain } that reply
d. She **informed the parents that** the day care center would be closed for the holiday.	d. Other common verbs used in reported speech that have an indirect object are: inform notify remind } someone that . . . promise
Compare: She **said,** "I love you." She **said to her daughter,** "I love you."	In an exact quote, we use *say* or *say to someone*. We do not usually use *tell* in an exact quote. *Wrong:* She *told,* "I love you."

EXERCISE 22 Fill in the blanks with *said* or *told*.

EXAMPLES He _____told_____ his children that they should study hard.

I _____said_____ that I was a very happy child.

1. I _____ that I wanted to learn more about raising children.

2. Dr. Spock _____ parents that they should trust their instincts.

3. John Watson _____ that parents should not hug their children.

4. Dr. Spock _____, "You know more than you think you do."

5. The mother _____ to her son, "Eat your vegetables."

6. The mother _____ her son that she would pick him up after school.

7. My parents _____ me that they wanted me to get a good education.

8. I called my parents last week and _____ them about my new roommate.

9. The little girl _____ to her mother, "I want to grow up to be just like you."

10. My parents _____ us to be honest.

EXERCISE 23 Change each sentence to reported speech. Follow the rule of sequence of tenses.

EXAMPLE Lisa said, "I need to put the kids to bed."

Lisa said that she needed to put the kids to bed.

1. Lisa said, "I have never read Dr. Spock's books."

_____

2. Lisa said to her friend, "I want to take my children to the zoo."

_____

3. Lisa said, "My children need to get exercise."

_____

4. Lisa and Paul said, "We will take our kids to the park tomorrow."

_____

5. Lisa said, "I forgot to give the kids their vitamins this morning."

_____

6. Lisa said, "The children went to bed early last night."

_____

7. Lisa said to her neighbor, "My son is in kindergarten."

_____

8. Lisa and Paul said, "Our son wants us to read him a story."

_____

9. Lisa said to Paul, "It's your turn to put the kids to bed."

_____

10. Lisa said to the teacher, "Our son's name is Tod."

_____

11. Tod said to his mother, "I don't want to go to bed."

_____

12. Tod said to his father, "I'm thirsty."

_____

13. Tod said to his friend, "I love my new bicycle."

_____

14. Tod said to his teacher, "I can write my name."

_____

15. Tod said to his friend, "My grandmother will buy me a toy."

_____

16. Lisa said to Tod, "You must go to bed."

_____

17. Tod said to his father, "I can't sleep."

_____

18. Tod said to his father, "I want to watch my favorite program on TV."

_____

19. Paul said to Tod, "You will not get enough sleep."

_____

20. Paul said to Tod, "I don't want to argue with you."

_____

9.11 | Exceptions to the Rule of Sequence of Tenses

Examples	Exceptions to the rule:
Parents **say** that Dr. Spock's book **is** their bible for raising children.	When the main verb is in the **present** tense, we do not change tenses.
Dr. Spock said that children **deserve** respect. Dr. Spock told parents that children **need** love.	In reporting a general truth, it is not necessary to follow the rule of sequence of tenses.
My brother has five children. He said that he **loves** (or **loved**) children. He said that he **wants** (or **wanted**) to have more children.	In reporting something that is still present, you can leave the tenses with no change or follow the rule of sequence of tenses.
Compare: a. Our teacher said that the test on Lesson 9 **will** (or **would**) be next week. b. My kindergarten teacher said that she **would** always remember me.	a. When the action has not happened yet, you can use *will* or *would*. b. When the action is past, use *would*.
A: I can't find my wallet. **B:** I didn't hear you. What did you say? **A:** I said I **can't** find my wallet.	When repeating speech immediately after it was said for someone who did not hear it, we do not usually follow the rule of sequence of tenses.
a. My mother said that she **was** born in 1948. b. My mother said that she **had** (or **had had**) a difficult childhood. c. She said that she lived (or had lived) in Poland when she was a child.	In reporting a statement about the past, it is not necessary to follow the rule of sequence of tenses if it is clear that the original verb was past. In sentence (a), it is clear that she said, "I **was** born in 1948" and not "I **am** born in 1948." It is rare to change *be* to past perfect if there is no confusion of time. In sentence (b), it is clear that she said, "I **had** a difficult childhood" not "I **have** a difficult childhood." In sentence (c), it is clear that she said, "I **lived** in Poland when I was a child."
Compare: a. She said that she **was** angry. b. She said that she **had been** angry, but that later she calmed down.	In sentence (a), she said, "I **am** angry." In sentence (b), she said, "I **was** angry." We change to past perfect in sentence (b) to show that the anger was gone by the time she said something about it.

EXERCISE 24 Circle the correct verb to complete these sentences. In a few cases, both answers are possible.

1. She said that she *will / would* come to the U.S. in 2001.

2. The teacher said that we *will / would* finish this lesson next week.

3. I always say that money *isn't / wasn't* as important as health.

4. She said that she *can't / couldn't* come to my party last week.

5. Pediatricians say that children *watch / watched* too much TV.

6. My little brother said that he *wants / wanted* to be president when he grows up.

7. Last semester our teacher said that we *will / would* have our final exam on Saturday, so all the students were unhappy. But they came anyway.

8. Our teacher last semester said that her name *is / was* Sandy and that she *wants / wanted* us to call her by her first name.

9. My doctor said that fatty food *is / was* bad for your health.

10. My boss said that he *lost / had lost* his keys.

11. Last Saturday, he said that he *needed / had needed* my help because he was moving that day.

9.12 | Reporting an Imperative

Examples	Explanation

"Trust yourself." Spock **told** parents **to trust** themselves.
 	
 "Sit down, please." She **asked** me **to sit** down.
	To report an imperative, an infinitive is used. Use *ask* for an invitation or request. Use *tell* for a command or instruction. Don't use *say* to report an imperative.
	    Wrong: She *said me to sit* down.
	 Use an object after *tell* or *ask*.
	    Wrong: He *told to close* the door.

"Don't hit your children." The doctor told us **not to hit** our children.	For a negative, put *not* before the infinitive.

Language Note:
Don't forget to change the pronouns and possessive forms in the infinitive phrase.
   "Show **your** children love."
   He told us to show **our** children love.

   "Give **me your** book."
   He asked me to give **him my** book.

EXERCISE 25 Change these imperatives to reported speech. Use *asked* or *told* + an object pronoun.

EXAMPLE   The mother told her children, "Study for your test."
The mother told them to study for their test.

1. The son said to his mother, "Read me a story."

   _____

2. She told the babysitter, "Don't let the kids watch TV all day."

   _____

3. The girl said to her father, "Buy me a doll."

   _____

4. The mother said to her child, "Eat your vegetables."

   _____

5. The father said to his daughter, "Help me in the garage."

   _____

6. The girl said to her parents, "Take me to the zoo."

   _____

7. The dentist said to the boy, "Brush your teeth after every meal."

   _____

8. I said to my parents, "Don't spoil your grandchildren."

   _____

9. The girl said to her mother, "Comb my hair."

   _____

10. The father said to his daughter, "Do your homework."

    _____

11. The father said to his teenage daughter, "Don't come home late."

    _____

12. The father said to his son, "Always be a gentleman."

    _____

EXERCISE 26 Circle the correct word to complete this story about a babysitter.

Last month I babysat for a family that lives near me. It was my first

babysitting job. They (*said* / *told*) that the children (*would* / *will*) sleep
            (example)   (1)

through the night and not cause any problems. But Danielle, the three-

year-old girl, woke up at 9 and (*said* / *told*) that (*I* / *she*) (*can't* / *couldn't*)
                                        (2)   (3)   (4)

sleep. I (*said* / *told*) her that I (*will* / *would*) read (*her* / *you*) a story. Every
            (5)   (6)   (7)

time I finished the story, she (*said* / *told*) me (*read* / *to read*) (*her* / *me*)
                                  (8)   (9)   (10)

another one. She finally fell asleep at 10. Then Estelle, the five-year-old,

started crying. When I went to her room, she told me that (*I* / *she*)
                                                              (11)

(*has seen* / *had seen*) a monster in the closet. I tried to (*tell* / *say*) her that
        (12)   (13)

there (*aren't* / *weren't*) any monsters in her closet, but she didn't stop
          (14)

crying. I wanted to call the parents and tell them that Estelle (*is* / *was*)
                                                                    (15)

upset and that she (*is* / *was*) crying. They had given me their cell phone
                      (16)

number and told me (*call* / *to call*) (*us* / *them*) in case of any problem,
                        (17)   (18)

but when I called, there was no answer. Later they told me that they

(*must* / *had to*) turn off their cell phone because they were at a concert.
    (19)

They said (*we* / *they*) (*would* / *will*) be home by 11. But they
              (20)   (21)

didn't come home till 1 a.m. They called and told me that the concert

(*has started* / *had started*) an hour late. I called my mother and told
          (22)

her that I (*can't* / *couldn't*) leave because the parents hadn't come home.
              (23)

She told me (*don't / not to*) worry. She said that it (*is / was*) my respon-
(24)   (25)

sibility to stay with the kids until the parents came home. When they

finally got home, they told me that (*we / they*) (*don't / didn't*) have any
(26)   (27)

money to pay (*you / me*) because they (*have forgotten / had forgotten*)
(28)   (29)

to stop at a cash machine. They said that (*they / we*) (*would / will*)
(30)   (31)

pay (*you / me*) (*next / the following*) week.
(32)   (33)

When I got home, my mother was waiting up for me. I told her that I

(*don't / didn't*) ever want to have children. She laughed and told me that
(34)

the children's behavior (*wasn't / isn't*) unusual. She told me that (*you / I*)
(35)   (36)

(*will / would*) change (*my / your*) mind some day. I (*said / told*) her
(37)   (38)   (39)

that I (*don't / didn't*) want to babysit ever again. She told me that I
(40)

(*will / would*) get used to it.
(41)

BEING AN AU PAIR

Before You Read

1. Have you ever taken care of small children?

2. Do you know anyone who works in child care?

Read the following article. Pay special attention to reported questions.

Five years ago, when I was 18 years old and living in my native Estonia, I read an article about an "au pair" program in the U.S. This is a program where young people, mostly women between the ages of 18 and 25, go to live in the U.S. with an American family for a year to take care of their small children. In the process, these young people can improve their English, learn about American culture, and travel in the U.S.

When I heard about it, I became very excited and asked my mother **if I could join.** At first she said, "Absolutely not." She asked me **why I wanted to leave our family for a year.** I told her that it would be an opportunity for me to improve my English. I have always wanted to be an English teacher in Estonia, but my English was far from perfect. My mother said she would talk it over with Dad, and they finally agreed to let me go.

After filling out the application, I had an interview. The interviewer asked **why I wanted to be an au pair.** She also asked me **whether I knew how to drive.** Sometimes an au pair has to drive kids to school and to play dates. I told her that I had just gotten my license. I asked her **how many hours a week I would have to work**, and she said 45. I wanted to know **if I would get paid,** and she said I would be paid about $200 a week. I also wanted to know **if I would have the opportunity to go to school in the U.S.,** and she said, "Yes." She told me that the family would have to help pay for my schooling. I asked her **if I had to do housework,** and she said no, that my job was only to take care of the kids: wake them up, get them dressed, give them breakfast, take them to school, and help them with homework.

I was so excited when I was accepted.

My year in the U.S. (in Lansing, Michigan) was wonderful. The family treated me like a member of their family, taking me with them on trips and other family outings. I met other au pairs from around the world and have made many new friends. My English is 100 percent better now.

Friends often ask me **if I am happy that I spent a year in the U.S.,** and I say, "This was the opportunity of a lifetime."

Did You Know?

Parents today spend 22 hours a week less with their kids than parents did in 1969.

9.13 | Noun Clauses as Reported Questions

When we report a question, we follow the rule of sequence of tenses if the main verb is in the **past tense** (*asked, wanted to know, tried to understand*, etc.). Remember: Reported speech is a paraphrase of what someone has said. The exact words are not important or not remembered. The idea is more important than the exact words.

Wh-* Questions with auxiliaries or *be	
"How old are you?" She asked me **how old I was.** "Where will I go to school?" I asked her **where I would go to school.** "What's your name?" She asked me **what my name was.**	Use statement word order—put the subject before the verb. Use a period at the end. An object (*me, him, her*, etc.) can be added after *asked*.
Wh-* Questions with *do / does / did	
"Why do you want to be an au pair?" She asked me **why I wanted to be an au pair.** "How did you hear about the program?" She asked me **how I had heard about the program.**	Remove *do / does / did* in the noun clause. Use statement word order—put the subject before the verb.
***Wh-* Questions about the subject**	
"Who taught you to drive?" She asked me **who had taught me to drive.** "What happened?" She asked me **what had happened.**	There is no change in word order in questions about the subject.
Yes / No* Questions with auxiliaries or *be	
"Will I have time to go to school?" I asked her **if I would have time to go to school.** "Can I take classes?" I asked her **whether I could take classes or not.** "Am I responsible for housework?" I asked **whether I was responsible for housework.**	Add the word *if* or *whether* before reporting a *yes / no* question. You can add *or not* at the end. Use statement word order—put the subject before the verb.
Yes / No* Questions with *do / does / did	
"Do I have to do housework?" I asked her **whether I had to do housework.** "Does your mother approve?" She asked me **if my mother approved.** "Did you receive the application?" She asked me **if I had received the application.**	Remove *do / does / did*. Use statement word order—put the subject before the verb.

Language Notes:
1. If the *ask* phrase is in the present tense, do not follow the rule of sequence of tenses. Keep the same tenses as the original question.

   "**Are** you happy that you **spent** a year in the U.S.?"

   Friends often ask me if I **am** happy that I **spent** a year in the U.S.
2. For exceptions to the rule of sequence of tenses, see Section 9.11.

   She asked me if Estonia is in Europe.

EXERCISE 27   These are some questions the interviewer asked the au pair candidate. Change these questions to reported speech.

EXAMPLE   How old are you?

She asked me _how old I was._

1. Have you discussed this with your parents?

   She asked me _____

2. Do you have experience with small children?

   She asked me _____

3. When did you graduate from high school?

   She asked me _____

4. Do you have younger sisters and brothers?

   She asked me _____

5. Do you speak English?

   She asked me _____

6. Have you ever traveled to another country?

   She asked me _____

7. Do you have a driver's license?

   She asked me _____

8. How long have you had your driver's license?

   She asked me _____

9. Did you receive our brochure?

   She asked me _____

10. What are your plans for the future?

    She asked me _____

11. Have you ever left your parents before?

    She asked me _____

EXERCISE 28 These are some questions the au pair candidate asked the interviewer.

EXAMPLE How much will I get paid?

She asked her _how much she would get paid._

1. Will I have my own room?

   She asked her _____

2. How many children does the family have?

   She asked her _____

3. How old are the children?

   She asked her _____

4. Are the children in school?

   She asked her _____

5. Should I get an international driver's license?

   She asked her _____

6. What is the climate like in Michigan?

   She asked her _____

7. Does the family have a computer?

   She asked her _____

8. Can I e-mail my own family every day?

   She asked her _____

9. When will I get a vacation?

   She asked her _____

10. How much is the airfare?

    She asked her _____

11. Who will pay for the airfare?

    She asked her _____

12. Where can I study English?

    She asked her _____

EXERCISE 29 Change these questions to reported speech.

EXAMPLE The babysitter asked the child, "Do you feel sick?"

The babysitter asked the child _if he felt sick._

1. The babysitter asked the parents, "What time will you be home?"

   The babysitter asked the parents _____

2. The babysitter asked the parents, "Where are you going?"

   The babysitter asked the parents _____

3. The children asked the babysitter, "What's your name?"

   The children asked the babysitter _____

4. The babysitter asked the little boy, "How old are you?"

   The babysitter asked the little boy _____

5. The babysitter asked the parents, "Have the kids eaten dinner yet?"

   The babysitter asked the parents _____

6. The children asked the babysitter, "Do we have to go to bed at 8 p.m.?"

   The children asked the babysitter _____

7. The babysitter asked the parents, "Should I give the kids a snack before bed?"

   The babysitter asked the parents _____

8. The children asked the babysitter, "Do you want to play a game with us?"

   The children asked the babysitter _____

9. The children asked the babysitter, "Can we watch TV?"

   The children asked the babysitter _____

10. The parents asked the babysitter, "Have you ever taken care of an infant before?"

    The parents asked the babysitter _____

11. The babysitter asked the parents, "Do you have a phone number where I can reach you?"

    The babysitter asked the parents _____

12. The babysitter asked the parents, "Can I use your telephone?"

    The babysitter asked the parents _____

9.14 | Noun Clauses After Other Past Tense Verbs

Examples	Explanation
Dr. Spock *decided* that **he would write a book.**	If the verb in the main clause is past tense (*thought, knew, believed, wondered, realized, decided, imagined, understood, was sure,* etc.), follow the rule of sequence of tenses in Section 9.9.
He *thought* that **he could help parents feel more comfortable with their kids.**	
He *knew* **that he wanted to help parents.**	
The au pair *didn't know* **if she would be happy in the U.S.**	
She *wondered* **what her life would be like in the U.S.**	
Her mother *wasn't sure* **whether she should let her daughter to go the U.S. or not.**	

EXERCISE **30** ABOUT YOU Fill in the blanks and discuss your answers. Follow the rule of sequence of tenses.

EXAMPLE Before I came to this city, I thought that *everybody here was unfriendly,* but it isn't true.

1. Before I came to this city (or the U.S.), I thought that _____
   _____, but it isn't true.

2. Before I came to this city (or the U.S.), I didn't know that _____
   _____

3. Before I came to this city (or the U.S.), I was worried that _____
   _____

4. When I lived in my hometown, I was afraid that _____
   _____

5. When I came to this school, I was surprised to learn that _____
   _____

6. When I came to this school, I realized that _____
   _____

7. When I was younger, I never imagined that _____
   _____

8. Before I came to the U.S. (or this city), I wondered _____
   _____

EXERCISE 31 ABOUT YOU Fill in the blanks to tell about you and your parents when you were a child.

EXAMPLE   When I was a child, I dreamed that _____*I would be a movie star.*_____

1. My parents told me that _____

2. My parents hoped that _____

3. My parents thought that _____

4. When I was a child, I dreamed that _____

5. When I was a child, I thought that _____

6. When I was a child, I didn't understand _____

7. When I was younger, I never imagined that _____

8. When I was younger, I wondered _____

9. When I was younger, I didn't know _____

10. When I was younger, I couldn't decide _____

EXERCISE 32

Combination Exercise. The author of this book remembers this true story from her childhood. Change the words in parentheses to reported speech.

When I was about 6 years old, I had the measles.[3] My mother told me

_____*to stay in the bedroom*_____ because it was dark in there. She said
        (example: "Stay in the bedroom.")

_____. My bedroom was near
        (1 "I don't want the bright light to hurt your eyes.")

the dining room of the house. My mother told me _____

_____ because it was dark in
        (2 "You can go into the dining room.")

there. She told me _____ because
                          (3 "Don't go into the living room.")

it was too light there. The TV was in the living room and she thought

_____.
        (4 "The brightness of the TV can hurt your eyes.")

My sister Micki was three years older than I and liked to bully[4] me. She had already had the measles, so she wasn't afraid of getting

sick. She came to the door of my bedroom and asked me _____

_____. I told her
        (5 "Do you know why you can't go into the living room?")

[3] *Measles* is an illness that children often get. The medical name is rubeola.
[4] To *bully* means to act cruel to someone who is smaller and more helpless.

_____. She said, "The living room is
(6 "I don't understand.")

for living people. The dining room is for dying people, and you're gonna
die." Of course, I believed her because she was 9 years old and knew

much more than I did. I didn't understand that _____

_____ .
(7 " 'Dining' means 'eating,' not 'dying'.")

Today we can laugh about this story, but when I had the measles, I was

afraid that _____ .
(8 "I will die.")

EXERCISE 33

Combination Exercise. This is a composition written by a former
au pair. Change the words in parentheses ( ) to reported speech.

    Two years ago, when I was 18 and living in my native Poland, I didn't

know exactly ___*what I should do*___ with my life. I had just graduated
(example: "What should I do?")

from high school and I couldn't decide _____ .
(1 "Should I go to college or not?")

I was not sure _____. A neighbor
(2 "What do I want to do with my life?")

of mine told me _____ and
(3 "I had the same problem when I was your age.")

decided to go to the U.S. for a year to work as an "au pair." She asked me

_____ . I told
(4 "Have you ever heard of the au pair program in America?")

her that _____ . She told me that
(5 "I haven't.")

_____ , helping them take care
(6 "I lived with an American family for a year.")

of their two small children. I asked her _____ .
(7 "How much will this program cost me?")

She laughed and told me _____
(8 "You will earn about $200 a week, get your own room, and

_____ . She also told me _____
get three meals a day.")   (9 "You will have a chance to travel in the U.S.")

I asked her _____ , and she said
(10 "Was it a good experience for you?")

_____ . She said _____
(11 "It has changed my life.")

_____and _____
(12 "I have gained a new understanding of people.")

_____. I asked her _____
(13 "My English has improved a lot.")   (14 "Is the work very hard?")

and she said _____ but that _____.
(15 "It is.")   (16 "It is very rewarding.")

I looked up *au pair* on the Internet and found out how to apply. I

told my parents that _____.
(17 "I am thinking about going to America for a year.")

At first they told me _____. They thought that
(18 "Don't go.")

_____ and that __ _____.
(19 "You are too young.")   (20 "You don't have any experience.")

I reminded them _____ _____
(21 "I have babysat many times for our neighbors' kids.")

and that by working in America _____.
(22 "I will get even more experience.")

I also told them that _____ _____,
(23 "My English will improve if I live with an American family.")

My parents finally agreed to let me go. I filled out the application, had
an interview, and was accepted.

I told my parents _____. I promised them
(24 "Don't worry.")

_____.
(25 "I will keep in touch with you by e-mail almost every day.")

When I arrived, my American family explained to me _____

_____ _____. They had two small kids, and I had to wake them
(26 "What do I have to do?")

up, make them breakfast, and take them to school in the morning. I asked

them _____, and they laughed. They told
(27 "Do I have to wait for them at school?")

me _____.
(28 "While the kids are in school, you can take English classes at a local college.")

I told them _____ _____,
(29 "I don't have enough money to pay for school.")

but they told me _____. So that's what
(30 "We will pay for your classes.")

I did. I met students from all over the world. I also had a chance to
travel to many American cities with other au pairs. When the year was

over, I was very sad to leave my new family, but we promised _____

_____. They told me

(31 "We will stay in touch.")

_____.

(32 "You will always be welcome in our house.")

    Now I am back home and in college, majoring in early childhood

education. My parents told me _____.

(33 "We are happy we let you go to America.")

They can see that I've become much more confident and mature.
Becoming an au pair in America was one of the best experiences of
my life.

SUMMARY OF LESSON 9

Direct statement or question	Sentence with included statement or question	Use of noun clause or infinitive
She loves kids. She is patient.	I know **that she loves kids.** I'm sure **that she is patient.**	A noun clause is used after verbs and adjectives.
Talk to your children. Don't be so strict.	It is essential **that you talk to your children.** He recommends **that we not be so strict.**	A noun clause is used after expressions of importance. The base form is used in the noun clause.
Is the baby sick? What does the baby need?	If don't know **if the baby is sick or not.** I'm not sure **what the baby needs.**	A noun clause is used as an included question.
What should I do with the crying baby? Where can I get information about the "au pair" program?	I don't know **what to do with the crying baby.** Can you tell me **where to get information about the "au pair" program?**	An infinitive can replace *should* or *can*.
You know more than you think you do. Do you have children?	Dr. Spock said, **"You know more than you think you do."** **"Do you have children?"** asked the doctor.	A noun clause is used in an exact quote to report what someone has said.
I will read a book about child care. Do you have experience with children?	She said **that she would read a book about child care.** She asked me **if I had experience** with children.	A noun clause is used in reported speech to paraphrase what someone has said.
Trust yourself. Don't give the child candy.	He told us **to trust ourselves.** He told me **not to give the child candy.**	An infinitive is used to report an imperative.

1. Use *that* or nothing to introduce an included statement. Don't use *what*.

   that
   I know ~~what~~ she likes to swim.

2. Use statement word order in an indirect question.

   it is
   I don't know what time ~~is it~~.

   I don't know where (lives) your brother.

3. We *say* something. We *tell* someone something.

   told
   He ~~said~~ me that he wanted to go home.

   said
   He ~~told~~, "I want to go home."

4. Use *tell* or *ask*, not *say*, to report an imperative. Follow *tell* and *ask* with an object.

   told
   I ~~said~~ you to wash your hands.

   me
   She asked ˄ to show her my ID card.

5. Don't use *to* after *tell*.

   He told ~~to~~ me that he wanted to go home.

6. Use *if* or *whether* to introduce an included *yes/no* question.

   if
   I can't decide ˄ I should buy a car or not.

   whether
   I don't know ˄ it's going to rain or not.

7. Use *would*, not *will*, to report something that is past.

   would
   My father said that he ~~will~~ come to the U.S. in 1995.

8. Follow the rule of sequence of tenses when the main verb is in the past.

   wanted
   When I was a child, my grandmother told me that she ~~wants~~ to travel.

9. Don't use *so* before a noun clause.

   He thinks ~~so~~ the U.S. is a beautiful country.

10. Use the base form after expressions showing importance or urgency.

> *be*
> It is urgent that you ~~are~~ on time for the meeting.

> *review*
> I suggested that the teacher ~~reviewed~~ the last lesson.

11. Use *not* + base form to form the negative after expressions showing importance or urgency.

> *not*
> Doctors recommend that small children ~~don't~~ watch TV.

12. Use a period, not a question mark, if a question is included in a statement.

> I don't know what time it is~~?~~

13. Use correct punctuation in an exact quote.

> He said, "I love you."

14. Don't use a comma before a noun clause (EXCEPTION: an exact quote).

> He knows~~,~~ that you like him.

15. *Don't* isn't used in reporting a negative imperative.

> *not to*
> He told me ~~don't~~ open the door.

LESSON 9 TEST/REVIEW

PART 1 Find the mistakes with the underlined words, and correct them. Not every sentence has a mistake. If the sentence is correct, write *C*.

EXAMPLES   I don't know where ~~does~~ your brother live .
                                                              is ^

"What do you want?" asked the man.   **C**

1. I'd like to know what I need to study for the final exam.

2. She is happy what her daughter got married.

3. I don't know what you want.

4. He said me that he wanted my help.

5. I don't know what time is it.

6. The president said, "There will be no new taxes."

7. I don't know what to do.

8. I don't know where should I go for registration.

9. I told you not to leave the room.

10. The weatherman said that it will rain on Sunday, but it didn't.

11. Do you think so New Yorkers are friendly people?

12. Do you think I'm intelligent?

13. I don't know she understands English or not.

14. He asked me how do I feel.

15. He told that he wanted to speak with me.

16. He said to his father, "I'm an adult now."

17. I didn't know that learning English would be so hard.

18. Before I started looking for a job, I thought that I will find a job right away, but I didn't.

19. He told to me that he wanted to buy a car.

20. He said me to open the window.

21. She told me don't use her computer.

22. I didn't understand what did I need to do.

23. It is important that you be here before 9 o'clock.

24. I recommend that you not give the answers to anyone.

25. I suggest that my friend visits me during vacation.

26. My counselor advised that I didn't take so many credit hours.

PART 2 Find the mistakes with **punctuation** in the following sentences. Not every sentence has a mistake. If the sentence is correct, write *C*.

EXAMPLES He said, "I can't help you."

He said, "I have to leave now."   **C**

1. I don't know what time it is?

2. Do you know what time it is?

3. I'm sure, that you'll find a job soon.

4. The teacher said I will return your tests on Monday.

5. I didn't realize, that you had seen the movie already.

6. He asked me, "What are you doing here?"

7. "What do you want," he asked.

8. "I want to help you," I said.

9. I told him that I didn't need his help.

10. Can you tell me where I can find the bookstore.

PART 3 Fill in the blanks with an included question.

EXAMPLE   How old is the president?

Do you know _____ *how old the president is?* _____

1. Where does Jack live?

I don't know _____

2. Did she go home?

I don't know _____

3. Why were they late?

Nobody knows _____

4. Who ate the cake?

I don't know _____

5. What does "liberty" mean?

I don't know _____

6. Are they working now?

Can you tell me _____

7. Should I buy the car?

I don't know _____

8. Has she ever gone to Paris?

I'm not sure _____

9. Can we use our books during the test?

Do you know _____

10. What should I do?

I don't know _____

PART 4 Change the following sentences to reported speech. Follow the rule of sequence of tenses or use the infinitive where necessary.

EXAMPLE   He said, "She is late."

He said that she was late. _____

1. She said, "I can help you."

_____

2. He said, "Don't go away."

_____

3. He said, "My mother left yesterday."

_____

4. She said, "I'm learning a lot."

_____

5. He said, "I've never heard of Dr. Spock."

_____

6. He said, "Give me the money."

_____

7. They said to me, "We finished the job."

_____

8. He said to us, "You may need some help."

_____

9. He said to her, "We were studying."

_____

10. He said to her, "I have your book."

_____

11. He said to us, "You should have called me."

_____

12. He said to his wife, "I will call you."

_____

13. He asked me, "Do you have any children?"

_____

14. He asked me, "Where are you from?"

_____

15. He asked me, "What time is it?"

_____

16. He asked me, "Did your father come home?"

_____

17. He asked me, "Where have you been?"

_____

18. He asked me, "Will you leave tomorrow?"

_____

19. He asked me, "What do you need?"

_____

20. He asked me, "Are you a student?"

_____

21. He asked us, "Can you help me today?"

_____

22. He asked us, "Who needs my help?"

_____

EXPANSION ACTIVITIES

Classroom Activities

1. Write questions you have about the topics in the readings of this lesson. Express your questions with *"I wonder . . . "* Compare your questions in a small group.

EXAMPLES I wonder why parents spend so much less time with their children than they used to.

I wonder why it is so hard to raise a child.

2. What advice did your parents, teachers, or other adults give you when you were younger? Write three sentences. Share them in a small group.

EXAMPLES My mother told me to be honest.

My grandfather told me that I should always respect older people.

_____

_____

_____

Talk About it

1. How is your philosophy of raising children different from your parents' philosophy or methods?

2. Do you think parents should or shouldn't hit children when they misbehave?

3. Did your parents read to you when you were a child?

4. Did you have a lot of toys when you were a child?

5. Do you think children today behave differently from when you were a child?

6. Is it hard to raise children? Why?

7. Read the following poem. Discuss the meaning.

> Your children are not your children.
> They are the sons and daughters of Life's longing for itself.
> They come through you but not from you,
> And though they are with you, yet they belong not to you.
> You may give them your love but not your thoughts.
> For they have their own thoughts.
> You may house their bodies but not their souls,
> For their souls dwell in the house of tomorrow, which you cannot
>   visit, not even in your dreams.
> You may strive to be like them, but seek not to make them like you.
> For life goes not backward nor tarries with yesterday.
> You are the bows from which your children as living arrows are
>   sent forth.
>
> . . .
>
> Let your bending in the archer's hand be for gladness;
> For even as he loves the arrow that flies, so he loves also the bow
>   that is stable.

> Kahil Gibran (From *The Prophet*)

Write About it

1. Write a paragraph about an interesting conversation or argument that you had or that you heard recently.

> **EXAMPLE** Last week I had a conversation with my best friend about having children. I told her that I didn't want to have children. She asked me why I was against having kids. . . .

2. Write about an unpopular belief that you have. Explain why you have this belief and why it is unpopular.

> **EXAMPLES** I believe that there is life on other planets.
>
> I believe that schools shouldn't have tests.

3. Write about a belief you used to have that you no longer have. Explain what this belief was and why you no longer believe it to be true.

> **EXAMPLES** I used to believe that communism was the best form of government.
>
> I used to believe that marriage made people happy.

4. Write about a general belief that people in your native culture have. Explain what this belief means. Do you agree with it?

   EXAMPLES In my native country, it is said that it takes a village to raise a child.

   In my native culture, it is believed that wisdom comes with age.

5. Write a short fable or fairy tale that you remember. Include the characters' words in quotation marks. See the folk tale on page 393 for an example.

6. Write about an incident from your childhood, like the one in Exercise 32.

Outside Activities

1. Interview a classmate, coworker, or neighbor about his or her childhood. Find out about this person's family, school, house, activities, and toys. Tell the class what this person said, using reported speech.

2. Interview a friend, coworker, or neighbor who has a child or children. Ask him or her these questions:

   What's the hardest thing about raising a child?
   What's the best thing about raising a child?

   Report this person's answers to the class.

Internet Activities

1. At a search engine, type in *parents, parenting,* or *family*. What kind of information can parents get about raising children from a Web site? Bring this information to class.

2. At a search engine, type in *au pair*. Find out how to apply for an au pair program. Bring an application to class.

3. For information about parenting and children, find these Web sites by typing in their names at a search engine:

   Zero to Three
   I am your child

   Find some information about children that surprises you. Bring this information to class.

4. At a search engine, type in *day care center* and the name of the city where you live. Find out five facts about a specific day care center. Bring this information to class.

 Additional Activities at **http://elt.thomson.com/gic**

LESSON

10

GRAMMAR

Unreal Conditions—Present
Real Conditions vs. Unreal Conditions
Unreal Conditions—Past
Wishes

CONTEXT: Science or Science Fiction?

Time Travel
Traveling to Mars
Life 100 Years Ago
Science or Wishful Thinking?

Before You Read

1. Do you think time travel is a possibility for the future?

2. Can you name some changes in technology or medicine that happened since you were a child?

Read the following article. Pay special attention to unreal conditions.

If you **could travel** to the past or the future, which time period **would** you **visit?** What would you like to see? **Would** you **want** to come back to the present? If you **could travel** to the past and prevent your grandfather from meeting your grandmother, then you **wouldn't be** here, right? These ideas may seem the subject of science fiction movies and novels now, but believe it or not, physicists are studying the possibility of time travel seriously.

About 100 years ago, Albert Einstein proved that the universe has not three dimensions but four—three of space and one of time. He proved that time changes with motion. A moving clock ticks more slowly than one that does not move. Einstein believed that, theoretically, time travel is possible. If

Albert Einstein 1879–1955

you **wanted** to visit the Earth in the year 3000, you **would have to** get on a rocket ship going at almost of the speed of light,[1] go to a star 500 light years away, turn around and come back at that speed. When you got back, the Earth **would be** 1,000 years older, but you **would** only **be** ten years older. You **would** be in the future.

However, using today's technologies, if you **wanted** to travel to the nearest star, it **would take** 85,000 years to arrive. (This assumes the speed of today's rockets, which is 35,000 miles per hour.) According to Einstein, you can't travel faster than the speed of light. While most physicists believe that travel to the future is possible, many believe that travel to the past will never happen.

Science and technology are evolving at a rapid pace. **Would** you **want** to travel to the future to see all the changes that will occur? **Would** you **be** able to come back to the present and warn people of future earthquakes or accidents? These ideas, first presented in a novel called *The Time Machine*, written by H.G. Wells over 100 years ago, are the subject not only of fantasy but of serious scientific exploration. In fact, many of today's scientific discoveries and explorations, such as traveling to the moon, had their roots in science fiction novels and movies.

Did You Know?

In 1955, Albert Einstein died at the age of 76. He had requested that his body be cremated but that his brain be saved and studied for research.

Read what people have said in the past about the future.

"Heavier-than-air flying machines are impossible."
  (Lord Kelvin, president, Royal Society, 1895)

"There is no reason for any individual to have a computer in their home."
  (Ken Olsen, president, chairman, and founder of Digital Equipment Corp., 1977)

"The telephone has too many shortcomings to be seriously considered as a means of communication. The device is inherently of no value to us."
  (Western Union internal memo, 1876)

"Airplanes are interesting toys but of no military value."
  (Marshal Ferdinand Foch, French commander of Allied forces during the closing months of World War I, 1918)

"Who . . . wants to hear actors talk?"
  (Harry M. Warner, Warner Brothers, 1927)

"Everything that can be invented has been invented."
  (Charles H. Duell, commissioner, U.S. Office of Patents, 1899)

[1] The *speed of light* is 299,792,458 meters per second (or 186,000 miles per second).

10.1 | Unreal Conditions—Present

An unreal condition is used to talk about a hypothetical or imagined situation.

Examples	Explanation

If we **had** a time machine, we **could travel** to the future or past.
    (Reality: We **don't have** a time machine.)
 	
If I **could travel** to the past, I **would visit** my ancestors.
    (Reality: I **can't travel** to the past.)
 	
If we **didn't have** computers, our lives **would be** different.
    (Reality: We **have** computers.)
	An unreal condition in the **present** describes a situation that is not real now.
	
	Use a past form in the *if* clause and *would* or *could* + base form in the main clause.

If we **could travel** at the speed of light, we**'d be able** to visit the future. If I **visited** my great-great-great-grandparents, they**'d be** very surprised to meet me.	All pronouns except *it* can contract with *would*: *I'd, you'd, he'd, she'd, we'd, they'd.*
If time travel **were** possible, many people **would do** it. If we **were** time travelers, we**'d see** the future.	*Were* is the correct form in the condition clause for all subjects, singular and plural. However, you will often hear native speakers use *was* with *I, he, she,* and *it.*
If I **were** you, I**'d study** more science.	We often give advice with the expression *"If I were you . . ."*
What if you could travel to the future? **What if** you had the brain of Einstein?	We use *what if* to propose a hypothetical situation.
If you **had** Einstein's brain, what **would** you **do?** If you **could** fly to another planet, **would** you **go?**	When we make a question with conditionals, the *if* clause uses statement word order. The main clause uses question word order.

Punctuation Note:
When the *if* clause precedes the main clause, a comma is used to separate the two clauses. When the main clause precedes the *if* clause, a comma is not used.

    If I had Einstein's brain, I would be smarter. (Comma)
    I would be smarter if I had Einstein's brain. (No comma)

EXERCISE 1   ABOUT YOU   Answer the following questions with *I would*. Give an explanation for your answers.

EXAMPLE   If you could meet any famous person, who would you meet?

I would meet Einstein. I would ask him how he discovered his theory

of relativity.

1. If you could travel to the past or the future, which direction would you go?

   _____

2. If you could make a clone of yourself, would you do it? Why or why not?

   _____

3. If you could travel to another planet, would you want to go?

   _____

4. If you could change one thing about today's world, what would it be?

   _____

5. If you could find a cure for only one disease, what would it be?

   _____

6. If you could know the day of your death, would you want to know it?

   _____

7. If you could have the brain of another person, whose brain would you want?

   _____

8. If you could be a child again, what age would you be?

   _____

9. If you could change one thing about yourself, what would it be?

   _____

10. If you could meet any famous person, who would it be?

   _____

11. If you could be any animal, what animal would you be?

   _____

EXERCISE **2** Fill in the blanks with the correct form of the verb in parentheses ( ) to complete these conversations. Use *would* + base form in the main clause. Use the past tense in the *if* clause.

EXAMPLE **A:** What ___*would you do*___ if you ___*were*___
(you/do)   (be)

the mayor of this city?

B: If I ___*were*___ the mayor, I
(be)

___*would create*___ enough parking spaces for everyone.
(create)

1. **A:** If you _____ make a copy of yourself,
(can)

_____ it?
(you/do)

   B: My wife says that one of me is enough. If she _____
(have)

two of me, it _____ her crazy.
(drive)

2. **A:** If you _____ come back to Earth in any form
(can)

after you die, how _____ back?
(you/come)

   B: I _____ back as a dog. Dogs have such an easy life.
(come)

   A: Not in my native country. There are many homeless dogs.

   B: I _____ as an American dog.
(only/come back)

3. **A:** If you _____ choose to have a boy or girl baby,
(can)

what _____?
(you/choose)

   B: I _____. I _____ to
(not/choose)   (not/want)

interfere with nature.

4. **A:** What _____ if you _____
(you/do)   (have)

a lot of money?

   B. I _____ my family first. Then I
(help)

_____ a nice house and car.
(buy)

5. A: If you _____ look like any movie star,
(can)

who _____?
(you/look like)

B: I _____ a young Harrison Ford.
(look like)

6. A: If I _____ find a way to teach a person a
(can)

foreign language in a week, I _____ a million
(make)

dollars.

B: And I _____ your first customer.
(be)

7. A: If you _____ be invisible for a day,
(can)

what _____?
(you/do)

B: I _____ to my teacher's house the day she
(go)

writes the final exam.

8. A: What _____ if you _____
(you/do)   (not/have)

a TV?

B: I think I _____ crazy if
(go)

I _____ a TV.
(not/have)

9. A: Why are you writing your composition by hand?

B: I don't know how to type. I _____ my
(type)

compositions on the computer if I _____ type fast.
(can)

A: If I _____ you, I _____ a
(be)   (take)

keyboarding class to learn to type.

10. A: What _____ if you _____
(you/do)   (can/travel)

to the past or future?

B: I _____ to the past.
(go)

A: How far back _____?
(you/go)

B: I _____ to the nineteenth century and stay there.
(go)

A: Why?

B: If I _____ in the nineteenth century, I
(live)

_____ work. My life _____ easy.
(not/have to)   (be)

A: Yes, but if you _____ in the nineteenth
(live)

century, you _____ vote.
(not/be able to)

11. A: It _____ nice if people _____
(be)   (can)

live forever.

B: If people _____, the world
(not/die)

_____ overpopulated. There
(be)

_____ enough resources for everybody.
(not/be)

A: I didn't think of that. If the world _____
(be)

overpopulated, I _____ a parking space!
(never/find)

EXERCISE 3 Fill in the blanks with the correct form of the verb in parentheses
( ) to complete this conversation.

A: If you ___*could*___ change one thing about yourself,
(example: can)

what _____?
(1 it/be)

B: I _____ thinner. If I _____
(2 be)   (3 lose)

about 30 pounds, I _____ much happier—
(4 be)

and healthier. If I _____ so much, I
(5 not/eat)

_____ weight.
(6 lose)

A: Diet is not enough. You need to get exercise too. You can start right
now with exercise. Let's go jogging every day after work.

B: If I _____ so tired after work,
            (7 be/not)

    I _____ jogging with you. But I work
        (8 go)

    nine hours a day and it takes me two hours to commute[2]. So I'm too tired at the end of the day.

A: Can't you get any exercise at your job?

B: If I _____ a different kind of job,
            (9 have)

    I _____ more exercise. But I sit at a desk all day.
        (10 get)

A: How about going swimming with me on Saturdays? I go every Saturday. Swimming is great exercise.

B: If I _____ how to swim, I _____
          (11 know)   *(12 go)*

    with you. The problem is I don't know how to swim.

A: You can take lessons. My gym has a pool and they give lessons on the weekends. Why don't you sign up for lessons?

B: I'm too busy with the kids on the weekends. If I

    _____ kids, I _____ much
        (13 not/have)   *(14 have)*
    more free time.

A: If I _____ you, I _____ to
        (15 be)   *(16 try)*
    simplify my life.

EXERCISE 4   ABOUT YOU Make a list of things you would do if you had more time. You may share your sentences in a small group or with the entire class.

EXAMPLES   *If I had more free time, I'd read more novels.*

             I'd visit my grandmother more often if I had more free time.

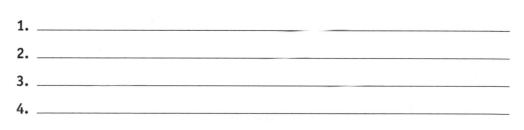

1. _____

2. _____

3. _____

4. _____

---

[2] To *commute* means to travel from home to work and back.

EXERCISE 5 ABOUT YOU Make a list of things you would do differently if you spoke or understood English better. You may share your sentences in a small group or with the entire class.

EXAMPLES <u>*If I spoke English fluently, I wouldn't come to this class.*</u>

<u>*I wouldn't be so nervous when I talk on the telephone if I*</u>

<u>*understood English better.*</u>

1. _____

2. _____

3. _____

EXERCISE 6 Fill in the blanks to tell what the following people are thinking.

EXAMPLE One-year-old: If I _____*could*_____ walk, I _____*would walk*_____ into the kitchen
(can)   (walk)

and take a cookie out of the cookie jar.

1. Two-year-old: If I _____ talk,
(can)

I _____ my mother that I hate peas.
(tell)

2. 14-year-old: I _____ happier if
(be)

I _____ drive.
(can)

3. 16-year-old: If I _____ a car, my friends and
(have)

I _____ out every night.
(go)

4. 19-year-old: I _____ a private university if
(attend)

I _____ a lot of money.
(have)

5. 25-year-old: If I _____ married, my parents
(be)

_____ about me so much.
(not/worry)

6. 35-year-old mother: I _____ more time for
(have)

myself if my kids _____ older.
(be)

7. 60-year-old grandmother: If I _____

(not/have)

grandchildren, my life _____ so interesting.

(not/be)

8. 90-year-old: If I _____ young today,

(be)

I _____ learn all about computers and other

(have to)

high-tech stuff.

9. 100-year-old: If I _____ you the story of

(tell)

my life, you _____ it.

(not/believe)

10. The dog: If I _____ talk, I

(can)

_____ "Feed me a steak."

(say)

EXERCISE 7 ABOUT YOU Complete each statement.

EXAMPLES If I studied harder, _I would get better grades._ _____

If I were the president, _I would lower taxes._ _____

1. If I were the English teacher, _____

2. If I could live to be 200 years old, _____

3. If I could predict the future, _____

4. If I were rich, _____

5. If I could be a child again, _____

6. If I could change places with any other person in the world, _____

_____

7. My life would be better if _____

8. I'd be learning English much faster if _____

9. I'd study more if _____

10. I'd travel a lot if _____

11. I'd be very unhappy if _____

12. I wouldn't borrow money from a friend unless _____

_____

EXERCISE 8 ABOUT YOU Answer each question with *yes* or *no*. Then make a statement with an unreal condition.

EXAMPLES Do you have the textbook?

Yes. If I didn't have the textbook, I wouldn't be able to do this exercise.

Is this lesson easy?

No. If it were easy, we wouldn't have to spend so much time on it.

1. Are you an American?

   _____

2. Do you know how to use the Internet?

   _____

3. Do you work on Sundays?

   _____

4. Do all the students in this class speak the same language?

   _____

5. Does the teacher speak your native language?

   _____

6. Are you taking other courses this semester?

   _____

7. Do you have a high school diploma?

   _____

8. Do you have a car?

   _____

9. Do you live far from school?

   _____

10. Do you have a job?

    _____

11. Do you speak English perfectly?

    _____

12. Do you have a computer?

    _____

10.2 | Implied Conditions

Examples	Explanation
I **would** never lie to a friend. **Would** you jump in a river to save a drowning person? She **would** never leave her children with a babysitter.	Sometimes the condition (the *if* clause) is implied, not stated. In the examples on the left, the implication is "if you had the opportunity" or "if the possibility presented itself."
Would you **want** to live without today's technologies? **Would** you **want** to travel to another planet? **Would** you **want** to have Einstein's brain? I **wouldn't want** to live for 500 years, **would** you?	*Would want* is used to present hypothetical situations. The *if* clause is implied.

EXERCISE 9 ABOUT YOU Answer these questions and discuss your answers.

1. Would you give money to a beggar?
2. Would you marry someone from another country?
3. Would you buy a used computer?
4. Would you lend a large amount of money to a friend?
5. Would you open someone else's mail?
6. Would you lie to protect a friend?
7. Would you tell a dying relative that he or she is dying?
8. Would you want to travel to the past or the future?
9. Would you want to live more than 100 years?
10. Would you want to visit another planet?
11. Would you want to live on the top floor of a hundred story building?
12. Would you want to go on an African safari?

EXERCISE 10 ABOUT YOU Answer these questions.

EXAMPLE What would you do if a stranger on the street asked you for money?
I would say, "I'm sorry. I can't give you any."

1. What would you do if you found a wallet in the street with a name and phone number in it?

_____

2. What would you do if you lost your money and didn't have enough money to get home by public transportation?

_____

3. What would you do if you saw a person in a public park picking flowers?

_____

4. What would you do if a cashier in a supermarket gave you a ten-dollar bill in change instead of a one-dollar bill?

_____

5. What would you do if you hit a car in a parking lot and no one saw you?

_____

6. What would you do if you saw another student cheating on a test?

_____

7. What would you do if your doctor told you that you had six months left to live?

_____

8. What would you do if you lost your job and couldn't pay your rent?

_____

9. What would you do if your best friend borrowed money from you and didn't pay you back?

_____

10. What would you do if your best friend told your secret to another person?

_____

TRAVELING TO MARS

Before You Read

1. Are you interested in exploration of different planets?

2. Do you think there is life on other planets?

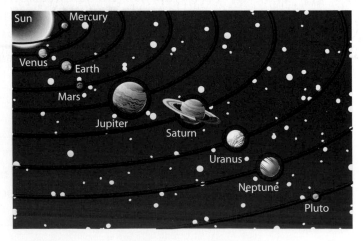

Exploration on Mars, our closest planetary neighbor, has already begun. In 2004, Spirit Rover landed on Mars to gather information about possible life-forms there, to study the climate and geology of the planet, and to prepare for human exploration in the not-so-distant future of our neighbor. Before anyone goes to Mars, however, more needs to be learned.

Going to Mars is more difficult than going to the moon. **If** astronauts go to Mars, they **will be have** to return within a given time period. **If** they **don't come** back within this period of time, they **will miss** their chance. **If** astronauts have a problem with their equipment, they **will not be able** to rely on a message from Earth to help them. Because of the distance from Earth, it can take about 40 minutes from the time a message goes out from Earth until it is received on Mars. Also, a visitor to Mars will have to be gone for at least three years because of the distance and time necessary to travel.

If you **had** the chance to go to Mars, **would** you go?

Spirit Rover

10.3 | Real Conditions vs. Unreal Conditions

Examples	Explanation
If astronauts **go** to Mars, they **will have** to return within a given time period. **If** they **have** problems, they **will have** to solve them by themselves. **If** a person goes to Mars, he **will be** gone for three years.	The sentences on the left describe a real possibility for the **future**. Notice that for real possibilities, we use the present tense in the *if* clause and the future tense in the main clause.

If you **were** on Mars, you **would weigh** about one-third of what you weigh on Earth.
 If you **could** go to Mars, **would** you **go**?
 If you **met** a Martian, what **would** you **do** or **say**?
	The statements to the left are about hypothetical or imaginary situations in the **present**. They are not plans for the future.
	     Reality: You are not on Mars now.
	     Reality: You can't go to Mars now.
	 Notice that we use the past tense in the *if* clause and *would* or *could* in the main clause.

EXERCISE 11   Fill in the blanks with the correct form of the verb in parentheses ( ). Both real conditions and unreal conditions are used.

EXAMPLES   The government is planning to send astronauts to Mars in the near future. If an astronaut _____<u>decides</u>_____ to go to Mars, he or she
      (decide)

_____<u>will be</u>_____ away from family for at least three years.
    (be)

If I _____<u>saw</u>_____ a Martian, I _____<u>would shake</u>_____ his hand.
   (see)   (shake)

1. I'm thinking of going to California next month. If I

_____, I _____ back
        (go)   (bring)

a souvenir for you.

2. If I _____ go to Mars, I _____
        (can)   (bring)

back a rock as a souvenir.

3. If the weather _____ nice today,
        (be)

I _____ out. But it's raining now.
   (go)

4. If the weather _____ nice this weekend,
        (be)

we _____ for a walk in the forest.
   (go)

5. The temperature on Mars is very cold. If it _____ (not/be)

so cold, maybe it _____ sustain life.
(can)

6. My sister is thinking about getting married soon. If she

_____ married in the summer, she
(get)

_____ an outdoor wedding.
(have)

7. My brother hates the woman next door. He _____
(not/marry)

her if she _____ the last woman on Earth.
(be)

8. My mother may visit me next week. If she _____
(come)

here, I _____ her to an art museum.
(take)

9. Sue's father died when she was a child. If her father

_____ here, he _____
(be)   (be)

so proud of her.

10. Our cat just had six kittens. If you _____ a kitten,
(want)

we _____ you one.
(give)

11. We love our dog. She's like a member of the family. We

_____ our dog if you _____
(not/sell)   (pay)

us a million dollars.

12. She may get some money from her parents. If her parents

_____ her some money, she
(send)

_____ some new clothes.
(buy)

13. She's always dreaming about winning the lottery. If she

_____ the lottery, she _____
(win)   (quit)

her job.

14. If I _____ a child, I _____
(be)   (play)

video games all day.

15. My son is thinking about a career in medicine. If my son

_____ a doctor when he grows up, we
(become)

_____ so happy.
(be)

16. I study a lot. If I _____, I _____
(not/study)   (not/pass)

this course.

17. My brother is a great student and will probably get a scholarship.

If he _____ a scholarship, he _____
(get)   (go)

to the University of Wisconsin.

EXERCISE 12 *Combination Exercise.* Fill in the blanks with the correct form of
the verb in parentheses ( ).

A: If you ___could___ change one thing in your life,
(example: can)

what _____?
(1 you/change)

B: I _____ younger.
(2 be)

A: You're not very old now. You're just in your 30s.

B: But if I _____ younger,
(3 be)

I _____ so many responsibilities.
(4 not/have)

Now I have two small children who need all my attention.

A: What _____ if you _____ kids?
(5 you/do)   (6 not/have)

B: I _____ golf all day on Saturday. And I
(7 play)

_____ late on Sunday mornings.
(8 sleep)

A: Are you sorry you had kids?

B: Of course not. I love them very much. If I _____
(9 not/have)

them, I _____ very unhappy. But I'm just
(10 be)

dreaming about a simpler, easier time.

A: It _____ nice if we _____
(11 be)   (12 can)

go back in time and make some changes.

Before You Read

1. Can you imagine what life was like 100 years ago? 1,000 years ago?

2. Would you want to live at a different time in history? Would you want to visit a different time in history? What period in history would you want to visit?

Read the following article. Pay special attention to unreal conditions in the past.

Did You Know?

The average life expectancy for someone born in the U.S. in the year 1900 was 47 years. For someone born in the year 2000 it was 75. Today the leading cause of death is heart disease.

Most of us are amazed by the rapid pace of technology at the beginning of the twenty-first century. We often wonder what life will be like 20 or 50 or 100 years from now. But do you ever wonder what your life **would have been** like if you **had been** alive 100 years ago?

If you **had lived** around 1900 in the U.S., you **would have earned** about $200–$400 a year. You probably **wouldn't have graduated** from high school. Only 6 percent of Americans had a high school diploma at that time. If you **had been** a dentist or an accountant, you **would have made** $2,500 a year. If you **had been** a child living in a city, you **might have had** to work in a factory for 12–16 hours a day.

If you **had gone** to a doctor, he probably **would not have had** a college education. Only 10 percent of doctors at that time had a college degree. And if you **had had** a baby at that time, it **would have been** born at home. If you **had gotten** an infection at that time, you probably **would have died** because antibiotics had not yet been discovered. The leading causes of death at that time were pneumonia, influenza, and tuberculosis.

What about your home? If you **had been living** 100 years ago, you probably **wouldn't have had** a bathtub or a telephone. You **would have washed** your hair about once a month.

Do you think you **would have been** happy with life 100 years ago?

10.4 | Unreal Conditions—Past

Examples	Explanation
If you **had been** alive 100 years ago, you **would have made** about $200 a year. If you **had lived** 100 years ago, you probably **wouldn't have graduated** from high school.	An unreal condition can describe a situation that is not real in the **past**. Use the past perfect in the *if* clause and *would have* + past participle in the main clause.
If you **had gotten** an infection, you **could have died.** If you **had had** a baby, it **might have died** young.	*Could* or *might* can be used in the main clause instead of *would*.
If I **had known** that learning English *was going* to be so hard, I **would have studied** it in my country. If **I had realized** how hard I *would have to* work as a waitperson, I **would have gone** to college.	A noun clause can be used within an *if* clause (after *know, realize,* etc.). Follow the rule of sequence of tenses in the noun clause. (See Section 9.9.)
If my great-grandparents **had been able to** come to the U.S. 100 years ago, our lives **would have been** easier.	In the *if* clause, use *had been able to* for the past perfect of *could*.
a. If you **were** born 100 years ago, your life **would have been** different. OR b. If you **had been** born 100 years ago, your life **would have been** different.	Sometimes we don't change to the past perfect, especially with the verb *be*, if it is clear that the action is past. It is clear that you *were* born in the past. Sentences (a) and (b) have the same meaning.

Language Notes:

1. In informal speech, *have* after *could, would,* or *might* is pronounced like *of* or /ə/. Listen to your teacher pronounce the sentences above with fast, informal pronunciation.

2. In very informal conversational English, you often hear *would have* in both clauses.

   If I *would have known* about the problem, I *would have told* you. (Informal)

   If I *had known* about the problem, I *would have told* you. (Formal)

EXERCISE 13 Fill in the blanks with the correct form of the verb about life in the U.S. 100 years ago.

EXAMPLE If you _____*had been*_____ a doctor 100 years ago, you
               (be)

_____*wouldn't have been*_____ rich.
      (not/be)

1. If you _____ a baby 100 years ago, it probably
          (have)

_____ at home.
   (be/born)

442   Lesson **10**

2. If you _____ an infection, you
(get)

probably _____.
(die)

3. If you _____ around 1900,
(live)

you probably _____ high school.
(not/finish)

4. You _____ a car if you
(not/have)

_____ in the U.S. 100 years ago.
(live)

5. Your president _____ Theodore Roosevelt if you
(be)

_____ in the U.S. 100 years ago.
(live)

6. If you _____ to travel to another city,
(need)

you _____ by train.
(travel)

7. You probably _____ if you
(work)

_____ child 100 years ago.
(be)

EXERCISE 14 A middle-aged woman is telling her daughter how the young lady's life would have been different if she had grown up in the late fifties. Fill in the blanks with the correct form of the verb in parentheses ( ) to complete the story.

It's great that you're thinking about becoming a doctor or astronaut. When I was your age, I didn't have the opportunity you have today.

You can be anything you want, but if you ___*had been*___ a woman
(example: be)

growing up in the fifties, your opportunities _____ limited.
(1 be)

If you _____ to college, you probably
(2 go)

_____ in nursing or education, or you
(3 major)

_____ a secretarial course.
(4 take)

You probably _____ married in your
(5 get)

early twenties.

If you _____ pregnant, you probably
      (6 get)

_____ your job. You probably
      (7 quit)

_____ two or more children. Your husband
      (8 have)

_____ to support you and the children. But today,
      (9 work)

you have the opportunity to continue working after you have children.

Technology _____ different too. Your house
            (10 be)

_____ one TV and one phone. Because we had only
      (11 have)

one TV, the family spent more time together. You _____
                                                    (12 not/have)

a computer or a cell phone.

If you _____ up in the fifties, your life
      (13 grow)

_____ completely different.
      (14 be)

10.5 | Mixed Tenses in Condition Statements

We can mix a present condition with a past result, or a past condition with a
present result.

Present Condition (Use simple past)	Past Result (Use *would have* + past participle)
If I **were** you,	I **wouldn't have bought** that old computer.
If I **had** a car,	I **would have taken** you to the airport last week.
If I **were** rich,	I **would have bought** a big house when I came to the U.S.

Past Condition (Use past perfect)	Present Result (Use *would* + base form)
If you **had lived** during the fifties,	you **would have** a different way of looking at the world now.
If I **hadn't come** to the U.S.,	I **would be living** with my parents now.
If she **hadn't lost** her job last month,	she **would be able** to take a vacation now.

EXERCISE 15   Fill in the blanks with the correct form of an appropriate verb.
These sentences have mixed tenses.

EXAMPLE   She just came to the U.S., so she doesn't speak English perfectly. If she

_____*had come*_____ here a long time ago, she _____*would speak*_____

English much better.

1. He invested a lot of money in a good stock, and now he's rich.

   If he _____ in that stock, he _____

   rich today.

2. Luckily she didn't marry her high school boyfriend. If she

   _____ him, she _____

   happy now.

3. I passed the last course, and now I'm in this course.

   I _____ in this course if I _____

   the last course.

4. The car you bought is terrible. If I _____ you,

   I _____ that car.

5. She didn't see the accident, so she can't tell you what happened.

   She _____ you what happened if she

   _____ the accident.

6. You didn't come to class yesterday, so you don't understand the

   teacher's explanation today. You _____ the

   teacher's explanation today if you _____ to class
   yesterday.

7. She has a lot of work to do, so she got up early. If she

   _____ so much work, she

   _____ in bed all morning.

8. She doesn't have a car, so she didn't drive you to the hospital. If she

   _____ a car, she _____
   you to the hospital yesterday.

9. I didn't learn English as a child. If I _____

   English as a child, I _____ so many problems
   with it now.

EXERCISE 16   ABOUT YOU Complete each statement with a past or present
result.

EXAMPLES   If I had taken the TOEFL test last year, _I wouldn't have passed it._

If I hadn't brought my book to class today, _I wouldn't be able to do_
this exercise.

1. If I hadn't taken this course, _____

2. If I hadn't taken beginning English, _____

3. If I hadn't come to class today, _____

4. If I hadn't studied for the last test, _____

5. If I hadn't paid last month's rent, _____

6. If I had been born 200 years ago, _____

EXERCISE 17 ABOUT YOU Complete each statement with a past or present condition.

EXAMPLES I would have saved money if *I had bought a used book.*

I would have studied last night if *we were having a test today.*

1. I would have stayed after class yesterday if _____

_____

2. I would have stayed home today if _____

_____

3. I would have done better on the last test if _____

_____

4. The teacher would have explained the last lesson again if _____

_____

5. I would have taken an easier course if _____

_____

6. I would have studied English when I was a child if _____

_____

7. My parents would have been disappointed in me if _____

_____

EXERCISE 18 Fill in the blanks with the correct form of an appropriate verb. Some sentences have mixed tenses.

EXAMPLES I took a wrong turn on the highway. I arrived at the meeting one hour late.

If I ____*hadn't taken*____ a wrong turn on the highway, I

____*would have arrived*____ at the meeting on time.

1. I forgot to set my alarm clock, so I didn't wake up on time.

I _____ on time if I

_____ my alarm clock.

2. She didn't pass the final exam, so she didn't pass the course. If she

_____ the final exam, she

_____ the course.

3. I didn't see the movie, so I can't give you any information about it.

If I _____ the movie, I

_____ you some information about it.

4. He loves her, so he married her. If he _____

her, he _____ her.

5. She didn't hear the phone ring, so she didn't answer it. She

_____ the phone

if she _____ it ring.

6. He left his keys at the office, so he couldn't get into the house. If he

_____ his keys at the office,

he _____ into the house.

7. I don't have much money, so I didn't buy a new coat. I

_____ a new coat if I

_____ more money.

8. He didn't take the medicine, so his condition didn't improve. If he

_____ the medicine, his

condition _____ .

9. I didn't have my credit card with me, so I didn't buy the computer I

saw last week. I _____ the computer

if I _____ my credit card with me.

EXERCISE 19 Complete each statement.

EXAMPLES If I had a million dollars, _I would travel around the world._

If I had a computer, _I would have typed my last composition._

1. People would live longer if _____

_____

2. I wouldn't have to work if _____

_____

3. If we had had a test on this lesson last week, _____

_____

4. If I could visit any country in the world, _____

   _____

5. If everyone lived to be 150 years old, _____

   _____

6. If I had lived in the nineteenth century, _____

   _____

SCIENCE OR WISHFUL THINKING?

Before You Read

1. Do you wish for things you don't have in your life?

2. Would you want to live for 150 years?

Read the science news articles and the conversation that follows. Pay special attention to *wish* and the verbs that follow it.

In laboratory experiments, scientists at the University of Connecticut have been able to double the life span of fruit flies from 70 days to 140 days. They have been able to produce mice that live 30 percent longer than the average mouse. If these experiments worked in humans, it would mean that we would be able to live up to 150 years.

A 63-year-old California woman gave birth to a baby. The woman is believed to be the oldest woman ever to give birth. She went through a program of in-vitro fertilization[3] at the University of Southern California.

If you wish your loving cat had nine lives, you can make your dream come true. A U.S. company announced the start of its cat-cloning service. For $50,000 you can have your darling cat cloned.

[3] *In-vitro fertilization* is a surgical procedure to help a woman conceive a baby.

A: I **wish** I **were** younger. I **wish** I **didn't have to** get old and sick. Science can do so much these days. I **wish** they **could find** a way to keep us young.

B: I read an article about how scientists are working to extend our lives. It's possible that soon people will be able to live 150 years.

A: I wouldn't want to be 150 years old and sick. I **wish** I **could be** 21 forever.

B: I don't think scientists will ever find a way to make us any younger than we are now. The best they can do is extend our lives and keep us healthier longer. What would you do differently if you were 21?

A: I would be going to parties on weekends. I wouldn't have so many responsibilities. I **wouldn't have to** take care of children. I started to have my children when I was in my early twenties. I **wish** I **had waited** until I was older.

B: My aunt is 55 and just got married for the first time a few years ago. She **wishes** she **had gotten** married when she was young and she **wishes** she **had had** children. But now she's too old.

A: I'm not so sure about that. I read an article about a 63-year-old woman who gave birth to a baby with the help of science.

B: That's amazing! What will science do for us next?

A: Scientists have started to clone animals.

B: I used to have a wonderful dog. I miss her. I **wish** I **could have** cloned her. But it's too late. She died 10 years ago.

A: Technology in the twenty-first century is moving so fast, isn't it? Don't you **wish** you **could come** back in 1,000 years and see all the changes in the world after that period of time?

B: I read an article that says that if we could travel at almost the speed of light, we could leave the Earth and come back a thousand years from now.

A: I wouldn't want to live in the future. I just **wish** I **could visit** the future. All our friends and relatives would be long dead if we left the present.

10.6 | Wishes

We often wish for things that are not real or true.

Examples	Explanation
Present **Reality:** I **don't have** a dog. **Wish:** I wish (that) I **had** a dog. **Reality:** We **have** to get old. **Wish:** I wish (that) we **didn't have** to get old. **Reality:** I **can't live** 150 years. **Wish:** I wish I **could live** 150 years.	Use a **past** tense verb to wish for something in the **present**. After *wish*, you can use *that* to introduce the clause, but it is usually omitted.
Past **Reality:** I **didn't know** my grandparents. **Wish:** I wish I **had known** them. **Reality:** My aunt **didn't have** kids when she was young. **Wish:** She wishes she **had had** kids when she was young. **Reality:** My favorite dog died years ago. I **couldn't clone** my dog. **Wish:** I wish I **could have cloned** her.	Use a **past perfect** verb to wish for something in the **past**. If the real situation uses *could*, use *could have* + past participle after *wish*.
Formal: I wish I **were** younger. **Informal:** I wish I **was** younger.[4] **Formal:** I wish it **were** Sunday. **Informal:** I wish it was Sunday.	With *be*, *were* is the correct form for all subjects. In conversation, however, you will often hear native speakers use *was* with *I, he, she,* and *it*.
I'm not young, but I wish I were. I don't have a car, but I wish I **did.** I didn't bring my photo album to the U.S., but I wish I **had.** I couldn't go to the party last week, but I wish I **could have.**	We can use an auxiliary verb (were, did, had, etc.) to shorten the *wish* clause.
Wish you were here! John Smith 123 Bay Road Cutchogue NY, 11935 37	When people on vacation send postcards to friends and relatives, they sometimes write these words.

Usage Note:
In conversation, you often hear Americans use *would have* + past participle for past wishes.
> Formal: I wish you *had told* me the truth.
> Informal: I wish you *would have told* me the truth.

[4]Many native speakers consider *was*, in this case, to be incorrect.

EXERCISE 20 Fill in the blanks to make a wish about the present.

EXAMPLE Today isn't Friday. I wish it _____*were*_____ Friday.

1. You're not here with me. I wish you _____ here.

2. I have to work 60 hours a week. I wish I _____ work so much.

3. I can't speak English perfectly. I wish I _____ English perfectly.

4. I don't have a car. I wish I _____ a car.

5. You're going on vacation to Hawaii, but I can't go with you. I wish I _____ with you.

6. I'm not rich. I wish I _____ rich.

7. I have a lot of responsibilities. I wish I _____ so many responsibilities.

8. I don't have time to read much. I wish I _____ more time to read.

9. I'm not 18 years old. I wish I _____.

10. Do you wish you _____ to be 150 years old?

11. I can't speak French. I wish _____ French.

EXERCISE 21 ABOUT YOU Fill in the blanks to complete each statement.

EXAMPLE I wish I had _more time to spend with my family._

1. I wish I were _____

2. I wish I knew how to _____

3. I wish I didn't have to _____

4. I wish I had _____

5. I wish I could _____

EXERCISE 22 Fill in the blanks to make a wish about the past.

EXAMPLE You didn't see the movie. I wish you _had seen it._

1. I didn't know it was your birthday. I wish I _____. I would have baked you a cake.

2. I didn't go to the concert. Everyone said it was wonderful. I wish I _____.

3. I didn't see the parade. I wish I _____ it.

4. I studied German in high school. I wish I _____

_____ English instead.

5. I didn't see his face when he opened the present. I wish I _____

_____ his face.

6. I lost my favorite ring. I was wearing it at the party. I wish I _____

_____ it at home.

7. I told Larry my secret, and he told all his friends. I wish I _____

_____ him my secret.

8. I forgot to bring my photo album when I moved to this city. I wish

I _____ it.

EXERCISE 23 *Combination Exercise.* Fill in the blanks with the correct form of the verb in parentheses ( ) in each of the conversations below. Some wishes are about the present, some are about the past.

EXAMPLE   **A:** I wish I _____ *had* _____ good vision.
                        (have)

B: You *can* have perfect or near perfect vision. Why don't you try laser surgery?

A: What can that do for me?

B: A lot. I had it two years ago, and I don't need glasses anymore. I wore glasses since I was a child. I wish they _____ *had had* _____ this surgery
                                                                                    (have)

years ago. Now I can see first thing in the morning, read, drive, and play sports without wondering where my glasses are.

1. A: I wish I _____ thin.
                              (be)

B: Why don't you try a diet?

A: I've tried every diet. Nothing works.

B: You need to exercise every day.

A: I'm too tired when I get home from work. I wish scientists

_____ find a pill that would make me thin
                        (can)

with no effort on my part.

2. A: I've been bald since I was 25 years old. I wish I

_____ bald.
                        (be/not)

B: They say bald men are very manly.

A. I don't care what they say. I wish I _____ hair.
(have)

I wish someone _____ find a cure for

baldness.

3. A: It's so expensive to call my country. I wish I

_____ talk to my family every day.
(can)

B: You can. Just get a microphone for your computer and you can chat with them online for free.

A: I wish I _____ how to do that.
(know)

B: Don't worry. I'll show you.

4. A: I wish I _____ older.
(be)

B: Why? No one wants to get old.

A: I didn't say old. I just said "older." Older people have more experience and wisdom.

B: I wish we _____ have the wisdom of old
(can)

people and the bodies of young people.

A: If everyone stayed young and no one died, where would we find space on the Earth for all the new babies born every day?

B: We could colonize Mars.

5. A: Wish I _____ travel to the future.
(can)

B: Why?

A: I would be able to see future problems and then come back and warn people about them.

B: I wish I _____ go to the past.
(can)

A: Why?

B: I would like to meet my grandparents. I never knew them. I wish

I _____ them, but they died before I was born.
(knew)

6. A: We saw a great movie last night about time travel.

B: I wish I _____ with you, but I had to study
(can/go)

for my biology test.

7. **A:** I studied Italian when I was a child. I wish I

_____ English.
    (study)

B: I wish I _____ born in the U.S. Then English
           (be)

would be easy.

8. **A:** I wish I _____ college before getting married.
              (finish)

B: But you have a great husband.

A: I know. But I wish I _____ a few years. Now
                  (wait)

I have no education and a lot of responsibilities.

B: You can finish college now.

A: I wish I _____ , but with my two kids, there's no
              (can)

time.

9. **A:** I'm an only child. I wish I _____ a sister or brother.
                    (have)

B: Maybe you will someday.

A: I don't think so. My mom is in her fifties already.

B: With today's biological technologies, older women can still have
kids.

A: Maybe so. But she doesn't have the energy to raise a small child.

10.7 | Wishing for a Desired Change

Examples	Explanation
I wish you **wouldn't watch** so many science fiction movies. I wish you **would take** a science course. Your hair is too long. I wish you **would cut** it.	*Would* + base form is used after *wish* to show that a person wants something different to happen in the future. It shows a desire for change.
Compare: a. I wish I **could** travel to the past. (I can't travel to the past.) a. I wish I **were** young. (I'm not young.) b. I wish my parents **would come** to the U.S. (I want them to come to the U.S.) b. I wish you **wouldn't talk** so much about the past. (I want you to stop talking about the past.)	a. *Wish* without *would* is not a desire for change but an expression of discontent with the present situation. b. *Wish* with *would* shows a desire for change.

EXERCISE 24 Fill in the blanks to show a desire that someone do something differently. Answers may vary.

EXAMPLE My parents are going back to my country. I wish they _would stay here._

1. Are you leaving so soon? I wish you _____ for a few more hours.

2. My son doesn't want to clean his room. I wish he _____ _____ his room.

3. My daughter wants to use the Internet all day. I wish she _____ _____ with her friends instead of sitting in front of the computer all day.

4. Some students are talking so loudly in the library that I can't think. I wish they _____.

5. My son's hair is so long. I don't like long hair on a boy. I wish he _____ his hair.

6. The teacher gives a lot of homework. I wish she _____ _____ so much homework.

7. My friend doesn't want to go to the party with me. I wish he _____ _____ to the party with me.

EXERCISE 25 A man is complaining about his apartment situation. Fill in the blanks with the correct form of the verb in parentheses ( ). Include *would* if you think he is hoping for a change. Don't include *would* if you think there is no possibility of change.

EXAMPLES I wish my neighbors __would be__ more quiet.
(be)

I wish the walls __were__ thicker.
(be)

1. I wish my landlord _____ more heat.
(give)

2. I wish the people upstairs from me _____ (no/walk) around so much at night.

3. I wish the landlord _____ the hallways more often.
(clean)

4. I wish the building _____ an elevator.
(have)

5. I wish there _____ more trees and flowers around (be) the building.

6. I wish the landlord _____ my rent every year.
(not/raise)

7. I wish my kitchen _____ larger.
(be)

8. I wish I _____ a gas stove, not an electric stove.
(have)

9. I wish the apartment _____ sunnier.
(be)

10. I wish I _____ rich enough to buy a house.
(be)

11. I wish I _____ air-conditioning.
(have)

12. I wish I _____ move, but I can't.
(can)

EXERCISE 26   ABOUT YOU   Fill in the blanks to complete these statements. Your wish can include a desire for a change (by using *would*) or it can simply state that you're unhappy with the way things are right now.

EXAMPLES   I wish the class _didn't have so many students._

I wish my parents _would let me go out with my friends._

1. I wish my family _____

2. I wish the teacher _____

3. I wish my neighbors _____

4. I wish the government _____

5. I wish more people _____

6. I wish my apartment _____

EXERCISE 27   A student is complaining about her class. Fill in the blanks with the correct form of the verb. Include *would* if you think she hopes for a change. Don't include *would* if you think there is no possibility of change. Both present and past wishes are included.

EXAMPLES   I wish the teacher _____didn't give_____ so much homework.
(not/give)

I wish the teacher _____would spend_____ more time on conditionals.
(spend)

1. I wish I _____ skip ESL and go into regular
(can)
English.

2. I wish the book _____ the answers in the back.
   (have)

3. I wish I _____ more attention to learning
   (pay)
   English when I was in my native country.

4. I wish I _____ a dictionary in my native country.
   (buy)
   Dictionaries are much cheaper there.

5. I wish I _____ my counselor's advice and
   (take)
   registered early. I couldn't get into the biology class I wanted.

6. I wish I _____ my dictionary to class today.
   (bring)
   We're going to write a composition, and I need to check my
   spelling.

7. I wish the teacher _____ us use our books
   (let)
   during a test.

8. I wish we _____ write so many compositions.
   (not/have to)

9. I wish the students in the back _____ quiet.
   (be)
   They're always making so much noise.

10. I wish I _____ the teacher's brain. Then I would
    (have)
    know English perfectly

EXERCISE 28

Combination Exercise. A mother (M) is complaining to her son (S).
Fill in the blanks with the correct form of the words in parentheses
( ) to express their wishes.

M: You never visit. I wish you _____*would visit*_____ me more
   (example: visit)
   often. I'm not going to live forever, you know.

S: I *do* visit you often. Isn't once a week often enough?

M: Some day I won't be here, and you'll say to yourself, "I wish I

   _____ my mom more often."
   (1 visit)

S: Mom, you're only 48 years old.

M: Who knows how long I'll be here? There are no guarantees in life.
   My own mother died when I was a teenager. I wish she

   _____ to see you and your sister.
   (2 live)

S: I do too. But what can we do?

M: I wish you _____ married already.
(3 be)

S: Mom, I'm only 25 years old. There's plenty of time to get married.

M: Well, your sister's only 23, and she's already married.

S: I wish you _____ comparing me to my sister.
(4 stop)

She has different goals in life. Besides you don't like Shari's husband.

M: You're right. I wish she _____ a better man.
(5 marry)

S: There's nothing wrong with Paul. He's a good husband to her.

M: We'll see. You know, I wish you _____ your hair.
(6 cut)

It's too long.

S: Mom. I'm old enough to decide how long to wear my hair.

M: You're too thin. I wish you _____ more.
(7 eat)

S: I eat enough. When I was a teenager, you said I was too fat.

M: I'm still your mother. I wish you _____ to me.
(8 listen)

S: I *do* listen to you. But I've got to live my own life.

M: Sometimes you act like a child and tell me you're old enough to make your own decisions. Then you tell me you're too young to get married.

S: I'm not too young to get married. I just don't want to now. I want to be a rock musician.

M: I wish you _____ a real job.
(9 find)

S: It *is* a real job.

M: You didn't finish college. I wish you _____ your
(10 get)

degree. How are you ever going to find a real job?

S: You don't need a college degree to be a rock musician.

M: Well, I hope I live long enough to see you married, with a good job.

S: With today's technologies, you'll probably live to be 150 years old and not only see me married, but also see your great-great-great-grandchildren married.

M: I wouldn't want to live so long.

S: You wouldn't? Just think, you'll be 150 years old and I'll be 127. You'll still be telling me how to live my life. That would make you happy, wouldn't it?

SUMMARY OF LESSON 10

1.

Unreal Conditions—Present	
Verb → Past	**Verb → *Would / Might / Could* + Base Form**
If I **were** an astronaut,	I **would go** to Mars.
If I **could** live to be 150 years old,	I **would know** my great-great-grandchildren.
If I **spoke** English perfectly,	I **might have** more opportunities.
If I **could** travel to the past,	I **could meet** my ancestors.
If she **didn't have** children,	she **would have** more free time.
If I **were** in Hawaii,	I **would be** on a beach right now.
If we **didn't have** advanced technology,	we **wouldn't be** able to explore space.

2.

Unreal Conditions—Past	
Verb → Past Perfect	**Verb → *Would / Might / Could* + Have + Past Participle**
If you **had lived** 100 years ago,	you **wouldn't have had** a computer.
If a doctor **had lived** 100 years ago,	he **could have practiced** medicine without a college degree.
If you **had gotten** an infection,	you **might have died.**
If my father **had** not **met** my mother,	I **wouldn't have been** born.

3.

Mixed Tenses	
Present Condition	**Past Result**
If she **were** rich,	she **would have sent** her kids to private school.
If I **had** your phone number,	I **would have called** you yesterday.
If I **were** you,	I **would have quit** my job a long time ago.
Past Condition	**Present Result**
If she **had married** him,	she **would be** very unhappy now.
If I **had stayed** home today,	I **wouldn't be reviewing** this lesson.

4.

Real Possibilities for the Future	
Condition	**Future Result**
If we **explore** Mars,	we **will learn** a lot.
If I **go** to New York,	I **will send** you a postcard.
If she **is** late,	she **will miss** the meeting.

5.

Wishes	
Present	**Past**
I wish I **were** younger.	I wish I **had studied** English when I was younger.
I wish I **could** be a child again.	I wish I **had been** a better student when I was a child.
I wish you **would** cut your hair.	I wish my parents **would have let** me go to the party last week.

EDITING ADVICE

1. Don't use *will* with an unreal condition.

   If I ~~will be~~ rich, I would buy a house.
   (were)

2. Don't include *be* if you have another verb.

   If I knew more English, I would ~~be~~ find a better job.

3. Always use the base form after a modal.

   She would ~~has~~ called you if she had your phone number.
   (have)

4. Use the past perfect, not the present perfect, for unreal conditions and wishes.

   If she ~~has~~ studied harder, she wouldn't have failed the test.
   (had)

   I wish I ~~have~~ seen that movie.
   (had)

5. For a real condition, use the simple present tense in the *if* clause.

   If I ~~will~~ have time tomorrow, I will write my composition.

PART 1 Find the mistakes with the underlined words, and correct them. Not every sentence has a mistake. If the sentence is correct, write *C*.

EXAMPLES What ~~will~~ ^{would} you do if you had a million dollars?

I wouldn't be able to visit my friends if I <u>didn't have</u> a car. **C**

1. I don't have much money. If I <u>have</u> a lot of money, I'd travel around the world.

2. I <u>will be</u> happier if my family were here.

3. I don't have any time. If I had time, <u>I'd help</u> my friend today.

4. If I <u>could meet</u> the president, I would tell him that he's doing a great job.

5. I'm unhappy because my daughter can't come here. I <u>will be</u> happy if my daughter could live with me.

6. I wish I <u>could speak</u> English perfectly.

7. If I <u>will be</u> you, I would buy a new car.

8. If I didn't have to study English, I <u>would be have</u> more free time.

9. I have a car. I wouldn't be able to find a job here if I <u>don't have a car</u>.

10. If she hadn't repaired the brakes on her car, she <u>might have had</u> an accident.

11. The teacher <u>would has explained</u> the grammar more slowly if she had had more time.

12. I came here when I was 40 years old. I wish I <u>had come</u> here when I was younger.

13. Can you help me?—Sorry. If I could, I <u>would</u>.

14. If I <u>would be</u> young, I would have more energy.

15. I'm sorry I didn't call you yesterday. I <u>would call</u> you if I hadn't been so busy.

16. I didn't know about the party so I didn't go. I wish I <u>have known</u> about it.

17. Mary hates Paul. She wouldn't marry him even if he <u>were</u> the last man on Earth.

18. I wish you <u>would call</u> me more often.

19. If you <u>are</u> late for tomorrow's test, you will not have enough time to finish it.

20. What would you do if you <u>find</u> a wallet with a lot of money in it?

21. I got an invitation to my sister's graduation. I <u>wouldn't have been able to</u> go without the invitation.

22. I heard you saw a great movie last night. I wish I <u>have gone</u> with you.

23. If he <u>has been</u> more careful, the accident wouldn't have happened.

24. If he <u>will have</u> time next weekend, he will help his brother.

PART 2 Fill in the blanks to complete the conversation.

A: Are you happy you came to the U.S.?

B: Yes, I'm glad I'm here. But I wish I _____*had come*_____ here when
(example)

my brother came here 15 years ago.

A: Why?

B: Well, now I'm 40 years old, and it's harder to learn English and find a good job. I didn't study English when I was a child. I wish I

_____ it when I was younger.
(1)

A: But your brother learned English quickly.

B: He was only 18 when he came here. Now he speaks English well, has

a small business, and owns a big house. If I _____
(2)

here when he came here, I _____ successful
(3)

now. But now I have to start everything from the beginning. I wish

I _____ to start so many new things at my age.
(4)

A: Did your parents come here too?

B: No. My parents are alone in my country. I've asked them to come

here. I wish they _____ here, but they're too old
(5)

to make such a big change. If they _____ here,
(6)

they _____ have to go to school to learn English.
(7)

They're in their late seventies. If they _____ here,
(8)

their life _____ much more difficult than it is now.
(9)

A: There are a lot of things I wish _____ different
(10)

in my life too.

B: What, for example?

A: I got married when I was only 18. I wish I _____
(11)
married so young. And I had my first son when I was only 20. I'm attending college now, and it's hard with so many family responsibilities. I wish I _____ to college when I
(12)
was 18.

B: It's too bad we can't go back and start our lives again. I wish I

_____ back and use the knowledge I have now
(13)
to make better choices.

A: Who knows . . . we may live to be 150 years old and have time to do

all the things we wish we _____ do.
(14)

B: If everyone _____ to be 150 years old, the world
(15)

_____ very crowded and there _____
(16)   (17)
enough food or other resources for everybody.

A: Maybe you're right. We should just do the best we can with the time we have.

PART 3 Some of the following sentences contain real conditions; some contain unreal conditions. Write the letter of the correct words to fill in the blanks.

1. I _____ drive to Canada if I had a car.
   a. were   **b.** will   **c.** would   **d.** would be

2. I might go shopping next Saturday. If I _____ shopping next Saturday, I'll buy you a scarf.
   a. will go   **b.** went   **c.** would go   **d.** go

3. If I _____ you, I'd move to a different apartment.
   a. were   **b.** am   **c.** will be   **d.** would be

4. I can't help you. I would help you if I _____.
   a. can   **b.** could   **c.** will be able to   **d.** would

5. I might have to work next Monday. If I have to work,
   I _____ be able to come to class.
   a. wouldn't   **b.** won't   **c.** weren't   **d.** wasn't

6. My life would be easier if I _____ more English.
   a. knew   **b.** know   **c.** will know   **d.** would know

7. She has three children. She has no time to study. If she
_____ children, she would have more time to study.
   a. doesn't have   b. weren't have
   c. wouldn't have   d. didn't have

8. It's raining now. If it _____ now, I'd go for a walk.
   a. isn't raining   b. doesn't raining
   c. weren't raining   d. wouldn't raining

9. She wouldn't tell you the secret even if you _____
her a million dollars.
   a. would be pay   b. paid   c. will pay   d. pay

10. If I could live in any city in the world, I _____
in Paris.
   a. will live   b. would have lived   c. would live   d. live

11. I don't have a house. I wish I _____ a house.
   a. had   b. will have   c. have had   d. have

12. I can't drive a car. I wish I _____ a car.
   a. could drive   b. can drive   c. would drive   d. will drive

13. If I had known how difficult it was to learn English,
I _____ it when I was young.
   a. would study   b. would studied
   c. would had studied   d. would have studied

14. He never exercised and was overweight. He had a heart attack and
died when he was 50 years old. If he _____
better care of himself, he might have lived much longer.
   a. would take   b. took   c. had taken   d. will take

15. He needs more driving lessons before he can take the driver's
license test. If he _____ the test last week, he
would have failed it.
   a. were taken   b. would take   c. has taken   d. had taken

16. I didn't have time to call you yesterday. I _____
you if I had had more free time.
   a. would call   b. will call   c. would have called   d. would called

17. He was driving without a seat belt and had a car accident. He
was seriously injured. If he had been wearing his seat belt, he
_____ such a serious injury.
   a. might not have had   b. wouldn't had
   c. didn't have   d. hadn't had

18. Nobody told me we were going to have a test today. I wish
someone _____ me.
   a. would tell   b. had told   c. would told   d. were told

19. Why didn't you tell me about your move last week? If you had told me, I _____ you.

    a. could have helped   **b.** could help

    c. could helped   **d.** could had helped

20. My roommate talks on the phone all the time. I wish he

    _____ on the phone so much.

    a. won't talk   **b.** wouldn't talk

    c. doesn't talk **d.** wouldn't have talked

EXPANSION ACTIVITIES

Classroom Activities

1. Do you think the world would be better or worse if . . . ? Form a small group and discuss your reasons.

    a. If there were no computers?

    b. If everyone were the same religion or race?

    c. If everyone spoke the same language?

    d. If we could live to be about 150 years old?

    e. If people didn't have to work?

    f. If families were allowed to have only one child?

    g. If every job paid the same salary?

2. Fill in the blanks. Share your sentences in a small group.

    a. If I could change one thing about myself (or my life), I'd change

    _____

    b. If I lost my _____, I'd be very upset.

    c. Most people would be happier if _____ _____

    d. If I could travel to the past, _____

    e. If I could travel to the future, _____

    f. The world would be a better place if _____

    g. I wish I were _____ years old.

3. Fill in the blanks and explain your answers.

    If I had known _____,

    I would (not) have _____

    EXAMPLE If I had known that I needed computer skills in the U.S., I would have studied computers in my native country.

4. Fill in the blanks and explain your answer.

    a. I didn't _____, but I wish I had.

    b. I _____, but I wish I hadn't.

5. Write some sentences about your job, your school, your apartment, or your family. What do you wish were different? Share your answers in a small group.

   EXAMPLES I have to work on Saturdays. I wish I didn't have to work on Saturdays.

   My son watches TV all day. I wish he would play with his friends more.

6. On a piece of paper or index card, finish this sentence:

   I would be happier if _____.

   The teacher will collect the cards or papers and read each statement. The rest of the class has to guess who wrote it. (Many people will write "*if I were rich,*" or "*if I knew more English,*" so try to think of something else.)

7. Name something. Form a small group and discuss your responses.

   EXAMPLE Name something you wish had never happened.
   I wish the war had never happened.

   a. Name something you wish you had done when you were younger.

   b. Name something you wish you had studied when you were younger.

   c. Name something your family wishes you had done differently.

   d. Name something you wish you had known before you came to this city.

   e. Name something you wish your parents had done or told you.

   f. Name something you wish you had never done.

   g. Name something you wish had never happened.

Talk
About it

1. If you could meet anyone in the world, who would you want to meet?

2. If you had the brain of another person, who would you be?

3. Since Albert Einstein's death in 1955, his brain has been kept in a jar for study. If it were possible to create a new Einstein from a brain cell, would it be a good idea to do so? Why or why not?

4. If you had the possibility of making a clone of yourself or a member of your family, would you do it? Why or why not?

5. If you could live 200 years, would you want to?

6. If we could eliminate all diseases, would the Earth be overpopulated?

7. In Lesson Six, we read about Tim Berners-Lee, the creator of the World Wide Web. He has never made any money from the Web. Do you think he would have tried to make money on his idea if he had known how popular the Web was going to become?

8. What entirely new things do you think might be possible in the future?

9. Read the following poem and discuss its meaning.

> There was a young lady named Bright,
> Who traveled far faster than light.
> She left one day
> In a relative way
> And returned the previous night.

Write About it

1. Write about personality traits or bad habits you have. Write how your life would be different if you didn't have these traits or habits. (Or you can write about the habits or traits of another person you know well.)

   EXAMPLES If I exercised, my health would be better.
   If my son weren't so lazy, he'd be able to accomplish much more in his life.

2. Write about an important event in history. Tell what the result would or might have been if this event hadn't happened.

3. Write about how your life would have been different if you had stayed in the same place your whole life.

4. Write about some things in your life that you are not happy about. How would you want to change your life?

Outside Activities

1. Ask a native speaker of English to answer the questions in the first classroom activity. Report this person's answers to the class.

2. Rent one of these movies: *Cocoon, Sleeper, Back to the Future, AI (Artificial Intelligence), Contact,* or *Kate and Leopold.* Write a summary.

Internet Activities

1. At a search engine, type in *time travel.* Find an interesting article to bring to class.

2. At a search engine, type in *H.G. Wells The Time Machine.* Find a summary of this 1895 novel.

3. At a search engine, type in *aging.* Find an interesting article to bring to class. Summarize it.

Additional Activities at **http://elt.thomson.com/gic**

Appendices

APPENDIX A

Noncount Nouns

The following groups of words are classified as noncount nouns.

Group A. Nouns that have no distinct, separate parts. We look at the whole

air	cheese	lightning	paper	tea
blood	cholesterol	meat	pork	thunder
bread	coffee	milk	poultry	water
butter	electricity	oil	soup	yogurt

Group B. Nouns that have parts that are too small or insignificant to count

corn	hair	rice	sand	sugar
grass	popcorn	salt	snow	

Note: Count and noncount nouns are grammatical terms, but they are not always logical. *Rice* is very small and is a noncount noun. *Beans* and *peas* are also very small but are count nouns.

Group C. Nouns that are classes or categories of things

food (vegetables, meat, spaghetti)	makeup (lipstick, rouge, eye shadow)
furniture (chairs, tables, beds)	homework (compositions, exercises, reading)
clothing (sweaters, pants, dresses)	jewelry (necklaces, bracelets, rings)
mail (letters, packages, postcards, fliers)	housework (washing dishes, dusting, cooking)
fruit (cherries, apples, grapes)	money or cash (nickels, dimes, dollars)

Group D. Nouns that are abstractions

advice	experience	intelligence	nature	trouble
art	fun	knowledge	noise	truth
beauty	happiness	life	nutrition	unemployment
crime	health	love	patience	work
education	help	luck	pollution	
energy	information	music	time	

Group E. Subjects of study

biology	geometry	history
chemistry	grammar	math (mathematics)*

*****Note:** Even though *mathematics* ends with *s*, it is not plural.

Notice the quantity words used with count and noncount nouns

Singular Count	Plural Count	Noncount
a tomato	tomatoes	coffee
one tomato	**two** tomatoes	**two cups of** coffee
	some tomatoes	**some** coffee
no tomato	**no** tomatoes	**no** coffee
	(with questions and negatives) **any** tomatoes	**any** coffee
	a lot of tomatoes	**a lot of** coffee
	(with questions and negatives) **many** tomatoes	**much** coffee
	a few tomatoes	**a little** coffee
	several tomatoes	**several** cups of coffee
	How many tomatoes?	**How much** coffee?

The following words can be used as either count nouns or noncount nouns. However, the meaning changes according to the way the nouns are used.

Count	Noncount
Oranges and grapefruit are **fruits** that contain a lot of vitamin C.	I bought some **fruit** at the fruit store.
Ice cream and butter are **foods** that contain cholesterol.	We don't need to go shopping today. We have a lot of **food** at home.
He wrote a **paper** about hypnosis.	I need some **paper** to write my composition.
He committed three **crimes** last year.	There is a lot of **crime** in a big city.
I have 200 **chickens** on my farm.	We ate some **chicken** for dinner.
I don't want to bore you with all my **troubles.**	I have some **trouble** with my car.
She went to Puerto Rico three **times.**	She spent a lot of **time** on her project.
She drank three **glasses** of water.	The window is made of bulletproof **glass.**
I had a bad **experience** during my trip to Paris.	She has some **experience** with computer programming.
I don't know much about the **lives** of my grandparents.	**Life** is sometimes happy, sometimes sad.
I heard a **noise** outside my window.	Those children are making a lot of **noise.**

Uses of Articles

Overview of Articles

Articles tell us if a noun is definite or indefinite.			
	Count		**Noncount**
	Singular	**Plural**	
Definite	**the** book	**the** books	**the** coffee
Indefinite	**a** book	**(some / any)** books	**(some / any)** coffee

Part 1. Uses of the Indefinite Article

A. To classify a subject

Examples	Explanation
Chicago is **a** city. Illinois is **a** state. Abraham Lincoln was **an** American president. What's that? It's **a** tall building.	• Use *a* before a consonant sound. • Use *an* before a vowel sound. • You can put an adjective before the noun.
Chicago and Los Angeles are cities. Lincoln and Washington were American presidents. What are those? They're tall buildings.	Do not use an article before a plural noun.

B. To make a generalization about a noun

Examples	Explanation
A dog has sharp teeth. **Dogs** have sharp teeth. **An elephant** has big ears. **Elephants** have big ears.	Use the indefinite article (*a / an*) + a singular count noun or no article with a plural noun. Both the singular and plural forms have the same meaning.
Coffee contains caffeine. **Milk** is white. **Love** makes people happy. **Money** can't buy **happiness.**	Do not use an article to make a generalization about a noncount noun.

C. To introduce a new noun into the conversation

Examples	Explanation
I have **a cell phone.** I have **an umbrella.**	Use the definite article *a / an* with singular count nouns.
Count: I have **(some) dishes.** Do you have **(any) cups?** I don't have **(any) forks.** **Noncount:** I have **(some) money** with me. Do you have **(any) cash** with you? I don't have **(any) time.**	Use *some* or *any* with plural nouns and noncount nouns. Use *any* in questions and negatives. *Some* and *any* can be omitted.
There's **an elevator** in the building. Are there **any restrooms** on this floor? There isn't **any money** in my checking account.	*There* + a form of *be* can introduce an indefinite noun into a conversation.

Part 2. Uses of the Definite Article

A. To refer to a previously mentioned noun

Examples	Explanation
There's **a dog** in the next apartment. **The dog** barks all the time.	We start by saying *a dog*. We continue by saying *the dog*.
We bought **some grapes.** We ate **the grapes** this morning.	We start by saying *some grapes*. We continue by saying *the grapes*.
I need **some sugar.** I'm going to use **the sugar** to bake a cake.	We start by saying *some sugar*. We continue by saying *the sugar*.
Did you buy **any coffee?** Yes. **The coffee** is in the cabinet.	We start by saying *any coffee*. We continue by saying *the coffee*.

B. When the speaker and the listener have the same reference

Examples	Explanation
The dog has big ears. **The cats** are sleeping. **The milk** is sour. Don't drink it.	The object is present, so the speaker and listener have the same object in mind.
a. **The teacher** is writing on **the blackboard** in **the classroom**. b. **The president** is talking about taxes. c. Please turn off **the lights** and shut **the door** and **the windows** before you leave **the house**.	a. Students in the same class have things in common. b. People who live in the same country have things in common. c. People who live in the same house have things in common.
The house on the corner is beautiful. I spent **the money you gave me.**	The listener knows exactly which one because the speaker defines or specifies which one.

C. When there is only one in our experience

Examples	Explanation
The sun is bigger than **the moon.** There are many problems in **the world.**	The *sun*, the *moon*, and the *world* are unique objects. There is only one in our immediate experience.
Write your name on **the top** of the page. Sign your name on **the back** of the check.	The page has only one top. The check has only one back.
The Amazon is **the longest** river in the world. Alaska is **the biggest** state in the U.S.	A superlative indicates that there is only one.

D. With familiar places

Examples	Explanation
I'm going to **the store** after work. Do you need anything? **The bank** is closed now. I'll go tomorrow.	We use *the* with certain familiar places and people—*the bank, the zoo, the park, the store, the movies, the beach, the post office, the bus / train, the doctor, the dentist*—when we refer to the one that we habitually visit or use.

Language Notes:
1. Omit *the* after a preposition with the words *church, school, work,* and *bed.*

   He's **in church.**

   I'm going **to school.**

   They're **at work.**

   I'm going **to bed.**
2. Omit *to* and *the* with *home* and *downtown.*

   I'm going **home.**

   Are you going **downtown** after class?

E. To make a formal generalization

Examples	Explanation
The shark is the oldest and most primitive fish. **The bat** is a nocturnal animal.	To say that something is true of all members of a group, use *the* with singular count nouns.
The computer has changed the way people deal with information. **The cell phone** uses radio waves.	To talk about a class of inventions, use *the*.
The heart is a muscle that pumps blood to the rest of the body. **The ear** has three parts: outer, middle, and inner.	To talk about an organ of the body in a general sense, use *the*.

Language Note:
For informal generalizations, use *a* + a singular noun or no article with a plural noun.

Compare:

   The computer has changed the way we deal with information.

   A computer is expensive.

   Computers are expensive.

Part 3: Special Uses of Articles

No Article	Article

Personal names:
   John Kennedy
   George Bush
	The whole family:
	   the Kennedys
	   the Bushes

Title and name:
   Queen Elizabeth
   Pope John Paul
	Title without name:
	   the Queen
	   the Pope

Cities, states, countries, continents:
   Cleveland
   Ohio
   Mexico
   South America
	Places that are considered a union:
	   the United States
	   the former Soviet Union
	Place names: the _____ of _____
	   the Republic of China
	   the District of Columbia

Mountains:
   Mount Everest
   Mount McKinley
	Mountain ranges:
	   the Himalayas
	   the Rocky Mountains

Islands:
   Coney Island
   Staten Island
	Collectives of islands:
	   the Hawaiian Islands
	   the Philippines

Lakes:
   Lake Superior
   Lake Michigan
	Collectives of lakes:
	   the Great Lakes
	   the Finger Lakes

Beaches:
   Palm Beach
   Pebble Beach
	Rivers, oceans, seas, canals:
	   the Mississippi River
	   the Atlantic Ocean
	   the Dead Sea
	   the Panama Canal

Streets and avenues:
   Madison Avenue
   Wall Street
	Well-known buildings:
	   the Sears Tower
	   the Empire State Building

Parks:
   Central Park
   Hyde Park
	Zoos:
	   the San Diego Zoo
	   the Milwaukee Zoo

Seasons:
   summer   fall   spring   winter
   Summer is my favorite season.
Note: After a preposition, *the* may be used.
   In (the) winter, my car runs badly.
	Deserts:
	   the Mojave Desert
	   the Sahara Desert

Continued

Directions:
    north   south
    east   west
	Sections of a piece of land:
	    the Southwest (of the U.S.)
	    the West Side (of New York)

School subjects:
    history   math
	Unique geographical points:
	    the North Pole the Vatican

Name + *college* or *university*:
    Northwestern University
    Bradford College
	The University (College) of _____
	    the University of Michigan
	    the College of DuPage County

Magazines:
    Time   *Sports Illustrated*
	Newspapers:
	    the *Tribune* the *Wall Street Journal*

Months and days:
    September
    Monday
	Ships:
	    the *Titanic*
	    the *Queen Elizabeth II*

Holidays and dates:
(month + day):
    Thanksgiving   July 4   Mother's Day
	The day of (month):
	    the Fourth of July
	    the fifth of May

Diseases:
    cancer   AIDS
    polio   malaria
	Ailments:
	    a cold a toothache
	    a headache the flu

Games and sports:
    poker   soccer
	Musical instruments, after *play:*
	    the drums the piano
	    Note: Sometimes *the* is omitted.
	    She plays (the) drums.

Languages:
    French
    English
	The _____ language:
	    the French language
	    the English language

Last month, year, week, etc. = the one
before this one:
    I forgot to pay my rent last month.
    The teacher gave us a test last week.
	The last month, the last year, the last
	week, etc. = the last in a series:
	    December is the last month of the year.
	    Summer vacation begins the last
	    week in May.

In office = in an elected position:
    The president is in office for four years.
	In the office = in a specific room:
	    The teacher is in the office.

In back / in front:
    She's in back
    of the car.
 	
	In the back / in the front:
	    He's in the back of the bus.

The Verb *Get*

Get has many meanings. Here is a list of the most common ones:

- get something = receive

  I got a letter from my father.
- get + (to) place = arrive

  I got home at six.

  What time do you get to school?

- get + object + infinitive = persuade

  She got him to wash the dishes.

- get + past participle = become

get accustomed to	get dressed	get scared
get acquainted	get engaged	get tired
get bored	get hurt	get used to
get confused	get lost	get worried
get divorced	get married	

  They got married in 1989.

- get + adjective = become

get angry	get nervous	get upset
get dark	get old	get well
get fat	get rich	
get hungry	get sleepy	

  It gets dark at 6:30.

- get an illness = catch

  While she was traveling, she got malaria.

- get a joke or an idea = understand

  Everybody except Tom laughed at the joke. He didn't get it.

  The boss explained the project to us, but I didn't get it.

- get ahead = advance

  He works very hard because he wants to get ahead in his job.

- get along (well) (with someone) = have a good relationship

  She doesn't get along with her mother-in-law.

  Do you and your roommate get along well?

- get around to something = find the time to do something

  I wanted to write my brother a letter yesterday, but I didn't get around to it.

Continued

- **get away** = escape

  The police chased the thief, but he got away.

- **get away with something** = escape punishment

  He cheated on his taxes and got away with it.

- **get back** = return

  He got back from his vacation last Saturday.

- **get back at someone** = get revenge

  My brother wants to get back at me for stealing his girlfriend.

- **get back to someone** = communicate with someone at a later time

  The boss can't talk to you today. Can she get back to you tomorrow?

- **get by** = have just enough but nothing more

  On her salary, she's just getting by. She can't afford a car or a vacation.

- **get in trouble** = be caught and punished for doing something wrong

  They got in trouble for cheating on the test.

- **get in(to)** = enter a car

  She got in the car and drove away quickly.

- **get out (of)** = leave a car

  When the taxi arrived at the theater, everyone got out.

- **get on** = seat yourself on a bicycle, motorcycle, horse; enter a train, bus, airplane

  She got on the motorcycle and left.

  She got on the bus and took a seat in the back.

- **get off** = leave a bicycle, motorcycle, horse, train, bus, airplane

  They will get off the train at the next stop.

- **get out of something** = escape responsibility

  My boss wants me to help him on Saturday, but I'm going to try to get out of it.

- **get over something** = recover from an illness or disappointment

  She has the flu this week. I hope she gets over it soon.

- **get rid of someone or something** = free oneself of someone or something undesirable

  My apartment has roaches, and I can't get rid of them.

- **get through (to someone)** = communicate, often by telephone

  She tried to explain the harm of eating fast food to her son, but she couldn't get through to him.

  I tried to call my mother many times, but her line was busy. I couldn't get through.

- **get through with something** = finish

  I can meet you after I get through with my homework.

Continued

- get together = meet with another person
  I'd like to see you again. When can we get together?
- get up = arise from bed
  He woke up at 6 o'clock, but he didn't get up until 6:30.

APPENDIX D

Gerund and Infinitive Patterns

1. Verb + Infinitive

They need **to leave.**
I learned **to speak English.**

agree	claim	know how	seem
appear	consent	learn	swear
arrange	decide	manage	tend
ask	demand	need	threaten
attempt	deserve	offer	try
be able	expect	plan	volunteer
beg	fail	prepare	want
can afford	forget	pretend	wish
care	hope	promise	would like
choose	intend	refuse	

2. Verb + Noun / Object Pronoun + Infinitive

I want you **to leave.**
He expects me **to call** him.

advise	convince	hire	require
allow	dare	instruct	select
appoint	enable	invite	teach
ask	encourage	need	tell
beg	expect	order	urge
cause	forbid	permit	want
challenge	force	persuade	warn
choose	get	remind	would like
command	help*		

*Note: After *help*, *to* is often omitted: "He helped me (to) move."

3. Adjective + Infinitive

They are happy **to be** here.
We're willing **to help** you.

afraid	disturbed	lucky	sorry
ashamed	eager	pleased	surprised
amazed	foolish	prepared	upset
careful	fortunate	proud	willing
content	free	ready	wrong
delighted	glad	reluctant	
determined	happy	sad	
disappointed	likely	shocked	

4. Verb + Gerund

I enjoy **dancing**.
They don't permit **drinking**.

admit	detest	miss	resent
advise	discuss	permit	resist
anticipate	dislike	postpone	risk
appreciate	enjoy	practice	stop
avoid	finish	put off	suggest
can't help	forbid	quit	tolerate
complete	imagine	recall	understand
consider	keep (on)	recommend	
delay	mention	regret	
deny	mind	remember	

5. Expressions with *go* + Gerund

He **goes fishing** every Saturday.
They **went shopping** yesterday.

go boating	go hiking	go sightseeing
go bowling	go hunting	go skating
go camping	go jogging	go skiing
go dancing	go sailing	go swimming
go fishing	go shopping	

6. Preposition + Gerund

Verb + Preposition + Gerund
We talked about **moving**.
I look forward to **having** my own apartment.

adjust to	concentrate on	forget about	refrain from
argue about	depend on	insist on	succeed in
believe in	(dis)approve of	look forward to	talk about
care about	dream about	object to	think about
complain about	feel like	plan on	worry about

Adjective + Preposition + Gerund
I'm fond of **traveling**.
She's not accustomed to **eating** alone.

accustomed to	famous for	interested in	sure of
afraid of	fond of	lazy about	surprised at
appropriate for	good at	proud of	tired of
ashamed of	grateful to . . . for	responsible for	upset about
concerned about	guilty of	sorry about	used to
excited about	(in)capable of	suitable for	worried about

Verb + Object + Preposition + Gerund
I thanked him for **helping** me.
I apologized to him for **forgetting** his birthday.

accuse . . . of	devote . . . to	prevent . . . from	suspect . . . of
apologize to . . . for	forgive . . . for	prohibit . . . from	thank . . . for
blame . . . for	keep . . . from	stop . . . from	warn . . . about

Gerund After Preposition in Certain Expressions
Who's in charge of **collecting** the papers?
What is your reason for **coming** late?

impression of	in favor of	in the middle of	requirement for
in charge of	instead of	need for	technique for
in danger of	interest in	reason for	the point of

7. Noun + Gerund

He has difficulty **speaking** English.
She had a problem **finding** a job.
She spent three weeks **looking** for an apartment.

Use a gerund after the noun in these expressions:

have a difficult time	have a hard time
have difficulty	have a problem
have experience	have trouble
have fun	spend time / money
have a good time	there's no use

8. Verb + Gerund or Infinitive (with little or no difference in meaning)

They like **to sing.**　　　　I started **to read.**
They like **singing.**　　　　I started **reading.**

attempt	intend
begin	like
can't stand	love
continue	neglect
deserve	prefer
hate	start
hesitate	

APPENDIX E

Verbs and Adjectives Followed by a Preposition

Many verbs and adjectives are followed by a preposition.

accuse someone of	(be) ashamed of	count on
(be) accustomed to	(be) aware of	deal with
adjust to	believe in	decide on
(be) afraid of	blame someone for	depend on / upon
agree with	(be) bored with / by	(be) different from
(be) amazed at / by	(be) capable of	disapprove of
(be) angry about	care about / for	(be) divorced from
(be) angry at / with	compare to / with	dream about / of
apologize for	complain about	(be) engaged to
approve of	concentrate on	(be) excited about
argue about	(be) concerned about	(be) familiar with
argue with	consist of	(be) famous for

Continued

Many verbs and adjectives are followed by a preposition.		
feel like	(be) mad about	(be) sorry about
(be) fond of	(be) mad at	(be) sorry for
forget about	(be) made from / of	speak about
forgive someone for	(be) married to	speak to / with
(be) glad about	object to	succeed in
(be) good at	(be) opposed to	(be) sure of / about
(be) grateful to someone for	participate in	(be) surprised at
(be) guilty of	plan on	take care of
(be) happy about	pray to	talk about
hear of	(be) prepared for	talk to / with
hope for	prevent someone from	thank someone for
(be) incapable of	prohibit someone from	(be) thankful to someone for
insist on / upon	protect someone from	think about / of
(be) interested in	(be) proud of	(be) tired of
(be) involved in	recover from	(be) upset about
(be) jealous of	(be) related to	(be) upset with
(be) known for	rely on / upon	(be) used to
(be) lazy about	(be) responsible for	wait for
listen to	(be) sad about	warn someone about
look at	(be) satisfied with	(be) worried about
look for	(be) scared of	worry about
look forward to	(be) sick of	

APPENDIX F

Direct and Indirect Objects

Word Order with Direct and Indirect Objects

The order of direct and indirect objects depends on the verb you use.

```
       IO         DO
He told his friend the answer.
```
```
              DO          IO
He explained the answer to his friend.
```

The order of the objects sometimes depends on whether you use a noun or a pronoun object.

```
 S   V     IO        DO
He gave the woman the keys.
```
```
 S   V    DO   IO
He gave them to her.
```

Each of the following groups of words follows a specific pattern of word order and preposition choice. In some cases, the connecting preposition is *to*; in some cases, *for*. In some cases, there is no connecting preposition.

She'll serve lunch *to* her guests.
She reserved a seat *for* you.
I asked him a question.

Group 1 **Pronouns affect word order. The preposition is *to*.**

Patterns: He gave a present to his wife. (DO to IO)
He gave his wife a present. (IO / DO)
He gave it to his wife. (DO to IO)
He gave her a present. (IO / DO)
He gave it to her. (DO to IO)

Verbs:

bring	lend	pass	sell	show	teach
give	offer	pay	send	sing	tell
hand	owe	read	serve	take	write

Group 2 **Pronouns affect word order. The preposition is *for*.**

Patterns: He bought a car for his daughter. (DO for IO)
He bought his daughter a car. (IO / DO)
He bought it for his daughter. (DO for IO)
He bought her a car. (IO / DO)
He bought it for her. (DO for IO)

Verbs:

bake	buy	draw	get	make
build	do	find	knit	reserve

Group 3 **Pronouns don't affect word order. The preposition is *to*.**

Patterns: He explained the problem to his friend. (DO to IO)
He explained it to her. (DO to IO)

Verbs:

admit	introduce	recommend	say
announce	mention	repeat	speak
describe	prove	report	suggest
explain			

Group 4 **Pronouns don't affect word order. The preposition is *for*.**

Patterns: He cashed a check for his friend. (DO for IO)
He cashed it for her. (DO for IO)

Verbs:

answer	change	design	open	prescribe
cash	close	fix	prepare	pronounce

Group 5 **Pronouns don't affect word order. No preposition is used.**

Patterns: She asked the teacher a question. (IO / DO)
She asked him a question. (IO / DO)
It took me five minutes to answer the question. (IO / DO)

Verbs:

ask	charge	cost	wish	take (with time)

Spelling and Pronunciation of Verbs

Spelling of the -s Form of Verbs

Rule	Base Form	-s Form
Add *s* to most verbs to make the -*s* form.	hope eat	hopes eats
When the base form ends in *s*, *z*, *sh*, *ch*, or *x*, add *es* and pronounce an extra syllable, /əz/.	miss buzz wash catch fix	misses buzzes washes catches fixes
When the base form ends in a consonant + *y*, change the *y* to *i* and add *es*.	carry worry	carries worries
When the base form ends in a vowel + *y*, do not change the *y*.	pay obey	pays obeys
Add *es* to *go* and *do*.	go do	goes does

Pronunciation of -s Form
The -s form has three pronunciations.

We pronounce /s/ if the verb ends in these voiceless sounds: /p t k f/.
  hope—hopes   pick—picks
  eat—eats   laugh—laughs

We pronounce /z/ if the verb ends in most voiced sounds.
  live—lives   read—reads   sing—sings
  grab—grabs   run—runs   borrow—borrows

When the base form ends in *s*, *z*, *sh*, *ch*, *x*, *se*, *ge*, or *ce*, we pronounce an extra syllable, /əz/.
  miss—misses   watch—watches   change—changes
  buzz—buzzes   fix—fixes   dance—dances
  wash—washes   use—uses

These verbs have a change in the vowel sound.
  do /du/—does /dʌz/
  say /seɪ/—says /sɛz/

Spelling of the *-ing* Form of Verbs

Rule	Base Form	*-ing* Form
Add *-ing* to most verbs. **Note:** Do not remove the *-y* for the *-ing* form.	eat go study	eating going studying

For a one-syllable verb that ends in a consonant + vowel + consonant (CVC), double the final consonant and add *ing*.	p l a n
	  | | |
	 C V C
	
	 s t o p
	  | | |
	 C V C
	
	 s i t
	 | | |
	 C V C
		planning
		
		 stopping
		
		 sitting

Do not double a final *w*, *x*, or *y*.	show mix stay	showing mixing staying
For a two-syllable word that ends in CVC, double the final consonant only if the last syllable is stressed.	refér admít begín	referring admitting beginning
When the last syllable of a two-syllable word is not stressed, do not double the final consonant.	lísten ópen óffer	listening opening offering
If the word ends in a consonant + *e*, drop the *e* before adding *ing*.	live take write	living taking writing

Spelling of the Past Tense of Regular Verbs

Rule	Base Form	*-ed* Form
Add *ed* to the base form to make the past tense of most regular verbs.	start kick	started kicked
When the base form ends in *e*, add *d* only.	die live	died lived
When the base form ends in a consonant + *y*, change the *y* to *i* and add *ed*.	carry worry	carried worried
When the base form ends in a vowel + *y*, do not change the *y*.	destroy stay	destroyed stayed

Continued

Rule	Base Form	-ed Form
For a one-syllable word that ends in a consonant + vowel + consonant (CVC), double the final consonant and add -ed.	s t o p | | | C V C p l u g | | | C V C	stopped plugged
Do not double a final w or x.	sew fix	sewed fixed
For a two-syllable word that ends in CVC, double the final consonant only if the last syllable is stressed.	occúr permít	occurred permitted
When the last syllable of a two-syllable word is not stressed, do not double the final consonant.	ópen háppen	opened happened

Pronunciation of Past Forms That End in -ed
The past tense with -ed has three pronunciations.

We pronounce a /t/ if the base form ends in these voiceless sounds: /p, k, f, s, š, č/.

jump—jumped	cough—coughed	wash—washed
cook—cooked	kiss—kissed	watch—watched

We pronounce a /d/ if the base form ends in most voiced sounds.

rub—rubbed	charge—charged	bang—banged
drag—dragged	glue—glued	call—called
love—loved	massage—massaged	fear—feared
bathe—bathed	name—named	free—freed
use—used	learn—learned	

We pronounce an extra syllable /əd/ if the base form ends in a /t/ or /d/ sound.

wait—waited	want—wanted	need—needed
hate—hated	add—added	decide—decided

APPENDIX H

Capitalization Rules

- The first word in a sentence: **My** friends are helpful.

- The word "I": My sister and **I** took a trip together.

- Names of people: **Michael Jordan**; **George Washington**

- Titles preceding names of people: **Doctor (Dr.) Smith**; **President Lincoln**; **Queen Elizabeth**; **Mr. Rogers**; **Mrs. Carter**

- Geographic names: the **U**nited **S**tates; **L**ake **S**uperior; **C**alifornia; the **R**ocky **M**ountains; the **M**ississippi **R**iver

  Note: The word "the" in a geographic name is not capitalized.

- Street names: **P**ennsylvania **A**venue (**A**ve.); **W**all **S**treet (**St**.); **A**bbey **R**oad (**R**d.)

- Names of organizations, companies, colleges, buildings, stores, hotels: the **R**epublican **P**arty; **H**einle **T**homson; **D**artmouth **C**ollege; the **U**niversity of **W**isconsin; the **W**hite **H**ouse; **B**loomingdale's; the **H**ilton **H**otel

- Nationalities and ethnic groups: **M**exicans; **C**anadians; **S**paniards; **A**mericans; **J**ews; **K**urds; **E**skimos

- Languages: **E**nglish; **S**panish; **P**olish; **V**ietnamese; **R**ussian

- Months: **J**anuary; **F**ebruary

- Days: **S**unday; **M**onday

- Holidays: **C**hristmas; **I**ndependence **D**ay

- Important words in a title: **G**rammar in **C**ontext; **T**he **O**ld **M**an and the **S**ea; **R**omeo and **J**uliet; **T**he **S**ound of **M**usic

  Note: Capitalize "the" as the first word of a title.

APPENDIX I

Plural Forms of Nouns

Regular Noun Plurals

Word Ending	Example Noun	Plural Addition	Plural Form	Pronunciation
Vowel	bee banana	+ s	bees bananas	/z/
s, ss, sh, ch, x, z	church dish box watch class	+ es	churches dishes boxes watches classes	/əz/
Voiceless consonants	cat lip month book	+ s	cats lips months books	/s/

Continued

Word Ending	Example Noun	Plural Addition	Plural Form	Pronunciation
Voiced consonants	card pin stove	+ s	cards pins stoves	/z/
Vowel + y	boy day key	+ s	boys days keys	/z/
Consonant + y	lady story party	y + ies	ladies stories parties	/z/
Vowel + o	video radio	+ s	videos radios	/z/
Consonant + o	potato hero	+ es	potatoes heroes	/z/
Exceptions: photos, pianos, solos, altos, sopranos, autos, avocados				
f or fe	leaf knife	f + ves	leaves knives	/vz/
Exceptions: beliefs, chiefs, roofs, cliffs, chefs, sheriffs				

Irregular Noun Plurals

Singular	Plural	Explanation
man woman mouse tooth foot goose	men women mice teeth feet geese	Vowel change (**Note:** The first vowel in *women* is pronounced /I/.)
sheep fish deer	sheep fish deer	No change
child person	children people (OR persons)	Different word form

Continued

Singular	Plural	Explanation
	(eye)glasses belongings clothes goods groceries jeans pajamas pants / slacks scissors shorts	No singular form
alumnus cactus radius stimulus syllabus	alumni cacti OR cactuses radii stimuli syllabi OR syllabuses	*us → i*
analysis crisis hypothesis oasis parenthesis thesis	analyses crises hypotheses oases parentheses theses	*is → es*
appendix index	appendices OR appendixes indices OR indexes	*ix → ices* OR *→ ixes*
bacterium curriculum datum medium memorandum criterion phenomenon	bacteria curricula data media memoranda criteria phenomena	*um → a* *ion → a* *on → a*
alga formula vertebra	algae formulae OR formulas vertebrae	*a → ae*

Metric Conversion Chart

Length

When You Know	Symbol	Multiply by	To Find	Symbol
inches	in	2.54	centimeters	cm
feet	ft	30.5	centimeters	cm
feet	ft	0.3	meters	m
yards	yd	0.91	meters	m
miles	mi	1.6	kilometers	km

Metric

When You Know	Symbol	Multiply by	To Find	Symbol
centimeters	cm	0.39	inches	in
centimeters	cm	0.03	feet	ft
meters	m	3.28	feet	ft
meters	m	1.09	yards	yd
kilometers	km	0.62	miles	mi

Note:
1 foot = 12 inches
1 yard = 3 feet or 36 inches

Area

When You Know	Symbol	Multiply by	To Find	Symbol
square inches	in^2	6.5	square centimeters	cm^2
square feet	ft^2	0.09	square meters	m^2
square yards	yd^2	0.8	square meters	m^2
square miles	mi^2	2.6	square kilometers	km^2

Metric

When You Know	Symbol	Multiply by	To Find	Symbol
square centimeters	cm^2	0.16	square inches	in^2
square meters	m^2	10.76	square feet	ft^2
square meters	m^2	1.2	square yards	yd^2
square kilometers	km^2	0.39	square miles	mi^2

Weight (Mass)

When You Know	Symbol	Multiply by	To Find	Symbol
ounces	oz	28.35	grams	g
pounds	lb	0.45	kilograms	kg
Metric				
grams	g	0.04	ounces	oz
kilograms	kg	2.2	pounds	lb

Note: 16 ounces = 1 pound

Volume

When You Know	Symbol	Multiply by	To Find	Symbol
fluid ounces	fl oz	30.0	milliliters	mL
pints	pt	0.47	liters	L
quarts	qt	0.95	liters	L
gallons	gal	3.8	liters	L
Metric				
milliliters	mL	0.03	fluid ounces	fl oz
liters	L	2.11	pints	pt
liters	L	1.05	quarts	qt
liters	L	0.26	gallons	gal

Temperature

When You Know	Symbol	Do This	To Find	Symbol
degrees Fahrenheit	°F	Subtract 32, then multiply by $\frac{5}{9}$	degrees Celsius	°C
Metric				
degrees Celsius	°C	Multiply by $\frac{9}{5}$, then add 32	degrees Fahrenheit	°F

Sample temperatures

Fahrenheit	Celsius	Fahrenheit	Celsius
0	– 18	60	16
10	– 12	70	21
20	– 7	80	27
30	– 1	90	32
40	4	100	38
50	10		

Comparative and Superlative Forms

Comparative and Superlative Forms			
	Simple	**Comparative**	**Superlative**
One-syllable adjectives and adverbs	tall	taller	the tallest
	fast	faster	the fastest
Exceptions:	bored	more bored	the most bored
	tired	more tired	the most tired
Two-syllable adjectives that end in -y	easy	easier	the easiest
	happy	happier	the happiest
	pretty	prettier	the prettiest
Other two-syllable adjectives	frequent	more frequent	the most frequent
	active	more active	the most active
Some two-syllable adjectives have two forms.	simple	simpler	the simplest
		more simple	the most simple
	common	commoner	the commonest
		more common	the most common

Note: These two-syllable adjectives have two forms: *handsome, quiet, gentle, narrow, clever, friendly,* and *angry.*

Adjectives with three or more syllables	important	more important	the most important
	difficult	more difficult	the most difficult
-*ly* adverbs	quickly	more quickly	the most quickly
	brightly	more brightly	the most brightly
Irregular adjectives and adverbs	good / well	better	the best
	bad / badly	worse	the worst
	far	farther / further*	the farthest / furthest
	little	less	the least
	a lot	more	the most

* **Note:** *Farther* is for distances. *Further* is for ideas.
I live *farther* from school than you do.
She doesn't want to discuss the matter *further*.

The Superlative Form

Subject	Verb	Superlative Form + Noun	Prepositional Phrase
Alaska	is	the biggest state	in the U.S.
California	is	the most populated state	in the U.S.

The Comparative Form

Subject	Linking Verb[1]	Comparative Adjective	*Than*	Noun / Pronoun
She	is	taller	than	her sister (is).
She	seems	more intelligent	than	her sister.

Subject	Verb Phrase	Comparative Adverb	*Than*	Noun / Pronoun
I	speak English	more fluently	than	my sister (does).
I	sleep	less	than	you (do).

Comparisons with Nouns

Subject	Verb	Comparative Word + Noun	*Than*	Noun / Pronoun
I	work	fewer hours	than	you (do).
I	have	more time	than	you (do).

Equatives with Adjectives and Adverbs

Subject	Linking Verb	*As*	Adjective	*As*	Noun / Pronoun
She	isn't	as	old	as	her husband (is).
She	looks	as	pretty	as	a picture.

Subject	Verb Phrase	*As*	Adverb	*As*	Noun / Pronoun
She	speaks English	as	fluently	as	her husband (does).
He	doesn't work	as	hard	as	his wife (does).

Equatives with Quantities

Subject	Verb	*As Many / Much*	Noun	*As*	Noun / Pronoun
She	works	as many	hours	as	her husband (does).
Milk	doesn't have	as much	fat	as	cream (does).

Subject	Verb	*As Much As*	Noun / Pronoun
Chicken	doesn't cost	as much as	meat (does).
I	don't drive	as much as	you (do).

[1] The linking verbs are *be, look, seem, feel, taste, sound,* and *seem.*

Equatives with Nouns

Pattern A

Subject	Verb	*The Same*	Noun	*As*	Noun / Pronoun
She	wears	the same	size	as	her mother (does).
She	isn't	the same	height	as	her brother (is).

Pattern B

Subject & Subject	Verb	*The Same*	Noun
She and her mother	wear	the same	size.
She and her brother	aren't	the same	height.

Similarities using *Like / Alike*

Pattern A

Subject	Linking Verb	*Like*	Noun / Pronoun
Sugar	looks	like	salt.
Regular coffee	tastes	like	decaf.

Pattern B

Subject & Subject	Linking Verb	*Alike*
Sugar and salt	look	alike.
Regular coffee and decaf	taste	alike.

Glossary of Grammatical Terms

- **Adjective** An adjective gives a description of a noun.

  It's a *tall* tree.   He's an *old* man.   My neighbors are *nice*.

- **Adverb** An adverb describes the action of a sentence or an adjective or another adverb.

  She speaks English *fluently*.   I drive *carefully*.

  She speaks English *extremely* well.   She is *very* intelligent.

- **Adverb of Frequency** An adverb of frequency tells how often the action happens.

  I *never* drink coffee.   They *usually* take the bus.

- **Affirmative** means *yes*.

- **Apostrophe '** We use the apostrophe for possession and contractions.

  My *sister's* friend is beautiful.   Today *isn't* Sunday.

- **Article** The definite article is *the*. The indefinite articles are *a* and *an*.

  I have *a* cat.   I ate *an* apple.   *The* president was late.

- **Auxiliary Verb** Some verbs have two parts: an auxiliary verb and a main verb.

  He *can't* study.   We *will* return.

- **Base Form** The base form, sometimes called the "simple" form, of the verb has no tense. It has no ending (*-s* or *-ed*): *be, go, eat, take, write.*

  He doesn't *know* the answer.   I didn't *go* out.

  You shouldn't *talk* loudly.

- **Capital Letter** A B C D E F G . . .

- **Clause** A clause is a group of words that has a subject and a verb. Some sentences have only one clause.

  She found a good job.

  Some sentences have **a main clause** and a **dependent clause.**

MAIN CLAUSE	DEPENDENT CLAUSE (**reason clause**)
She found a good job	because she has computer skills.
MAIN CLAUSE	DEPENDENT CLAUSE (**time clause**)
She'll turn off the light	before she goes to bed.
MAIN CLAUSE	DEPENDENT CLAUSE (***if* clause**)
I'll take you to the doctor	if you don't have your car on Saturday.

- **Colon :**

- **Comma ,**

- **Comparative Form** A comparative form of an adjective or adverb is used to compare two things.

    My house is *bigger* than your house.

    Her husband drives *faster* than she does.

- **Complement** The complement of the sentence is the information after the verb. It completes the verb phrase.

    He works *hard.*   I slept *for five hours.*   They are *late.*

- **Consonant** The following letters are consonants: *b, c, d, f, g, h, j, k, l, m, n, p, q, r, s, t, v, w, x, y, z.*

    NOTE: *y* is sometimes considered a vowel, as in the world *syllable.*

- **Contraction** A contraction is made up of two words put together with an apostrophe.

    He's my brother.   *You're* late.   They *won't* talk to me.

    (*He's* = he is)   (*You're* = you are)   (*won't* = will not)

- **Count Noun** Count nouns are nouns that we can count. They have a singular and a plural form.

    1 pen — 3 pens   1 table — 4 tables

- **Dependent Clause** See **Clause**

- **Direct Object** A direct object is a noun (phrase) or pronoun that receives the action of the verb.

    We saw *the movie.*   You have *a nice car.*   I love *you.*

- **Exclamation Mark !**

- **Frequency Words** Frequency words are *always, usually, often, sometimes, rarely, seldom,* and *never.*

    I *never* drink coffee.   We *always* do our homework.

- **Hyphen** –

- **Imperative** An imperative sentence gives a command or instructions. An imperative sentence omits the word *you.*

    Come here.   *Don't be* late.   Please *sit* down.

- **Indefinite Pronoun** An indefinite pronoun (*one, some, any*) takes the place of an indefinite noun.

    I have a cell phone. Do you have *one*?

    I didn't drink any coffee, but you drank *some.* Did he drink *any*?

- **Infinitive** An infinitive is *to* + base form.

    I want *to leave.*   You need *to be* here on time.

- **Linking Verb** A linking verb is a verb that links the subject to the noun or adjective after it. Linking verbs include *be, seem, feel, smell, sound, look, appear,* and *taste.*

    She *is* a doctor.   She *seems* very intelligent.   She *looks* tired.

- **Modal** The modal verbs are *can, could, shall, should, will, would, may, might,* and *must.*

  They *should* leave.   I *must* go.

- **Negative** means *no.*

- **Nonaction Verb** A nonaction verb has no action. We do not use a continuous tense (*be* + verb *-ing*) with a nonaction verb. The nonaction verbs are: *believe, cost, care, have, hear, know, like, love, matter, mean, need, own, prefer, remember, see, seem, think, understand,* and *want.*

  She *has* a laptop.   We *love* our mother.

- **Noncount Noun** A noncount noun is a noun that we don't count. It has no plural form.

  She drank some *water.*   He prepared some *rice.*

  Do you need any *money*?

- **Noun** A noun is a person (*brother*), a place (*kitchen*), or a thing (*table*). Nouns can be either count (*1 table, 2 tables*) or noncount (*money, water*).

  My *brother* lives in California.   My *sisters* live in New York.

  I get *mail* from them.

- **Noun Modifier** A noun modifier makes a noun more specific.

  fire department   *Independence* Day   *can* opener

- **Noun Phrase** A noun phrase is a group of words that forms the subject or object of the sentence.

  A very nice woman helped me at registration.

  I bought *a big box of candy.*

- **Object** The object of the sentence follows the verb. It receives the action of the verb.

  He bought *a car.*   I saw *a movie.*   I met *your brother.*

- **Object Pronoun** Use object pronouns (*me, you, him, her, it, us, them*) after the verb or preposition.

  He likes *her.*   I saw the movie. Let's talk about *it.*

- **Paragraph** A paragraph is a group of sentences about one topic.

- **Parentheses ( )**

- **Participle, Present** The present participle is verb + *-ing.*

  She is *sleeping.*   They were *laughing.*

- **Period .**

- **Phrase** A group of words that go together.

  Last month my sister came to visit.

  There is a strange car *in front of my house.*

- **Plural** Plural means more than one. A plural noun usually ends with *-s*.

    She has beautiful *eyes*.

- **Possessive Form** Possessive forms show ownership or relationship.

    Mary's coat is in the closet.   *My* brother lives in Miami.

- **Preposition** A preposition is a short connecting word: *about, above, across, after, around, as, at, away, back, before, behind, below, by, down, for, from, in, into, like, of, off, on, out, over, to, under, up, with.*

    The book is *on* the table.

- **Pronoun** A pronoun takes the place of a noun.

    I have a new car. I bought *it* last week.

    John likes Mary, but *she* doesn't like *him*.

- **Punctuation** Period . Comma , Colon : Semicolon ; Question Mark ? Exclamation Mark !

- **Question Mark** ?

- **Quotation Marks** " "

- **Regular Verb** A regular verb forms its past tense with *-ed*.

    He *worked* yesterday.   I *laughed* at the joke.

- ***s* Form** A present tense verb that ends in *-s* or *-es*.

    He *lives* in New York.   She *watches* TV a lot.

- **Sense-Perception Verb** A sense-perception verb has no action. It describes a sense.

    She *feels* fine.   The coffee *smells* fresh.   The milk *tastes* sour.

- **Sentence** A sentence is a group of words that contains a subject[2] and a verb (at least) and gives a complete thought.

    SENTENCE: She came home.

    NOT A SENTENCE: When she came home.

- **Simple Form of Verb** The simple form of the verb, also called the base form, has no tense; it never has an *-s, -ed,* or *-ing* ending.

    Did you *see* the movie?   I couldn't *find* your phone number.

- **Singular** Singular means one.

    She ate a *sandwich*.   I have one *television*.

- **Subject** The subject of the sentence tells who or what the sentence is about.

    My sister got married last April. *The wedding* was beautiful.

- **Subject Pronouns** Use subject pronouns (*I, you, he, she, it, we, you, they*) before a verb.

    They speak Japanese.   *We* speak Spanish.

---

[2] In an imperative sentence, the subject *you* is omitted: *Sit down. Come here.*

- **Superlative Form** A superlative form of an adjective or adverb shows the number one item in a group of three or more.

    January is the *coldest* month of the year.

    My brother speaks English the *best* in my family.

- **Syllable** A syllable is a part of a word that has only one vowel sound. (Some words have only one syllable.)

    change (one syllable)   after (af·ter = two syllables)

    look (one syllable)   responsible (re·spon·si·ble = four syllables)

- **Tag Question** A tag question is a short question at the end of a sentence. It is used in conversation.

    You speak Spanish, *don't you?*   He's not happy, *is he?*

- **Tense** A verb has tense. Tense shows when the action of the sentence happened.

    SIMPLE PRESENT: She usually *works* hard.

    FUTURE: She *will work* tomorrow.

    PRESENT CONTINUOUS: She *is working* now.

    SIMPLE PAST: She *worked* yesterday.

- **Verb** A verb is the action of the sentence.

    He *runs* fast.   I *speak* English.

    Some verbs have no action. They are linking verbs. They connect the subject to the rest of the sentence.

    He *is* tall.   She *looks* beautiful.   You *seem* tired.

- **Vowel** The following letters are vowels: *a, e, i, o, u. Y* is sometimes considered a vowel (for example, in the word *syllable*).

APPENDIX M

Alphabetical List of Irregular Verb Forms

Base Form	Past Form	Past Participle	Base Form	Past Form	Past Participle
be	was / were	been	bid	bid	bid
bear	bore	born / borne	bind	bound	bound
beat	beat	beaten	bite	bit	bitten
become	became	become	bleed	bled	bled
begin	began	begun	blow	blew	blown
bend	bent	bent	break	broke	broken
bet	bet	bet	breed	bred	bred

Continued

Base Form	Past Form	Past Participle	Base Form	Past Form	Past Participle
bring	brought	brought	grow	grew	grown
broadcast	broadcast	broadcast	hang	hung	hung[3]
build	built	built	have	had	had
burst	burst	burst	hear	heard	heard
buy	bought	bought	hide	hid	hidden
cast	cast	cast	hit	hit	hit
catch	caught	caught	hold	held	held
choose	chose	chosen	hurt	hurt	hurt
cling	clung	clung	keep	kept	kept
come	came	come	know	knew	known
cost	cost	cost	lay	laid	laid
creep	crept	crept	lead	led	led
cut	cut	cut	leap	leapt / leaped	leapt / leaped
deal	dealt	dealt	leave	left	left
dig	dug	dug	lend	loaned / lent	loaned / lent
dive	dove / dived	dove / dived	let	let	let
do	did	done	lie	lay	lain
draw	drew	drawn	light	lit / lighted	lit / lighted
drink	drank	drunk	lose	lost	lost
drive	drove	driven	make	made	made
eat	ate	eaten	mean	meant	meant
fall	fell	fallen	meet	met	met
feed	fed	fed	mistake	mistook	mistaken
feel	felt	felt	overcome	overcame	overcome
fight	fought	fought	overdo	overdid	overdone
find	found	found	overtake	overtook	overtaken
fit	fit	fit	overthrow	overthrew	overthrown
flee	fled	fled	pay	paid	paid
fly	flew	flown	plead	pleaded / pled	pleaded / pled
forbid	forbade	forbidden	prove	proved	proven / proved
forget	forgot	forgotten	put	put	put
forgive	forgave	forgiven	quit	quit	quit
freeze	froze	frozen	read	read	read
get	got	gotten	ride	rode	ridden
give	gave	given	ring	rang	rung
go	went	gone	rise	rose	risen
grind	ground	ground	run	ran	run

Continued

[3] *Hanged* is used as the past form to refer to punishment by death. *Hung* is used in other situations: She *hung* the picture on the wall.

Base Form	Past Form	Past Participle	Base Form	Past Form	Past Participle
say	said	said	swear	swore	sworn
see	saw	seen	sweep	swept	swept
seek	sought	sought	swell	swelled	swelled / swollen
sell	sold	sold	swim	swam	swum
send	sent	sent	swing	swung	swung
set	set	set	take	took	taken
sew	sewed	sown / sewed	teach	taught	taught
shake	shook	shaken	tear	tore	torn
shed	shed	shed	tell	told	told
shine	shone / shined	shone / shined	think	thought	thought
shoot	shot	shot	throw	threw	thrown
show	showed	shown / showed	understand	understood	understood
shrink	shrank / shrunk	shrunk / shrunken	uphold	upheld	upheld
shut	shut	shut	upset	upset	upset
sing	sang	sung	wake	woke	woken
sink	sank	sunk	wear	wore	worn
sit	sat	sat	weave	wove	woven
sleep	slept	slept	wed	wedded / wed	wedded / wed
slide	slid	slid	weep	wept	wept
slit	slit	slit	win	won	won
speak	spoke	spoken	wind	wound	wound
speed	sped	sped	withhold	withheld	withheld
spend	spent	spent	withdraw	withdrew	withdrawn
spin	spun	spun	withstand	withstood	withstood
spit	spit	spit	wring	wrung	wrung
split	split	split	write	wrote	written
spread	spread	spread			
spring	sprang	sprung			
stand	stood	stood			
steal	stole	stolen			
stick	stuck	stuck			
sting	stung	stung			
stink	stank	stunk			
strike	struck	stuck / stricken			
strive	strove	striven			

Note:

The past and past participle of some verbs can end in -ed or -t.

burn	burned or burnt
dream	dreamed or dreamt
kneel	kneeled or knelt
learn	learned or learnt
spill	spilled or spilt
spoil	spoiled or spoilt

The United States of America: Major Cities

The United States of America

AL Alabama	HI Hawaii	MA Massachusetts	NM New Mexico	SD South Dakota
AK Alaska	ID Idaho	MI Michigan	NY New York	TN Tennessee
AZ Arizona	IL Illinois	MN Minnesota	NC North Carolina	TX Texas
AR Arkansas	IN Indiana	MS Mississippi	ND North Dakota	UT Utah
CA California	IA Iowa	MO Missouri	OH Ohio	VT Vermont
CO Colorado	KS Kansas	MT Montana	OK Oklahoma	VA Virginia
CT Connecticut	KY Kentucky	NE Nebraska	OR Oregon	WA Washington
DE Delaware	LA Louisiana	NV Nevada	PA Pennsylvania	WV West Virginia
FL Florida	ME Maine	NH New Hampshire	RI Rhode Island	WI Wisconsin
GA Georgia	MD Maryland	NJ New Jersey	SC South Carolina	WY Wyoming
				DC* District of Columbia

*The District of Columbia is not a state. Washington, D.C. is the capital of the United States.
Note: Washington, D.C., and Washington state are not the same.

North America

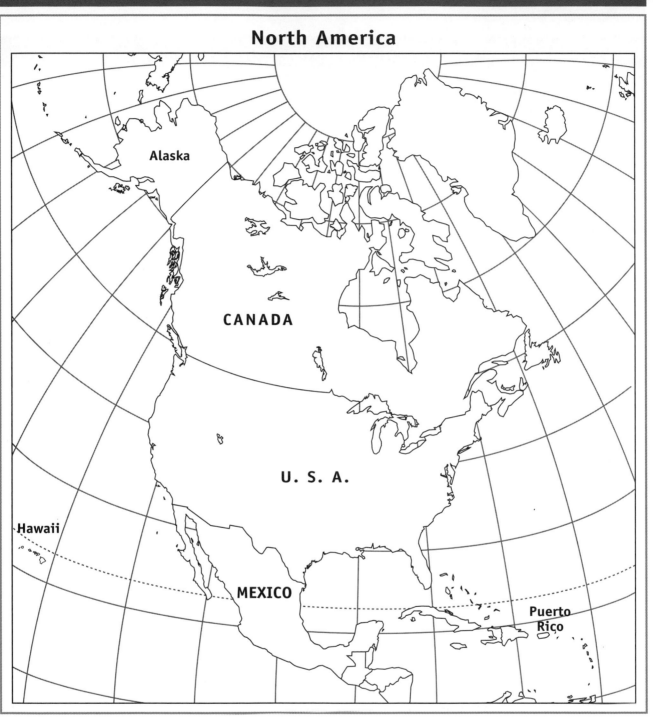

Alaska

CANADA

U. S. A.

Hawaii

MEXICO

Puerto Rico

Index

Photo Credits

1, Royalty Free/CORBIS; *2*, Taxi/Getty Images; *9*, Superstock; *19*, Brian Lee/CORBIS; *22*, Bill Freeman/PhotoEdit; *32*, Kathy McLaughlin/The Image Works; *57*, *top left*, Mike Blake/Reuters/CORBIS, *bottom left*, PA/Topham/The Image Works, *right*, UPPA/Topham/The Image Works; *58*, Bettmann/CORBIS; *60*, Reuters/CORBIS; *65*, Los Angeles Daily News/Sygma/CORBIS; *68*, Library of Congress; *69*, *top*, Hulton Deutsch Collection/CORBIS, *bottom*, Tom Wagner/Sygma/CORBIS; *70*, *top*, Photofest, *bottom*, Roman Soumar/CORBIS; *73*, *top*, Bettmann/CORBIS, *bottom*, Photofest; *76*, Jose Luis Pelaez, Inc./CORBIS; *77*, *top*, Bettmann/CORBIS, *bottom*, Douglas Kirkland/CORBIS; *80*, Tatiana Markow/Sygma/CORBIS; *81*, Bob Daemmrich/The Image Works; *83*, Photofest; *84*, Topham/The Image Works; *85*, *left*, Bettmann/CORBIS, *right*, Kenneth James/CORBIS; *86*, Peter Hvizdak/The Image Works; *97*, Steven K. Doi/ZUMA/CORBIS; *99*, William G. Hartenstein/CORBIS; *101*, Bettmann/CORBIS; *108*, Bettmann/CORBIS; *109*, Ralph White/CORBIS; *111*, Hulton-Deutsch Collection/CORBIS; *118*, Jim Mahoney/The Image Works; *119*, Royalty Free/ThinkStock LLC; *121*, Bettmann/CORBIS; *125*, Ralph White/CORBIS; *149*, Bill Lai/The Image Works; *150*, Laura Doss/CORBIS; *152*, Alison Wright/The Image Works; *161*, James Marshall 2004/The Image Works; *162*, David Young Wolff/PhotoEdit; *166*, Helen King/CORBIS; *167*, Royalty Free/CORBIS; *183*, Bettmann; Stanley Tretick, 1963/CORBIS; *184*, Topham/The Image Works; *185*, Bettmann/CORBIS; *192*, CORBIS; *194*, Bettmann/CORBIS; *197*, *left*, Bettmann/CORBIS, *right*, Bettmann/CORBIS; *203*, Bettmann/CORBIS; *204*, *top*, Bettmann/CORBIS, *bottom*, Bettmann/CORBIS; *223*, LWA-Jay Newman/CORBIS; *224*, David Young Wolff/PhotoEdit; *231*, Catherine Wessel/CORBIS; *236*, Nathaniel Welch/CORBIS; *237*, Kin Cheung/Reuters/CORBIS; *242*, Topham/The Image Works; *250*, Ed Quinn/CORBIS; *251*, AP/Wide World Photos; *253*, Andrea Comas/Reuters/CORBIS; *260*, AP/Wide World Photos; *273*, Rick Friedman/CORBIS; *274*, Underwood and Underwood/CORBIS; *277*, Darren Modricker/CORBIS; *281*, Michael Mulvey/Dallas Morning News/CORBIS; *282*, Christopher Sohm; Chromosohm Inc./CORBIS; *284*, Royalty Free/CORBIS; *285*, Courtesy of the Carnegie Library; *287*, Marilyn Humphries/The Image Works; *289*, Royalty Free/CORBIS; *296*, AP/Wide World Photos; *309*, Alaska Stock; *313*, Courtesy of Global Volunteers; *315*, Harvard University Gazette; *327*, Morton Beebe/CORBIS; *328*, Bettmann/CORBIS; *334*, *left*, Wendy Stone/CORBIS, *right*, Loren Anderson/CORBIS; *335*, Loren Anderson/CORBIS; *341*, Bettmann/CORBIS; *344*, Skjold Photographs/CORBIS; *345*, Reuters/CORBIS; *350*, Ariel Skelley/CORBIS; *351*, Roy McMahon/CORBIS; *357*, Laura Dwight/CORBIS; *371*, Taxi/Getty Images; *373*, Ariel Skelley/CORBIS; *377*, Pat Doyle/CORBIS; *379*, Kevin Cozad/CORBIS; *380*, Darien Modricker/CORBIS; *390*, Douglas Kirkland/CORBIS; *404*, Roy Morsch/CORBIS; *405*, Steve Prezant/CORBIS; *424*, Bettmann/CORBIS; *437*, Fred Prouser/Reuters/CORBIS; *441*, *top*, CORBIS, *bottom*, Hulton Archive/Getty Images; *444*, Myrleen Ferguson Cate/PhotoEdit; *448*, Royalty Free/CORBIS